CONSTITUTIONAL ARGUMENT AND INSTITUTIONAL STRUCTURE IN THE UNITED STATES

US constitutional jurisprudence often conflates two distinct enquiries: how to interpret the Constitution and how to allocate interpretive authority. This book explains the distinct role of judgements about interpretive authority in constitutional practice. It argues that these judgements do not determine what qualifies as good constitutional argument, and cannot substitute for it. Rather, they specify the division of labour between the political branches and the judiciary in forming applicable constitutional determinations.

This explanation of the structure of constitutional reasoning sets the stage for the development of a normative theory about each enquiry. The book advances a theory of substantive constitutional argument. It argues that constitutional interpretation is a special kind of practical reasoning, aiming to construct and specify morally sound accounts of the Constitution and surrounding constitutional practice. Yet, this task is entrusted to a scheme of institutions, as agents of free and equal citizens. The standard of review is an interlocking component of that scheme, regulating the judicial assignment. As such, it should aim to facilitate best performance of the overall interpretive task, so that the judicial process settles on appropriate constitutional determinations; grounded on morally sound reasons that reach all citizens and uphold the fundamental commitments to freedom and equal citizenship.

Constitutional Argument and Institutional Structure in the United States

Nicholas Papaspyrou

•HART•
OXFORD • LONDON • NEW YORK • NEW DELHI • SYDNEY

HART PUBLISHING
Bloomsbury Publishing Plc
Kemp House, Chawley Park, Cumnor Hill, Oxford, OX2 9PH, UK

HART PUBLISHING, the Hart/Stag logo, BLOOMSBURY and the Diana logo are trademarks of Bloomsbury Publishing Plc

First published in Great Britain 2018

A catalogue record for this book is available from the British Library.

Library of Congress Cataloging-in-Publication data

Names: Papaspyrou, Nicholas, author.

Title: Constitutional argument and institutional structure in the United States / Nicholas Papaspyrou.

Description: Oxford [UK] ; Portland, Oregon : Hart Publishing, 2018. | Includes bibliographical references and index.

Identifiers: LCCN 2017051101 (print) | LCCN 2017051418 (ebook) | ISBN 9781509917198 (Epub) | ISBN 9781509917174 (hardback : alk. paper)

Subjects: LCSH: Constitutional law—United States—Interpretation and construction. | Constitutional law—United States—Philosophy. | Federal government—United States. | State, The. | Separation of powers—United States. | Democracy—United States.

Classification: LCC KF4552 (ebook) | LCC KF4552 .P37 2018 (print) | DDC 342.73—dc23

LC record available at https://lccn.loc.gov/2017051101

ISBN: HB: 978-1-50991-7-174
ePDF: 978-1-50991-7-181
ePub: 978-1-50991-7-198

Typeset by Compuscript Ltd, Shannon
Printed and bound by CPI Group (UK) Ltd, Croydon, CR0 4YY

MIX
Paper from responsible sources
FSC® C013604

To find out more about our authors and books visit www.hartpublishing.co.uk. Here you will find extracts, author information, details of forthcoming events and the option to sign up for our newsletters.

ACKNOWLEDGEMENTS

I was fortunate enough to discuss the thoughts ultimately developed in this work with many admirable teachers while pursuing my doctoral studies at Harvard Law School. I am primarily indebted to Frank Michelman for his support and insightful comments, as well as to Todd Rakoff and Thomas Scanlon, who shaped the way I think about administrative law and practical philosophy respectively. My work is influenced by the ideas and advice of Ronald Dworkin, who had in fact proposed to me to examine the distinction between interpretive authority and interpretive substance, and by the philosophy of Joseph Raz, with whom I had unforgettable tutorial lessons at Balliol College, Oxford. My jurisprudential outlook is largely shaped by my efforts to navigate between their highly influential, yet sharply contrasting positions. I have also benefited from discussing early chapters with Richard Fallon, Larry Sager, Fred Schauer, David Shapiro and Mattias Kumm. President Procopis Pavlopoulos and Nicos Alivisatos from Athens first introduced me in public law and have been a continuous source of support throughout the last 25 years. Acknowledgment is well deserved by three anonymous readers, who helped me improve the functional balance of the overall manuscript and qualify hasty generalisations, and by the editors of Hart Publishing. Finally, gratitude is owed to family and close friends for their forbearance and encouragement. The support and enthusiasm of my parents and my brother, and the love of Anastasia, Ioanna, Dimitris and John made assumption of this project and completion of this book possible.

Early pieces of this work were written in the congenial environment of the Harvard Center in Ethics and the Professions. The stimulating suggestions of my graduate fellows at the Center and of Arthur Applbaum were more than helpful. I also acknowledge the financial support of the Alexander Onassis Foundation, the Basil and Elise Goulandris Museum of Fine Arts and the British Academy.

CONTENTS

ANALYTICAL TABLE OF CONTENTS

PART 3: CONSTITUTIONAL DOCTRINE

INTRODUCTION

This book attempts to shed light on the architecture of interpretive reasoning in American constitutional law. Its driving objective is to single out the two main inquiries in the field—*how to interpret the Constitution* and *how to allocate interpretive responsibility and authority*; and to frame them in a way that respects the integrity of each inquiry, while also showing how they are to be assembled in a unified conception of the field. It seeks to explain the fact that institutionalised interpretation, for instance judicial interpretive reasoning in the process of judicial review, involves both institutional considerations about the division of interpretive labour between the political branches and the judiciary, and substantive judgements about the content of the law.

On this analytic basis, it sets forth a normative theory on the structure of constitutional reasoning, by locating the interpretive activity under the fundamental pursuit of political justice and the commitments to constitutional legitimacy and political democracy. It defends the thesis that the latter commitments may not be understood apart from an encompassing account of public reason and political justice: in a just society public reason is the deliberative reason of a political community of free and equal citizens with the power to exercise their equal liberty and to engage in moral reflection about its protective scope. Constitutional reasoning is a special kind of public reasoning, seeking to identify and specify pertinent constitutional norms—especially norms about the very scope of constitutional liberty and equal protection—through dialectic, interpretive reception of the Constitution and of its history of authoritative exposition. The provisional settlement of such interpretive issues is entrusted to a scheme of public institutions, operating as agents of free and equal citizens. Hence, institutions of constitutional implementation, courts in particular, are well advised to interpret their institutional mandate—including the requisite inter-branch synergy and reciprocity—so that they best fulfil this task, and with a view to settle on the more appropriate constitutional determinations, upon reasons that reach citizens as free and equal.

We may set the stage for this analysis by introducing, first, a few famous debates recently conducted before the Supreme Court of the United States; bringing to the fore major controversies between process and substance, history and reason, policy and principle. And we will conclude this book by revisiting judicial doctrine, the multi-faceted scheme of applicable standards of judicial review, with a view to explaining the interplay between substantive and institutional norms and ideas, and to unearthing implicated shortcomings and underlying sensibilities.

I. Supreme Debates

In a historic decision issued on 26 June 2015, the Supreme Court held that States are constitutionally required to license a marriage between two persons of the same sex (*Obergefell v Hodges*).[1] On the majority's broad reading of the constitutional text and history, the fundamental liberties protected by the due process clause 'extend to certain personal choices central to individual dignity and autonomy, including intimate choices defining personal identity and beliefs'. The Court reasoned that the identification and protection of these liberties is an enduring part of the judicial duty to interpret the Constitution. That responsibility requires courts 'to exercise reasoned judgment in identifying interests of the person so fundamental that the State must accord them its due respect'.

Justice Kennedy, writing for the majority, acknowledged that history and tradition guide and discipline this inquiry but are not dispositive, as the generations that wrote and ratified the Bill of Rights and the Fourteenth Amendment did not presume to know the extent of freedom in all of its dimensions, and so they entrusted to future generations a charter protecting the right of all persons to enjoy liberty 'as we learn its meaning'. The Court then engaged in a constructive reading of its case law on the right to marry and determined that the principles supporting it apply with equal force to same sex couples. It concluded that the traditional limitation of marriage to opposite-sex couples, while having seemed natural and just for generations, is inconsistent with the central meaning of the fundamental right to marry and that such inconsistency 'is now manifest'. The Court engaged in similar analysis under the Fourteenth Amendment's guarantee of equal protection and concluded that denial of same-sex marriage abridges central precepts of equality as well.

The holding was fiercely contested by a minority of four judges. Their dissenting opinions focused on two main themes. On the one hand, liberty interests not enumerated in the Constitution were said to deserve special constitutional protection only so long as they are 'so rooted in the traditions and conscience of our people as to be ranked as fundamental'. And proper performance of this task involves the employment 'of neutral principles of constitutional law'. If, on the other hand, the judiciary proceeds on the basis of its own 'understanding of what freedom is and must become', it effectively subordinates 'the *People's* understanding of liberty, at the time of ratification or even today, to the reasoned judgment of a committee of nine unelected lawyers'. 'This practice of constitutional revision by an unelected committee of nine … robs the People of the most important liberty they asserted in the Declaration of Independence and won in the Revolution of 1776: the freedom to govern themselves'.

[1] *Obergefell v Hodges*, 576 US __ (2015).

The minority elaborated on both themes. Justice Scalia scorned the majority for comfortably 'concluding that every State violated the Constitution for all of the 135 years between the Fourteenth Amendment's ratification and Massachusetts' permitting of same-sex marriages in 2003' and all four dissenting justices emphasised that the issue has been at the centre of public debate and political decision making. 'What matters is that the process established by those who created the [civil] society has been honored. … That process has been honored here. The definition of marriage has been the subject of heated debate in the States. Legislatures have repeatedly taken up the matter on behalf of the People, and 35 States have put the question to the People themselves.'

The Chief Justice, concerned about the broader legitimacy of the Court, confirmed that claimants 'make strong arguments rooted in social policy and considerations of fairness'. He even confessed that if he were a legislator, he 'would certainly consider that view as a matter of social policy'. Yet, he emphasised that the judiciary is ill-equipped to impose it upon the political process.

But what makes the claim in controversy a matter of policy? The majority presented it as a matter of high principle, reflecting the foundational commitment of the polity to freedom and equal citizenship. The Chief Justice was well aware that philosophical reflection is pertinent in assessing the merits of the issue. Yet, invoking the specter of the *Lochner* Court (the discredited invocation by the Court a century ago of high principle and common law values to block socioeconomic legislation), the Chief Justice stressed that the Constitution is made for people of fundamentally differing philosophical views. 'Then and now, this assertion of the "harm principle" sounds more in philosophy than law. The elevation of the fullest individual self-realization over the constraints that society has expressed in law may or may not be attractive moral philosophy. But a Justice's commission does not confer any special moral, philosophical, or social insight sufficient to justify imposing those perceptions on fellow citizens under the pretense of "due process." There is indeed a process due on issues of this sort—the democratic process'. As a result, 'whatever force that belief may have as a matter of moral philosophy, it has no more basis in the Constitution than did the naked policy preferences adopted in *Lochner*'. And the Chief Justice concluded: the 'majority's decision is an act of will, not legal judgment'.

The majority did not let this argument without rebuttal. Acknowledging that democracy is the appropriate process for change, it noted that extensive deliberation has taken place in society and the political process, and emphasised that delay in recognition of a fundamental right, whose validity has become manifest, would let claimants, seeking equal dignity in the eyes of the law, suffer lingering and irreversible pain and humiliation. The moral gravity of the subject matter necessitated judicial settlement.

This case is paradigmatic of some of the most profound debates in constitutional theory. In approaching constitutional text and precedent, how are we to think about the relevance of contestable philosophical issues of political justice and fairness? What is the force of considerations like history and tradition? And, assuming that constitutional notions like liberty and equal treatment are entrusted to future generations, as they learn their meanings, what is the institutional role of the political and the judicial process in expounding such meaning? Are judges well advised to exercise independent, reasoned judgement, or is the constitutional legitimacy of the result reached simply dependent upon due operation of the political process? And finally, what are the respective roles of policy and principle in constitutional adjudication; how do they help us to distinguish between judicial reasoning proper and acts of will?

The reader should not assume that constitutional adjudication exhibits the Manichean logic implied in the way *Obergefell* framed these profound questions. On the one hand, there are many areas of constitutional law where these supreme debates have played out their contested implications and constitutional doctrine has attained a high degree of settlement; and fields where judicial passivity is treated to be the norm. The main example is the minimal standard of review applicable in socioeconomic legislation. Legislative classifications that do not burden enumerated rights or fundamental liberties, nor implicate suspect groups receive only superficial judicial attention. In an uncontested formulation of the applicable standard of review, socioeconomic legislation 'carries with it a presumption of rationality that can only be overcome by a clear showing of arbitrariness and irrationality' (*Hodel v Indiana*).[2] Absent truly exceptional circumstances, it would cause much surprise were a federal court to invoke an argument of principle, or history, or tradition, or claim the virtues of the judicial process over the federal or state legislatures in this field.

Most importantly, we need to interpolate a third possibility, silenced by the gravity and simplicity of the subject matter in *Obergefell*, and ignored by their absence in *Hodel*. The garden-variety of more refined, theme-specific standards of review, tailoring the structure of constitutional interests to local configurations of policy and principle, of tradition and reason, and the intensity of review to corresponding assessments of institutional competency and legitimacy. Still, in such cases, the issues debated in *Obergefell* stand in the background, by way of purported justification, and often surface back in an endless process of doctrinal specification or revision—gradual or punctuated, contested or consensual.

The recent case law on affirmative action illustrates this third possibility, in all its complexity. In *Fisher v University of Texas at Austin (Fisher I)* (2013),[3] Justice Kennedy, writing for a broad majority of conservative and liberal justices, construed past decisions of the Court for the purpose of articulating the standard controlling race-sensitive university admissions policies. The earlier cases were battlefields of contrasting conceptions of constitutional principle regarding the meaning of racial equality and of different assumptions about the role of the judicial process in their pursuit. The prevailing view was that, while the educational

[2] *Hodel v Indiana*, 452 US 314, 331–32 (1981) (involving heavy requirements imposed upon surface coal mining operations conducted on prime farmland).

[3] *Fisher v University of Texas at Austin*, 570 US __ (2013).

benefits of student body diversity may constitute a compelling state interest, the employment of racial classifications in their pursuit is subject to strict judicial scrutiny. The *Fisher* Court assumed the task of specifying a comprehensive and relatively consensual standard under such precedent.

On the *Fisher* construal of precedent, a university must clearly demonstrate that such policies pursue unquestionably legitimate and substantial interests and that employment of racial classifications is necessary to their accomplishment. In this regard and assuming the educational benefits from student-body diversity to be the stated purpose, a court may give 'some, but not complete' deference to a university's judgement that student-body diversity is essential to its educational mission, provided that diversity is not defined as mere racial balancing and there is a reasoned, principled explanation for the academic decision. However, once the University has established that its goal of diversity is consistent with strict scrutiny, the University must prove, without the benefit of deference, that the means it chose to attain that diversity are narrowly tailored to its goal, that admissions processes 'ensure that each applicant is evaluated as an individual and not in a way that makes an applicant's race or ethnicity the defining feature of his or her application', and that no workable race-neutral alternatives would produce the educational benefits of diversity.

This complex doctrinal formula reflects a sensibility distinct from the grand narratives of history and reason, democracy and judicial elitism. Analysis is focused on the category of permissible conceptions of diversity and on the proper degree of judicial scrutiny and deference to universities making complex judgements of necessity. The Court was aware of the entanglement of policy and principle and understood that the appropriate synergy between the academic and the judicial process is a delicate issue. On a reasonable reading, the underlying idea was to tie the degree of institutional deference over educational decisions to the task of ensuring fair treatment. Universities have experience and expertise over judgements of educational necessity. Yet, they are also subject to more subtle vices, to imperceptible use of means impermissible, so that judicial attentiveness is crucial—even at the risk of some judicial over-enforcement.

On judicial methodology, the opinion was a fusion of doctrinal reasoning with a strategy to reach compromising common ground on the operation of underlying issues of principle, while postponing contestation to the level of applying the standard on the facts of the case after remand. Justice Ginsburg felt uneasy with both aspects of this methodology and dissented. Three years later, she unreservedly joined the decision of the Court on the merits of the case (*Fisher II*, 2016).[4] The policy in question was held to pass strict scrutiny. Justice Kennedy was satisfied, while conservative justices dissented. 'Something strange has happened since our prior decision in this case', they remarked. And different conceptions of principle, contrasting ideas about the relation between race neutrality and racial equality, resurfaced.

[4] *Fisher v University of Texas at Austin*, 579 US __ (2016).

This book attempts to shed light on the structure of such debates and the ways they affect constitutional doctrine, by proposing a set of more generic ideas about what I perceive to be rather fundamental elements of constitutional reasoning. The following sections present a brief, though dense, summary of the main thesis.

II. The Substantive Structure of Constitutional Interpretation

A. An Aporia

Constitutional theory has identified various modes of argumentation employed in American interpretive practice (so-called arguments from the constitutional text, precedent, structure, history, political morality and public political culture). It has also suggested that these modes do not operate independently and that an interpretive judgement is not supposed to aggregate their individual vectors.[5] In *Obergefell*, for instance, we wouldn't sensibly ask how well each outcome would fare along the dimension of history and the dimension of reason and then aggregate respective rankings. Practitioners may also appreciate that they shall tailor the way they treat each factor to the reasons for paying attention to them. Still, they lack, I fear, a satisfactory account of the way history, tradition or independent reason matter and make sense together, as elements of an overall interpretive argument.

In my opinion, this defect is explicable in the light of uncertainty about the character of legal interpretation and its location in the realm of practical reasoning. And this uncertainty can be attributed to the difficulties of delineating the appropriate relation between the commitment to constitutional authority, on the one hand, and the pursuit of political justice, on the other. Without some sense of how constitutional legitimacy relates to justice and how history matters in this relation, we lack critical intellectual resources for approaching a matter as thorny as the one raised in *Obergefell*, when local traditions appear recalcitrant to the intuitive demands of justice or, even worse, when many of us are tempted to understand the claims of litigants as generic claims of policy rather than as claims of constitutional justice.

Part One of this work addresses this underlying source of confusion by attempting to locate constitutional interpretation within the wider chart of practical reasoning and by defending a normative thesis about the governing ideas. In carrying out this project, I focus on the fact that constitutional interpretation is a species of

[5] See Richard Fallon, 'A Constructivist Coherence Theory of Constitutional Interpretation' (1987) 100 *Harv L Rev* 1189 and Philip Bobbitt, *Constitutional Fate: Theory of the Constitution* (Oxford, Oxford University Press, 1982) and *Constitutional Interpretation* (Oxford, Basil Blackwell, 1991) 28–30.

practical reasoning, that is to say, reasoning about how to conduct ourselves and arrange public institutions. As a kind of practical reasoning, it is shaped by a pertinent stock of values, concerns and commitments. Humans try to understand and explain the practical reasons they have over a specified domain against the backdrop of concerns and commitments about what is worth respecting and achieving. Accordingly, it is of paramount importance that we identify the pertinent stock of concerns and commitments that frame constitutional interpretation as a kind of human practical reasoning. An explanation of this normative framework would then highlight the general normative structure that is needed so that constitutional interpretation may serve its appropriate role.

B. Summary of the Argument

Constitutional law addresses fundamental issues about the exercise of public power. Practical reasoning about how public power is to be exercised is subject to *public reason* and is ideally performed in the light of attractive conceptions of political justice.

However, constitutional interpretation does not aim at explaining public reason *per se*. Its subject matter is constitutional *law*—the law's take on some fundamentals of public reason. In this sense, constitutional interpretation is a special kind of practical reasoning: it is reasoning about the content of an *institutional normative system*. An institutional normative system is not necessarily a valid system of norms. Yet, in reasoning about its content, we believe or *assume* so. We assume the authority of constitutional law (that is to say, we assume that under public reason the exercise of public power is subject to existing constitutional law) and we try to explain the practical reasons that constitutional law (supposedly) gives its subjects.

The process of explaining these reasons is underdetermined by text, precedent and understandings prevalent in constitutional practice. In fact, constitutional interpretation is a constructive enterprise of practical deliberation through which reflective practical reason constructs accounts of the normative reach and import we acknowledge to constitutional practice. This conception of the character of constitutional interpretation is a function of the reflective and critical ways in which argumentative constitutional practices receive and interact with the constitutional text and the history of its authoritative exposition.

Given the constructive nature of constitutional interpretation, we proceed to explain the normative principles to govern interpretive construction. The driving idea is that, in interpreting the Constitution, we are supposed to respond to the reasons for upholding constitutional legitimacy under public reason and political justice. The general aim is to construct *morally sound* accounts of the Constitution, along with surrounding practice of authoritative constitutional exposition, so that public power would be exercised in *better compliance* with *public reason* and *political justice*. This aim is understood against the placement of constitutional legitimacy under political justice. A morally sound account is supposed to redeem the commitment that, given the institutional world inherited, by following the normative import of the Constitution, public power would be exercised in better compliance with political justice.

Under this general aim, I emphasise two complementary features of interpretive reasoning: the employment of practice-dependent considerations serving the rationale for endorsing the authoritative status of constitutional text and precedent even if they lack ideal content, and sensitivity to the very justice of constitutional content. And I argue that, in determining the contours and proper adjustment of these elements, and in specifying the rules and principles that constitutional law provides us with, we engage in delicate exercises of moral reasoning under conditions of political legitimacy. Thus, the debate over the role of history and tradition in arguments of principle, as in *Obergefell*, is ultimately a question about the reasons for upholding the scheme of constitutional law under political justice, and about their implications for the ways we receive and interact with text and past practice.

III. The Institutional Architecture of Constitutional Interpretation

A. An Aporia

A second, particularly troubling source of confusion and contestation affecting constitutional practice, judicial review in particular, relates to the employment of institutional constraints in judicial reasoning. Is a court's assessment of a fundamental liberty affected by the settlement reached or not reached in the political process? Is a court's determination about the necessity of affirmative action measures affected by the university's reasoned judgement in the affirmative? Although questions of this sort are prevalent in adjudication, the pertinent issues are often mishandled or misunderstood. There are, most importantly, two recurrent, contradictory, and equally misguided dispositions: to treat issues of *institutional structure* as self-justified, and to collapse them to issues of *interpretive substance*.

For instance, it is common to assume that the judge is supposed to adjudicate on independent interpretation of applicable law, as 'it is emphatically the province and duty of the judicial department to say what the law is'.[6] At the same time, conceding that the judiciary lacks the legitimacy to review certain assessments of fact or value, these very same judges may ironically conclude that these considerations do not pertain to legal reasoning. Failing to distinguish between the necessity to rest their judgment on an interpretation of the law and the supposed necessity to rest it on their independently constructed interpretation of the law, judges often

[6] *Marbury v Madison*, 5 US 137, 177 (1803).

adopt an account of legal reasoning that is little more to a context specific account of judicial reasoning. And failing to distinguish between *judicial reasoning* and *legal reasoning*, they often drop their convictions of constitutional value and adopt new ones to operate smoothly under a fully independent standard of review. This leads to a distorted picture of the substantive interpretive question and of normative constitutional theory itself.

Thus, failure to distinguish between a substantive norm of 'reasonableness' and a standard of review calling for 'proof of clear unreasonableness' gives the impression that constitutional law is silent over ordinary socioeconomic legislation. And this culture has repercussions throughout constitutional law. It provides an excuse, for instance, to the conservative minority in *Obergefell* for disclaiming the constitutional nature of the pertinent questions of substance (treating them as issues of social policy) and for avoiding direct confrontation with the constitutional deliberations of the political process under a proper standard of review. And it silences the claim of the liberal minority in many affirmative action cases that there is a legitimate, inclusionary constitutional vision of equal protection, emerging in the political process; and that the limitations of the judicial role in its primary enforcement do not deprive it of its constitutional status. Judicial cognizance, on the other hand, that there exists constitutional space beyond judicial doctrine would set the stage for a constructive debate about institutional structure; about the proper synergy between the political and the judicial branches in constitutional implementation; and about the critical hedge of the judicial process in safeguarding certain commitments of principle.

Even when we recognise the distinctive role of institutional constraints, we are often tempted to assume that they involve trade-offs with considerations of substance; that judges somehow have to balance constitutional rightness with separation-of-powers principles. In this assumption, we fail to see that institutional considerations do not operate on the same level with substantive ones. Institutional considerations are of a *higher-order*: they are supposed to *structure* the role of substantive interpretive judgements of different bodies in institutionalised reasoning—rather than to rival them.

A sense of rivalry between structure and substance supports a culture of infidelity to structure, experienced in opportunistic treatment of standards of review. Trade-offs imply loss to rightness. In agony to avoid such loss, we are tempted to assess the applicable standard of review on the sole basis of the preferred outcome on the merits. Thus, we criticise a decision for not showing adequate deference to judgements of Congress that appear persuasive; inclined, next time, to argue for safeguarding the integrity of judicial review against alarming legislative pronouncements. This in turn reinforces an equally problematic response: treating standards of review as self-justified—even if they fail miserably to produce appropriate resolutions.

Resolving the above puzzles requires that we locate judicial reasoning within the wider chart of constitutional reasoning; and, in this course, that we rationalise the institutional dimension of judicial reasoning. This is the task of Part Two.

B. Summary of the Argument

The institutional nature of law and the constructive nature of constitutional interpretation establish the distinctive character of the following normative inquiry: how is the task of constitutional construction to be assigned to the various institutions charged with applying constitutional law? This question is analytically distinct from the debate regarding the substantive structure of constitutional reasoning. Hence, there is an analytic distinction between institutional structure and interpretive substance and, from the point of view of the reviewing court, a corresponding distinction between judicial reasoning (as structured by the resolution to the institutional question) and the wider realm of constitutional reasoning.

With regard to judicial review, the institutional question is salient in debates about the intensity of review, including the degree of deference to the political branches and to the administration. This issue, I argue, is best understood as involving the institutional scheme structuring the substantive judgements of various institutions for the purpose of resolving the pertinent dispute. Indeed, in making public policy, at least in ideal cases, the political branches often give content to ideas of liberty and equal protection. They do so both when they further the underlying causes and when they limit. And even though they do not often articulate their constitutional premises, they make, or at least proceed upon value judgements of constitutional significance. Intensity of review, properly understood, relates to the institutional structuring of these judgements and of requisite judgements of the reviewing court in forming the applicable constitutional determination.

To understand the nature and normative justification of institutional norms of this sort, we employ the perspective of the reviewing court and examine the normative commitments and pursuits framing judicial reasoning: the fundamental commitment that public power be exercised on the basis of public reason and political justice, and the commitment to the public and joint nature of authoritative interpretive construction.

Proper recognition of features like the existence of reasonable pluralism over constitutional interpretation and the role of public institutions as the collective arms of the political community ground the institutional dimension of judicial reasoning. They show that, under public reason and political justice, the judge may have most reason to exercise judicial review on the basis of an institutional scheme that may diverge from a fully independent standard of review. Such a scheme takes the form of institutional norms of a higher order with regard to the substantive judgements at issue. These norms *structure substantive judgements of different bodies* in the process of settling on the applicable interpretation of the law. This sets the stage for exposing the category mistake made by those who argue for trade-offs between substance and institutional structure.

At the same time, the pursuit of political justice frames the deliberation involved in determining which institutional scheme is preferable: ideally, the one ensuring better compliance with public reason and political justice. Institutional allocation may be the product of chance, luck, power or deliberate design. Yet, the reviewing court has reason to craft and apply those institutional norms that promote better compliance with political justice. I argue that in the paradigmatic case this implies the pursuit of *appropriate interpretations of the law,* of best serving the fundamental desiderata of constitutional interpretation under public reason and political justice.[7] I also discuss the relevance of systemic considerations, including the constitutional integrity of the political and the judicial processes, under the very same overarching pursuit, as well as the implications of uncertainty for outcome-oriented institutional choice.

An important lesson of this justificatory account is that, while institutional norms exhibit a certain kind of priority with regard to the substantive arguments on the interpretive issue at hand, the justification of institutional norms presupposes some conception about the general aims of constitutional interpretation. In this sense, structure depends upon substance. After I discuss the conceptual difficulties involved in this insight, I briefly examine the two main tensions that pertain to the design and interpretation of institutional norms: the tension between functional specialisation and institutional checks (chapter eight) and the tension between the commitment to political equality and to other aspects of political justice (chapters nine and ten).

On the latter issue, I advance the idea that, in deliberating about the more appropriate institutional process, we appeal to reasons that reflect the bonds of reciprocity among co-equal and free members of a political community with diverging views about political justice. This commitment underlies the requirement that the appropriate structure shall, among other things, respect the fundamental interest of each citizen to participate in public life and through the exercise of deliberative responsibility affect the formation of public policy and, secondly, treat each citizen as having the capacity for a sense of justice that is worthy of equal respect. At the same time, it also demands that we understand these ideas as elements of a broader principle mandating that government recognises and secures to each citizen a scheme of equal liberty, where the political and the non-political dimension are mutually adjusted.

On this frame, I discuss how the pursuit of democratic responsiveness affects the appropriate standard of review. And I argue that the appropriate process shall be well-suited to engage in a dialogue with the citizenry, a dialogue that is open and conducted on reasons that in good faith reach all citizens as free and equal. Thus, the cornerstone of the debate in *Obergefell*, to take a characteristic example, was precisely about the proper role of the Court in engaging with a political community of free and equal citizens on the implications deriving from this very fundamental commitment to equal citizenship.

[7] This was the main argument advanced in my doctoral dissertation, *Institutions of Justice: The Institutional Assignment of Interpretive Labor in Public Law Litigation*, SJD thesis, Harvard University (2000).

IV. A Topography of Judicial Doctrine

Institutional norms are often operationalised in the form of judicial doctrine, imposing self-discipline in the institutional reasoning of courts, while also setting in motion path dependent processes of institutional elaboration and contestation. Having reviewed basic analytic features, benefits and weaknesses of such processes in Part Two (chapter seven), I attempt in Part Three a survey of the practised field, aiming to highlight the interplay of institutional and substantive ideas.

My main argument is that much of American constitutional doctrine has a dual character, involving both an institutional and a substantive function. First, it has a substantive dimension; it provides an interpretation *of the normative content of substantive constitutional law*. That interpretation sometimes covers only part of applicable law, capturing only violations of a certain kind or magnitude. In this sense, constitutional doctrine may diverge from exhaustive formulations of applicable constitutional law, covering only judicially enforced law. Secondly, *it regulates the applicable scope and intensity of review, organizing the pertinent judicial assignment*. That institutional norm specifies the substantive constitutional judgements that courts are directed to make themselves and the way they are structured with relevant judgements of the reviewed body, in the process of forming an overall constitutional determination and resolving the dispute at hand.

An important objective of this work is to explain the operation of these features, while accommodating the rhetoric about judicial sovereignty over the law. At the same time, it aims to explain the contestation experienced in the field over the institutional dimension of constitutional doctrine. Such contestation may relate to the capacities and performance of judicial and political institutions. But quite often it is due to competing conceptions of political justice as the design and interpretation of an institutional scheme is mainly assessed on the appropriateness of the outcomes it is expected to produce.

Understanding the relation between the institutional and the substantive function of constitutional doctrine also enables us to detect noteworthy inconsistencies of approach. The theory of judicial under-enforcement, for instance, illuminates that there may be more to constitutional law than limited judicial competence and legitimacy perceives. And institutional considerations calling for searching review are often confused with overreaching substantive constraints, a point calling for re-examination of the substantive parameters of over-protection. Finally, appreciation of the institutional nature of constitutional doctrine provides us with a much better perspective in dealing with thorny issues of judicial *supremacy*: the asserted authority of judicial doctrine over future governmental conduct, and over complementary mechanisms of constitutional enforcement, like the mandate of Congress to enforce the reconstruction amendments. And, given the availability of such mechanisms, it brings to the surface the tension between absolutist claims to judicial supremacy and the proper synergy among the branches of the federal government in the joint project of constitutional construction.

Institutional considerations are not supposed to compete with substance, but to serve it. Recognition of their proper space is crucial for avoiding loss in constitutional vision. And it forces us to be critical over their proper content. Reasons for deference or for independent review are not self-justifying, as public institutions do not exercise privileges; they serve public functions, subject to public reason and political justice. The institutional scheme established by doctrine is to be assessed on the ways it organises a functional process: the process of engagement with interpretive pluralism with a view to settlement on appropriate constitutional constructions under public reason and political justice.

In the final chapter of this book, I engage in the task of unearthing sensibilities lying beneath the broader doctrinal frame and its institutional underpinnings. The starting point is the appearance of a puzzling *discontinuity* with regard to the intensity of review over issues of law between constitutional and agency-administered statutory law, as agencies are empowered with conditional interpretive authority over ambiguous statutory schemes they administer. This contrast enables us to single out two important features of constitutional doctrine, inviting us in turn to explore explanatory conjectures. In constitutional law the determination of the applicable standard of review is theme-specific as the standard is built into the doctrinal explication of the law, whereas in administrative law a uniform frame applies across the board and has an explicitly institutional nature. Moreover, in constitutional law, doctrine often reflects (in its content) or prescribes (in its operation) a high level of judicial scrutiny over issues of constitutional principle, whereas agencies are entrusted with broad interpretive responsibility over issues of statutory policy within their generic mandate.

I conclude offering a tentative argument about the salient sensibilities behind this frame. I discuss, in a genealogical fashion, dominant perceptions of institutional competency and institutional mistrust and I highlight the development of *a penetrating sense of moral significance* in much of constitutional law, along with the perception that principled and judicially articulated schemes are available for appropriate judicial engagement. In this context, I explore the idea that the domain of constitutional rights constitutes a domain of *principle*, structuring the realm of permissible public policy—as the violation of such rights inflicts upon right-holders a *wrong* that is crucially different from the kind of *loss* incurred in unwise or unbalanced combinations of substitutable components of public policy.

My argument does not imply that the scope and implications of this sensibility are anyhow settled in constitutional practice; on the contrary, they are the subject-matter of critical debate and contestation. And, as our reflections on the constructive nature of constitutional interpretation (chapter four) and on the substantive commitments of institutional reasoning (chapter six) would bring us to expect, that debate is ultimately accountable to competing visions of political justice, and to the operation of contrasting conceptions of constitutional legitimacy and democracy thereunder.

V. Methodological Prolegomena

Having established a normative conception about the character, the substantive, and the institutional structure of constitutional interpretation, we may claim that we have framed a general normative account of the field; and, hopefully, that we have explained how the pursuit of political justice and the commitments to constitutional legitimacy and political democracy are assembled in this domain under public reason, rather than left around, as independent variables pulling apart interpretive principles and straining the pursuit of integrity in constitutional practice. But before we embark upon this task, it is helpful to clarify certain methodological presuppositions.

The account proposed here is primarily an endeavour in critical self-understanding. We adopt the internal perspective, the perspective of raising arguments about the content of the law within the practice. We understand them as arguments of practical reason. And we abstract from specific disputations, aiming to make best sense of constitutional reasoning in its generality, given fundamental features and commitments of the practice and their placement under practical reason. But we cannot even begin to sketch such an account without engaging with ideas about practical reason and about how constitutional law may be considered authoritative thereunder. And we cannot frame normative ideas guiding constitutional reasoning without giving further content to constitutional legitimacy, political democracy and public reason.

Accordingly, the analysis to follow does not aspire to value neutrality. But it would be quite misleading to assume that all the normative arguments I employ are of the same category. Everything depends on what is claimed at each stage in the exposition. Sometimes, the argument seeks coherence in light of relatively formal features of legal practice and practical reason. The more formal the analysis becomes, the more I aspire to what is often called analytical jurisprudence. But even an analysis of formal features of practical reason is not value neutral. Elsewhere, the argument engages into substantive argument about principles underlying the law and discusses the content that institutional structures need to have to serve them. In doing so, I make an effort to proceed on a high level of generality. In this sense, the argument retains critical force, while allowing for its endorsement by readers who hold a reasonable variety of substantive ideas. Yet, there are also places where I specify a bit more the operative concepts (ie, by thickening the account of political equality in chapter nine) or the appropriate content of institutional norms (ie, by clarifying and criticising prevailing assumptions concerning the appropriate standard of review). Along this spectrum, there is a continuum of analysis—as we move from a formal explanation of fundamental features of a practice to an account of the justification of particular institutional and substantive arguments within the practice.

In the wider framework of legal ideas, this work attempts to assemble, refine and structure ideas developed by three distinct schools of thought: the legal process school that reigned in the American legal academia in the 1950s, the long tradition of reasoned, principle-seeking interpretation, and the contractualist school of normative political theory. Ever since the 1960s, the two main strands of the legal process school—emphasis on process and purposive interpretation—have been thought to be in sharp tension. In the 1960s and 1970s process-based ideas were withering away and an account of legal interpretation that emphasises the service to the justification of the interpreted norm was gaining ascent. In the more recent misty times, process-based ideas have resurfaced, in a misleading blending with purpose-agnostic institutional analysis. Against that background, this exposition may be understood as an endeavour in reconciliation—guided and tested against the commitment to political justice.

The reader should be aware though that adoption of this perspective comes at a price. As this book engages in critical synthesis of ideas implicit in these three discourses, it detaches itself, in import if not in intent, from alternative currents of thought. For instance, our approach may not appear congenial to students of constitutional practice who show deep scepticism about public rationality, doubt the attractiveness of political justice as a structuring value or approach the law in fundamentally voluntaristic terms. It is not my purpose here to show that such competing schemes of thought are deficient—other than perhaps by structuring in an attractive and balanced scheme what we take to be fundamental normative commitments of American constitutional practice.

Finally, as I read the pages that follow, I acknowledge the influence of philosophical pragmatism. In an important sense, practice is primary in philosophy. We cannot exercise philosophy from Sirius, aiming to discover what facts and values there are. We start from the fact that we participate in multiple practices and that we care about our fundamental interests: the interest in living in a just political community and the interest in leading lives we deem to be worthwhile. Human knowledge is the product of this interaction. Faced with a social world we do not fully grasp, we construct explanatory accounts of our practices and form principles of justice to guide our social and political conduct in furtherance of our fundamental interests.[8]

[8] The constructivist character of human knowledge and the role of values in the process of construction do not imply the lack of objectivity of the knowledge produced. See Hilary Putnam, 'Pragmatism and Moral Objectivity' in his *Words and Life* (Cambridge, Harvard University Press, 1994) 151–81, and 'Objectivity and the Science/Ethics Distinction' in his *Realism with a Human Face* (Cambridge, Harvard University Press, 1990) 163–78.

Part 1

Interpretive Substance

1

Textual Primacy and Precedential Force: The Institutional Anchorage of Constitutional Law

Constitutional interpretation may be understood as the intellectual activity of explaining the content of constitutional law. In discussing its structure, we need a general idea about its subject matter, about main features of constitutional law that the interpretive activity is supposed to respect and bring out. In this chapter, I focus on the two fundamental institutional blocks of American constitutional law, the primacy of the written Constitution and the ubiquity of judicial precedent. Their salience captures fundamental commitments of constitutional practice so that any account of constitutional interpretation ignoring them would not fit the practice. In explaining this idea, I discuss how textual primacy and precedential force dovetail with two fundamental dimensions of constitutional law, that is, its institutional nature and its interpretive character.

I. The Institutional, Interpretive and Preemptive Dimensions of Constitutional Law

As a preliminary matter, we need to single out three fundamental features that constitutional law, in its very nature as law of the land, does possess: its institutional, interpretive and preemptive character. Here is how I propose to integrate these features.

Constitutional norms, like all legal norms, are members of an *institutional system* of norms. Constitutional law is a *system* of norms that is *practised* in the political community and its lawmaking and law-applying institutions. In this sense, constitutional law has an *institutional* dimension.[1] It is anchored in social

[1] The 'practice theory' of law was famously defended by HLA Hart in *The Concept of Law*, 2nd edn (Oxford, Oxford University Press, 1994) in support of legal positivism. The weak version employed here accepts the basic institutional insight of the theory while dropping much of its conventionalist baggage; yet, even in this elementary version, it is committed to a weak separation thesis in holding that legal norms do not necessarily constitute valid practical reasons that subjects of law truly have.

practices of recognition like law enforcement and adjudication. This dimension has important implications. It explains why the law does not necessarily consist of practical reasons that subjects of law do have. It is institutional practice that claims so. In this sense, the law consists of practical reasons that subjects of law are *supposed* to have by virtue of the membership of these norms in the relevant institutional system.

At the same time, the institutional nature of law does not imply that membership of a norm in a legal system is determined by mere reference to and systematisation of these practices of social recognition. As Ronald Dworkin has famously argued,[2] recognitional practices have an argumentative nature, being committed in complex and contested ways to standards related to the reasons for accepting law's authority. The supreme debates discussed in the introduction—the arguments and counterarguments supporting or disputing certain conceptions of constitutional liberty and equal treatment on underlying ideas about the function of the Constitution in a democracy, etc—are just emblematic performances of the kind of reflection that is in principle applicable and often becomes operational throughout constitutional practice. This insight is fundamental in questioning the idea that constitutional law has some pre-interpretive, socially determined content. It is the very argumentative confrontation of law-applying institutions with constitutional text and traditions that supplies such content. We may call this the *interpretive* dimension of law. Within this frame, legal interpretation explains the content of the law by bringing out the pertinent normative signification rooted in institutional, yet fragmented and argumentative practices of recognition.

The way the interpretive dimension of law interrelates with the institutional nature of law is a matter of significant contention between positivists and non-positivists. I will discuss my own, rather eclectic views on this subject in section IV below and throughout chapter four. Here I want to emphasise that any legitimate account shall fit what we may call the *preemptive* dimension of law. Constitutional norms, like all legal norms, are supposed to have *preemptive* force in the practical reason of subjects of law. Subjects of law are supposed to comply with the law rather than follow the (possibly diverging) reasons they would directly endorse by exercising independent practical reasoning without the mediation of law.[3] Public institutions are supposed to comply with freedom of speech, even if they were to form a different conception about the liberties of the person were they to

[2] Dworkin's most elaborate account is presented in his magisterial *Law's Empire* (Cambridge, Harvard University Press, 1986).

[3] The preemptive function of legal norms has been elaborated by Joseph Raz. See Joseph Raz, *The Morality of Freedom* (Oxford, Oxford University Press, 1986) 57–62 and 'Authority, Law and Morality' (1985) 68 *Monist* 295–324 (legal reasons are supposed to be preemptive reasons for action in the sense that they preempt—incorporate and take the place of—some or all of the reasons that independently apply to us). Raz's version of the preemption thesis is stricter than the one adopted here in excluding consideration of the preempted reasons in the process of determining the content of existing law (ch 4, s V).

exercise independent reasoning about this subject matter. Legal norms fulfil this preemptive function by virtue of their first feature, namely, the fact that they are rooted in practices of institutional recognition; in practices that focus upon and uphold the normative significance of certain facts of political history like, in the First Amendment case, the ratification of the Constitution, the enactment of the First Amendment to the Constitution, the history of judicial exposition of the First Amendment, etc.

These features of constitutional norms help us clarify the nature of the *legal authority* that constitutional law has. Constitutional law has supposed authority in the political community in the following sense: practices of *institutional recognition* rest on the fundamental assumption that constitutional law is authoritative over its subjects; and that subjects of law have the most reason to comply with such law rather than follow the determinations each of them would adopt were they to deliberate directly on each regulated matter by exercising independent practical reasoning.

Constitutional norms serve this function by carrying out the (supposed) normative signification rooted and upheld in certain practices of institutional recognition. We may now approach these practices of upholding and enforcing the Constitution more closely, to unearth some of their fundamental commitments.

II. The Written Constitution and Supreme Court Precedent

American constitutional practice, judicial practice in particular,[4] is committed to two salient normative propositions. First, determinations inscribed in the constitutional text constitute the primary authoritative source of a distinctive body of supreme law.[5] Second, along with constitutional text, a set of pronouncements made in the practice of constitutional enforcement, mainly Supreme Court precedent, also partake in the positive authoritative base of constitutional law.[6]

[4] On the salience of judicial recognitional practices, see Joseph Raz, *The Authority of Law: Essays on Law and Morality* (Oxford, Oxford University Press, 1979) 107–08 and Christopher Kutz, 'The Judicial Community' (2001) 11 *Phil Issues* 462. Matthew Adler, 'Popular Constitutionalism and the Rule of Recognition: Whose Practices Ground U.S. Law?' (2006) 100 *NW U L Rev* 719 counterargues that there are multiple, partly overlapping, recognitional practices. Even so, such multiplicity would not diminish the value of examining the normative structure of a salient institution: the institutional system of legal norms practised as such by the courts of law, whose adjudicatory function is upheld by the officials of the political community.

[5] On the centrality of the constitutional text see Frederick Schauer, 'The Constitution as Text and Rule' (1987) 29 *Wm & Mary L Rev* 41.

[6] See Richard Fallon, *Implementing the Constitution* (Cambridge, Harvard University Press, 2000) 111–26 (arguing that American constitutional law consists of the written Constitution and an unwritten one that supplements or mediates the former), David Strauss, 'Common Law Constitutional Interpretation' (1996) 63 *U Chicago L Rev* 877 (arguing that the constitutional law practised in the US

Under existing judicial practice, the Court's interpretations are awarded qualified authoritative force over officials charged with applying the law under the doctrines of *res judicata* and *stare decisis*. Even a Supreme Court Justice is conditionally bound to follow them despite the fact that they may differ from her best (independent) interpretive judgement. As the Court itself has repeatedly pronounced, *stare decisis* 'carries such persuasive force that we have always required a departure from precedent to be supported by some special justification'.[7]

Our account shall not discriminate against any of these two propositions. We may bring them together and conceive of constitutional law as the corpus of legal norms that carry out the (supposed) normative import of the Constitution, along with the surrounding practice of authoritative constitutional exposition. I do not claim that this formulation is the only satisfactory one; yet, it provides us with an operational idea, sufficient for what is to follow. Reasonable variation is to be kept in the background and I understand that accommodation can be provided by the reader herself, without affecting the core ideas of this work.

What is important is that this thin account enables us to locate constitutional norms institutionally and to explain how they serve their preemptive function: constitutional norms carry out the normative signification of the Constitution, along with its history of authoritative exposition. They are grounded in: (a) the status of the Constitution as the primary authoritative source of constitutional law along with the status of Supreme Court precedent as conditionally authoritative source of constitutional law, and (b) the fact that they carry out the Constitution's normative signification. The status of the Constitution, along with judicial precedent, as the authoritative sources of constitutional law, in turn, is a fundamental commitment of constitutional practice.

III. The Contested Import of Text and Precedent

The account adopted here does not reduce constitutional interpretation to the task of providing a literary exegesis of the constitutional text and precedent. While this is one interpretive option that has received attention by conservative scholars

is best explained as a *sui generis* common law system) and *The Living Constitution* (Oxford, Oxford University Press, 2010), and David Shapiro, 'The Role of Precedent in Constitutional Adjudication: an Introspection' (2008) 86 *Texas L Rev* 929, 942 ('the suggested dichotomy between the Constitution and a decision or line of decisions interpreting it is in some respects significantly misleading').

[7] *Dickerson v United States*, 530 US 428, 443 (2000). Fallon adds: 'throughout constitutional history, Supreme Court Justices have assumed with near unanimity that they are legally authorized and sometimes bound to follow precedents, sometimes even when prior cases were themselves erroneous at the time of their decision. Indeed, I know of no Justice in the history of the Supreme Court who has persistently questioned precedent-based decision-making'. Richard Fallon, 'Legitimacy and the Constitution' (2005) 118 *Harv L Rev* 1787, 1821–22.

and judges, the normative import of text and precedent is thoroughly contested in constitutional practice, inviting constructive interpretation.

Recognition of the authoritative status of the text does not imply commitment to textualism. The normative import of the Constitution is underdetermined by the positive determinations inscribed in its text and is hotly debated in argumentative constitutional practice.[8] The same applies, notoriously enough, to precedent.[9]

I will discuss the nature and implications of positive under-determinacy in chapter four. I indicate here, by way of example, that fundamental features of American constitutional law, like judicial review and substantive due process, lack express textual support or fit uncomfortably with their purported textual grounding. *Marbury v Madison's* holding on judicial review does not have express textual support. It can more plausibly be understood as carrying out the normative import of the Constitution as a whole by effectuating the various substantive norms rooted therein. And, in John Ely's famous remark, the substantive dimension of the 'due process of law' clauses 'sounds like a contradiction in terms—sort of like "green pastel redness"'.[10] Both issues are now covered by established precedent. Yet, the underlying contestation resounds in myriads of controversies about how to give concrete meaning to the scope and intensity of judicial review and to the dimensions of protected liberty.

Recognition of the authoritative status of text and precedent does not commit us even to the way these two sources of law combine in supporting overall interpretive judgements about the law. Neither is there institutional convergence in the practice about such a way. It is perhaps fair to say that the practice is fundamentally committed, on the one hand, to the text's *primacy* and, on the other, to the *conditional* nature of precedential authority. Thus, interpretive practice is not treated as standing on an equal par with the determinations embodied in constitutional text since precedent is *in principle* taken not to supersede contrary constitutional text.[11] Furthermore, precedent is supposed to be responsive to the written Constitution. The fact that a precedent does not offer an attractive construction of the Constitution is treated as a legitimate, though not necessarily conclusive, argument against the precedent. Yet, beyond this basic ground of understanding, there is wild disagreement in the practice over the appropriate structure of text and precedent

[8] See Frederick Schauer, 'Constitutional Invocations' (1997) 65 *Fordham L Rev* 1295, 1309 (as a matter of judicial practice, moral text often produces non-moral adjudication and non-moral text often produces moral adjudication).

[9] See, eg, Karl Llewellyn, *The Common Law Tradition: Deciding Appeals* (Boston, Little, Brown & Co, 1960) 62–91. For an overview of the literature in the constitutional field see Shapiro, above n 6.

[10] John Hart Ely, *Democracy and Distrust: A Theory of Judicial Review* (Cambridge, Harvard University Press, 1980) 18.

[11] See Fallon, above n 6, ch 3. See also Strauss (1996), above n 6, at 899. David Strauss, discussing cases where the text seems inconsistent to well-established principles of constitutional law, argues that 'the claim about the anomalies is not that it is impossible to read the language in a way that is consistent with the established principles. We *do* read it that way; in a sense, that is precisely the point. The claim is rather that the established principles are inconsistent with the most straightforward or natural reading'. David Strauss, 'Foreword: Does the Constitution Mean What it Says?' (2015) 129 *Harv L Rev* 1, 29.

in the light of competing explanations for the special role and primacy of the written Constitution over judicial gloss and for the conditionally binding character of past judicial interpretations of the Constitution. In fact, while any account of constitutional interpretation ignoring the positive authoritative nature of text and precedent would not fit fundamental features of constitutional practice, the appropriate structure of text and precedent (including the appropriate structure between judicial and non-judicial precedent), as well as the precise nature and conditions of precedential authority and their variation with regard to multiple kinds of officials are the subject of contested constitutional interpretation.

For instance, one may discern a divide in the literature between conceptions of constitutional interpretation that take reliance on precedent as the starting point of analysis, which may then be trumped by overriding justifications, and conceptions that accept such reliance provided that the respective precedent rests upon a reasonable reading of the Constitution.[12] This leads to the further distinction between treating precedent as supplementing versus treating precedent as merely mediating between current practice and the text. Finally, even on the very understanding of textual primacy, there is divergence between the orthodoxy holding that nothing irreconcilable with the text can properly be considered part of constitutional law and those, like Dworkin, willing to argue that precedent and practice over time can in principle supersede even so basic a piece of interpretive data as the Constitution's text when no way of reconciling both text and practice in an overall constructive interpretation can be found.[13] All these accounts are reasonably presented as dovetailing (at least in part) with elements of institutional practice and as offering legitimate interpretations of structural aspects of existing constitutional law.

IV. The Grounds of Textual and Precedential Authority

A. Interpretive Institutional Acceptance

I assume that the ideas presented in section II above, or a reasonable variant thereof, fairly capture certain elementary features of American constitutional law. Indeed, I will employ them as a building block for what follows. Yet, it is important to pause for a moment on their grounding. This will enable us to clarify somehow the intricate relationship between the institutional and the interpretive dimensions of constitutional law.

[12] See Shapiro, above n 6, at 933–35 (distinguishing between those who rely on precedent 'only if' and those who rely 'unless').

[13] Contrast Ronald Dworkin, *Justice in Robes* (Cambridge, Harvard University Press, 2006) 128–29 with Laurence Tribe, 'Comment' in Antonin Scalia, *A Matter of Interpretation: Federal Courts and the Law* (Princeton, Princeton University Press, 1997) 77.

Richard Fallon has argued that the authoritative status of constitutional precedent, as well as of the Constitution itself, lies upon *institutional acceptance*.[14] This approach is faithful to the institutional nature of law and, indeed, provides the starting point for understanding the grounds of textual and precedential authority. Yet, I doubt that even the thin account of constitutional law presented in this chapter can be established by mere reference to and by systematisation of the facts of institutional acceptance exhibited in constitutional practice. Institutional acceptance is interpretive. If a litigant presents a constitutional claim flatly contradicting the basic precepts of *Marbury*, for instance, a judge may not explain its rejection merely by noting that all other judges accept *Marbury* as a matter of course. Rather, textual and precedential authority is ultimately grounded on *interpretive argument*: a kind of normative argument that interprets constitutional practice and affirms the centrality of these features in the light of the fundamental commitment of the practice to constitutional legitimacy.

In this section, I wish to discuss the shape of such an argument, developed, by necessity, from the standpoint of somebody who does accept (or assume) the fundamental normative commitments of the practice and is asked to explain the salience of text and precedent. But first, I need to clarify what is at stake in the debate about the interpretive nature of this argument.

Our task is to make best sense of constitutional practice and of its fundamental normative commitments. The institutional practice of upholding norms of constitutional law is a normative practice. It is widely accepted that judges do not necessarily follow the applicable scheme of norms merely because others also do so.[15] In fact, they are best seen as doing so in the light of normative reasons for accepting constitutional law as legitimate, reasons that vary among officials. Thus, we may distinguish between the *content of the law* and the *reasons for accepting such law as legitimate*.

The paradigmatic jurisprudential question is whether such reasons affect the content of the law or whether they operate only as background conditions for the operation of the practice. I will argue in chapter four for the former. As a general matter, what other judges have accepted in the past about the content of the law is not treated in the practice as conclusive with regard to law's demands. Institutional

[14] Richard Fallon, 'Constitutional Precedent viewed through the Lens of Hartian Jurisprudence' (2008) 86 *N Car L Rev* 101. See also Kent Greenawalt, 'The Rule of Recognition and the Constitution' (1987) 85 *Mich L Rev* 621, and Frederick Schauer, 'Precedent and the Necessary Externality of Constitutional Norms' (1994) 17 *Harv J L & Pub Pol'y* 45.

[15] Joseph Raz, 'On the Authority and Interpretation of Constitutions' in Larry Alexander (ed), *Constitutionalism: Philosophical Foundations* (Cambridge, Cambridge University Press, 1998) 157, 161–62. See also Julie Dickson, 'Is the Rule of Recognition Really a Conventional Rule?' (2007) 27 *Oxford Journal of Legal Studies* 373–402 and Andrei Marmor, 'Legal Conventionalism' in Jules Coleman (ed), *Hart's Postscript* (Oxford, Oxford University Press, 2001) 193, 211 ('Does this mean that the reasons for following a set of constitutive conventions consist in the fact that others follow it too? Not necessarily. We cannot explain people's reasons for engaging in a conventional practice just by reference to a desirability for uniformity of action … Nevertheless, conventional rules exist only if they are actually practiced by the pertinent community').

acceptance of propositions of constitutional law is not treated in the practice as sufficient and indeed conclusive ground for their validity. As Ronald Dworkin has famously argued, constitutional practice is argumentative, committed to standards related to the reasons for accepting constitutional law as legitimate. I will expand on this idea and defend the thesis that the content of constitutional law is characterised by what we may call constructive dependence upon our reflective practical reason, including the reasons behind supposed constitutional legitimacy, and their operation in carrying out the normative signification of constitutional practices. This argumentative character is reflected in a standing commitment to reflect, reject or defend even established propositions about the content of constitutional law on the basis of deliberative considerations that extend beyond bare text and precedent and that are not reducible to claims about institutional endorsement. Given the pluralism experienced over these underlying considerations, this argumentative character is reflected further in the actual disagreement over the content of constitutional norms, including disagreement over the force of text and precedent.

For the purposes of this chapter one, our question is more focused: do reasons for upholding the legitimacy of constitutional law affect the endorsement of the thin account presented in section II above as a valid account of American constitutional law? Do reasons of this kind affect endorsing the salience of text and precedent in constitutional practice? Or, is their supposition merely a general background condition for the legal authority of constitutional practice and of whatever content such practice recognises as a matter of social fact? Assuming the overall constructive dependence of the content of constitutional law upon reflective practical reason I defend in chapter four, the narrow question we face here is whether such constructive dependence also applies to this very abstract account of American constitutional law or whether the salience of text and precedent is settled conventionally in the practice.

A tempting reply would be to treat the abstract account as settled by some set of social conventions constituting constitutional practice that legal institutions, for independent background reasons of political morality, consider or treat as binding and legitimate. This reply would explain disagreement over details by distinguishing between the abstract account itself and its 'specification'. The abstract account provides the conventional form, while constructive reflection and disagreement is pertinent in filling the substance.[16] The salience of text and precedent is settled by convention, their import is a matter of interpretation. Say, the core principle of *Marbury* on judicial review, or the core principle of *stare decisis* is settled by

[16] Professor Coleman has made the related claim that the existence of a conventional constitutional rule is compatible with disputes about its content that are subject to resolution by moral argument. Jules Coleman, *The Practice of Principle: in Defense of a Pragmatist Approach to Legal Theory* (Oxford, Oxford University Press, 2001) ch 7. Ronald Dworkin, in reply, has argued that such a view trivialises legal positivism and eviscerates legal conventionalism. Dworkin, above n 13, at 193–94.

convention, but the details of constitutional doctrine are subject to interpretative reasoning.

Can such a distinction be sustained? I believe not. For the distinction to make sense, we would need to be able to independently specify a conventional component that would somehow channel the moral argument involved in the specification of content. Any such inquiry, nonetheless, would misunderstand both the kind and depth of the controversy experienced in the practice and of its relation to the more abstract question. We have seen that constitutional practice experiences contestation and engages in thorough reflection on the very nature and force of textual primacy and precedential force. Claimants disagree over how text and precedent matter and over why they matter. And they consider that their arguments on why they matter are legitimate considerations in determining how they matter. Given such internal reflection and contestation, the social fact that there is in the practice convergence to the effect that text and precedent *somehow* matter cannot in itself establish the authoritative salience of text and precedent.

Now, one could insist that we still have a rudimentary idea that text and precedent somehow matter? Can't this support a distinction between what matters, settled by convention, and how they matter, open to argument in the light of why they matter? I suggest not. It immediately invites the question, what 'somehow' means. And I cannot see how one is to settle this without appeal to why text and precedent matter.

I obviously don't deny that text and precedent matter and that there is convergence in the practice that this is so. And I don't even deny that positivists are right that the fact of convergence is of significance both for the existence of the constitutional order and for settling textual and precedential salience. But institutional convergence does not in itself determine such salience.

B. Affirming the Fundamental Role of Text and Precedent

But if this is so, if appeal to practical reason is needed, how can we explain that institutional convergence amounts to something more than a temporary equilibrium in the argumentative struggle among competing thicker constitutional accounts, an equilibrium that may destabilise at their next internal restructuring? The answer to this question lies in the fact that, given the nature of both contestation and convergence, and in the light of the operating reasons for valuing text and precedent, the authoritative salience of text and precedent does constitute a *fundamental* normative commitment of the overall practice; but this conclusion implies and stands sensitive to argument of practical reason, developed from within the practice, to the effect that a departure from such an account would fundamentally undermine the reasons behind the legitimacy of operating constitutional practice.

For instance, there are voices in the academia arguing for a radical reconstruction of constitutional practice along originalist or textualist approaches and against the 'corrupting influence of precedent'.[17] Their rejection as a matter of applicable law cannot depend merely on their descriptive inadequacy as to actual judicial practice. In rejecting a strong textualist argument claiming, say, that the common law-like scheme of constitutional exposition is an aberrational, non-fundamental element of the practice, one has to counterclaim, in a process of morally engaged argumentation, that (among perhaps other possible defects) such a textualist argument fails as an interpretation of fundamental normative commitments of constitutional practice. In making this claim, one has to employ some morally non-neutral structure of constitutional legitimacy and engage with it in order to bring out such commitments of the practice in the light of its supposed legitimacy. Thus, the validity of the thin account of constitutional law presented here is ultimately dependent upon constructive practical reason engaged in the process of carrying out the fundamental normative commitments of American constitutional practice.

We now need to explain how the fact of recognitional convergence around the salience of text and precedent is implicated in this constructive enterprise. As mentioned (section I), constitutional practice is committed to the idea that subjects of law are supposed to comply with the scheme of constitutional norms upheld in the practice rather than follow the reasons they would directly endorse by exercising independent practical reasoning. In doing so, they are best seen as supposing that certain facts about the practice, including the efficacious recognition and enforcement of the relevant scheme of norms, are an important consideration in upholding, in connection with further considerations like the sufficient justice of its content, the legitimacy of constitutional law. Recognitional convergence around the salience of text and precedent may reasonably be seen as having a central role in this process so as to support the interpretive conclusion that such salience reflects fundamental normative commitments of the practice.

This argument, of course, has to be made in more detail and its content would evidently vary with the conception of legitimacy each practitioner holds. All we can do here is propose a rationalisation that makes best sense of the normative commitments of a practitioner, as we see them, while allowing ample scope for debate over the details. Thus, the argument, to be successful, would have to single out certain features of this institutional convergence: the respective normative beliefs are deeply entrenched in the normative practice; they stand in relations of mutual support with a vast number of concrete propositions of law held in the practice; their endorsement exhibits stability and temporal continuity; moreover, they are interwoven into a collective belief-structure: it is shared knowledge among its holders that these beliefs are largely shared (in reasonable variants) and treated as normatively significant in the practice. And they reflect appreciation

[17] See Gary Lawson, 'The Constitutional Case against Precedent' (1994) 17 *Harv JL & Pub Pol'y* 23 and Michael Stokes Paulsen, 'The Intrinsically Corrupting Influence of Precedent' (2005) 22 *Const Commentary* 289.

that continuation of the practice, despite its possible defects, is a matter of political and moral significance. In the light of such and other related features, a plausible (in light of moral reason) way to make sense of this recognitional convergence is to conceive of the special status of the Constitution and of its surrounding practice of authoritative exposition as reflecting fundamental normative commitments of constitutional practice. And as recognitional efficacy and stability has to be understood within an encompassing account of constitutional legitimacy, the argument, in its fully-fledged form, would also have to show how such fundamental convergence around the salience of text and precedent fits with other relevant considerations (sufficient justice of their content, democratic pedigree, etc, see chapter two, section I(B)) in support of the overall commitment, implied in the practice, to the legitimacy of American constitutional law. Finally, it should be stressed that such an argument would be continuous with more engaged argumentation, singling out specific facts about textual primacy and precedential force and explicating how each element matters and how they are best combined in support of specific interpretive arguments about the law.

One clarification remains to be made. The opening aspiration of this chapter was to capture some features of the constitutional practice that any account of constitutional interpretation ignoring them *would not fit* the practice. I hope that the argumentation advanced shows that the notion of 'fit' shall not be understood as referring to descriptive accuracy. In claiming that any account of constitutional interpretation failing to capture the special status of text and precedent would not fit constitutional practice, we are to be understood as claiming that such an account would not dovetail with fundamental normative commitments of the practice. Thus, in employing accounts of constitutional interpretation exhibiting such failings, one would find himself, for better or worse, being immersed into another practice.

2

The Authority of Constitutional Law

In the previous chapter, I discussed the legal nature of constitutional norms, emphasising their institutional dimension. Given that dimension, the legal authority of constitutional norms shall not be confused with their (normative) authority, political legitimacy and ideal content. This chapter presents the latter concepts and discusses the kind of considerations grounding each feature of constitutional norms.

I. Constitutional Authority, Political Legitimacy and Public Reason

A. The Relevance of Political Legitimacy

I argued that the legal authority of constitutional law lies in the *institutional recognition* of its normative authority and I clarified that such recognition is interpretive and argumentative. However, the fact of institutional recognition cannot and does not establish whether the supposed authority of constitutional law is in fact justified and whether institutional practices rest on sound assumptions. On the contrary, these are quintessential moral issues. Humans assess their conduct by employing practical reasoning. In the exercise of public power, they are subject to public reason. If constitutional law is to have any authority over us, such authority cannot be grounded in claims or beliefs of officials; it would have to be grounded in public reason, and relevant claims have to be defended or defeated in requisite argument.

In this chapter, I will discuss the kind of considerations involved in examining whether constitutional law has the normative authority assumed in the social practices of institutional recognition. The arguments are not meant to be conclusive, but will hopefully illuminate the kind of pertinent considerations. This is of importance for any theory of constitutional interpretation since, as we will see, in performing this cognitive activity, we assume constitutional authority and, hence, we assume the existence of the pertinent grounding. Accordingly, proper understanding of the kind of considerations grounding constitutional authority is helpful in assessing the rationality and placement of constitutional interpretation in practical reasoning (see chapter three), as well as in illuminating the moral engagement involved in conducting constitutional interpretation (see chapter five).

The starting point for any discussion of constitutional authority is the realisation that the content of constitutional law often *falls short of being ideal.* Despite the refinement that the interpretive process often contributes, constitutional norms seldom approach perfection. This, however, does not imply that constitutional norms cannot have authority to guide human conduct. For instance, in certain subject areas, most officials charged with applying the law are less likely to come up, individually and effectively, with more appropriate resolutions than the ones the law provides them with. This is especially so wherever the coordinated application and enforcement of some constitutional policy matters more than its content (judged independently). In such cases, non-ideal constitutional norms normally have authority over these officials.[1]

Having said that, most of constitutional law differs from 'traffic regulation' and related coordination games since it structures the distribution of political and social power and addresses fundamental issues of political morality. In the majority of cases, especially in fundamental rights jurisprudence, independent content is more important than coordinated enforcement, and it is hard to show that certain institutions, say Congress, may not sometimes come up with superior resolutions over issues of constitutional significance than those the law provides.

In such cases, we need a more nuanced concept to assess constitutional authority. The concept of political legitimacy is, I think, the best candidate available. The idea is that if a set of conditions is satisfied, the *political legitimacy* of the constitutional structure provides an independent ground supporting the conditional and qualified authority of constitutional law. It is in fact arguable that, under conditions of political legitimacy and within a certain range, we have a general though conditional duty to comply with *non-ideal* constitutional law rather than to follow the determinations we would endorse were we to deliberate directly by exercising independent practical reasoning.

B. Political Legitimacy and Political Justice

The conditions, scope and rationale underlying such a duty are clarified in the light of public reason. Endorsement of this argument is not committed upon any tendentious conception of public reason. The purpose is to explain the kind of

[1] See Joseph Raz, *The Morality of Freedom* (Oxford, Oxford University Press, 1986) 53. On the coordinative function of constitutionalism see Russell Hardin, *Liberalism, Constitutionalism and Democracy* (Oxford, Oxford University Press, 1999). On the importance of coordinative enforcement against constitutional violations see B Weingast, 'The Political Foundations of Democracy and the Rule of Law' (1997) 91 *American Political Science Review* 245–63.

moral considerations that are relevant in assessing political legitimacy, rather than to perform specific assessments.

Still, for this purpose, it is illuminating to somehow thicken the operative account and employ the concept of political justice. I understand the concept broadly enough to cover both the democratic basis and the substantive justice of the content of public policy. In this broad sense, political justice may be seen as a fundamental political value for a political community of free and equal citizens.[2] It reflects the very nature of public power as the collective power of such a political community and the proper political bonds linking its members as free and equals. Accordingly, it matters for all exercise of public power and, in principle, it is not to be compromised by competing policy considerations, as it expresses the deepest commitment to equal citizenship. Finally, it does not merely set limits to the exercise of public power; neither does it exhaust applicable political reasons. Rather, it structures the (irreducibly plural) realm of political values by guiding our determination of the admissibility, relevance and structure of competing political reasons. It provides us with an argumentative structure that can help us determine, for instance, whether strong collective beliefs about the morality of same-sex marriage may permissibly be invoked in determining its legal status, or whether universities may pursue student-body diversity by employing racial classifications in the admissions process and, if so, how pertinent commitments to diversity and racial equality are to be understood and permissibly structured.

On this frame, we may claim that under public reason the *exercise of public power shall be governed by principles of political justice.* This commitment has inspired the more respectable moments of American constitutional history from the founding era[3] onwards and, I think, reflects the considerate convictions many of us have about the *appropriate* exercise of public power.[4] Similarly, the conditions, scope and rationale behind a duty to comply with non-ideal constitutional law are to be assessed in the light of political justice, as the issues raised by the question of political legitimacy are paradigmatically issues of political justice so understood; they address at the very core the nature of the political bonds among the members of the political community and their implications for compliance under potentially non-ideal law.

Our societies experience a wide pluralism of opinion over the considerations grounding political legitimacy and their application. This in turn reflects disagreement over political justice and the content of public reason. Such pluralism

[2] The broader idea is Rawlsian, although it is not committed to any specific conception of public reason. For Rawls' own conception, specifying the realm of permissible political reasons, see John Rawls, *Political Liberalism* (New York, Columbia University Press, 1993, 1996) 212 ff and *The Law of Peoples With 'The Idea of Public Reason Revisited'* (Cambridge, Harvard University Press, 1999) 129 ff.

[3] *The Federalist,* No 51 (James Madison, 'justice is the end of government').

[4] See John Rawls, *A Theory of Justice*, rev edn (Cambridge, Harvard University Press, 1999) 3–4 ('justice is the first virtue of social institutions, as truth is of systems of thought. Being first virtues of human activities, truth and justice are uncompromising').

underlies, as I will argue in chapters four and five, much of interpretive disagreement; and partly accounts for the interpretive nature of constitutional practices. Some of us emphasise the democratic pedigree of the law and argue that citizens have a prima facie duty to comply with constitutional choices that have prevailed in fair political processes. Others stress considerations of stability and efficacious enforcement of a constitutional scheme. And finally, many others point out that a legitimate regime shall employ modes of institutional reasoning that appeal to the status of its citizens as free and equal and satisfy certain substantive requirements of equal liberty.

I assume that any reasonable conception of legitimacy shall somehow accommodate all three perspectives and it is fair to say that core elements of all three are implicit in actual constitutional discourse and case law. But we need to be aware of a fundamental difference of emphasis between conceptions that prioritise issues of *just content* and conceptions that focus on *partly content-independent* factors, like democratic pedigree or efficacy. This has important implications for the acceptable margin of judgement we allow to political institutions and for the degree of injustice that renders a constitutional choice incapable of grounding a duty to public compliance. It is of paramount importance whether we consider an (otherwise democratic) regime legitimate provided it satisfies certain minimal requirements of fair criminal procedure or whether we condition its legitimacy on the defendants being invested with a full set of protections that minimise the risk of wrongful conviction.

At the same time, any manichaean dichotomy here will fail to do justice to considerate ideas about constitutional legitimacy. Fair democratic procedures presuppose collective reflection and due deliberation and a certain degree of public-spiritedness. Efficacy is viable only upon public endorsement of just content. And equal liberty includes equal political liberty. I discuss my own views on the relation between democracy and equal liberty in chapter nine. The main idea is that in a democracy political institutions are to be understood as the collective arms of free and equal citizens. And their operations shall rest upon the idea that each citizen has a capacity to develop a sense of justice worthy of equal respect. At the same time, equal political liberty does not require indifference to the substantive justice of constitutional law as democracy and liberty largely presuppose one another and reflect a joint commitment to equal liberty. And I will argue further in chapter fourteen that there is a dominant sensibility in constitutional rights jurisprudence to the effect that protection of fundamental rights reflects the elementary relation between free and equal citizens as joint tenants in sovereignty. It is respect for this commitment that *structures* the very idea of the common good that democratic policies pursue.

For reasons of such kind, I assume that considerate ideas of legitimacy would include elements of all three accounts. For instance, on an account that I would be prepared to defend, important considerations for assessing political legitimacy under political justice include: (a) the *efficacious recognition* of the constitutional structure by most members of the political community and its efficacious *enforcement* by the officials of the respective community, (b) under conditions of *fair political responsiveness* (over the amendment, interpretation and application of the structure), (c) its enforcement in compliance with the rule of law, (d) the *sufficient* (though not necessarily *full) justice* of its content and (e) the institutionalisation of a reasonable process of constitutional *amendment*.

The original democratic pedigree of the Constitution is also important. Some overemphasise this point. Founding eras in the Western world usually praise themselves for achieving a kind of constitutional self-government: the people giving themselves a Constitution. This idea has a powerful mobilising force. And in successful constitutional experiments it invites us to ponder on the fact that such eras set in motion processes of public formation, commitment and contestation that brought us to the present state of affairs. At the same time, it may well turn out that some of the claims may be fictitious and the normative force may well diminish over time. We shall not forget that the longest-lasting empires in European history, the Byzantine and the German empire, claimed that the power of their emperors was constitutionally based on a transfer of imperium by the Roman populus. This example evidently does not apply to us. Yet, it offers a reminder: for old Constitutions, as far as democracy is concerned, it is equally important that the present status of the Constitution is reasonably perceived to reflect and, in turn, to give effect to the equal political standing of its citizens.

The important point for present purposes is the distinction between *sufficient justice* and *full justice*. 'Sufficient justice' refers to constitutional content not unacceptably distanced from the requirements of political justice.[5] If so, the argument from political legitimacy may appear puzzling. It proposes that in many circumstances we have reason to refrain from acting on (what we take to be) a more just though unconstitutional political principle. Different conceptions of political legitimacy have their own ways to approach this difficulty. Following John Rawls, I would propose that, under political justice, the appropriate political relation among reasonable members of a political community and, in particular, the bonds of civility and reciprocity among them do justify the existence of such a reason.[6] The basic assumption is that a decent constitutional structure is accepted and efficaciously practised by most members of the political community under conditions of fair political responsiveness. Reasonable members of such a community

[5] Rawls has argued that political legitimacy is a weaker notion than political justice. See Rawls (1996), above n 2, at 428. See also R Fallon, 'Legitimacy and the Constitution' (2005) 118 *Harv L Rev* 1787, 1798 ('minimal theories of moral legitimacy define a threshold above which legal regimes are sufficiently just to deserve the support of those who are subject to them in the absence of better, realistically attainable alternatives').

[6] See Rawls, above n 4, at 311–12. See also Dworkin's account of political legitimacy, focused on the notion of community of principle, in his *Law's Empire* (Cambridge, Harvard University Press, 1986) 190–206. For competing, more sceptical accounts of the justified scope of political authority and of a general (even prima facie) duty to obey the law, see Raz, above n 1, at 70–109, Leslie Green, *The Authority of the State* (Oxford, Oxford University Press, 1988), and John Simmons, *Justification and Legitimacy: Essays on Rights and Obligations* (Cambridge, Cambridge University Press, 2001).

are supposed to appreciate the significance of the following two facts. First, there is a range of reasonable disagreement over the best resolution of contested issues of political justice.[7] Unanimous endorsement of the ideal arrangement is incompatible with open and viable democracies and perhaps with free human spirit as such. Secondly, given the duty of publicity and the salience of constitutional issues, extra-constitutional revisionism carries with it significant risks, including transition costs, unstable outcomes,[8] and disruption of public trust.

In such conditions, the bonds of civility and reciprocity require that we comply with *reasonable* (even though not ideal) constitutional law. Such compliance is a way to realise the good of living in a sufficiently just political community under conditions of reciprocity and despite the fact of reasonable disagreement over the requirements of political justice. Moreover, such compliance is normally qualified in covering reasonable law.[9] And it does not preclude political conduct aiming at a more just Constitution through a reasonable amending process.

C. The Charge of Constitutional Moralism

We may pause at this point to take note of a rather widespread concern about the employment of abstract moral concepts, like the concept of political justice, in assessing the legitimacy of constitutional structures. It might seem that by employing this moralistic vocabulary, we are attempting somehow to smuggle into constitutional theory a certain normative picture with undemocratic implications and a conceptual vocabulary with alienating potential.

Bernard Williams has emphasised that political philosophy often takes the form of what he calls 'Political Moralism', a sensibility putting the moral *before* the political and assuming that it is the task of public institutions to implement moral principles.[10] This is often associated with a conception of public reason that fails to take modern social formations and historical contingencies as fundamental and disables us from mobilising ideas that make sense to us given our collective projects and pursuits.

[7] See Rawls (1999), above n 2, at 137.

[8] See Joseph Raz, 'On the Authority and Interpretation of Constitutions' in Larry Alexander (ed), *Constitutionalism: Philosophical Foundations* 157, 169–76 (Cambridge, Cambridge University Press, 1998), and Fallon, above n 5, at 1798, on constitutional efficacy and stability. Game theory-inspired political science has rightly emphasised that constitutional stability requires constitutional self-enforcement, which in turn normally implies (a) that a sufficient degree of coordination is in place, and (b) that the respective agents would consider the existing structure preferable over alternative, ideal ones, (for example, because such structures are feared to be unstable—see D Acemoglu, G Egorov & K Sonin, 'Dynamics and Stability of Constitutions, Coalitions and Clubs' (2012) 102 *American Economic Review* 1446).

[9] See Rawls (1996), above n 2, at 308–12. See also Dworkin, above n 6, at 214 (a community of principle can claim moral legitimacy; yet, its claims may be defeated by the demands of justice).

[10] Bernard Williams, *In the Beginning Was the Deed: Realism and Moralism in Political Argument* (Princeton, Princeton University Press, 2007) 2–3.

From a democratic perspective, Jeremy Waldron adds that by treating substantive conceptions of public reason as natural, we ultimately strip the public of their fundamental moral power to *settle*, through democratic processes, applicable public reasons for their societies.[11] And we are brought into a conceptual terrain lacking in argumentative resources needed to scrutinise assertive elitist claims, like the *Obergefell* edict on the duty of courts to implement the precepts of liberty 'as we learn its meaning'.

Proper treatment of the merits and relevance of abstract moral theory in normative political reasoning is beyond of scope of this book. But it is important to keep these concerns in mind and feel confident that the notions of public reason and of political justice do not impoverish our normative outlook in constitutional matters. Although these concepts are not value-neutral, they are largely operational concepts that enable us to engage in constructive debate about pertinent ideals, concerns and commitments; and as loci for focused disagreements over such contested commitments. The substantive arguments we employ in giving content to these notions may well fit historical contingencies, and we may well take care that our theorising springs from the society's moral horizon and responds to actual concerns and commitments. Abstract reasoning would have its proper place, as we need normative reasoning to be critical of its own historical contingencies—especially in quintessential issues of moral concern, like the fundamental liberties of persons. But at the end of the day, abstract principles as such do not claim any metaphysical priority over more local commitments, nor do they imply that concrete ways of exercising public power are unjust or illegitimate *because* they fail to implement abstract principles of political justice. Abstract principles grow out of more local concerns, in the process of explaining more fully and at a general level the pertinent considerations.

The same concern for harmony applies to the content of such principles and to the very idea of 'matters of principle' that is central in 'moralistic' constitutional jurisprudence. Such principles, like the idea of equal liberty or equal freedom as exemplified in *Obergefell*, play an important structuring role in the irreducibly plural realm of political values by guiding determination of the admissibility, relevance and structure of competing reasons. Yet, in this process, we may well take care that reasoning from principle does not overwhelm the policies and pursuits that a political community actually wishes to pursue. And if a happy ending cannot obtain, we may have to consider whether questionable policies are not truly public, but betray fundamental commitments that, when honoured, enable the community to speak in the name of its members as free and equal.

[11] Jeremy Waldron, *Law and Disagreement* (Oxford, Oxford University Press, 1999) esp part two. See also Richard Bellamy, 'The Democratic Qualities of Courts: A Critical Analysis of Three Arguments' (2013) 49 *Representation* 333–46.

I will return to this issue in the end of the book, pointing out that, at any rate, affirming the entanglement of principle and policy provides us with superior intellectual resources than dropping this distinction altogether (chapter fourteen, section IV(B)).

Similarly, as I explained above and I will discuss in more detail in chapter nine, the value of political justice also reflects the democratic basis of public power and illuminates the value of fair democratic procedures. In fact, an important driving concern of this book is the idea that, under political justice, and given reasonable pluralism over its content, judicial reasoning over issues of constitutional law shall pay due attention to the input from public discourse and the operation of democratic processes. What appears to me indefensible, on the other hand, is that we can get rid of the substantive concept of public reason and of political justice and satisfy us with procedures. Without employing fundamental moral commitments, like the commitment to equal citizenship, we are incapable of assessing both processes of public decision-making, and the decisions such processes make (chapter nine, sections I–II and chapter ten, section II).

II. Political Justice and Ideal Constitutional Law

I argued that in some circumstances political legitimacy supports a duty to comply with reasonable, though non-ideal, constitutional law. If the applicable circumstances obtain, such compliance satisfies public reason. I then thickened the operative account of public reason employing the concept of political justice, in order to specify somehow the applicable circumstances. The driving idea is that such duty to comply may be defended only under the general principle that the exercise of public power be governed by principles of political justice; never as an exception to this principle.

Having examined how the pursuit of political justice affects the stance towards existing non-ideal constitutional law, let us now briefly touch upon the way this general principle applies to the enactment and amendment of the Constitution and to the considerations grounding its ideal content. My aim is just to make the pertinent contrast without any ambition to sketch a theory of constitutional design.

Constitutional law establishes the basic public institutions, confers upon them the authority to exercise public power and stipulates fundamental directives guiding that exercise. In enacting or amending the Constitution, participants in the debate deliberate over two kinds of choices: First, over the issues to regulate on the constitutional level and, secondly, over their appropriate regulation. In both choices, there is reason to set up a constitutional scheme expected to make it more likely that public power would be exercised *in compliance with public reason and political justice.*

Again, this idea does not imply a 'moralistic' perspective. In considering the *scope* of the written Constitution we take note of the fact that proper content is partly dependent upon local contingencies and should be responsive to the actual formation of considerate and time-specific political judgements in the citizenry. Considerations of this sort advise that many choices should not be entrenched in the text of the Constitution. Rather they should be left to the better judgement of the constituted branches of government. At the same time, we also attend to various issues of political structure, strategy, continuity, etc. A Constitution needs to self-enforcing and efficacious and to provide for certainty and social peace. Finally, since constitutional design is paradigmatically conducted under extreme uncertainty, we pay attention to issues of gravity and reversibility of error.

Yet, while many of these considerations address effectiveness and quality of outcome, they can only be assessed against a background pursuit of political justice. Strategy and effectiveness is related to just outcomes. And justice is often implicated in more direct ways. For example, the intergenerational allocation of political responsibility, the very question whether founding fathers may bind future generations over major issues of policy or principle, is a quintessential issue of political justice in itself. Considerations about distribution of risk of error also raise fundamental issues of fairness.

At any rate, reasons for deferring resolution show that even ideal constitutional law does not exhaust in scope the domain of political justice.[12] And many of the areas constitutional law does cover are not issues of political justice themselves (federalism, policy commitments of a national character, etc) though they implicate, for the very reasons mentioned above, considerations of justice.

In deliberating about *the content* of competing proposals, we do not appeal to what the polls say. Ideally, each of us forms his own substantive judgement about which proposal makes best sense under public reason, and political justice. Yet, we also face *reasonable pluralism* over the substantive requirements of political justice. This fact makes it of paramount importance to distinguish substantive argumentation about *ideal content* from institutional argumentation about the *ideal process* charged with selecting and enacting the more attractive proposal.

In deliberating about ideal institutional process, we also operate within an argumentative structure shaped by considerations of political justice. Political justice reflects the commitment that we conceive public power as the collective power of free and equal citizens. On this conception, in deliberating about the more appropriate institutional process, we shall appeal to reasons that

[12] See Rawls (1996), above n 2, at 227–30 and Larry Sager, 'The Domain of Constitutional Justice' in Larry Alexander (ed), *Constitutionalism: Philosophical Foundations* (Cambridge, Cambridge University Press, 1998) 235–70 (the set of pertinent concerns forms a subset of political justice, which Sager aptly calls the realm of *constitutional justice*).

reflect the bonds of reciprocity among co-equal and free members of a political community with diverging views on political justice. Considerations of this kind underlie, I think, the view many of us have that appropriate process shall, among other things (quality, efficacy, etc), respect the fundamental interest of each citizen to participate in public life and through the exercise of deliberative responsibility affect the exercise of public policy and treat each citizen as having the capacity for a sense of justice that is worthy of equal respect.[13] This generic idea applies to the processes of constitutional interpretation as well—in more nuanced ways, to be discussed in chapters nine and ten.

[13] See Rawls (1996), above n 2, at 205–06 and Rawls, above n 4, at 310–24 and 404 (fn 39).

3

Constitutional Interpretation as a Distinctive Kind of Practical Reasoning

I. The Assumption of Constitutional Legitimacy

Let us suppose we are addressees of the law inquiring about the practical reasons we have in deciding about our social conduct. So situated, we normally have reason to know *the practical reasons that constitutional law supposedly gives us*. In this course, we often engage in constitutional interpretation, the kind of reasoning that establishes explanations about the content of applicable constitutional law, about the rights, powers and duties the law of the Constitution provides us with. And I suggest that we understand this activity broadly to cover both abstract interpretive reasoning and reasoning about the reach of constitutional law to concrete factual patterns.

A difficulty in approaching this kind of reasoning arises from the fact that the law does not necessarily consist of practical reasons that subjects of law do have. It is institutional practice that claims as much. Some of us fully endorse its claims. Others may be more reserved. Joseph Raz has offered here an important insight. In reasoning about the content of the law, we *assume* the authority of the law over us. We assume that we have a duty to follow the reasons provided by the law rather than the reasons we would independently endorse were we to deliberate in its absence. Thus, on the assumption that the law has authority over us, we inquire about the practical reasons it supposedly gives us.[1]

Similar logic applies if we are not addressees ourselves, but reason about what the law requires from its addressees. We assume law's authority over them, and so forth. Equally, in developing a normative thesis about the general structure of constitutional interpretation, as we do here, we need to reason from the interpretive perspective and therefore assume the authority of constitutional law. On this assumption, we examine the distinctive location constitutional interpretation

[1] See Joseph Raz, *Practical Reason and Norms*, 2nd edn (Princeton, Princeton University Press, 1990) 175–77.

(supposedly) has in human practical reasoning and the needs, concerns and commitments it (supposedly) responds to.

An important point from this discussion is that the institutional nature of law does not alter the fact that interpretive reasoning about the law is an instance of practical reasoning. It proceeds from a normative standpoint (employed by assumption or full endorsement) and aims at explaining the content of practical reasons.

Now, as the law does not fully determine our conduct, we also evidently reason beyond the requirements of law. The former kind of reasoning establishes propositions about the practical reasons provided by law and the latter about practical reasons on issues not preempted by law. How does the former kind differ from the latter? The answer lies in the institutional nature of law. In inquiring about the law, we inquire about normative import rooted in practices of institutional recognition. Legal interpretation is a kind of practical reasoning that purportedly carries out such normative import. In American constitutional practice, the Constitution, along with Supreme Court precedent, is recognised as the positive authoritative source of constitutional law and we claimed this to be a fundamental commitment of the practice. Accordingly, constitutional interpretation is a kind of practical reasoning that purportedly *carries out the normative import of the Constitution and of its history of authoritative exposition.*

In performing this inquiry, we are (supposedly) committed to the authoritative status of the Constitution (along with the conditionally authoritative status of judicial precedent). In doing so, we also assume that there are sufficient reasons grounding such authority. This commitment and the relevant concerns it responds to explain why constitutional interpretation is both a kind of practical reasoning and a distinctive one: it is pretty much straightforward practical reasoning for all those of us who do share this commitment. The rest of us perform it on such an assumption.

II. The Place of Constitutional Interpretation in Human Practical Reasoning

A. Constitutional Interpretation as a Rational Engagement

I have discussed the supposed place of constitutional interpretation with the practical reasoning of somebody who shares or assumes the authority of constitutional law in order to bring out those features of the activity that single it out as a distinctive kind of practical reasoning. In the following chapters, I employ this idea to study the nature and general structure of constitutional interpretation. Before doing so, we shall check whether this way of proceeding exposes constitutional interpretation as a *defective* form of practical reasoning. Humans conduct their affairs on practical reasons they actually *endorse* rather than simply assume. So what if one does not share constitutional legitimacy? Has constitutional interpretation any place in the practical reasoning of individuals who want to find out what practical reasons they truly (rather than supposedly) have?

My reply proceeds with two steps. First, the assumption of constitutional legitimacy does not render constitutional interpretation an irrational activity. True, it does not commit us to the authority of the law and, hence, to the authority of the norms established through our interpretive engagement. There is no choice over this assumption since our task is one of explaining the content of an institutional system of norms whose authority is supposed in practices of institutional recognition. At the same time, this assumption does not disable us from exercising *independent practical reasoning* and determining what, in our opinion and all things considered, we have most reason to do. In fact, we may first specify what the law requires from us (by reasoning from the point of view of someone who shares its authority), and then determine what course of action we have most reason to follow.

There is a difficulty though, that will become apparent in chapter five. As I will argue there, in the process of interpreting constitutional materials, we need to construct the more plausible rationale behind the Constitution's authoritative status from the point of view of somebody who endorses such status (chapter five, section II). Therefore, constitutional interpretation makes sense as a *rational* enterprise so long as the constitutional materials are of such content that it is feasible to construct the pertinent rationale and apply it in carrying out their normative import. Indeed, the very coherence of constitutional interpretation depends on the ability to locate constitutional legitimacy under public reason and pursue, on this basis, interpretive deliberation over existing non-ideal constitutional structures.

B. Constitutional Interpretation as an Engagement of Relevance

We still need to examine the *relevance* of constitutional interpretation so understood in the practical reasoning of individuals who want to find out what practical reasons they truly have. Much depends on our stance towards existing constitutional law. No one would dispute the relevance of constitutional interpretation in the practical reasoning of those who do independently and unconditionally *endorse* the authority of existing constitutional law under public reason and want to make best use of it. But what about the practical reasoning of citizens and officials who do not accept existing constitutional law unconditionally?[2]

[2] This challenge was raised to me by David Kennedy in discussion.

I have suggested that, under conditions of political legitimacy, citizens may arguably have a conditional and qualified general duty to comply with existing (non-ideal) constitutional law (chapter two, section I). Constitutional interpretation constitutes an important part of the practical reasoning of those who independently consider that under public reason they have such a duty. Indeed, before determining whether a particular application falls within this general duty, they need to know the law and, to do so, they may have to interpret it. In this course, they assume that the duty of compliance covers the case before them. But once they have formed an interpretive judgement, they no longer need that assumption. If explicit deliberation is needed, they may independently examine whether the relevant norm, even as it stands after the best interpretive reconstruction available, is so unacceptable that compliance with it is not required.

But does it really make sense to engage in such an enterprise if one is not an official, authorised to issue a binding pronouncement of the law? Does it make sense to adopt the interpretive standpoint if we know that, in the end of the day, the interpretive judgement of a third party, perhaps unmoved by the account proposed by us, will bind us?

The short reply is that a conscientious citizen who acknowledges normative force to the law of the Constitution—conditional or not, has an interest in engaging in genuine reasoning about its content. She may have prudential reason to consider also how the institutional arbiters of her conduct are expected to reason themselves; yet this does not negate the relevance of her direct inquiry. After all, rational performance of this inquiry will enable her to defend her convictions about constitutional rights and duties and criticise officials for reaching misguided determinations of law.

This brings us to a fundamental point about the reasons explaining the content of constitutional powers, freedoms and duties: their publicity. In an open society, such reasons are in principle available to the cognizance of all, citizens and officials alike. In a democratic polity, they are available to all citizens, whether addressees of the pertinent norm or bystanders who care about constitutional legality. In this sense, both addressees of the law and members of the citizenry at large have reason to engage in constitutional interpretation; their engagement provides the public frame within which institutional interpretation (the topic of Part Two of this book) takes place. And a robust public frame becomes all the more important once we appreciate the deliberative and moral nature of the interpretive inquiry—the task of the remainder of Part One.

Of course, the viability of this outlook presupposes an argumentative institutional structure (especially as regards the adjudicatory process) that is indeed fairly responsive to argument about appropriate interpretation of the law. In fact, political legitimacy would normally entail that much as well—as a basic requirement of the rule of law. In such circumstances, even if we know that our interpretive judgement may not ultimately be controlling, we have reason to engage in the interpretive activity, as understood here, exercising the human power to criticise and, potentially, to persuade.

At the same time, the situation is dramatically different with regard to an unjust Constitution (including the case where the constitutional structure is unresponsive to interpretive argument). If so, citizens and officials alike have a strong moral reason to modify the practice. In determining their conduct, they have reason to appeal directly to the effectiveness of alternative courses of action in promoting their vision of political justice, and to their moral duties towards people immediately affected by their conduct.

4

Constitutional Constructivism and Practical Deliberation

I have argued that constitutional interpretation aims at explaining the content of constitutional law by bringing out the normative signification of the written Constitution, along with its history of authoritative exposition. Constitutional interpretation is *directed* at constitutional text and precedent and is supposed to bring out and specify *their normative import*. In this sense, the positive determinations inscribed in the constitutional text and pronounced in authoritative constitutional practice provide the focal source of constitutional interpretation.

In this chapter, I argue, first, that text and precedent *underdetermine* the normative import of the Constitution, and, secondly, that the task of bringing out such import involves *practical deliberation*. Constitutional interpretation is a creative process of practical deliberation aiming at bringing out the normative import of the Constitution and of its history of authoritative exposition. In affirming this position, I also address the positivist reply that the deliberation involved in this creative process is a distinctive kind of reasoning that aims at developing or modifying the law, as opposed to reasoning about the content of existing law. In chapter five, I offer a general account of the considerations that (should) govern the pertinent deliberation and of their normative structure.

I. Identifying Constitutional Norms

A. Positive Under-determinacy

Text and precedent underdetermine the very *identification* of constitutional rules and principles. In a sense, this is both plain and trivial. A wild variety of normative schemes carrying out the normative import of the Constitution as a whole, along with the history of its authoritative exposition, is intellectually conceivable. At a minimum, certain structural features of constitutional sources indicate that a plurality of mutually incommensurable normative schemes could conceivably be presented as fitting text and precedent. In the absence of any canonical, authoritative structuring of text and precedent and in the face of textual, as well as precedential determinations in tension, considerations extending beyond bare text and precedent are needed to select among such competing schemes. Even when these structural features are not at play, there is a multiplicity of ways a set of historical facts (the ratification of the written Constitution, its recognition in precedent-based practices of adjudication, etc) could be treated as having normative significance for contemporary political institutions.

But is it enough to state that many different ways to approach the Constitution are *conceivable*? Shall we not locate text and precedent within the actual institutional practice of upholding and applying constitutional norms? As Larry Tribe has convincingly argued, next to the 'visible' written Constitution and precedent, there exists an 'invisible' set of background assumptions, a 'vast and deep ocean of ideas, propositions, recovered memories and imagined experiences'[1] that help us fix what the visible Constitution requires. Moreover, constitutional practice experiences a certain degree of institutional convergence, confidence and stability over the identification of many constitutional norms and, therefore, over the operation of the pertinent determinants. Along with the institutional recognition of the status of text and precedent as authoritative sources of constitutional law, there is also abundant institutional convergence over various propositions concerning the identity of many constitutional norms and confidence in constitutional judgements over new cases.

It is therefore essential that any account of positive under-determinacy has to accommodate the fact of convergence and this sense of confidence. At the same time, it also has to accommodate another factum of constitutional practice, namely the fact that, along with convergence, there is institutional interpretive disagreement over various aspects of the Constitution's normative ambit and over the identification of many constitutional norms. Does this further factum explain positive under-determinacy? At any rate, what is the nature and scope of the under-determinacy involved?

B. Interpretive Institutional Divergence

Let us begin with interpretive disagreement and proceed by recalling famous examples. The more evident one relates to the debate over whether the Constitution's normative ambit encompasses the normative *principles* that underlie a set of relevant clauses or even a single concrete constitutional provision.[2]

[1] Laurence Tribe, *The Invisible Constitution* (Oxford, Oxford University Press, 2008) 9. See also C Bradley & N Siegel, 'Constructed Constraint and the Constitutional Text' (2015) 64 *Duke Law Journal* 1213 (arguing that the very naturalness in our approach to the visible text and in our perceptions of its clarity are often due to such background assumptions).

[2] See Laurence Tribe, 'Comment' in Antonin Scalia, *A Matter of Interpretation: Federal Courts and the Law* (Princeton, Princeton University Press, 1997) 68–72 ('the task of deciding which provisions to treat as generative of constitutional principles broader or deeper than their specific terms [like the

Participants in the practice wildly differ over this issue, as well as over the content of the pertinent principles. In some cases, they read a broad provision narrowly while in others they carry out broader visions of political morality. And they keep on, debating, converging and diverging over both methodology and substance.

The paradigmatic controversy is substantive due process. Few dicta reverberate more deeply and also more controversially in constitutional practice than Justice Harlan's claim that 'the full scope of the liberty guaranteed by the Due Process Clause cannot be found in or limited by the precise terms of the specific guarantees elsewhere provided in the Constitution. This "liberty" is not a series of isolated points … It is a rational continuum which, broadly speaking, includes a freedom from all substantial arbitrary impositions and purposeless restraints, and which also recognizes … that certain interests require particularly careful scrutiny of the state needs asserted to justify their abridgment';[3] in a tradition that goes back to Chief Justice Coke, who projected a broad liberty principle and, expanding upon an Edwardian statutory precedent of more limited scope, constructively read the due process of law principle in the Magna Carta.[4] The *Obergefell* holding discussed in the introduction, invoking a broad principle of personal liberty to ground the protected status of same-sex marriage, is merely the more recent step in this self-critical process.[5]

The same pattern of reflection and disagreement—sometimes fundamental—over the role and scope of principles is exhibited in various areas of constitutional

bill of attainder clause] … lies at the core of the interpretive enterprise'), Laurence Tribe, *American Constitutional Law*, 3rd edn, vol I (New York, Foundation Press, 2000) 49–51, and David Strauss, 'Foreword: Does the Constitution Mean What it Says?' (2015) 129 *Harvard L Rev* 1, 59–60 (2015).

[3] *Poe v Ullman*, 367 US 497, 543 (1961) (Harlan, J, dissenting).

[4] In *The Second Part of the Institutes of the Lawes of England. Containing the Exposition of Many Ancient, and other Statutes* (London, M Flesher & M Young, 1642) at 46, Coke famously concludes: 'No man shall be disseised, that is, put out of seison, or dispossessed of his free-hold (that is) lands, or livelihood, or of his liberties, or free customes, that is, of such franchises, and freedomes, and free customes, as belong to him by his free birth-right, unlesse it be by the lawfull judgement, that is, verdict of his equals (that is, of men of his own condition) or by the Law of the Land (that is, to speak it once for all) by the due course, and processe of Law'. Cap 29 of the Magna Carta (25 Edward I, c 9, 1297) reads, in modern English, 'NO Freeman shall be taken or imprisoned, or be disseised of his Freehold, or Liberties, or free Customs, or be outlawed, or exiled, or any other wise destroyed; nor will We not pass upon him, nor condemn him, but by lawful judgment of his Peers, or by the Law of the Land …'. And 28 Edward III, c 3 (1354) reads, 'That no Man of what Estate or Condition that he be, shall be put out of Land or Tenement, nor condemned, nor imprisoned, nor disinherited, nor put to Death, without being brought in Answer by due Process of the Law'.

[5] Compare *Obergefell v Hodges*, 576 US ___ (2015) (slip op, at 11) ('The generations that wrote and ratified the Bill of Rights and the Fourteenth Amendment did not presume to know the extent of freedom in all of its dimensions, and so they entrusted to future generations a charter protecting the right of all persons to enjoy liberty as we learn its meaning') to *Washington v Glucksberg*, 521 US 702, 720–21 (1997) (substantive due process inquiry focuses on whether a carefully described right is deeply rooted in the Nation's history and traditions) to *Cruzan v Director, Missouri Dep't of Health*, 497 US 261, 300 (1990) (Scalia, J, concurring) ('the Constitution has nothing to say about the subject').

law, ranging from federalism[6] to presidential powers;[7] and in ways that notoriously straddle the conservative-liberal divide.[8]

Another noteworthy example is encountered in the interpretive design of *prophylactic rules*. Prophylactic rules are supplementary norms that aim at ensuring conformity to other (primary) constitutional norms by dictating or proscribing conduct that is not dictated or proscribed by the latter norms themselves. For example, the constitutional right against unreasonable searches protected by the Fourth Amendment has been supplemented by an exclusionary principle precluding the employment in criminal trials of evidence gathered in violation of the constitutional right. The primary purpose of this exclusionary norm 'is to deter future unlawful police conduct and thereby effectuate the guarantee of the Fourth Amendment against unreasonable searches and seizures'.[9]

Two features of prophylactic rules are important for our purposes. First, even if they are not explicitly stated in constitutional text, they are norms of constitutional law,[10] effectuating the principles underlying other constitutional norms that are anchored in the constitutional text. Accordingly, they are identified through constitutional interpretation. Secondly, as their purpose is to strengthen the efficacy of

[6] For instance, in *Alden v Maine*, 527 US 706 (1999), a 5–4 conservative majority of the Court read, over a fierce dissent, a broad principle of State residuary sovereignty in the constitutional structure. It then constructed norms of State immunity to effectuate this principle, even though such norms 'neither derive from nor [are] limited by the terms of the Eleventh Amendment' (at 713). As the majority had announced a few years before in *Blatchford v Native Village of Noatak*, 501 US 775, 779 (1991), 'we have understood the Eleventh Amendment to stand not so much for what it says, but for the presupposition of our constitutional structure which it confirms'.

[7] Compare the opinion of the Court in *Zivotofsky v Kerry*, 576 US __ (2015) delivered by Justice Kennedy ('the Nation must have a single policy regarding which governments are legitimate in the eyes of the United States and which are not. … That voice must be the President's. Between the two political branches, only the Executive has the characteristic of unity at all times.' (slip op, at 11)) with the dissent of the conservative minority ('It is possible that this approach will make for more effective foreign policy, perhaps as effective as that of a monarchy. It is certain that, in the long run, it will erode the structure of separated powers that the People established for the protection of their liberty.' (Scalia, J, dissenting, at 15)).

[8] For a nice contrast, compare the exchange of views in *Zivotofsky*, ibid, with the exchange in *Hamdan v Rumsfeld*, 548 US 557 (2006) ('Concentration of power puts personal liberty in peril of arbitrary action by officials, an incursion the Constitution's three-part system is designed to avoid. It is imperative, then, that when military tribunals are established, full and proper authority exists for the Presidential directive.') (Kennedy, J, concurring in part, at 638) and ('the structural advantages attendant to the Executive Branch—namely, the decisiveness, "activity, secrecy, and dispatch" that flow from the Executive's "unity," … led the Founders to conclude that the "President ha[s] primary responsibility—along with the necessary power—to protect the national security and to conduct the Nation's foreign relations."') (Thomas, J, dissenting, at 679).

[9] *United States v Calandra*, 414 US 338, 347 (1974). See more generally David A Strauss, 'The Ubiquity of Prophylactic Rules' (1988) 55 *U Chi L Rev* 190.

[10] *Dickerson v United States*, 530 US 428, 437–43 (2000) (*Miranda* announced a constitutional rule to secure Fifth Amendment rights. Congress may not legislatively supersede such a decision interpreting and applying the Constitution). *cf* Justice Stewart's argument that the '[exclusionary] rule is constitutionally required, not as a 'right' explicitly incorporated in the Fourth Amendment's prohibitions, but as a remedy necessary to ensure that those prohibitions are observed in fact.' Potter Stewart, 'The Road to *Mapp v Ohio* and Beyond: The Origins, Development and Future of the Exclusionary Rule in Search-and-Seizure Cases' (1983) 83 *Colum L Rev* 1365, 1389.

the primary norms, they are largely grounded on considerations of strategy. The second point is a contested one. In the area of criminal procedure, for example, liberal members of the Court have argued that violation of the prophylactic norm often 'implicates the same constitutional concerns' as the violation of the primary norm.[11] But the conservative view that has prevailed is more revealing for our argument. On this view, prophylactic norms are accountable to policy judgements based on assessment of social and institutional fact and cost-benefit analysis,[12] that is to say, to considerations that are paradigmatically characterised by divergence of approach. And their initial endorsement is subject to withdrawal, as shifting majorities make their own calculus and may well conclude that 'the marginal benefits of [the rule] … (viz, the number of confessions obtained coercively that are suppressed by its bright-line rule and would otherwise have been admitted) are dwarfed by its substantial costs (viz, hindering society's compelling interest in finding, convicting, and punishing those who violate the law)'.[13]

How are we to account for such systemic interpretive divergence? I propose, following Dworkin, that we bypass parochial explanations about, say, possible occasional gaps or inconsistencies in text or precedent and focus on a fundamental feature of pluralistic institutional life: its reflective and argumentative nature.

Constitutional law attempts to settle relations of political authority against a backdrop of social and political conflict of interests. But formal pieces of institutional history, like the enactment of a written Constitution, are only part of the story of constitutional settlement. Their reception by the political and the judicial branches of government, as well as by the citizenry at large, shapes the way they are perceived and interpreted throughout institutional life. Yet, it is naïve to suppose that courts and Congresses, citizens and litigants simply take institutional history for granted and do not bring back, in their reception and continuous interaction with such history, elements of the underlying conflicts. Indeed, such continuous reception is reflective and critical, often disharmonious, sometimes conflictual. Furthermore, constitutional law is a cultural phenomenon, reflecting visions, ideas and habits of thought as they develop in public culture. Our perception of its content exhibits the inherent fragility of interaction with such cultural norms and understandings, in particular those of moral significance.

What are the implications of these fundamental facts for constitutional practice? Recall that constitutional practice is both institutional and normative. It is institutional in the sense that public bodies uphold and apply the constitutional scheme; it is normative in the sense that they do so in the light of normative reasons. And such reasons vary among officials. Deliberative institutions faced with the task of comprehending and carrying out the normative ambit of constitutional

[11] *United States v Leon*, 468 US 897, 933 (1984) (Brennan, J, dissenting).

[12] See *Montejo v Louisiana*, 556 US 778 (2009) (emphasising the policy driven character of constitutional prophylaxis) and *Davis v United States*, 564 US 229, 237 (2011) ('For exclusion to be appropriate, the deterrence benefits of suppression must outweigh its heavy costs').

[13] *Montejo*, ibid, at 793.

text and precedent reflect upon the relevant reasons for upholding it. They reflect upon the grounds of constitutional legitimacy. And such reflection often engages, at least to some extent, the justice of the law itself. This reflection, in turn, informs the normative reach and import they acknowledge to the constitutional sources they treat as authoritative. This process leads to disputations within constitutional practice. Such disagreements may focus on whether we should amend the Constitution and, in extraordinary times, they may even challenge the legitimacy of the constitutional practice en block. Still, in ordinary times, they are internalised and take the form of disputations about the content of applicable constitutional law. The major debates of our times about fundamental rights and federalism reflect disagreement about how to construe the normative relevance of the Constitution on these matters in the light of competing views about why to treat it as authoritative, blended with competing visions of political morality and political structure. Disputants in such internal arguments accept constitutional legitimacy but perceive it in different ways. Their differences involve different conceptions about both the force of history and practice and different assessments about the substance of constitutional content.

This phenomenon explains how disputations about matters of justification become internalised in genuine interpretive disagreement about constitutional law. Accordingly, the content of constitutional law is treated as sensitive, in an argumentative manner, to considerations that extend beyond bare text and precedent and that are not reducible to what rules and principles public institutions happened to have endorsed in institutional history. In all these instances, we may not carry out the normative import of the Constitution without engaging in *deliberation* extending beyond and, indeed, structuring positive text and precedent. In this sense, the identification of constitutional rules and principles is a *constructive* enterprise; it constructs accounts of text and precedent in the light of applicable considerations of justification. Moreover, the requisite deliberation is of a *practical* and indeed *normative* nature since it aims at carrying out the normative import of the Constitution, along with its history of authoritative exposition, in our practical reason.

C. Interpretive Institutional Convergence

The emphasis on interpretive disagreement may tempt us into thinking that positive under-determinacy occurs whenever interpretive convergence runs out or breaks down. On this account, pockets of interpretive contestation, actual or conceivable, are situated next to a set of conventionally constituted constitutional norms that are available and practised. Such norms are in principle capable of identification without reference to the primary reasons for upholding the legitimacy of the practice or the reasons that have shaped the practice in its process of historical evolution. In this sense, constitutional practice is partly autonomous and path-dependent, determined by historical contingencies and the way a variety of factors (including moral considerations) operated in its path and fixed the identity and content of much of constitutional law that is now available to us without justificatory recourse to these factors.[14] Shall we accept this dualistic picture of constitutional practice?

A good candidate for testing this conventionalist explanation is what Professor Fallon has called 'ordinary adjudication', areas where courts purport to apply established doctrine as a matter of routine.[15] No doubt, considerations of principle 'hover always in the background' and 'dominate the interstices of doctrinal argument and guide contestable judgments'.[16] Yet, in ordinary cases we are in principle capable of identifying and specifying the applicable norms, at least to some extent, without the necessary intermediation of any interpretive explanation, at least not of the kind of explanation involved in areas of 'extraordinary adjudication'.

Let us grant that interpretive contestation in extraordinary adjudication and in the interstices of ordinary adjudication does not establish the interpretive character of constitutional rules in areas of interpretive convergence.[17] Much depends on the nature of interpretive convergence itself. In this regard, Professor Dworkin has presented two interrelated arguments, one drawing upon features of interpretive divergence and another addressing directly interpretive convergence.

First, Dworkin has pointed out that interpretive disagreement often involves 'theoretical' disagreement, disagreement over the considerations that make propositions of law true 'not just at the margin but in the core as well'.[18] While much has been said about the narrow or wide, borderline or pivotal scope of actual disagreement, the point here, as I see it, is that such disagreement highlights a source of *potentially pervasive* disagreement about the truth of any specific proposition of law and this in turn, given the engagement of contestable deliberative argument, indicates pervasive positive under-determinacy.

This argument is not conclusive. The existence of such 'theoretical' disagreement does not in itself establish that its pervasive implications are in fact operational within the practice. Perhaps the practice has conventionally settled on specific propositions of law whose legal validity is not affected by arguments of disharmony with justificatory considerations applied elsewhere. A revisionary interpretation may still be available, but it will be just that: revisionary.

The second argument focuses directly on the nature of convergence and the kind of considerations that ground established and uncontested propositions of constitutional law. Dworkin has claimed that instances of convergence are

[14] For a carefully crafted defence of legal conventionalism see Andrei Marmor, *Positive Law and Objective Values* (Oxford, Oxford University Press, 2001).

[15] Richard Fallon, *Implementing the Constitution* (Cambridge, Harvard University Press, 2000) 102 ff.

[16] Fallon, ibid, at 43 and 109.

[17] See Marmor, 'Legal Conventionalism' in Jules Coleman (ed), *Hart's Postscript* (Oxford, Oxford University Press, 2001) 198–99.

[18] Ronald Dworkin, *Law's Empire* (Cambridge, Harvard University Press, 1986) 43.

best explained by convergence in the operation of the underlying contestable deliberative judgements.[19]

I believe that this claim is in fact supported by the kind of argumentation we would be willing to offer, as participants in the practice, in examining and, let us suppose, rejecting a substantive challenge to an established proposition of law. We would not be disposed to assess and reject such a challenge on the *mere* ground that the proposition under review does in fact follow from the social facts of the constitutional practice (like the existence of institutional convergence around it and around related issues of law) in combination with the primary reasons that support the legitimacy of the practice as a whole (in our case, the legitimacy of the Constitution and of judicial precedent). To put it simply, we would not say: this is what the practice recognises as applicable law and hence, since we assume or share law's legitimacy, what we have reason to do in accordance therewith.

We would rather consider that we also need some further justificatory argument, linking these primary reasons to the content of the specific proposition at issue. No doubt, such argument may indicate that uncontroversial doctrinal settlement, surrounded by deep-seated background assumptions, suffices, in the circumstances, to uphold the proposition as carrying out the normative import of the Constitution. But even this argument would be a practical and indeed a normative one, and its validity would not be *reduced* to the social facts of the practice alone and to the supposed legitimacy of the practice as a whole.

I will argue that there is a third element in any satisfactory explanation of institutional convergence, namely that the underlying evaluative considerations have a built-in 'convergence-directedness', so that the ensuing convergence is not merely an overlap of idiolectic constitutional visions (see section IV, below). But first, we need to examine two noteworthy objections that may be raised against the argument we have advanced so far.

First, it may be argued that the value dependence involved here is of a trivial nature. True, the reasons applicable in constitutional practice are somehow dependent upon some value framework. But what is at play here is a stable evaluative framework that makes it possible to ordinarily understand and apply much of constitutional law without engaging into constitutional interpretation.[20] The rest is an over-intellectualised picture of constitutional practice.

I fear that this objection trivialises the political values involved in the constitutional realm and the reflective capacities of pluralistic institutional

[19] Dworkin, ibid, at 135–40 (distinguishing between a consensus of convention and a consensus of independent conviction). This point is well appreciated in localised debates. See Frederick Schauer, 'Precedent' (1987) 39 *Stanford L Rev* 571, 585–87 (sense of precedential determinacy attributed in part to convergence in the norms and values of the underlying constitutional culture).

[20] *cf* Marmor's sound argument that the requirement that legal rules are intelligible against the background of certain purposes shall not be confused with the argument that the content of legal rules is determined by reference to underlying purposes, nor with the further argument that understanding the former always presupposes understanding the latter. Andrei Marmor, *Interpretation and Legal Theory*, rev edn (Oxford, Hart Publishing, 2005) 113.

life. It is true that we often understand and apply propositions of constitutional law without appealing to any further explanation. Yet, the kind of argumentation involved when pressed to explain why we take a constitutional proposition in review to be true, why, say, we affirm that there is a constitutional norm protecting the freedom of speech against the States despite the absence of an express provision to this effect in the Constitution, is of a reflective nature. As constitutional legitimacy is a moral concept, as this concept is normally taken to be sensitive to the substantive content of the law and as public institutions operate against a backdrop of argumentative pluralism, it would be naïve to assume that these institutions simply take established conceptions for granted. Rather, they take endorsement of the constitutional proposition at issue to be open to legitimate critical challenge, even if such challenge is neither experienced, not contemplated. This point is easy to overlook because diverse moral outlooks often support treating an established interpretive conclusion or understanding as appropriate—despite non-ideal substantive content.

Thus, no matter how confident we are about the proposition concerned, we (at least ideally) appreciate that the justificatory considerations involved in questions of this subject matter are of a contestable nature, that we may need to reflect upon their force and that such reflection is in principle capable to alter our understanding of what the normative import of the Constitution is. Even in areas where constitutional law appears settled, we experience a *standing commitment to reflect*, and defend or revise supposedly settled propositions of law on the basis of considerations that extend beyond bare text and precedent and that are not reducible to social patterns of institutional recognition and endorsement. In this sense, what is involved here is (latent or active, yet genuine) constructive dependence of the reasons applicable to the practice upon our reflective practical reason.

The second objection would hold that when an established proposition is called into question, what we simply have is a proposal to reconsider and potentially revise conventionally identified constitutional norms. Why not conclude that there is no positive under-determinacy there; merely a call for revision to be exercised by a revisionary interpretation of the law or to be rejected by adherence to the substantive evaluations behind the established account?

There is no doubt that there are pockets of established interpretive tradition and that an interpretation diverting therefrom may be considered as 'revisionary'. It departs from interpretations, understandings, doctrinal accounts, etc that prevailed or seemed persuasive to a certain institutional community. Yet, and putting aside the legal implications of precedential change, it would mischaracterise constitutional practice to say that, in doing so, the revisionary interpretation revises conventionally established law. I have argued that constitutional practice exhibits a standing dependence of constitutional norms upon reflective practical reason. Such reflective dependence is confirmed when interpretive institutions reach back and conclude that established understandings (including established methods of identifying constitutional norms) failed to carry out the normative import of the Constitution even during their unquestioned reign. In doing so, they do not merely conclude that the substantive determinations were wrong, as a matter of political justice; they may very well conclude that their predecessors also misunderstood the implications of their duty to comply with the law of the Constitution.

The underlying explanation ultimately relates to the way the normativity of constitutional law operates in self-critical, argumentative interpretive communities. In such communities, the primary reasons to uphold the legitimacy of constitutional law are not taken to be reduced to a general duty to comply with established tradition (including established methods to revise it). They rather include a variety of more intricate reasons that participants in the practice employ in determining whether propositions of law in question do indeed carry out the normative import of the Constitution along with its history of authoritative exposition, and hence fall within the ambit of the duty to comply with the law. Argumentative practices reflect the idea that the pertinent link is in principle subject to reasoned contestation on grounds extending beyond reference to the mere social fact of established tradition. Thus, in adopting a 'revisionary' interpretation, we hold that the pertinent normative import is determined by the considerations grounding such an interpretation as opposed to the considerations (positive or otherwise) that supposedly supported the interpretation we revisit and discard. And we are sometimes willing to hold that the normative import captured by the 'revisionary' interpretation had to be recognised even before the latter interpretation became established in the practice or acquired authoritative force. Similarly, once questioned and pressed to articulate our opinion, in affirming the traditional interpretation as expounding the pertinent normative import, we do not merely refer to the fact of prior institutional recognition; we rather make an interpretive judgement expressing our reflective endorsement of the traditional interpretation. Either way, under our duty to comply with the law of the Constitution, we do not treat interpretation settled by solid tradition as providing 'positive' determinacy on what the law requires from its subjects. And when we simply apply such an established interpretation without revisiting the matter, we are best understood as assuming that such reflective grounding is available.

If the arguments brought forward in this section are sound, we have reason to accept some fundamental unity in the positive under-determinacy and the interpretive constructivism involved both in cases where we adhere to established tradition and in cases where we depart therefrom. This point will be reinforced by the argument developed in chapter five for the common normative structure of constitutional interpretation. Whether the interpretive inquiry concludes with an innovative or a conservative interpretation is ultimately answerable to a unitary normative structure and to the more appropriate reading of the relevant positive sources thereunder.

II. Specifying Constitutional Norms

Positive under-determinacy applies to the specification of the content of an already identified constitutional norm as well. The most obvious explanation here relates to the employment of contestable concepts, like 'due' process or 'cruel' punishment.[21] The very use of such concepts consists in inviting users to engage in circumscribed deliberation about the practical reasons that we have in the relevant subject-matter. This operation is reinforced, in the constitutional domain, by their argumentative reception in the pluralistic political and institutional communities that apply them as constitutional concepts.

Consider the equal protection principle. Given the opaque and contestable nature of the language used and the reflective reception of such language by the legal institutions, the application of the principle normally follows an interpretation. An interpretation of the principle is a conception of the principle that explains how to identify particular applications of the principle.[22] An interpretation of equal protection, for instance, explains whether race can ever be a permissible factor in university admissions, provides us with standards to assess such permissibility, explains their application to sets of facts, etc.

What is the nature of such an interpretation? Text and precedent guide us, but do not settle the appropriate conception of the equal protection principle. The framers have not institutionally endorsed in the constitutional text any particular conception of equal protection and arguments from precedent are notoriously ambivalent and, at any rate, conditional. Competent users of the language may reach various diverging conceptions of the principle without linguistically misusing the concept. Thus, the relation between the appropriate conception of a concept and the concept itself is not one of sameness of meaning but one of substantive support. In determining the appropriate conception of the equal protection principle we engage in practical and, indeed, *normative deliberation*. Our judgement goes beyond positive text and precedent and addresses a normative issue, namely, the rights, powers and duties of subjects of law.

In fact, in our example, we engage in circumscribed moral deliberation since the equal protection principle is a moral principle.[23] And all major debates in the application of the principle, all the way down to the resolution of concrete cases,

[21] See WB Gallie, 'Essentially Contested Concepts' (1955–1956) 56 *Proceedings of the Aristotelean Society* 167–98.

[22] See Dworkin's 'Constitutional Cases' in his *Taking Rights Seriously* (Cambridge, Harvard University Press, 1977) 134–36. See also David Wiggins, 'Putnam's Doctrine of Natural Kind Words and Frege's Doctrines of Sense, Reference, and Extension: Can They Cohere?' in AW Moore (ed), *Meaning and Reference* (Oxford, Oxford University Press, 1993) 200 ff.

[23] See Ronald Dworkin, *Freedom's Law: The Moral Reading of the American Constitution* (Cambridge, Harvard University Press, 1996).

implicate moral ideas: whether the permissibility of racial classifications varies with the race of the persons benefited therefrom, whether the educational benefits from student body diversity constitute a compelling state interest, how policies in its pursuit may remain consistent with the fundamental principle that each applicant is treated as an individual worthy of equal respect, etc.

There is an apparently forceful objection here. In receiving contestable constitutional language, courts and legal culture refract its contestable function and shape its meaning in accordance with the prevailing institutional ethos. And they have done this for centuries. Thus, no matter how critical and fragmented the recognitional community is, history and legal practice provide us with quasi-conventionally prevalent modes of specification.

I acknowledge the objection but I think it does not discredit our main argument. True, there exist history-contingent modes of specification that explain much of interpretive convergence. Yet, the fact that legal institutions have been doing the pertinent normative deliberations all along, instilling in present practitioners a sense of naturalness for established interpretive assumptions and providing reasons for employing them, does not alter the moral nature of the specification. The fact that the equal protection principle is a legal principle and its meaning has been elaborated in path-dependent legal practices, as the *Fisher* example encountered in the introduction illustrates, does not alter its moral nature. On the contrary, established patterns and assumptions are in principle subject to critical examination on the basis of the moral nature of the principle to be specified and of the reasons against uncritically departing from them.

Indeed, each new case before the Court is an opportunity for a thorough analysis of the pertinent moral considerations. In *Parents Involved*, for instance, involving elementary school assignments, plurality and minority clashed ferociously on the principle and 'promise' of *Brown v Board of Education* and navigated differently among the subsequent case law. Their conflicting expositions resemble treatises of applied moral philosophy, informed by analysis of social fact. And the pivotal fifth vote of Justice Kennedy evinced the frustrating complexity of any effort to accommodate colour-blindness and equality: the employment of race to combat racial isolation displays the 'frustrating duality of the Equal Protection Clause', reflecting in turn 'the duality of our history and our attempts to promote freedom in a world that sometimes seems set against it'.[24]

We may of course be told that affirmative action jurisprudence is exceptional, exhibiting actual contest on moral grounds. In reply, let us consider, as we did in section I(C) above, the deliberative nature of constitutional specification in areas beyond actual contest.

Equal protection is a moral concept whose interpretation is indeed actually contested in constitutional discourse. Yet, the scope of under-determinacy is not

[24] *Parents Involved in Community Schools v Seattle School District No. 1*, 551 US 701, 797 (2007) (Kennedy, J, concurring).

determined by the scope of actual contest. A contestable concept is characterised by the inherent potential for generating disputes.[25] Moreover, as Susan Hurley has argued, there is a continuum between contestable and uncontestable concepts.[26] And many evaluative concepts whose extension appears to be settled in a specific community are in fact sensitive to underlying evaluations.[27] Such evaluations are in principle subject to reflection and revision in accordance with the practical concerns of the relevant interpretive community, the degree of internal cohesion and criticism, etc.

This is particularly so in constitutional law given the argumentative character of constitutional practices. Adjudicatory institutions do not receive and apply constitutional rules and principles uncritically. The moral and policy significance of a constitutional rule is always in the background and may give rise to doubt and contestation over the rule's import. A few decades ago, no one could reasonably foresee that adjudicatory practices would exercise their self-standing commitment to reflect and, given the nature of the moral principle implicated (right to marry), would alter through interpretation even core elements of the concept of marriage to include within it same sex couples.[28]

This sensitivity to reflective evaluation highlights the fact that the under-determinacy in consideration cannot be explained by mere reference to actual contest. It is ultimately explained by the reflective and critical ways in which the recognitional community receives and interacts with the constitutional text and its history of authoritative exposition. Such interaction may trigger interpretive doubt and potential contest even in cases where linguistic usage would appear settled.[29]

Before concluding, we may pause for a moment and examine whether the deliberative and, indeed, moral nature of constitutional interpretation is just a contingent feature of our interpretive methodologies; and whether we can dispense with it if we employ a neutral methodology, like originalism. I will discuss in the next chapter the normative issues that pertain to the choice of interpretive methodology. Whether the interpretive community should adopt the interpretive standpoint of the enacting generation is a fundamentally moral issue, subject to

[25] See Barry Clarke, 'Eccentrically Contested Concepts' (1979) 9 *British Journal of Political Science* 124.

[26] Susan Hurley, *Natural Reasons, Personality and Polity* (Oxford, Oxford University Press, 1989) 43–50 (noting also the usefulness of employing an intermediate category of conceivably contestable concepts, where we can imagine circumstances in which we would hesitate to claim that the deviant application is not an attempt to apply the concept).

[27] See John McDowell, 'Non-Cognitivism and Rule-Following', in his *Mind, Value, and Reality* (Cambridge, Harvard University Press, 1998) 201–03, and Hilary Putnam, *The Collapse of the Fact/Value Dichotomy and Other Essays* (Cambridge, Harvard University Press, 2002) 34–40.

[28] *Obergefell v Hodges*, 576 US __ (2015) (slip op, at 17) ('The limitation of marriage to opposite-sex couples may long have seemed natural and just, but its inconsistency with the central meaning of the fundamental right to marry is now manifest').

[29] *cf* Fred Schauer, 'On the Supposed Defeasibility of Legal Rules' (ed MDA Freeman, 1998) 51 *Current Legal Problems* (the law may fail us even if its language does not).

deliberation and contestation. But even if we put this matter aside for the moment, it is essential to refute this idea at its very core, especially given that opponents of originalism sometimes seem to assume the theoretical possibility of dispensing with critical argumentation.

Let us focus on the prohibition of cruel punishments. As early as 1910, the Court declared that 'in interpreting the Eighth Amendment, it will be regarded as a precept of justice that punishment for crime should be graduated and proportioned to the offense' and thoughtfully explained that 'a principle, to be vital, must be capable of wider application than the mischief which gave it birth. This is peculiarly true of constitutions.'[30] How is this principle to se specified? Under current doctrine, 'whether this requirement has been fulfilled is determined not by the standards that prevailed when the Eighth Amendment was adopted in 1791 but by the norms that "currently prevail." ... This is because "[t]he standard of extreme cruelty is not merely descriptive, but necessarily embodies a moral judgment."'[31]

Now, it is unclear to me how specification of cruelty by today's standards is a matter of moral judgement whereas reference to past standards transforms the nature of the enterprise into one of description. In both cases, the applicable norm can more plausibly be understood as incorporating a moral principle. All that differs is the person (or persons) making the pertinent moral judgement. The moral and constructive nature of this enterprise is not negated by the fact that the interpreter is not applying her own moral values, but the moral values prevailing within a certain social space, in the past or the present. In fact, current jurisprudence fuses existing public culture and potential moral consensus with independent assessment by the judiciary, and we may well assume that something of this sort would apply even if we were to employ the standpoint of a common law judge of the enacting era.

Even Justice Scalia would not have objected to this way of framing the debate. For him, the Eighth Amendment sets an abstract principle embodying the moral outlook of the enacting generation, 'abstracting ... the existing society's assessment of what is cruel'.[32] And the late Justice was quite clear that the assessment implicated in giving substance to the principle is a 'moral assessment'.[33]

Once we understand the matter this way, we may well rehearse all the arguments discussed in this chapter about consensual and self-critical elements in each moral outlook and about the way interpretive stability is compatible with moral dependence. The fact that the members of an early generation are not with us makes it impossible for them to show reflective sensitivity over the questions and

[30] *Weems v United States*, 217 US 349, 373 (1910).

[31] *Kennedy v Louisiana*, 554 US 407, 419 (2008).

[32] Antonin Scalia, *A Matter of Interpretation: Federal Courts and the Law* (Princeton, Princeton University Press, 1997) 143 (response to Ronald Dworkin).

[33] ibid, at 146 ('provision for the death penalty in a Constitution that sets forth the moral principle of "no cruel punishments" is conclusive evidence that the death penalty is not (in the moral view of the Constitution) cruel.').

arguments we would pose. Yet, this by no means alters the nature of the inquiry we would want them to engage with, and that we would have to engage with from within their outlook, for resolving the constitutional issues we face.

Let us conclude. The resolution of interpretive issues of constitutional law requires the employment of normative argument whose validity is not reduced to an exegesis of past positive authoritative endorsement.[34] When asked to explain how we determine and carry out the normative signification of the Constitution, we engage in *practical deliberation*. At the same time, the pertinent deliberation is of a distinctive kind: it is circumscribed in scope, directed at explaining and bringing out the (supposed) normative import of the Constitution.

This engagement of practical deliberation in the process of carrying out the Constitution's normative import shows that constitutional interpretation is not an activity of perceiving an independent order of constitutional norms (inscribed, say, in constitutional text and precedent). Rather, it is a *constructive* enterprise: we construct and defend accounts of constitutional law by engaging in practical deliberation about the more appropriate reading of the Constitution, along with its history of authoritative exposition.

III. The Truth in Conventionalism

The argumentative and constructive nature of constitutional law and of constitutional interpretation raises a host of fundamental issues. In the remaining sections of this chapter, I address three objections. First, our thesis on the role of deliberative reflection in explaining the content of constitutional law may appear to contradict the social contingency and conventionality that constitutional law, as an institutional artifact, has acquired in its historical evolution. Secondly, it may be said that it does not dovetail with the stability that constitutional law, as an institutional system of norms, enjoys in constitutional practice. For the same reason, it may be added, it also fails to explain how constitutional practice provides loci for genuine agreement and disagreement over the content of applicable law. Thirdly, it may be objected that, while the practical deliberation we have in mind is indeed implicated in argumentative constitutional practice, it is best understood as a kind of practical reasoning engaged with developing or modifying the law, as opposed to reasoning about the content of applicable law. As the discussion

[34] See *Planned Parenthood of Southeastern Pa v Casey*, 505 US 833, 849 (1992) (joint opinion of O'Connor, Kennedy, and Souter, JJ) ('the inescapable fact is that adjudication of substantive due process claims may call upon the Court [to] exercise … reasoned judgment … We accept our responsibility not to retreat from interpreting the full meaning of the covenant') and *Thornburgh v American College of Obstetricians*, 476 US 747, 789 (1986) (White, J, dissenting) ('The Constitution … is a document announcing fundamental principles in value-laden terms that leave ample scope for the exercise of normative judgment by those charged with interpreting and applying it').

becomes rather technical, the reader may skip it without loss in following the overall argument.

Legal conventionalists rightly emphasise that the fundamental norms of legal practice are under-determined by the primary values served by the practice. The main values (justice, social peace, policy effectiveness etc) may be served by a variety of interchangeable constitutional schemes. It is historical contingencies that have shaped the constitutional scheme actually practised.[35] It is history that largely accounts for text, precedent and established interpretive assumptions. Is our approach compatible with this insight?

In interpreting the Constitution, we assume constitutional legitimacy. In chapter two I explained why a non-ideal constitutional scheme can be legitimate and ground duties of compliance, provided it is efficaciously recognised and enforced in the political community and satisfies certain substantive conditions. In such a case, what we have most reason to do in issues within constitutional ambit depends upon path-dependent considerations related to the shape and content that constitutional practice has taken in the process of its historical evolution. If so, there is indeed an element of *contingency* in the content of such law. And this general idea does not apply only to the practice of upholding an arguably non-ideal written Constitution; it may justify alignment with a variety of second-best doctrinal solutions that structure ordinary adjudication[36] and explain the sense of appropriateness that we have developed in much of interpretive practice.

At the same time, it is essential to emphasise that political legitimacy operates under political justice, never as an exception to it. If constitutional law is legitimate, it is legitimate under political justice. Considerations of public reason in general, and political justice in particular, provide the reasons that supposedly justify upholding law's legitimacy and therefore the authority of the various claims that constitutional law makes upon us. Yet, considerations of political justice and political legitimacy are essentially contestable and, as a matter of fact, wildly contested in contemporary institutional life. Thus, it is reasonable to expect that the scope and kind of practice-dependent contingency that the public, deliberative institutions charged with enforcing constitutional law are willing to acknowledge to constitutional law is a contestable and often contested matter. This fundamental feature of actualised public reason is exhibited in the development of an argumentative constitutional practice and in the standing commitment of institutional life to deliberative reflection over the appropriate ways to carry out the normative import of the Constitution in social life.

In this process, contingency and deliberative reflection, convention and value are inextricably linked. And this is so even in areas of interpretive convergence. When alignment with interpretive tradition is questioned, we appeal to deliberative reflection. Such reflection may confirm our intuitive inclination that

[35] Marmor, above n 17, at 208 and 213–17.

[36] On the role of the second best in ordinary adjudication, see Fallon, above n 15, at 110.

considerations of political legitimacy justify adherence to established tradition, to the employment of inherited doctrinal webs or prevalent background assumptions. Sometimes, this may implicate assessment of ideas of continuity, stability and uniformity of application. Elsewhere, the operating forces of settlement may be so strong as to silence pleas for innovative tinkering altogether.

If I am allowed a metaphor, the fabric of constitutional law is a pale grey fabric, black with value and white with convention. But we do not have any persuasive reason for concluding that there are any quite black threads in it, or any white ones.[37]

IV. The Instability Thesis

If the content of constitutional law depends, in a constructive manner, upon the exercise of practical deliberation, one would expect (a) that changes in one's pertinent deliberative considerations could in principle effectuate changes in one's view of the content of the law, and (b) that, given the value pluralism experienced in society, members of the legal community could have, by and large, divergent views on the content of the law. The constitutional propositions they would hold, being embedded within thicker constitutional accounts, would often overlap. Yet, such overlap could be sporadic and often take the form of a temporary equilibrium among shifting wider accounts. If so, it is questionable whether a quasi-idiolectic conception of constitutional practice fits the kind of convergence we experience in the practice and, more generally, dovetails with law's stability, as a system of norms practised by the law-applying institutions of the political community.

Let us first qualify somehow the force of this objection. At a minimum, a degree of stability is ensured by mechanisms of institutional settlement through which closure is obtained in particular disputes and guidance is offered over the way similar disputes are to be resolved in near future. Moreover, the argumentative character of law serves an important legitimating function; by internalising disagreement, it enhances acceptance of the more fundamental elements of the constitutional structure;[38] by domesticating the interplay of competing values and accommodating it within legal discourse, it tames its disruptive potential; and,

[37] A paraphrase from Willard Van Orman Quine, 'Carnap and Logical Truth' in *Ways of Paradox and Other Essays*, rev edn (Cambridge, Harvard University Press, 1976) 132 ('the lore of our fathers is a fabric of sentences [which] develops and changes, through more or less arbitrary and deliberate revisions and additions of our own, more or less directly occasioned by the continuing stimulation of our sense organs. It is a pale grey lore, black with fact and white with convention. But I have found no substantial reasons for concluding that there are any quite black threads in it, or any white ones').

[38] See Fallon, 'Legitimacy and the Constitution' (2005) 118 *Harv L Rev* 1787, 1811 ('if constitutional meanings could not be experienced in various ways, then the fabric of acceptance that surrounds the Constitution might unravel').

at the same time, by enabling the dynamic, interpretive adjustment of the details of the structure, it facilitates the structure's systemic stability.[39]

Having made these qualifications, it is important to examine whether we may generalise the last point in order to deflate, though not refute, the instability thesis. As Ronald Dworkin has argued, interpretive concepts enable their holders to share them, while disagreeing about their proper interpretation and, accordingly, their applications.[40] Participating in a genuine debate over a proper application of a concept, holders of the concept treat themselves responsible to apply the appropriate interpretation *of* the pertinent concept. Thus, their potential disagreement is understood as disagreement over the proper interpretation and application of the concept they share. By generalising this idea, we obtain an account of how participants in an interpretive practice may be said to share the practice while disagreeing over many of its specific requirements, and therefore an account of how loci of genuine interpretive agreement and disagreement are possible.

On the account of Constitutional law defended here, the main interpretive locus is provided by the fundamental commitment to the authoritative status *of the Constitution, along with its history of authoritative exposition* (such status also being the product of interpretive reasoning, see chapter one, section IV). This basic commitment is further specified by various concrete interpretive propositions entrenched in the course of this historical process, providing in turn multiple more specific interpretive loci; in this sense, a web of interpretive loci is constructed.

Such interpretive loci often take the form of judicially crafted constitutional doctrine. Judicial doctrine provides institutional formality to interpretive propositions of an intermediate level of generality. Doctrine often constitutes what Sunstein has called incompletely theorised agreements,[41] facilitating local agreement while divergence remains over the underlying justifications. Once established as salient equilibria, they provide provisional loci for further interpretive specification and practice-dependent reasons for their preservation; they set in motion path-dependent processes of doctrinal elaboration and interstitial contestation. I will discuss the function, but also the limitations and weaknesses of such processes (as regards norms regulating the standard of judicial review) in chapter seven, sections III–V.

A scheme of this sort is capable of enabling the participants to a practice to share the practice. Yet, it does not determine whether this set of shared commitments is

[39] On dynamic institutional stability and incremental change see James Mahoney & Kathleen Thelen, 'A Theory of Gradual Institutional Change' in J Mahoney & K Thelen (eds), *Explaining Institutional Change: Ambiguity, Agency, and Power* (Cambridge, Cambridge University Press, 2010) 1–37.

[40] Dworkin, *Justice in Robes* (Cambridge, Harvard University Press, 2006) 11–12, 145–55, 224–25.

[41] Cass Sunstein, 'Incompletely Theorized Agreements' (1995) 103 *Harv L Rev* 1733 and 'Incompletely Theorized Agreements in Constitutional Law' (spring 2007) 74 *Social Research* 1. See also D Strauss, 'Common Law Constitutional Interpretation' (1996) 63 *U Chicago Law Review* 877, 910–13. On the limitations of incomplete theorisation see the forceful critique of Dworkin, above n 40, ch 2.

robust or shallow. It does not determine, for instance, whether the practice obtains an adequate degree of stability and convergence or whether participants merely share 'a common—and malleable—language of engagement' in struggles over distribution of rights and power, in David Kennedy's vivid expression.[42]

For example, initial endorsement of constitutional doctrine normally presupposes convergence on mid-level normative principles. Once established, doctrine provides practice-based reasons for its preservation. However, the mid-level principles themselves and their implications for supporting the doctrinal matter at issue are not self-standing, but depend on broader normative ideas that differ among practitioners. Therefore, it is reasonable to expect that the play of these ideas will exercise some independent force over treatment of analogous cases, or even over the doctrine's specification, in the light of the feature considered salient in each case. No doubt, practice-dependent reasons for valuing doctrinal stability limit such roles. But these very reasons are also contested themselves and often run out. In fact, they would turn out to be rather fragile unless doctrinal content is reasonable and argument-sensitive. And reasonableness obviously depends upon substantive visions of political justice and their endorsement within the judiciary and the wider constitutional culture.

Having obtained a sense of the ways such dependence leads to interpretive disagreement (section I(B) above), we may point out in the remaining part of this section various factors contributing to stability.

The degree of stability and convergence actually obtained in the practice largely depends upon the internal stability and interpersonal similarity in the underlying deliberative judgements. An important factor facilitating such similarity relates to the culture that develops within the judiciary, the operation of professional norms, and the expectancies about constitutional interpretation and doctrinal argument that, once they prevail, take a life of their own. Considerations of this sort make it possible in many cases to understand and apply the law without appealing to any interpretive explanation.

Furthermore, interpretive propositions, once stabilised, remain so despite shifts and discrepancies in the underlying deliberative judgements. There are a variety of reasons for this. One reason is cognitive uncertainty or inattention to the implications of such shifts. A second reason relates to strategic behaviour of litigants and judges in the light of the coordinative difficulties and risks associated with attempts to unpack the convergence already established and to establish a new stable equilibrium.[43] And there are also cohesion-enhancing moral reasons members of a legal community often share. We have already discussed, in this regard, how public reason often supports adherence to prevalent and

[42] David Kennedy, *A World of Struggle, How Power, Law and Expertise Shape Global Political Economy* (Princeton, Princeton University Press, 2016) 10.

[43] My argument here has been influenced by a more general argument concerning institutional stability in the face of parametric shift, proposed by A Greif & D Laitin in 'A Theory of Endogenous Institutional Change' (2004) 98 *American Political Science Review* 633, 636–38.

deep-seated understandings and to established doctrinal webs. Continuity, efficacy in recognition and enforcement, and the like, are considerations that matter under political legitimacy.

We shall add here another, rather subtle feature of constitutional practice: its discursive character as a significant co-determinant of mutual convergence and stability. Participants in genuinely discursive argumentation face an inherent pressure to appeal to reasons that are reasonably available for broader endorsement. This process is facilitated by the institutionalisation of adjudicatory institutions that are supposedly responsive to reasoned argument, at least as perceived by the prevailing culture; and it is kept alive, in the heydays of polarised jurisprudence, by the pivotal role of so-called 'moderate' judges, sensitive to the importance of reaching some reasonable common ground.

A genuine appeal to endorseability implies a commitment by the participant to his own fallibility. Indeed, we cannot make sense of a genuine interpretive practice of this sort without assuming that participants stand correctable in the light of applicable standards that they take to be (at least partly) external to their individual standpoint. This leads to a commitment to what Tyler Burge, making a related point concerning representational thought in general, has called a cognitive distance between individual standpoint and subject matter.[44] And although a commitment to correctability does not establish that participants would in fact be sensitive to reasoned arguments directed to them, it does provide a communicative frame facilitating such inter-personal sensitivity and enabling them to genuinely share a normative practice and to reach pockets of mutual convergence therein.

No doubt, there are limitations in the operation of such factors in normative discourse. First, participants acting strategically may often prefer, say, obtaining a committed majority on a divisive issue, rather than near-unanimity on shallow grounds. Secondly, even advocates of good faith often exhibit sensitivity towards a certain range of ideologically acceptable arguments; there may be recognition of cognitive distance between the personal and the impersonal standpoint, there may be commitment to correctability, yet, such commitment operates within substantive ideas we have about the applicable standards of reasonableness in the subject matter. This has implications for the conduct of public discourse as well: we often aim at persuading a certain range of listeners, those sensitive to acceptable standards of reasonableness.

As a result, stability and convergence comes on various levels and degrees. Yet, our task is not one of surveying the boundaries of consensus and dissensus in constitutional practice. We have to explain how the constructive nature of constitutional interpretation is compatible with a significant degree of stability that the practice is in fact taken to exhibit. And in this pursuit, considerations of the sort discussed here (constitutional culture, cognitive constraints, practice-dependent

[44] Tyler Burge, *Foundations of Mind* (Oxford, Oxford University Press, 2007) 24–26. See also Nicos Stavropoulos, *Objectivity in Law* (Oxford, Oxford University Press, 1996).

reasons and the discursive nature of constitutional argumentation, as reinforced by their institutionalisation) do explain, first, how interpretive convergence is possible and, secondly, how such convergence may reflect a *joint* commitment of participants as opposed to a mere overlap of thicker, idiolectic accounts. In fact, in an operating constitutional practice, such integrated convergence is normally exhibited in a large number of shared interpretive propositions at all levels of generality, including deeply entrenched ones that are to be treated as fundamental in the practice; and it is reflected in shared interpretive sensibilities and in the confidence we have in making constitutional judgements over new cases.

The account developed in this section explains, I hope, how the argumentative and constructive nature of constitutional law is compatible with the degree of stability that constitutional law, as an institutional system of norms, enjoys. In this way, it also contributes to our understanding of how the interpretive dimension of law is compatible with the institutional nature of law, of how the law can be the product of interpretive construction while being 'practised' by the lawmaking and the law-applying institutions of the political community.

V. Interpretation and Preemption

On the account defended here, the interpretive identification and specification of constitutional law is a constructive process requiring the circumscribed employment of normative deliberation. A traditional positivist reply here is that, while such a constructive enterprise is indeed involved in constitutional practice, it shall be distinguished from reasoning about the content of applicable law (interpretive or otherwise); it is rather better understood as a kind of practical reasoning engaged with developing or modifying the law. Improper expansion of the contours of this enterprise fails to fit the preemptive function of law.[45] The idea is that if explanatory identification of the law is constructive, then it would involve recourse to some of the very reasons that the law is supposed to preempt. For the same reason, it may be said that our account fails to explain how constitutional law can make a practical difference and provide epistemic guidance in the practical reasoning of subjects of law.[46]

The relation between legal interpretation and preemption is to remain one of the most intricate problems of jurisprudence. In this section, I will explain how

[45] 'If determining what the law is involves considerations about what the law is there to settle, how can [the law] compete with … that which the law is there to settle?' Andrei Marmor, *Interpretation and Legal Theory* (Oxford, Oxford University Press, 1992) 118. Compare it with 'Raz thinks law cannot be authoritative unless those who accept it *never* use their own convictions to decide what it requires … But why …?' Dworkin, above n 18, at 429. See also Dworkin, above n 40, at 198–211.

[46] Shapiro has suggested that only reasons capable of making such difference are capable of being legal norms. Scott Shapiro, 'Law, Morality and the Guidance of Conflict' (2000) 6 *Legal Theory* 127.

the account defended here is compatible with a weak version of preemption and argue that it makes good sense to read that version as implicit in argumentative constitutional practice. Finally, I will discuss some of the difficulties that positivist conceptions of interpretation face.

Constitutional norms carry out the (supposed) normative import of the Constitution. This property of constitutional norms explains their (supposedly) preemptive force in the practical reason of subjects of law. Subjects of law are supposed to follow the norms that possess this property, rather than the practical reasons they would directly endorse by exercising independent practical reasoning. The circumscribed practical deliberation involved, say, in the identification of constitutional principles differs from institutionally uncommitted practical reasoning by virtue of this very fact: it aspires to carry out the normative signification of the Constitution, along with its history of authoritative exposition.

On the account defended here, what has preemptive force in the practical reasoning of subjects of law is the constitutional norm, whose identity and content is fixed by a process of interpretive construction that differs in principle from independent practical reasoning about the same subject matter. Given the institutional nature of law, in accepting constitutional legitimacy, practical deliberation operates under a distinctive normative structure. This distinctive normative structure is capable of making a practical difference in our deliberation and the appropriate result of such interpretive deliberation is to be treated as authoritative over the result independent practical reasoning would reach on the same subject matter.[47]

No doubt, the fact that interpretive reasoning about the law involves practical deliberation signifies that the preemption law claims in our practical reasoning does not imply complete displacement of the underlying deliberative considerations. In this sense, our operative account of preemption is weak, so to speak. But we have good reason to consider that such a weak account dovetails the argumentative and fragmented character of constitutional practices. As I have tried to argue in this chapter, the normative import of argumentative constitutional practices cannot be established without recourse, active or by implication, to practical deliberation. Even the very determination of the degree of what we ordinarily call textual underdeterminacy is influenced by normative considerations about how to approach the text.[48] Our operative account of preemption has to fit this fact.

Let us recall that the law claims unconditional authority over its domain. We have discussed in chapter two the difficulties of succumbing to such an overreaching claim. At the same time, law-applying institutions act on the assumption of constitutional legitimacy. In receiving the written Constitution and its history of

[47] In this regard, the argument brought forward in the text differs from arguments claiming that the law is best understood as claiming special *force* rather than *preemption* over morality. See Stephen Perry, 'Second Order Reasons, Uncertainty, and Legal Theory' (1989) 62 *California L Rev* 913.

[48] Dworkin, above n 40, at 236 (the degree of eclipse that the law manages cannot be identified without recourse to morality).

authoritative exposition, they engage with it in various critical ways to make best sense of such a commitment to constitutional legitimacy under political justice. And they take the products of their interpretive engagement to carry out the very normative import they are supposed to apply. In this sense, the weak version of preemption reflects such efforts to secure the normativity of constitutional law.

Now, perhaps positivism has a convincing way to explain how strong preemption operates in such argumentative practices. Strong preemption rests upon the distinction between (a) reasoning aiming at establishing the content of positive law, and (b) reasoning implicated in modifying or developing the law. Positivism does not have to deny the salience of a constructive interpretive practice along the lines developed here; it may simply suggest that such an enterprise involves and synthesises (at various degrees) both elements of identifying existing positive law and of developing/modifying such law for the purpose of resolving the practical issue at hand.

Assessment of such a project is well beyond the scope of this book. But we may well take note of Joseph Raz's sophisticated treatment of constitutional interpretation[49] and indicate certain difficulties. Raz understands constitutional interpretation as a kind of reasoning aiming to establish the meaning of the constitution that (a) combines respect for fidelity to its traditional or current meaning, with (b) openness to novelty. Much of constitutional reasoning is interpretive, in this regard, because the moral considerations applicable include both moral reasons to secure continuity with the past and the present and moral reasons to rectify shortcomings and to avoid injustices. The applicable reasons often mix and, accordingly, our interpretation includes (at various degrees) both continuity and innovation.

So far, there is no principal tension between this account of interpretation and the one defended here. Continuity and innovation are indeed implicated in constitutional interpretation. And sometimes, as Raz adds, considerations of continuity may be the only applicable ones. Nonetheless, Raz argues, in some cases we have reason to 'interpret the constitution in ways that simply elucidate its content at the moment' and establish the meaning of constitutional law 'as it is'. Such an interpretation articulating the 'current meaning' constitutional provisions have in constitutional practice, called by Raz a conserving one, establishes the benchmark by which other interpretations, synthesising conserving and innovating elements, are compared.[50]

The main difficulty with this account lies in the idea of a conserving interpretation whose aim is to establish constitutional law 'as it is'. For the reasons brought forward in our rejection of conventionalism (section I(C) above), it is hard to see how we may make sense of such constitutional law 'as it is' as an authoritative normative system. The very content of the authoritative normative

[49] Raz, 'On the Authority and Interpretation of Constitutions' in Larry Alexander (ed), *Constitutionalism: Philosophical Foundations* (Cambridge, Cambridge University Press, 1998) 157.

[50] Raz, ibid, at 181 and 186.

system is fixed by a process of interpretive construction involving, among others, assessment of the relative force of moral considerations towards continuity and towards innovation.

An account of the law privileging just one factor, that is continuity, would often fail to provide us with the norms that we take to be authoritative—given our commitment to constitutional legitimacy. And it cannot explain why to attach some special jurisprudential role to that factor. After all, even in affirming a conservative interpretation of constitutional law as indeed carrying out the normative import of the Constitution on a subject matter, this affirmation is fixed by a process of interpretive construction answerable to our reflective practical reason; to our conclusion that the values of fidelity and continuity are controlling in the circumstances.

No doubt, we may distinguish between conservative and innovative interpretive judgements, ordinary and extraordinary ones, and the like. But such distinctions rest on the substantive content of the deliberative judgements involved, and the background consensus reached in the respective interpretive community.

There is a second difficulty also. Given the argumentative nature of constitutional practice, it is unclear how we may interpret constitutional practices with a view to specifying their supposed 'current meaning', without projecting into this enterprise our reflective and contestable moral understandings about the moral notions of constitutional fidelity and continuity and about the way 'current meaning' carries out the normative import of the Constitution. Therefore, even if we were to accept that 'current meanings' reflect the normative status of 'existing' law, it is unclear how their content could be articulated in a way compatible with a strong conception of constitutional preemption.

VI. The Vicissitudes of Interpretation

Before concluding this chapter, we may grasp this opportunity to indicate that similar difficulties afflict the related distinctions found in constitutional theory between so-called 'constitutional interpretation' and 'constitutional construction', and between 'interpretivism' and 'noninterpretivism'. The locus classicus of this debate is John Ely's famous assertion that the Court is sometimes employing a questionable form of reasoning ('noninterpretivism'), going beyond norms stated or clearly implicit in the written Constitution.[51] The abortion decision of *Roe v Wade* (1973) was, to his mind, the clearest example. Similarly, recent

[51] John Hart Ely, *Democracy and Distrust: A Theory of Judicial Review* (Cambridge, Harvard University Press, 1980) 1–2. On interpretation vs construction see Keith E Whittington, *Constitutional Construction: Divided Powers and Constitutional Meaning* (Cambridge, Harvard University Press, 1999). Lawrence Solum accepts the distinction between interpretation and construction, while emphasising that construction is both ubiquitous and ineliminable. 'Originalism and Constitutional Construction' (2013) 82 *Fordham L Rev* 453–537.

commentary distinguishes between the interpretive activity of determining the publicly available communicative content or linguistic meaning of the text at the time of enactment and subsequent construction of its legal implications for us.

No doubt, distinctions of this sort are employed for reasons beyond our current debate over preemption. They aim at curving out certain forms of constitutional reasoning and subjecting them to tougher standards of permissibility. But they share, in one form or another, the assumption that there is some default kind of interpretive reasoning that more innovative versions depart from. In this sense, these distinctions are variations of the distinction between conservative and innovative interpretive judgements. And the important point from the previous section is that both the option for and the option against the conservative approach are elements of the very same process of interpretive construction; and accountable to the very same normative ideas guiding this activity.

In fact, even the very determination of what such a conservative approach entails is an integral part of the interpretive process. For instance, original communicative content or meaning are ambiguous terms and their construal depends on a variety of considerations (who communicates, to whom, through what means, why is the addressee expected to pay attention, etc) answerable to the intellectual purposes at issue. There is no doubt that the enactment of the Constitution was a political fact and that all implicated agents had an understanding of what they were doing. Yet, we cannot single out one conception of the communicative meaning at stake as the default one for all purposes. Are we focusing on drafters or ratifiers? How do we aggregate individual intentions to ascribe common purpose? Do we care whether such actors took contemporaneous interpretive conventions or judicial interpretive practice for granted, or about their intent as to the construal of the moral concepts they employed in future times? Does it matter how the normative change they intended was understood by the addressees of the law at that time, or by the judicial community?

I do not deny that these are meaningful questions. In fact, one of the purposes of this Part One is to highlight that various interpretive considerations are not fungible elements, but have distinctive roles in an overall interpretive argument. But even approaching these questions, for the eventual purpose of explicating legal content[52]—whether now or even back then—is already part of the larger constructive activity, guided by the same fundamental commitments as every other part thereof. It is now high time to face these normative commitments directly.

[52] Solum defends the independence of 'communicative content' (ascertained through interpretation) over 'legal import' (determined through construction). He distinguishes the perspective of the judge from the perspective of the 'author of the legal text … Authors of legal texts care about the communicative content of their writings. From their perspective, it matters whether the judge acts in accord with the communicative content of the writing, or disregards it. In many cases, authors of legal texts have purposes that will be frustrated if the communicative content is ignored.' ibid, at 490. This is true. Yet, the inquiry into the content of the law is a distinctive inquiry and proceeds from a distinctive perspective: the perspective of somebody who inquires about the practical reasons that constitutional law gives its subjects. Whether and how the perspective of the author matters in this inquiry is a question to be addressed *from* this latter perspective. And on this point the judge has to engage with the framer on the same level.

5

The Pursuit of Political Justice

Given the constructive nature of constitutional interpretation, a central task of constitutional theory is to explain the normative principles to govern the process of interpretive construction. This chapter discusses the principal ideas.

The driving motif is that we have to bring together two fundamental insights: that in interpreting the Constitution we are supposed to respond to the reasons for upholding constitutional legitimacy; and that in doing so, we are operating under the force of public reason and political justice. Accordingly, the normative structure of constitutional interpretation depends upon the proper relation between constitutional legitimacy and political justice. This is fundamental in understanding the operation of practice-sensitive and content-sensitive interpretive arguments, as well as in realising that various argumentative modes employed are not self-justified; their grounds and operation are assessed in the light of the joint commitment to constitutional legitimacy and to the pursuit of political justice.

I. The General Aim

Like all practical reasoning, deliberation about the Constitution's normative import is conducted against the backdrop of and in response to a stock of concerns, pursuits and commitments about what is worth respecting and achieving in the relevant domain. The pertinent concerns, pursuits and commitments frame, so to speak, the service that constitutional interpretation (supposedly) performs to our practical reason.

What is the pertinent stock of concerns and commitments? First, constitutional interpretation is part of practical reasoning about the fundamental directives governing the exercise of public power. As such it is subject to *public reason* and the fundamental pursuit that public power would be exercised in compliance with such reason.

Given the conception of public reason employed in chapter two, constitutional interpretation is (ideally) governed by the pursuit that public power would be exercised in compliance with *political justice*. One clarification is needed here. Political justice evidently does not exhaust the irreducibly plural realm of political values. Yet, it is a fundamental political value, structuring in crucial respects the operation of other political values. Moreover, and subject to various qualifications made in chapter two, it provides the governing ideas in the domain of constitutional rights, as such rights exemplify the very commitment to equal citizenship and equal liberty that political justice aims to capture. Thus, in the rest of this book, I will often employ the pursuit of public reason and political justice interchangeably and I assume that we can easily make the necessary adaptations in areas like federalism, or separation of powers, where other political pursuits become pertinent either in conjunction with or against a background pursuit of political justice.

Secondly, the interpretive deliberation is conducted from a particular standpoint and aspires to identify and explain the content of legal norms: in determining the normative import of the Constitution, we are committed to the authoritative status of its text and the conditionally authoritative status of Supreme Court precedent. In fact, the very commitment to the authoritative status of the Constitution frames constitutional interpretation as a *distinctive* kind of practical reasoning—a kind of reasoning directed at the Constitution, along with its history of authoritative exposition, and aiming at carrying out its normative import.

Thus, at the interpretive standpoint, the supposed duty to comply with institutionally anchored law intersects the commitment that public power be exercised in compliance with public reason and political justice. This leads to the third point. These two commitments do not contradict one another since (we assume that) under public reason and political justice we have a duty to comply with law whose positive authoritative source is the Constitution, along with its history of authoritative exposition. This is so despite the fact that the content of such law may not be ideal! The rationale behind such duty is that by following the normative import of the Constitution, we (supposedly) exercise public power in compliance with public reason and political justice.

These three concerns and commitments, taken together, frame constitutional interpretation and highlight its objectives. Indeed, they counsel for the following account of constitutional interpretation's *general aim*. By combining the fact that the interpretive inquiry aims at carrying out the normative import of the Constitution with the fact that its ultimate pursuit is compliance with public reason and political justice, we may claim that the general aim of constitutional interpretation is to construct such an account of the Constitution, along with its history of authoritative exposition, that by following it *public power is exercised in better compliance with public reason and political justice.*

In this sense, our account belongs to a wider family of conceptions emphasising the moral basis of constitutional interpretation.[1] Yet, it distinguishes between

[1] *cf* the views of Ronald Dworkin (constitutional interpretation aspires to construct the scheme of principles of political morality that would provide the best moral justification of the constitutional practice and structure, and identify the content of constitutional norms flowing thereof) and John Rawls (constitutional interpretation aspires to fit the relevant body of constitutional materials and justify it in terms of the most reasonable public political conception of justice or a reasonable variant thereof). Dworkin, *Law's Empire* (Cambridge, Harvard University Press, 1986) 52 ff and 355 ff, Rawls, *Political Liberalism* (New York, Columbia University Press, 1993, 1996) 236.

such generic moral basis and the further claim that the aim of constitutional interpretation is the direct advancement of the just content of the law. To this issue we now turn.

II. The Conservative Element

A. Upholding Legitimacy under Political Justice

The most intractable problems arise in the process of performing this deliberative inquiry. In fact, much of existing interpretive disagreement may best be understood as disagreement over the role of considerations about the justice of the content of competing interpretations. Under the general aim stated above, are we to prefer the reading of text and precedent that is as close as possible to the substantive outcome political morality would independently favour? Or, would such an approach confuse legal reasoning with independent practical reasoning? If so, is constitutional interpretation properly constrained or even exclusively shaped by (partly) content-insensitive considerations, like history, ordinary linguistic understandings, or doctrinal reasoning?

For instance, we have to decide whether the right of same-sex couples to marry is a fundamental liberty protected by the due process clause. Are we to interpret the relevant provisions and related case law in such a way as to reach a plausible reading as close as possible to the substantive outcome best supported by conceptions of justice of the interpretive community, or in line with the way this moral issue has been understood in the history and traditions of the nation? Or, perhaps in an intermediate, more nuanced manner?

How are we to approach this issue? We may make progress by drawing our attention to the third consideration discussed above regarding the placement of the supposed commitment to constitutional authority within the commitment to public reason and political justice. Constitutional interpretation offers us accounts of the law, not of political morality. The law is supposed to have preemptive power in our practical reason. The idea behind recognising such power is that by following an appropriate account of the law we would (supposedly) act in better compliance with public reason (than by following the determinations we would endorse where we to deliberate directly on the pertinent question by exercising independent practical reasoning).

What invests then an appropriate account of constitutional law with this critical feature? How are we to conceive of an account of the Constitution's normative import under which compliance with political justice is better served? The written Constitution is (taken to be) of normative significance in virtue of some reasons, that is, the reasons (we supposedly have) to endorse its authoritative status. The rationale (so to speak) behind the Constitution's status explains why compliance with law anchored in the Constitution is (supposed to be) a duty of justice.

Thus, an account of the Constitution's normative import may not possess the critical feature unless it carries out that rationale.

We may now come to see how employment of considerations of legitimacy fits under the general aim. A reading of the Constitution that carries out the rationale behind the Constitution's authoritative status is supposed to be superior in terms of compliance with political justice to a reading that does not do so. Thus, in the very process of examining which account better responds to the pursuit of political justice, we are primarily guided by the reasons we have for upholding the Constitution's authority. Similar considerations apply with regard to judicial precedent and its conditionally authoritative status. And since the pertinent rationale behind the conditionally authoritative status of precedent may differ (as compliance with precedent is heavily related to 'rule of law' values and considerations of constitutional efficacy), what constitutional interpretation ultimately needs is a combined rationale of all its authoritative sources.

It should be stressed that although, in constructing and abiding by accounts of constitutional law that serve the pertinent rationales, we supposedly act under public reason and political justice, we need not assume that the better interpretation of the law expresses ideal principle. In deliberating about the normative import of the Constitution, we are deliberating about which account of the Constitution better serves the pursuit of public reason and political justice. However, this deliberation is conducted from a distinctive standpoint. We assume a duty of justice to comply with possibly *non-ideal* norms of law that carry out the normative import of the written Constitution, along with its history of authoritative exposition. By necessity, we also assume that there are reasons behind such duty, and that they fit within our conception of political justice. Accordingly, under political justice, the better interpretation of the law shall be responsive to the reasons for endorsing the authoritative status of the Constitution and the conditionally authoritative status of precedent. Unless it serves the pertinent reasons, an interpretation fails to express authoritative law, which is (at least) reasonable law partaking of a legitimate constitutional structure.

B. Deliberation on the Conserving Impact of Legitimacy

The authoritative status of text and precedent is largely (though not exclusively) related to practice-dependent features of the constitutional scheme like its contemporaneous recognition and enforcement, the history of the Constitution's authorship and ratification, the process of constitutional evolution and the embeddedness of the overall constitutional framework in the collective ethos of the Nation. Possession of such features partly explains why we have most reason under political justice to uphold such a scheme despite the fact that its content is (probably or, if you prefer, most likely) not ideal.

Given the socially contingent and partly content-independent nature of these features, constitutional interpretation, in serving the pertinent reasons, is distanced from considerations that appeal directly to the justice of the content of competing readings. For instance, in approaching which liberty interests are fundamental through the lenses of ideas that have received solid recognition in the ethos of the nation, we constrain the scope of our independent assessment. In constraining the direct examination of just content and, hence, in potentially distancing us from ideal principle, this element of constitutional interpretation is conservative. It suggests that, in interpreting the Constitution, we are not architects of the field. We are like the sailors on Neurath's boat who have to fix an item on the boat while the boat is afloat on the open sea.[2] But this is perhaps precisely what these sailors, as situated, have most reason to do.

At the same time, it by no means follows that we may identify and specify the reasons reflected in this conservative element and, more generally, the reasons for upholding the authority of the Constitution, without engaging in *moral deliberation*. While there is institutional endorsement of the Constitution's status as the positive authoritative source of legitimate law, there is social divergence over the underlying reasons. In chapter one I presented a minimal account arguing that the salience of text and precedent constitute fundamental commitments of the practice. But a full-fledged account of constitutional legitimacy is required here. Some may claim that the authoritative status of the written Constitution is justified by its contemporaneous institutional recognition only; by the virtues of stability and the risks of radical revisionism. Others may reply that the status of the text is partly justified by features related to its historical authorship and initial public endorsement, combined with the value of political continuity. Still others may emphasise the continuous responsiveness of text and precedent to surrounding social and political deliberations, and so forth. If interpretive reasoning is to proceed, the interpreter needs to construct and employ the more plausible rationale behind the authority of the written Constitution and deliberate about which interpretive accounts satisfy it.[3] It is not enough simply to suppose that such a rationale exists. Deliberation about the more plausible rationale is tested against the assumption of political legitimacy and the general aim of political justice. In explaining why, under political justice, we (supposedly) have a duty to comply with law grounded in the Constitution, we need to engage in moral argument. And even after forming an operating rationale, we continue such deliberation in the process of carrying out its implications in defending concrete interpretive propositions.

[2] Otto Neurath, 'Protocol Sentences' (1932), in Alfred Ayer (ed), *Logical Positivism* (New York, The Free Press, 1959) 201.

[3] For acknowledgment of the dependence of interpretive method upon considerations of constitutional legitimacy see also Jed Rubenfeld, 'Legitimacy and Interpretation' in Larry Alexander (ed), *Constitutionalism: Philosophical Foundations* (Cambridge, Cambridge University Press, 1998) 208–11 (the Constitution ought to be interpreted in accordance with the grounds of its legitimate authority; if interpreted otherwise, it loses its claim to legitimate authority), and Marmor, *Interpretation and Legal Theory*, rev edn (Oxford, Hart Publishing, 2005) ch 9 (the ways in which constitutional interpretation ought to be carried out must be sensitive to the main concerns about the legitimacy of a constitutional regime).

Understanding the nature of this conservative component helps us to distinguish it from the hard positive *facts* of text and precedent. The conservative component consists of a set of normative considerations for interpreting such social facts in ways that serve the rationale for treating them as authoritative in institutional life despite their (potentially) non-ideal content. In this sense, the account defended here confirms the claim made in the previous chapter that even what is ordinarily called textual or precedential under-determinacy is dependent upon our reflective practical reason and, in particular, upon deliberative considerations concerning the normative relevance of constitutional practices. The operating account of legitimacy will help us determine whether, for instance, ordinary or established understandings of the text are conclusive or not. Therefore, normative considerations of legitimacy apply throughout constitutional interpretation, both in ordinary cases where there is convergence over the relevance of text and precedent and in extraordinary ones; highlighting the operation of a common normative basis and explicating a kind of normative unity that interpretive constructivism enjoys in argumentative constitutional practices.

III. The Just Content

A. Inviting the Pursuit of Just Content

Recognition of the conservative element of constitutional interpretation shall not mislead us to ignore an equally vibrant innovative element. Considerations underlying the conservative element do not exhaust the applicable reasons but leave space for the engagement of considerations addressing the justice of the content of the law as well. I will advance two arguments to this conclusion, both driven by a proper understanding of constitutional legitimacy and by the argumentative character of constitutional interpretation. The two arguments may be combined into a more inclusive one once the concept of constitutional legitimacy is further specified.

First, a plausible rationale behind constitutional authority has to appeal, to some extent, to the substantive content of the constitutional scheme. In chapter two I suggested that a constitutional scheme would not normally be considered legitimate unless the 'sufficient' justice of its content is somehow secured. Moreover, much of constitutional law, paradigmatically fundamental rights, provides norms that, given their subject matter and content, are normally considered to set up a domain of 'principle' (no doubt, of disputed scope), structuring the realm of permissible public policy. Their violation inflicts upon right-holders a 'wrong' that is crucially different from the kind of *loss* incurred in unwise or unbalanced combinations of substitutable components of public policy (chapter fourteen, section IV).

The applicable rationale of constitutional legitimacy has to accommodate both features. Given the argumentative character of constitutional interpretation, interpretive deliberation about the content of the constitutional scheme we are supposed to uphold—in the light of, among others, these two features—is supposed to serve both the sufficient justice of the scheme and the integrity of the instituted domain of principle.

In fact, it is reasonable to expect that the pertinent rationale would engage the capacity of constitutional interpretation to identify, elaborate and advance the moral commitments of the constitutional scheme and perhaps even mitigate potential, dated shortcomings of the original textual structure. In Larry Sager's powerful terms, constitutional practice is best understood as justice-seeking.[4] On this approach, nicely exemplified in *Obergefell*, various clauses of the Constitutional text may best be understood as providing a solid ground for an ongoing process of moral deliberation (ie by incorporating moral principles), while related precedent may be treated as serving, despite its fallible and institutionally fragmented character, the task of offering guidance over the rational elaboration and over the consistent and judicially manageable implementation of such principles. To this extent, the rationale behind constitutional authority, taken as a consistent whole, would not disbar us from engagement into the justice of the content of competing interpretations; in fact, it would invite such engagement.

Even if one were not to follow Larry Sager that far, any sensible account of constitutional legitimacy would have to be weary of normative antinomies in issues of principle. For instance, Justice Kennedy in *Obergefell* attached special emphasis on the fact that 'the four principles and traditions … demonstrate that the reasons marriage is fundamental under the Constitution apply with equal force to same-sex couples.'[5] On this line of reasoning, selective and, indeed, arbitrary recognition of access to fundamental liberties, even if reflected in traditions of enduring popularity, would challenge the legitimacy of a legal scheme aiming to protect the liberty of the person.

Secondly, the practice-dependent reasons behind the text's authority and precedent's conditional authority would normally single out a set of permissible readings and demarcate a set of impermissible ones. They may also inform further deliberation in selecting among the permissible readings. Yet they often do not exhaust the deliberation needed; they do not determine a unique interpretive outcome.

[4] Lawrence Sager, *Justice in Plainclothes, A Theory of American Constitutional Practice* (New Haven, Yale University Press, 2004) 70 ff. On the relation to interpretive flexibility see also Marmor, above n 3, at 148 (constitutional legitimacy is dependent upon the interpretive flexibility allowed by the constitutional text and practice, that makes it possible to apply the Constitution's morally significant provisions in morally sound ways).

[5] *Obergefell v Hodges*, 576 US __ (2015) (slip op, at 12).

Indeed, the very idea of social contingency associated with constitutional legitimacy implies that a variety of potentially non-ideal constitutional schemes could (as far as their content is concerned) be considered legitimate, provided that they would carry out certain partly content-independent features that justify the duty to comply with the respective scheme. The efficacious recognition and enforcement of a constitutional scheme is arguably such a pertinent feature. Accordingly, we have reason to interpret the Constitution in ways that uphold this feature. However, the interpretive task is not one of determining whether an already specified constitutional scheme is legitimate. Rather, our task is one of determining which constitutional reading of a supposedly legitimate scheme better serves the pursuit of political justice, including the reasons for supposing such scheme to be legitimate. Now, positive under-determinacy is inherent in argumentative practices of recognition. In fact, we have attuned our expectations to a degree of interpretive disagreement and fluctuation. In this light, a set of mutually competing accounts of constitutional content would normally be compatible with the kind of efficacy that underlies the commitment to political legitimacy.

This is not to downplay the constraints that considerations of legitimacy impose, nor to deny the structural effects that various interpretive methodologies may have in the preservation or erosion of constitutional legitimacy. It is perfectly permissible, for instance, to argue that doctrinal tools are needed to channel and discipline the moral conflict inherent in the explication of open-ended constitutional text. In fact, by narrowing down moral and ideological contestation, such doctrinal disciplining may be necessary to preserve a polity-wide scheme of efficacious recognition and enforcement, worthy of our adherence. But this argument is normally incapable of demanding and even less of bringing about pervasive doctrinal determinacy and closure.

This idea is reinforced by a proper understanding of the pertinent practice-dependent reasons. In particular, I doubt that it makes sense to see the reasons supporting the conservative component as maximising ones. The uncritical pursuit of constitutional efficacy, for instance, is associated with constitutional vices, like constitutional rigidity and, at any rate, is potentially at the expense of ideal constitutional content. Accordingly, I would suggest that the respective reasons are best understood as reasons to secure that the interpretation reached sufficiently serves the concern for constitutional efficacy, rather than as reasons to maximise some independently defined parameters of efficacy. Once the values of constitutional legitimacy associated with practice-based constitutional efficacy are sufficiently served, there is no reason under political justice to pursue constitutional readings that potentially distance us even further from ideal principle.

More generally, argumentation of this kind shows that the practice-dependent reasons behind the authority of text and precedent would indicate permissible readings and exclude others, but would often fall short of dictating one unique interpretive outcome. If so, in deliberating about which account of the Constitution's normative import better serves the pursuit of political justice, constitutional legitimacy does not bar us from appealing directly to the justice of the content of competing accounts of the Constitution and to the fundamental concern that we be governed by constitutional norms that are as close to the ideal as possible. Under the general aim of constitutional interpretation defended here, we have most reason to read the authoritative sources of constitutional law in such ways that the resulting account better serves the pursuit of political justice. Once practice-dependent considerations for serving the rationale behind textual and precedential authority are satisfied, the resulting account better serves this pursuit if it is as just in content as possible.

B. Disciplining the Pursuit of Just Content

This brings us to the old conundrum: does interpretation discover or impose constitutional value?[6] Is the Constitution invested with inherent commitments of value that interpretation is supposed to discover and then creatively implement? Or is violent projection of purpose the leitmotif of the whole enterprise?

I hope that the argument advanced in chapter four shows that this distinction is quite misleading. Constitutional interpretation involves elements of both—through and through. At its very core, it reflects the argumentative, *dialectic* reception of constitutional history by incoming generations and interpreters. It is through this very reception that we understand the Constitution as exhibiting moral commitments about constitutional liberty and equality in the first place. And our more focused inquiries about what commitments are salient in explicating constitutional law today are at the very heart of this dialectic activity. Obviously actors engaged or implicated in making constitutional history had their own commitments and aspirations—and this is mirrored in various ways in the text itself. Our inquiries involve serious engagement with them, as well as with the constitutional visions that prevailed at various times in the history of the nation. Thus, the pertinent commitments and aspirations are neither discovered, nor projected upon text or history. They are ascribed to the Constitution in such dialectic processes. And what brings coherence to this enterprise—illuminating the force of the past and the contribution of the interpretive community—is the commitment to constitutional legitimacy: a normative commitment of its own.

For this very reason, appeal to just content does not curve out a separate domain of constitutional interpretation where constitutional legitimacy is irrelevant. No doubt, certain conceptions of constitutional interpretation will emphasise the innovative dimension, either globally or thematically. But there are limits. It would be inconceivable, for instance, to read into text and precedent whatever exotic requirements of justice happen not to contradict it. The constitutional inquiry is directed at the written Constitution, and its history of authoritative

[6] Ely, *Democracy and Distrust: A Theory of Judicial Review* (Cambridge, Harvard University Press, 1980) 43–72.

exposition, and aims at presenting *their* normative import as just in content as possible.[7] Similarly, in the realm of the mainstream, doctrinal tools, even though they often do not determine outcomes, they do discipline direct appeal to substantive moral argument. And by narrowing down moral and ideological contestation, they improve efficacy, stability and impartiality in the way ideas of substantive content enter into the process of constitutional implementation.

Most importantly, the value of political justice addresses both the *substantive* content and the democratic responsiveness of public policy. It is therefore open to reflective argument to determine what blending of these two pertinent dimensions of political justice shall inform interpretive constitutional construction. I will discuss this feature in Part Two (chapters nine and ten), as it is naturally linked with the institutional question about the distinctive role of the various branches of government in constitutional implementation. But it is important to emphasise here that considerations of political legitimacy affect the way we appeal to the justice of substantive constitutional content by requiring, for instance, that such appeal stands responsive to the citizenry as a corpus of free and equal citizens with the moral power to engage in moral reflection and argumentation over the exercise of their collective, public power. This element is not necessarily conservative, as public judgement may sometimes force us to liberate constitutional argument from the constraints of past practice. Yet, it reflects the familiar by now placement of political legitimacy under political justice, as is may require the interpreter to specify pertinent constitutional values, of liberty or of equality, in ways that, in his independent judgement, while reasonable, may fall sort of the ideal.

This task is not devoid of tensions or even of dilemmas. The death penalty jurisprudence provides an illuminating example. We have seen that the majority of the Court understands the Eighth Amendment's prohibition of cruel punishments as reflecting a precept of justice, grounded in the value of human dignity. The Court has accepted that current standards of justice are controlling, but it has also insisted that there is scope for independent judicial judgement to ensure that applicable standards do express respect to the dignity of the person. Now, after striking six death penalty schemes as unconstitutional in their operation in *Furman* (1972), the Court eventually accepted in *Gregg* (1976) that the death penalty is not categorically prohibited. In reaching this conclusion, the pivotal opinion of Justices Stewart, Powell and Stevens took note of the fact that both the framers and the enacting generation 'contemplated the continued existence of the capital sanction' and, most importantly, that there exists national conviction that the death penalty remains appropriate for certain crimes. 'The most marked indication of society's endorsement of the death penalty for murder is the legislative

[7] See Mark Greenberg, 'How Facts Make Law' (2004) 10 *Legal Theory* 157, 196–97 (a model of legal construction identifying the law with the set of morally best propositions that curves out specific exceptions to accommodate legal propositions upheld in institutional practices does not make it intelligible how such practices have normative significance).

response to *Furman*. The legislatures of at least 35 States have enacted new statutes that provide for the death penalty for at least some crimes that result in the death of another person.'[8] The Court evidently considered that a judgement contrary to such strong national conviction would not comport with ideas of constitutional legitimacy.

What is important to note here is that the *Gregg* Court apparently did not consider such national conviction to jeopardise what we call here the sufficient justice of the constitutional scheme. 'We cannot say that the judgment of the Georgia Legislature that capital punishment may be necessary in some cases is clearly wrong'.[9] On the other hand, Justices with a different conviction over substance made a different overall adjustment of the pertinent virtues of legitimacy. Justice Brennan, for instance, was unwilling to follow prevailing understandings as he was convinced that the punishment of death is incompatible with human dignity and violates 'the primary moral principle that the State, even as it punishes, treat[s] its citizens in a manner consistent with their intrinsic worth as human beings.'[10]

Eventually, the Court followed an intermediate path, narrowly tailoring the scope and process for imposition of the death penalty. As Justice Kennedy has acknowledged, 'our response to this case law, which is still in search of a unifying principle, has been to insist upon confining the instances in which capital punishment may be imposed.'[11] The aim is one of adjusting pertinent virtues of legitimacy under political justice. Given the conviction of the current majority (or at least of the Court's pivotal justices) that 'when the law punishes by death, it risks its own sudden descent into brutality, transgressing the constitutional commitment to decency and restraint',[12] this agonising effort is still in search of a unifying principle.

We may now complete the main argument of this section by suggesting how the conservative and the innovative element fit within a coherent account of constitutional interpretation. Both elements are supposed to contribute to the same general aim: the construction of such an account of the Constitution that by following it public power is exercised in better compliance with public reason and political justice. They are complementary dimensions of complex judgements of public reason about the normative significance of constitutional practices, with a view to presenting such significance in ways that better serve compliance with public reason and political justice. Accordingly, the crucial issue is to clarify the complementary role of each element in this pursuit.

The conservative element serves the pursuit of political justice in an indirect manner—through the commitment to the practice-dependent reasons for endorsing the status of constitutional text and of precedent. Considerations of just

[8] *Gregg v Georgia*, 428 US 153, 177 and 179–80 (1976) (joint opinion of Stewart, Powell, Stevens, JJ).
[9] ibid, at 186.
[10] ibid, at 230 (Brennan, J, dissenting).
[11] *Kennedy v Louisiana*, 554 US 407, 437 (2008).
[12] ibid, at 420.

content serve this pursuit in a direct manner—as practice-dependent reasons are properly adjusted with virtues of substantive content under an inclusive account of constitutional legitimacy.

Evidently, the appropriate scope of the two elements cannot be determined in a morally neutral way. It is dependent upon the applicable conception of constitutional legitimacy and the content of constitutional practice. And in determining the contours and proper adjustment of these elements, we engage in delicate exercises of moral reasoning—as we deliberate about what we have most reason to do under conditions of political legitimacy. Still, such reasoning is not institutionally uncommitted. The moral judgements implicated rest upon the assumption that constitutional law, as rooted in practices of institutional recognition, is authoritative. And ultimately, the appeal and coherence of this whole normative enterprise depends on our ability to locate constitutional legitimacy under political justice and to pursue practical deliberation, so structured, in the process of interpreting existing, non-ideal constitutional practices.

IV. Modes of Argumentation

The account defended here does not attempt to assess specific modes of constitutional argumentation, but to approach main aims and normative ideas. Yet, it is important to note that the basic structure frames the proper space and justification of various traditional modes of constitutional reasoning (arguments from text, doctrine, structure, history, traditions, constitutional ethos of the nation, etc). Such modes, properly understood, are not independent factors and a complete interpretive judgement is not supposed to rest on their aggregate strength. They make most sense if understood as operating under a normative structure serving the general aim of constitutional interpretation defended above. In fact, they largely reflect some of the concerns driving its conservative element. To this extent, their relevance is tested by their contribution in reading the Constitution in ways that carry out the rationale behind its authoritative status.

A. Originalism

For instance, the basic framework developed here is capable of structuring the debate over originalism. The reasons for upholding the Constitution today relate, to some degree, to the process and history of its enactment and to the placement of these formative events in the history of the nation. Thus, in interpreting the Constitution, we need to be responsive to the pertinent reasons and ensure that the interpretations reached serve the underlying rationale. In doing so, we need a conception of the normative significance the text may have by virtue of the process that produced it and of the way its enactment was implicated in the formation of the American political community. Once we have such a conception, we may then determine whether the underlying reasons under political justice direct us to pay requisite attention to original understandings regarding the Constitution's normative import. In this manner, we may determine whose original understandings matter (original intentions of framers, original understandings of the ratifiers, original public meaning of the linguistic community, etc),[13] how they matter, and at what level of specificity (abstract principle, mid-level conception, extension, etc).

Thus considerations of constitutional legitimacy are pertinent in guiding us over the relevance of the semantic meaning of the constitutional clauses as understood by the pertinent community, the expectations its members had as to appropriate applications, and the various conceptions for specifying the abstract language employed at intermediate levels of generality. For instance, constitutional text sometimes includes abstract moral concepts. What is their normative significance for public institutions of today? Ronald Dworkin has famously argued that we can make best sense of such terms as signifying commitment to pursuing the more appropriate moral conceptions of the respective moral concepts; and has claimed that it would defeat their point were we to treat them as signifying commitment to the specific applications the drafting community had in mind;[14] or commitment to the specific mid-level conceptions of these principles public morality of that day would uphold.[15] Perhaps. But in assessing what commitments *of* the founding generation are relevant, we need to know what the *present* commitments to the deeds of that generation are; starting from an idea about why the people *of today* are committed to treat the text bequeathed to them as authoritative in their present practices.

If, for instance, the debt to the framing generation is that they formed a political community of free and equal citizens and instituted a frame of principle that would enable future generations to elaborate moral ideas about political justice

[13] For an analysis of these distinctions, see Randy Barnett, 'An Originalism for Nonoriginalists' (1999) 45 *Loy LA L Rev* 611 and Keith Whittington, 'The New Originalism' (2004) 2 *Geo J L & Pub Pol'y* 599. For a comprehensive criticism of the original intentions school see Paul Brest, 'The Misconceived Quest for the Original Understanding' (1980) 60 *BUL Rev* 204. For subsequent attempts to reframe originalism see the seminal article of Antonin Scalia, 'Originalism: The Lesser Evil' (1989) 57 *U Cin L Rev* 849 and the more qualified works of Randy Barnett, *Restoring the Lost Constitution* (Princeton, Princeton University Press, 2003) and Keith E Whittington, *Constitutional Construction: Divided Powers and Constitutional Meaning* (Cambridge, Harvard University Press, 1999). More recent works of a critical nature are Jack Balkin, *Living Originalism* (Cambridge, Harvard University Press, 2011) and, defending a moral, nonoriginalist reading as the best way to justify fidelity to an imperfect Constitution, James Fleming, *Fidelity to our Imperfect Constitution: for Moral Readings and Against Originalisms* (Oxford, Oxford University Press, 2015).

[14] Dworkin, *Justice in Robes* (Cambridge, Harvard University Press, 2006) 117ff (distinguishing between semantic intentions and expectations as to applications).

[15] See Mitchell N. Berman, 'Originalism and Its Discontents (Plus a Thought or Two About Abortion)' (2007) 24 *Const Commentary* 383 (distinguishing between original principles and contemporary ones).

and to secure their judicially cognisable and manageable enforcement, then considerations about how that generation would have applied these ideas is of secondary importance. If, on the other hand, we consider ourselves committed to uphold the Constitution partly because the founding generation, at some point in time, managed to form a thick conception of certain moral principles and aimed to secure its enforcement in pathological eras of ideological division, demagogy, or political opportunism, then perhaps there could be an argument for a more conserving role; allowing for evolution, say, only in line with evolving national consensus. And more nuanced intermediate positions may call for narrow tailored, and possibly issue-specific, approaches.

Considerations of legitimacy are crucial for a related reason also; they disable us from appealing to the justice of the content of competing interpretations only to the extent necessary to serve the pertinent rationale. In a sense, this is recognised by some moderate originalists who argue that considerations of justice become relevant to the extent that the pertinent original understandings underdetermine the content of constitutional law.[16] However, the argument proposed here is more far-reaching. Virtues often come along with potential weaknesses. An adequate account would consider that both Constitution-making and interpretive reasoning constitute parts of the normative reasoning about the exercise of public power. In determining the appropriate content of each operation, we need to examine how to employ the synergistic effects of their combination under political justice. In considering the role of interpretive deliberation, we need to ponder on both the virtues and weaknesses the text may possess by virtue of the process that produced it. Only then may we determine the sense in which considerations relating to the constitution-making process should restrict present reflection and take steps to avoid perpetuating side-effects resulting from that process's inherent limitations.

It should be emphasised in this regard that the dependence of interpretive method upon considerations of constitutional legitimacy, in itself, does not aim to prejudge the force of originalism. In fact, scholars who are favourable to such dependence often differ substantially over whether original understandings serve the values behind constitutional legitimacy.[17] The point is perhaps better appreciated once we recognise that an interpretive method may serve constitutional legitimacy in indirect ways. For instance, if one were to establish that some form of originalism is necessary to secure constitutional efficacy and stability (on the ground, say, that the history of the Constitution's enactment has been instrumental in launching and is still instrumental in preserving such stability and social

[16] See Barnett, above n 13 and Whittington, above n 13.

[17] Compare Marmor, above n 3, at 158 ('the more we tie our deference to the constitution to the framers' particular role in its enactment, the more acute the problem of moral legitimacy becomes') with Barnett, above n 13 (defending deference to the original public meaning on considerations of legitimacy). The two scholars address different originalist methodologies. Yet, the comparison exhibits, I think, how diverging conceptions of constitutional legitimacy lead to divergence over the interpretive relevance of the founding era.

support), a cognisable prima facie argument for that form of originalism could be constructed. Still, in determining the limitations of such an argument and, in particular, the space it should leave open for the innovative component, one would have to engage in moral deliberation about the proper role of these virtues under political legitimacy. Interpretive stability, for instance, may easily become interpretive rigidity, undermining the critical force of constitutional principles,[18] a feature that may be considered essential for the sufficient justice of a constitutional scheme and, thus, for its legitimacy.

B. Text and Structure

Similarly, the structure defended here helps us examine the relevance of considerations like settled linguistic practice, settled special usage within legal community, and various textual canons in guiding and constraining deliberation about the Constitution's normative import. For instance, ordinary linguistic usage, far from yielding a natural interpretive baseline, is one among many available interpretive modalities, in need for justification. It could even be the case that restrictive readings that follow ordinary usage may sometimes betray the (supposed) duty to carry out the normative import of the Constitution given the underlying rationale behind constitutional authority.[19]

This could be so when there is divergence between ordinary usage and underlying purpose and public trust has developed in the effectuation of such purpose. There were times, for instance, when the prevailing sensibility in statutory interpretation was that 'frequently, however, even when the plain meaning did not produce absurd results but merely an unreasonable one "plainly at variance with the policy of the legislation as a whole", this Court has followed that purpose, rather than the literal words. When aid to construction of the meaning of words, as used in the statute, is available, there certainly can be no "rule of law" which forbids its use, however clear the words may appear on "superficial examination"'.[20] And this argument can be of particular force in constitutional law. No doubt, constitutional text is more carefully drafted. But constitutional law does not aim at narrowly defined policy results. And public trust in observance of diachronic moral commitments of the constitutional practice is normally understood to be of utmost importance.

[18] *cf* Mark Greenberg & Harry Litman, 'The Meaning of Original Meaning' (1998) 86 *Geo L J* 569 (fidelity to original practices themselves is inconsistent with an account of constitutional norms as principles).

[19] For a related argument regarding statutory interpretation, see Andrei Marmor, 'The Immorality of Textualism' (2005) 38 *Loy LA L Rev* 2063. See also the insightful essay of Frederick Schauer, 'Is Law a Technical Language?' (2015) 52 *San Diego L Rev* 501 (the ordinary versus technical language question cannot be determined without recourse to what law in general is aimed at achieving).

[20] *United States v American Trucking Assns., Inc.*, 310 US 534, 543–44 (1940).

If, on the other hand, the more plausible rationale behind the Constitution's authoritative status (or behind certain clauses) were to point, among others, to the function of the written Constitution in providing a focal point to coordinate impartially and efficaciously the behaviour of equal citizens with diverging views about political justice and with conflicting interests,[21] ordinary usage and similar interpretive modalities could sometimes be of controlling importance. An interpretation that substantially ignored the above-mentioned constraints could be said to fail to carry out this function and, in so doing, would not serve the pursuit of political justice. At the same time, the force of the relevant service would depend on many collateral considerations and, most importantly, on the content of interpretive practice and the expectations formed around it regarding the role of such interpretive constraints. For our purposes, what is important to emphasise is that, in dealing with this issue in a more informative manner, we need to assess the purported rationale under political justice and to examine which interpretive constraints serve it and how they serve it.

In the same manner, we need to appeal to the more plausible rationale for treating the constitutional text as authoritative in order to explain whether and how considerations of textual structure inform, expand or even qualify the force of arguments from discrete textual provisions. Let us consider the due process clause of the Fourteenth Amendment. On the face of the clause, a substantive reading of the clause is textually less natural than a procedural one.[22] Are we to say that the former is precluded by considerations of textual integrity? We may not duck the issue by claiming that a substantive reading is morally superior. The question we face is precisely whether we are precluded from addressing the justice of the content of this reading for the reasons discussed above (section II). At this point, we are asked to look elsewhere in the text: at the bill of rights, the Ninth Amendment and the 'privileges and immunities' clause. We are also reminded that the whole constitutional text is the primary positive authoritative source of the constitutional scheme.[23] And we are finally told that a substantive reading fits better in a morally appealing account of the constitutional text taken as a structured whole. Is this a permissible argument? To answer this question, we need to appeal to the more attractive rationale behind the text's status.

In addressing this issue, it may matter whether the pertinent constitutional provisions are to be understood as reflecting political compromises over the means to pursue contested mixtures of ends. Uncritical abstraction from means agreed

[21] *cf* Frederick Schauer, 'The Coordinating Function of Plain Meaning' (1994) *Sup Ct Rev* 231.

[22] For some, even 'eccentric'. Ely, above n 6, at 18 ('substantive due process is a contradiction in terms—sort of like "green pastel redness"').

[23] *cf* from the statutory context *King v Burwell*, 576 US __ (2015) ('when deciding whether the language is plain, we must read the words "in their context and with a view to their place in the overall statutory scheme" … If we give the phrase "the State that established the Exchange" its most natural meaning, there would be *no* "qualified individuals" on Federal Exchanges. But the Act clearly contemplates that there will be qualified individuals on *every* Exchange.' (slip op, at 9, 10)).

and interpretive projection of new ends may be said to dishonour the level of generality adopted at the founding era and devalue the commitment to the process followed at the Constitution's enactment.[24] In assessing this claim, as well as in drawing the pertinent distinctions to apply it, we need an account of the ways the enactment process affects the reasons for endorsing the authoritative status of the Constitution. Such an account will illuminate, for example, whether the relevant means are best seen as exclusive, demarcating the outer constitutional reach in the respective domain and exhausting the relevance of background principles, and if not, the kind of interpretive respect they deserve.

This problématique becomes even more pronounced when we move from the structure of the text to the practice of its authoritative exposition, and to the web of doctrinal loci established in the history of constitutional implementation. We encountered in chapter one a major debate between those who view precedent as mediating between text and application and those who perceive of it as supplementing the original text; and an even more profound debate between those attracted by versions of textualism and those who hold dear common-law fashions of constitutionalism.

Doctrinal intermediation and supplementation serve a variety of functions. We often focus on the extent doctrine restricts the direct pursuit of just content, in the course of facilitating the judicial administrability of abstract clauses or of narrowing down moral contestation. But judicial exposition also exhibits a critical feature of institutional life: the argumentative ways in which courts of law receive and interact with the formal pronouncements of the framing generation; often extending commitments of narrow scope to adjacent issues, bringing within the constitutional ambit rules that subsequent generations and their courts of law deem compelling by consistency of principle. Once these initially innovative pieces of constitutional practice become entrenched in the practice, they supply their own practice-dependent reasons for their preservation. Such reasons sometimes compete with sensible argument for radical, interpretive departures from the past. But they often also compete with reasons for restricting ourselves to the initial textual pigeonholes. What we need for the purpose of structuring textualist and doctrinal interpretive modalities, as well as for the purpose of setting the outer reach of both of them, is an inclusive conception of constitutional legitimacy.

C. Integrity

An extension of the argument from structure leads us to a respectable line of constitutional theory claiming that constitutional interpretation should be performed in the light of an inclusive moral account dovetailing and justifying the

[24] See John Manning, 'Federalism and the Generality Problem in Constitutional Interpretation' (2009) 122 *Harv L Rev* 2003. Although the focus of the article is on federalism, it structurally applies to fundamental rights jurisprudence as well.

constitutional text and surrounding institutional practice as a whole. Dworkin's adjudicative theory of integrity is a par excellence instance of this approach.[25]

As this approach stands in between textualist and doctrinal modes of reasoning, on the one hand, and purely innovative ones, on the other, it has been subjected to a kind of criticism fundamentally different from the kind discussed in the previous paragraphs. In particular, it has been questioned why, under political justice, we have most reason to act upon an inclusive set of 'legal' principles that, while lacking authoritative institutional approval (lacking textual or precedential pedigree), may lead to interpretive accounts that are not as just in content as competing alternatives?[26] Why, for instance, shall we extend the ideology governing certain clauses of the Constitution (even as construed under their most charitable construction) beyond instances that have received actual positive endorsement? Alternatively, if we end up with principles political morality would independently most favour, there may be suspicion that the pursuit of integrity is not genuine; that we have approached constitutional practice in a selective way to unearth our most cherished values of substance.

For our purposes, let us emphasise that this debate may better be approached under the standards of justification advanced here. Indeed, we have little reason to idealise adjacent legal fields and extrapolate from them principles of general applicability unless by doing so we serve the more plausible rationale behind constitutional legitimacy. If, for instance, the text reflects a set of unconnected political compromises, whose legitimacy rests upon considerations of social stability and the like, it is questionable whether we have reason to extend the underlying ideology beyond the actual deals struck. If, on the other hand, the more plausible rationale for upholding the authority of the Constitution over us relates in a significant way to the content of its underlying principles, as Dworkin obviously thought, interpreting the Constitution in their light may be justified under political justice.

I assume that many practitioners would locate themselves somewhere in between these positions. But there is a core of wisdom in the idea of integrity that they better hearken. As we seek to determine what we have most reason to do under conditions of constitutional legitimacy, we need to do our best so that our operating reasons (practice and content-dependent) and the way we have assembled them in our practical reasoning do not compromise, but serve political justice.

We may conclude this section by pointing out that various modes for structuring direct appeal to substantive moral argument are also accountable to the general aim of constitutional interpretation and the structuring role of political legitimacy in its pursuit. Indeed, constitutional practice employs various techniques for

[25] See Dworkin, above n 1.

[26] See Raz, 'The Relevance of Coherence', in his *Ethics in the Public Domain* (Oxford, Oxford University Press, 1994) 313, 325.

privileging certain deliberative judgements like those embedded in the constitutional ethos of public institutions or even of the nation at large,[27] or, on narrower accounts, those reflected in prevailing social practices and traditions. It occasionally also opts for excluding other categories of judgement (say, excluding appeal to divisive philosophical theories about the justice of substantive constitutional content).[28] Employment of such modes can be tested against considerations of political legitimacy that emphasise the good of living in a sufficiently just political community, enduring in time and history, under conditions of reciprocity and despite the fact of reasonable disagreement over the requirements of political justice.

In chapter ten (section I(D)), I will explore the idea that this good is served if we privilege ideas deeply embedded and proudly cherished in public culture while exercising critical responsibility over their principled conception and application. For our current purposes, we shall note a more generic difficulty. The relevance, under constitutional legitimacy, of the judgement of different generations and of the fact of reasonable pluralism among free and equal members of the present community raises significant challenges for the pursuit of integrity. Integrity is premised on the twin ideas that legitimacy and its internal elements do not compromise political justice and that a coherent scheme of principle can spring up from the interpretive engagement with the Constitution and its practices of recognition. The validity of these premises depends upon both the facts of constitutional practice and our conceptions of political justice. What is certain though is that the pursuit of integrity is an agonising endeavour and its fulfilment is always in peril; while jurisprudence often remains, in Justice Kennedy's vivid expression with regard to the death penalty, 'still in search of a unifying principle'.

D. Wrapping Up

Argumentation of moral character is needed to show whether and how certain of the modes discussed here do serve the pursuit of political justice by satisfying practice-dependent reasons for endorsing the authoritative status of text and precedent, like institutional efficacy and social support. Furthermore, even beyond the scope of practice-dependent reasons, considerations of legitimacy affect interpretive appeal to the justice of substantive constitutional content by requiring, for instance, that it stand responsive to the citizenry as a corpus of free and equal citizens with the moral power to engage in moral reflection and argumentation over the exercise of their collective, public power (see chapters nine and ten).

[27] See Philip Bobbitt, *Constitutional Interpretation* (Oxford, Basil Blackwell, 1991) 93 ff and Tribe, *American Constitutional Law*, 3rd edn, vol I (New York, Foundation Press, 2000) 70–78.

[28] See Cass Sunstein, 'Incompletely Theorized Agreements' (1995) 103 *Harv L Rev* 1733.

At the same time, arguments from political justice are critical in assessing what due respect to the pertinent values of legitimacy does not require, and how such values should be adjusted to considerations of just content. For instance, intricate issues of political morality surface in the process of specifying how to abstract relevant deliberative judgements from diverse and potentially conflicting social practices in a polity committed to equal citizenship; how to approach uncritical or argumentative practices; and what to make out of stagnant, fluctuating or evolving ones.[29] The duty of reciprocity in the face of moral disagreement presupposes commitment to equal citizenship. And this in turn may suggest that by strict adherence to the ways certain values are specified in prevailing social practices of some sort, we would not only overreach the very reasons behind appeal to such practices; we would also deprive ourselves of the critical capacity of constitutional interpretation to secure the sufficient justice of constitutional content.

This concern has powerful salience in cases implicating the tight nexus between fundamental liberty and equal protection, like those involving the exclusion of certain classes of persons from exercising a fundamental liberty. In Justice Kennedy's eloquent exposition in *Obergefell*, '*Loving* did not ask about a "right to interracial marriage"; *Turner* did not ask about a "right of inmates to marry"; and *Zablocki* did not ask about a "right of fathers with unpaid child support duties to marry." Rather, each case inquired about the right to marry in its comprehensive sense, asking if there was a sufficient justification for excluding the relevant class from the right. … If rights were defined by who exercised them in the past, then received practices could serve as their own continued justification and new groups could not invoke rights once denied'.[30]

Finally, scrutiny over the applicable reasons of political legitimacy and political justice facilitates supporting an argumentative mode *on the right reason*; and questions the consequentialist advice we often get to the effect that, in light of the fallibility of institutionalised interpretive reasoning, we may eventually get better outcomes if we apply an otherwise questionable (or, why not, even disreputable) interpretive mode.[31] We may extend this point beyond doctrine. If, say, we believe that the primary purpose of constitutional interpretation is to provide us with good moral readings of the Constitution, while we also deny that considerations of legitimacy favour originalism, it would be deeply unprincipled to adopt originalism for the mere reason that its results *happen* to better approximate on balance the results a moral reading would ideally reach. Such an approach, I fear, while possibly understandable in clearly controlled strategic moves, if extended

[29] Arguments from tradition in constitutional law are notoriously malleable. See JM Balkin, 'Tradition, Betrayal, and the Politics of Deconstruction' (1990) 11 *Cardozo L Rev* 1613, 1615.

[30] *Obergefell v Hodges*, 576 US __ (2015) (slip op, at 18).

[31] On constraints due to institutional fallibility, see the programmatic article of Cass Sunstein & Adrian Vermeule, 'Interpretation and Institutions' (2003) 101 *Mich L Rev* 885. As it will become apparent in part two of this book, although I largely share the proposed institutional turn, I consider it of paramount significance that it should be kept answerable to the general normative pursuits of constitutional reasoning.

as a general methodological principle, sacrifices the integrity of constitutional reasoning under its fundamental pursuits and commitments.[32]

V. Institutional Fallibility

We touched in the previous paragraph on the problem of institutional fallibility, warning against unprincipled consequentialist reasoning. We may be reminded at this stage that institutional fallibility counsels for lowering down the aspirations of philosophical ascent. Institutional fallibility, we are told, justifies distinguishing between ambitious projects of constitutional argumentation carried out by citizens and academicians and more minimalist methodologies appropriate for judges[33] and, let us add, public institutions in general.

Part Two of this work deals with the assignment of the interpretive project to public institutions and the distinctive input, including the propensity to err, expected from complementary institutions, with focus on the process of judicial review. We will have ample space to discuss whether judges should defer to legislatures over complex judgements of social fact or ambitious moral philosophising. The challenge I want to discuss here is more fundamental, affecting the totality of the legal process. Is it justified? Are we justified in adopting an across-the-board minimalist conception of constitutional reasoning out of concern for institutional fallibility over more ambitious projects?

I think we shall be very sceptical over such an approach. The law is an institutional system of norms. It is a fundamental feature of legal rules that they are recognised and enforced by a system of public institutions. Moreover, public law is a system of norms governing public institutions in the exercise of public power. This has two implications for our inquiry. First, the paradigmatic perspective is the institutional one. It does not make sense, at least in principle, to raise a sharp distinction between 'permissible' academic projects of constitutional interpretation and their institutionally 'permissible' replicas. If the former are incapable of institutional cognizance, they belong to an altogether different genre of thought. Secondly, when citizens advance arguments about constitutional content, including implicated arguments of political legitimacy and justice, they argue about the powers and constraints *applicable* to public institutions; thus, by implication, they make claims that public institutions are supposed to recognise—and are presumed capable of recognising—in their interpretive reasoning.

[32] *cf* Korsgaard's point that 'it is not quite right to say that what justice requires is that *the guilty should be punished*; rather what justice requires is that *the state should punish the guilty on account of his guilt*. This is why a lynching does *not* count as the next best thing'. Christine Korsgaard, *Self-Constitution: Agency, Identity, and Integrity* (Oxford, Oxford University Press, 2009) 151.

[33] Cass Sunstein, 'Second-Order Perfectionism' (2007) 75 *Fordham L Rev* 2867. See also Sunstein & Vermeule, above n 31.

But are public institutions capable of such cognizance? The argument of this book is explicitly developed from the institutional perspective and aims at organising considerations and commitments present, one way or another, in our common, public culture. Institutions of a polity partake in our common, public reason and they are in principle open to its critical force, including the kinds of arguments about political legitimacy and political justice described in this chapter. While discontent with institutional shortcomings in this process is part of the institutional experience, denial of the very capacity for such openness would be incompatible with fundamental facts about argumentative social practices and actualised public reason; it would even make the notion of shortcoming incoherent. It is too late in the day to turn back the enlightenment project.

Having said that, public institutions often do face uncertainty; and they need to be aware of their fallibility. Hence, constitutional theory needs to make space for ways of dealing with both uncertainty and fallibility. We will discuss this feature in Part Two as regards institutional reasoning (chapter six, section VI and chapter nine, section IV). One main idea is piecemeal experimentation and the employment of interim rules taking into account gravity and reversibility of error, as well as actual experience from past performance; and the selection of the proper time for settling fundamental issues of principle. Such processes, in turn, operate ideally within an environment that facilitates discursive openness, institutional dialogue and reversibility of choice.

No doubt, actual experience cuts both ways. The lessons from infamous cases, like *Red Scott v Sandford* (1857), *Lochner v New York* (1905) and *Plessy v Ferguson* (1895) are available to us as warning posts; as are the grave injustices from inaction, institutional pessimism, and doctrines of despair. 'Liberty finds no refuge in a jurisprudence of doubt'.[34]

In the light of fallibility, each institution is expected to adjust its reasoning in ways peculiar to its culture and function. For example, the judiciary employs various doctrinal tools in a wider scheme of path-dependent common-law constitutionalism. It has reason to attend to the judicial manageability of its doctrines, and to their institutional efficacy; and to be sensitive as to the necessity for adjustment. The distinction between ordinary and extraordinary adjudication (chapter four, section I(C)) is helpful in illuminating the importance of time frame and context for extraordinary choices. But even this very issue, the decision of whether the time is ready and knowledge adequate for putting traditional modes of argumentation at rest and resolving a fundamental issue of principle is not dissociated from the general structure developed here, the pursuit of political justice and the uncompromising elements thereunder. After all, our very argument in the previous section is that traditional modes of argumentation do not constitute necessary features of the general normative structure; their role is assessed in the light of the

[34] *Planned Parenthood of Southeastern Pa. v Casey*, 505 US 833, 844 (1992) (joint opinion of O'Connor, Kennedy, and Souter, JJ).

pursuit of justice, the commitment to constitutional legitimacy and the appropriate structure of these features in constitutional reasoning.

Finally, recognition of the permanence of institutional fallibility sometimes does not encourage cautionary experimental steps, but counsels for more ambitious in reach and justification, though more rigid in operation, precautionary frames. On the face of institutional fallibility, deep reflection on what the governing standard should be may well support both ambitiousness in reach and rigidity in content.

First Amendment jurisprudence is quite pertinent here. As the Court came to realise the vulnerability of First Amendment liberties and the propensity of institutions to err in engaging with them, it developed prophylactic rules of particular stringency. 'The objectionable quality of vagueness and overbreadth [depends] upon the danger of tolerating, in the area of First Amendment freedoms, the existence of a penal statute susceptible of sweeping and *improper* application. … These freedoms are delicate and vulnerable, as well as supremely precious in our society. The threat of sanctions may deter their exercise almost as potently as the actual application of sanctions. Because First Amendment freedoms need breathing space to survive, government may regulate in the area only with narrow specificity'.[35]

In settings involving freedoms deemed 'vulnerable' and 'supremely precious', institutional uncertainty about the appropriate specification and enforcement of constitutional requirements (coupled with subjective distrust over such processes) has led to rule-formalism, rather than minimalism; to constitutional doctrine over-protecting conduct in the light of 'law's conscious distrust of its own processes to make needed discriminations'.[36]

Similarly, in the death penalty jurisprudence, the Court has adopted a dual strategy of individualised decision making and categorical precaution. Faced with 'discretionary statutes pregnant with discrimination', the *Furman* Court held them unconstitutional in their operation, 'as discrimination is an ingredient not compatible with the idea of equal protection of the laws that is implicit in the ban on "cruel and unusual" punishments'.[37] Institutional fallibility, extending to the overall scheme of criminal justice, was linked with the risk of arbitrariness and discrimination. After eventually accepting that the death penalty is not categorically prohibited by the Constitution, the Court engaged in a process of articulating standards for guiding individualised determinations over the character and record of the individual offender and the circumstances of the particular offence. The Court adamantly rejected statutes that would render the death penalty mandatory under well-defined circumstances, as they 'would treat all persons convicted of a designated offense not as uniquely individual human beings, but as members of a

[35] *NAACP v Button*, 371 US 415, 432–33 (1963). See also Frederick Schauer, 'The Second-Best First Amendment' (1989) 31 *Wm & Mary L Rev* 1, 2–3.

[36] Harry Kalven, 'The New York Times Case: A Note on "The Central Meaning of the First Amendment"' (1964) *Sup Ct Rev* 191, 221.

[37] *Furman v Georgia*, 408 US 238, 256–57 (1972) (Douglas J, concurring).

faceless, undifferentiated mass to be subjected to the blind infliction of the penalty of death.'[38]

At the same time, the Court did accept certain categorical rules, but in the opposite direction—within a precautionary frame that is not minimalist, at least as to outcomes. It demanded that the death penalty be available for a very narrow class of crimes only and excluded various categories of offenders from its ambit. In a recent decision clarifying that States may not impose the death penalty to punish crimes against individuals not involving death, it conceded that 'the resulting imprecision and the tension between evaluating the individual circumstances and consistency of treatment have been tolerated where the victim dies.' Given that the applicable standards to confine the penalty's use remain 'indefinite and obscure', it pointedly refused to engage in a similar experimental 'process of articulating rational standards for crimes for which no one has been executed in more than 40 years [as this] would require experimentation in an area where a failed experiment would result in the execution of individuals undeserving of the death penalty'.[39]

The choice between casuistry and categorical protection was not made on shallow grounds. Management of the risk of error rested on consideration of implicated constitutional principles—a prerequisite for enlightened decision making about the content and protection of supremely precious freedoms.

VI. Conclusion

Constitutional interpretation is best understood as a reflective kind of practical reasoning. As such, it responds to applicable reasons, the reasons for upholding the authority of institutionally anchored law under political justice. From this standpoint, the interpretive community deliberates about the morally sounder accounts of text and precedent. These are accounts that serve practice-dependent reasons and virtues of just content in ways that redeem the commitment to political legitimacy; the commitment of the present community that, given the institutional world its members have inherited, by following the normative import of the Constitution, public power would be exercised in better compliance with political justice. In determining the contours and proper adjustment of such reasons, and specifying the rules and principles that constitutional law provides them with, they engage in delicate exercises of moral reasoning. They seek to avoid compromises in justice. And they often find themselves committed in an agonising, dialectic effort to establish principle against the recalcitrant backdrop of non-ideal practice.

[38] *Woodson v North Carolina*, 428 US 280, 304 (1976) (plurality opinion of Stewart, Powell, Stevens, JJ). See also *Miller v Alabama*, 567 US 460 (2012) (mandatory life without parole for juveniles violates the Eighth Amendment).

[39] *Kennedy v Louisiana*, 554 US 407, 440–41 (2008). See also *Graham v Florida*, 560 US 48 (2010) (the Eighth Amendment prohibits a sentence of life without parole for a juvenile convicted of a non-homicide offence).

Part 2

Institutional Architecture

The thesis defended in Part One addresses the general structure of *substantive constitutional argument*. Substantive interpretive argument is not to be equated with the inquiry of a public official about which substantive interpretation the official has most reason to rely upon in her official conduct, on the face of competing interpretations endorsed by other competent officials; or, in case he is charged with constructing the applicable interpretation himself, about what deference he has most reason to show to pertinent judgements of others. The latter inquiries include a second order *institutional component* that we now have to single out.

In a political democracy, public power is power held and exercised in trust. Public officials are supposed to exercise public power in their capacity as the collective arms of the free and equal members of the political community. We have argued in Part One that constitutional interpretation involves arguments of constitutional legitimacy and just content and that such arguments are explicable in terms of public reason and the pursuit of political justice. And it is a fact of constitutional practice that such arguments are subject to reasonable pluralism.[1] Given this fact, public reason and the very commitment to political justice may well preclude public officials from exercising public power on the basis of their fully independent interpretive judgement. In fact, their fundamental normative commitments may require that, in determining and specifying the applicable standard, officials show or allow space for adequate responsiveness to pertinent substantive judgements of others.

This may include responsiveness to public deliberation taking place among free and equal members of the political community who honour the bonds of reciprocity and deliberate about the more attractive specification of the requirements of political justice.[2] This is exhibited, for instance, in the Eighth Amendment jurisprudence on cruel and unusual punishments. As the Court noted in a significant death penalty case, 'in the [past] 13 years … the American public, legislators, scholars, and judges have deliberated over the question whether the death penalty

[1] For versions of this argument see Richard Fallon, *Implementing the Constitution* (Cambridge, Harvard University Press, 2000) 102–06 and Frank Michelman, *Brennan and Democracy* (Princeton, Princeton University Press, 1999).

[2] Michelman, ibid, at 59–60.

should ever be imposed on a mentally retarded criminal. The consensus reflected in those deliberations informs our answer to the question'.[3] It may also include intra-institutional responsiveness, that is, deference to certain judgements of other officials (ie, judicial deference to Congress), as evidenced in the various doctrinal standards of review courts craft and employ throughout constitutional litigation.[4]

This Part Two examines the nature and normative structure of the institutional inquiry. It builds and expands upon a basic insight about the relation between the substantive inquiry and the institutional one: once we have an account of the general structure of substantive constitutional argument, we may examine the appropriate *assignment of this task* to various public bodies, so that the institutional structure charged with reaching authoritative interpretations of the Constitution is best suited to successfully perform this task.

[3] *Atkins v Virginia*, 536 US 304, 307 (2002).

[4] See Fallon, above n 1, and 'Judicially Manageable Standards and Constitutional Meaning' (2006) 119 *Harv L Rev* 1274.

6

The Justification of Institutional Norms

I. Patterns of Institutional Assignment

The institutional nature of law and the constructive nature of constitutional interpretation highlight the distinctiveness of a task entrusted to law-applying institutions: the task of constructing applicable interpretations of the law.[1] In this sense *institutionalised interpretation* reflects a genuine division of normative labour between lawmaking and law-applying institutions. The normative character of the interpretive labour entrusted to law-applying institutions has been discussed in the preceding chapters. Its practical implications are confirmed in the politicisation of constitutional adjudication; similarly, as far as statutory interpretation is concerned, in the fact that political actors excluded from the winning coalition at the legislative stage organise to participate in the executing coalition and, by way of interpretation, contest, reshape, or at least get the best out of the initial policy choices.[2]

By and large, legal theory has overlooked the multiple patterns of assigning this project of construction to the system of public institutions; partly because it has failed to appreciate that this question is analytically distinct from the debate regarding the nature and substantive structure of constitutional reasoning; on the axiomatic assumption that the judge is supposed to adjudicate on the basis of constructions of law crafted on a fully independent basis. We will revisit this assumption, focusing upon judicial review over issues of constitutional law.

The traditional assumption is indeed that the judiciary, in performing its adjudicatory duties, is supposed to rely on interpretive judgements it performs on an *independent* basis. On this assumption, judgements of other bodies are merely 'potentially persuasive', in the sense that the judge would not adopt them unless

[1] See also Frederick Schauer, 'Authority and Indeterminacy' (1987) 29 *Nomos* 28 (legal indeterminacy is a source of interpretive authority).

[2] See Johannes Lindner & Berthold Rittberger, 'The Creation, Interpretation and Contestation of Institutions—Revisiting Historical Institutionalism' (2003) 41 *Journal of Common Market Studies* 445–73.

persuaded by them. What is important for our present purposes is that, first, this is an institutional scheme, and secondly, that it is one among many available alternatives.

In limited categories of issues, even a court of law may have to resolve a dispute on the basis of constitutional determinations of other bodies, for example by declining the power to review pertinent interpretive judgements made by the political and bureaucratic branches (see chapter eleven, section II on the political question doctrine). In such cases, we may say that the scope of judicial review is limited. True, courts may need to interpret the law themselves to determine whether the case before them falls under the stipulated exception. They may even need to interpret the interpretive judgement of the other body to specify how it applies to the case before them. But having done so, they are supposed to treat that judgement as *authoritative* in their practical reasoning. They are supposed to act on the basis of that interpretation, rather than on the interpretation they would independently form.

In a third scenario, a public body has interpretive authority over another body, which is nonetheless *limited in scope* or *conditional*. First, interpretive authority may be restricted to a particular issue partaking in an overall interpretive judgement (say, a material moral judgement or determination of social fact—remember that interpretive reasoning is understood broadly to cover the reach of constitutional law to concrete factual patterns). The court would still have to form the applicable interpretation, but defer in this process to certain material determinations of other bodies. Secondly, an overall interpretation may be *provisionally* authoritative over courts, that is to say, subject to challenge on some grounds only. Permissible grounds may relate to the process employed in reaching the provisionally authoritative judgement or to the substance of the judgement itself. For example, a court may have to rely on the interpretation offered, provided the latter is the result of a rational reasoning process, or does not raise concerns of a certain kind or magnitude. In the latter example, the court is supposed to review some aspects of the provisionally authoritative judgement (the structure of the substantive argument or the existence of a grave deficiency).[3] This in fact is familiar in the field of administrative law (chapter fourteen, section I) where various process- and substance-related qualifications are made: an agency interpretation offered in the course of litigation may not be controlling unless it reflects the agency's fair and considered judgement on the matter, etc.

Fourthly, a court of law may be supposed to act on independent interpretive judgement without recognising conditional authority to others. Yet, in the process of forming it, the court may be supposed to attach some normative significance

[3] Similarly, Raz argues that an authority serves its mediating role even if its subjects may ignore it in case of a clear mistake. Discerning a clear mistake does not require full substitution of judgement. See Joseph Raz, *The Morality of Freedom* (Oxford, Oxford University Press, 1986) 62.

to interpretive or auxiliary judgements of other bodies.[4] For example, in the pursuit of Professor Dworkin's ideal of integrity,[5] a judge has reason to construct an interpretation of the law that fits the past interpretive practice of the political community under pertinent moral principles. The precise kind and degree of fit required depends on the precise reasons for paying attention to past interpretive practice. The judge may independently consider such reasons. Yet, his interpretive judgement about the law is not fully independent; it may very well differ from the interpretive judgement he would form if he were to make all pertinent substantive determinations on a fully independent basis.

The list is not exhaustive. One can think of various intermediate ways of assigning interpretive labour. A court may be supposed to act upon interpretive judgements formed on an independent basis, but also provide explicit explanation for potential divergence of judgement. Or, if the court faces a requisite degree of uncertainty, it may have to act on the basis of the interpretation adopted by the reviewed body.

In fact, as I will argue in chapter twelve, various intricate institutional schemes are built into constitutional doctrine and applicable standards of review. Interpretive reasoning is not exhausted in the formation of an abstract interpretative proposition. In judicial enforcement of the Constitution, for instance, constitutional argument continues until courts make a specific determination about the matter in dispute. To rationalise this activity, courts form applicable doctrine. They design doctrine on an independent basis. Yet, such doctrine incorporates in its content and operation complex schemes of institutional synergy, exhibiting varying degrees of judicial scrutiny and deference over the diverse elements of this complex argumentative process.

These observations illuminate the multiplicity of ways in which past or parallel interpretive practice affects the reasoning of law-applying institutions, courts of law in particular. This recognition is especially important in refuting the received wisdom that public officials are always supposed to rely on interpretive judgement they construct on an independent basis. It illuminates the importance of recognising an analytic distinction between institutional structure and interpretive substance and, from the point of view of the court exercising judicial review, a corresponding distinction between judicial reasoning (as structured by the resolution to the institutional question) and the wider realm of constitutional reasoning. In fact, it invites us to single out a certain category of institutional norms and reasons that structure the substantive judgements of various bodies (mainly of the reviewing court and the body under review) in the process of resolving the relevant dispute. The operation and justification of these norms is the subject matter of this Part Two.

[4] For an illuminating attempt to capture the distinction between this scheme and the scheme of conditional interpretive authority in administrative law, see Peter Strauss, '"Deference" is Too Confusing—Let's Call Them "*Chevron* Space" and "*Skidmore* Weight"' (2012) 112 *Colum L Rev* 1143.

[5] *Law's Empire* (Cambridge, Harvard University Press, 1986) ch 7.

II. The Rationality of Institutional Norms

This diversity of institutional schemes may appear puzzling. If courts of law are supposed to act in compliance with the law and the law appears to be subject to more than one interpretation, courts have reason to act on the basis of the more appropriate interpretation of the law available. This proposition is, at least in paradigmatic cases, valid. Courts of law do not exercise privilege, nor have an inherent claim to interpretive autonomy, but perform a functional task in trust for the political community. And commitment to the rule of law colours this task in a paradigmatic manner.

In Part One I defended a thesis about the normative structure of establishing appropriate interpretations of the law. If so, if courts are supposed to act on the basis of the more appropriate interpretations and if there is a substantive structure governing them, is the institutional analysis we are ready to embark upon normatively redundant and potentially confusing?

The answer to this puzzle requires defence of two arguments. First, it requires that we distinguish conceptually between the claim that courts of law are supposed to act on the more appropriate interpretation of the law, and the further claim that they are supposed to act on the basis of their own, fully independent interpretive judgement; secondly, we need to argue that there is reasonable likelihood that courts of law act on the basis of the more appropriate interpretation of the law if, at least in certain categories of cases, they do not act on their own, fully independent interpretation of the law; if, in other words, they consider themselves bound by pertinent judgements of others in a joint process of constitutional construction.

We shall proceed with caution. Let us first clarify our perspective for the purposes of this inquiry. In this regard, we may share the wisdom of an ancient court of law, no longer in existence. In a unanimous holding, the Appellate Committee of the House of Lords expressed strong disapproval towards courtesy and comity in judicial review. 'The giving of weight to factors such as these is not, in our opinion, aptly described as deference: it is performance of the ordinary judicial task of weighing up the competing considerations on each side and according appropriate weight to the judgement of a person with responsibility for a given subject matter and access to special sources of knowledge and advice. That is how any *rational* judicial decision maker is likely to proceed.'[6] There is much to be said against the weight metaphor. Yet, the dictum captures an important insight. Treating the opinion of the body exercising primary jurisdiction as of particular normative significance is accountable to the reasons governing the exercise of judicial duty; it can be justified only as an element of rational judicial decision

[6] *Huang (FC) (Respondent) v Secretary of State for the Home Department*, [2007] UKHL 11, para 16.

making. Thus, our current perspective is the perspective of the judge deliberating under public reason about the most rational way to proceed in performance of his adjudicatory duties.

Now, a quite salient feature in this perspective is the fact of interpretive pluralism and potential disagreement. We have argued that legal interpretation is a constructive enterprise. Individuals committed to construct in good faith the more appropriate interpretation of the law may—and often do—produce diverging interpretations. No doubt, each of them would hold her interpretation to be superior to the interpretation offered by others. Similarly, each of us, assessing competing interpretations, may hold one interpretation to be superior to others. This fact of disagreement does not imply interpretive relativism. In fact, each of us would often think that others also have reason to accept the interpretation that in our opinion is the better one, explain why this is so and even account for the fact that others are not persuaded. Our explanation would invoke standards of success that are supposed to guide the interpretive activity. But given the activity's creative character, such standards are not reduced to the discovery of an independently existing 'interpretation proper'.

Given the fact of interpretive pluralism and the commitment to standards for assessing competing interpretations, we may distinguish in principle the social fact that a public institution holds an interpretive judgement from the quality of the judgement. We have no reason to equate the more appropriate interpretation of the law with the independent interpretive judgements that public institutions make. In fact, once we understand this distinction, we may suspect that some public institutions are more likely to produce better interpretive judgements in some fields of the law.

Let me present an artificial example that would help us see why this suspicion is plausible. Predictive judgements about social and economic consequences are often material in constructing an interpretive judgement about, say, the rationality of a regulatory statute employing classifications that substantially burden certain business interests. Given the lack of judicial competency and resources and assuming the absence of weakness of motivation, the legislative process would be more likely to produce an appropriate specification of rationality requirements than a reviewing court judging independently—even if the latter is restricted to the single task of assessing a specification already made and has the benefit of access to the legislative record. Even after we remove our *ceteris paribus* clause, introduce some educated guesses about motivation, procedural environment, etc, and succeed in disentangling separate aspects of the interpretive judgement, we may still conclude that the court will more likely implement constitutional requirements better if it reviews only some aspects of the legislative classifications—say, the employment of stigma-conferring distinctions, the evident lack of any public-purpose linkage, etc.

Once we move from assessments of social and economic fact to judgements of political value, we may appreciate a further feature of interpretive pluralism: its potentially *reasonable* character. Interpretations of the law are often to be assessed on the basis of the justice of their content (chapter five, section III). Yet, the justice of the content and hence the very appropriateness of an interpretation depend, in part, on whether the content is responsive to the deliberations of the citizenry in ways that respect the fundamental principles of equal citizenship. I will discuss the implications of this idea in chapters nine and ten. What is important to note here is that the political branches of government partake in this deliberative process and their interpretive judgements are expected to respond—one way or another—to relevant standards of interpretive success. In the face of reasonable interpretive pluralism, and given a conception of public institutions as the collective organs of the political community and of its citizens, a reasonable argument can be made that courts of law may act on the basis of the more appropriate interpretation of the law if, in certain categories of cases, they do not fully substitute their independent interpretive judgement, but operate under more nuanced standards of review.

The examples are impermissibly sweeping and clearly incomplete. Yet, they show that there is a genuine normative issue: there may be circumstances when, under public reason and political justice, the pursuit of exercising the adjudicatory power on the basis of an appropriate interpretation of the law is best served by institutional norms that differ from the fully independent standard of review.

I have framed the discussion in positive terms because I am arguing against apparent orthodoxy. We may add that, after all, the independent standard is not a natural default position itself. In cases of uncertainty, there is no independent reason showing that a court is more likely to reach appropriate interpretations by acting on an independent standard. Thus, we may generalise our point: there is a genuine normative issue about what institutional norm determining the standard of review courts have most reason to apply.

Recognition of this normative issue goes hand in hand with recognition that authoritative interpretive construction is a public and joint task, entrusted to the scheme of public institutions. Taken together, these points show that we have strong reason to inquire about how best to arrange the performance of this task and how to assess existing arrangements.

III. The Paradigmatic Justification of Institutional Norms

A. The General Aim

We claimed that courts are supposed to exercise their adjudicatory function on the basis of the more appropriate interpretations of the law. This premise lies at the very heart of the rule of law commitment of our societies. We then argued that this ɹit is not disserved by the employment of institutional reasoning about the ɔpriate scheme of interpretive assignment between courts and the political :hes; quite the contrary, it may thereby be served. The centrality of the rule v commitment shows that this very service also provides the paradigmatic cation[7] for institutional norms of this kind. We have most reason, other ; being equal, to assess competing schemes of interpretive responsibilities the pursuit of *establishing and acting upon appropriate interpretations of the* f best serving the fundamental desiderata of constitutional interpretation public reason and political justice.

ɜreas institutional reasoning can in theory be directed to a specific case is it rational for this court to proceed in the absence of an applicable rule'), :ional 'rules' are applicable to numerous cases by many bodies; they are by humans and they often fall short of the ideal. Institutional rules are o error. And they are often formalised in judicial doctrine, which limits vay of revision or deviation in future cases. These features of institutional invite us to distinguish between the aims of institutional design and the cy of applicable institutional rules. Our account has to address both s.

Aims of Design

ɔne, I argued that constitutional interpretation is supposed to construct ound accounts of the Constitution, along with the surrounding practice itative constitutional exposition, so that public power would be exercised ance with political justice. If so, we have reason to *design* institutional ɔf interpretive labour with a view to making it more likely that such te interpretations would be constructed and be relied upon.[8]

er may recognise a general influence from Raz, above n 3, at 53 (defending a thesis about ıstification' of authorities on the basis of their service to specifying the reasons applicable :ts). Although there are important differences (for instance on legitimacy), I believe that :eption is particularly helpful in understanding institutional norms. These norms are ɜrve constitutional practice by mediating between the pursuit of appropriate substantive ınd the proper role of distinct institutional processes to that result.

n's argument that the justification of the *overall* institution of judicial review has to be ...ıted. Ronald Dworkin, *Justice for Hedgehogs* (2011) 398 ('making it more likely that the community will settle on and enforce some appropriate conception of negative liberty and of a fair distribution of resources and opportunities, as well as of ... positive liberty'). See also Ronald Dworkin, *Freedom's Law: The Moral Reading of the American Constitution* (Cambridge, Harvard University Press, 1996) 34 ('I see no alternative but to use a result driven rather than a procedure-driven standard ... The best institutional structure is the one best calculated to produce the best answers to the essentially moral question of what the democratic conditions actually are, and to secure stable compliance with those conditions'). While I consider this insight to be fundamental, there are important differences of emphasis. This book does not consider outcome-oriented considerations as conclusive (section V, below), it has a built-in component of democratic responsiveness (ch 10), it emphasises the role of constitutional doctrine in operationalising complex schemes of allocating interpretive responsibility, it claims that such schemes are subject to continuous interpretive tinkering, etc.

Given that institutional rules are applied in numerically large cases and that a binary distinction between sound interpretations and the rest is not exhaustive of our evaluative concerns, this criterion should be understood broadly to include the general pursuit of better interpretations and the *avoidance of worse ones*, taking into account considerations like the likelihood and gravity of potential error and the merit of potential success.[9]

For instance, we know that both the legislative and the judicial process are prone to error. Suppose we are considering stipulating a searching standard of review that is expected to strike down a certain set of legislative measures. Suppose further we consider that the judicial process under this standard is as likely as the legislative process to reach a constitutionally appropriate result in this specific set of cases and that we are therefore unable to claim that such judicial screening will minimise error. We may still have reason to select a searching standard of review if it is likely that we thereby avoid 'grave' mistakes in the field, constitutional errors of a profound nature. If that is not the case, or if the standard carries along with it an equivalent likelihood of frustrating compelling public policies, we may have reason to opt for a more relaxed standard of review. In the example over regulatory policy mentioned in the previous section, we may well conclude that the risk of judicial error under a searching standard—say, frustrating significant regulatory aims—is more troubling than an equivalent risk of legislative error—say, overburdening a regulated entity. And this same logic applies to more nuanced approaches, tailoring the standard of review to theme-specific factors.

Now, in making comparisons of this sort, we need to keep in mind that justification is ultimately addressed to each citizen, on reasons that appeal to her status as an equal joint holder of sovereignty. This implies that considerations of gravity and likelihood of error need to take into account the standpoint of each citizen that may be adversely affected from our calculus. And it provides us with further criteria for design, in the aim that the institutional scheme selected 'reconciles' us with the *errors* it may produce.[10] Thus, we have reason to care about fairness in the allocation of risks of error, as well as to ensure that the institutional scheme respects the rights of litigants to present arguments and to have a reasoned explanation for the determinations involved in the resolution of the case.[11]

For instance, in the example over regulatory policy, adoption of a relaxed standard of review would also need a further argument explaining that it would not be unfair to prioritise avoidance of judicial overreach in the light, say, of various options the regulated entity may have to obtain redress for its legitimate

[9] The main insight has been offered by Fallon in his precautionary defence of judicial review. Richard Fallon, 'The Core of an Uneasy Case for Judicial Review' (2008) 121 *Harvard L Rev* 1693.

[10] The general idea comes from Lawrence Solum, 'Procedural Justice' (2004) 78 *S Cal L Rev* 181–321.

[11] See Alon Harel and Tsvi Kahana, 'The Easy Core Case for Judicial Review' (2010) 2 *Journal of Legal Analysis* 227–56.

claims through the political process; and the court would have, at any rate, the burden to explain that a cognizable rationale exists for what may eventually turn out to be a legislative error.

Moreover, since dysfunctional outcome-oriented institutional schemes are particularly likely to cause public distrust and discontent, it is important that the scheme selected is responsive to and does not disrespect the self-esteem and the equal political liberty of all citizens as joint holders of public power. Yet, I do think that the primary way for reconciliation with the likelihood of error would be to argue that the institutional rule was designed under a transparent process pursuing the fundamental aim of establishing and implementing appropriate interpretations of the law under political justice and public reason.

To avoid unnecessary complexity, in the rest of the book I use the simple idea that institutional schemes shall be designed with the aim of making it more likely that we reach and enforce appropriate interpretations—making the necessary qualifications in discussing specific issues, like precautionary approaches, fairness in the allocation of decision errors, etc.

C. The Legitimacy of Institutional Norms

Let us now suppose that an institutional norm is already in place and is practised as a legal norm. As I will argue in Part Three, constitutional law does provide us with a complex scheme of standards of review in the form of judicial doctrine. One function of such standards is to specify the interpretive responsibilities of courts and of the other branches in the process of constitutional implementation. Their legal status is grounded in precedent and they are accountable to the constitutional scheme with a view to effectuate it.

Under the paradigmatic thesis defended in this section, the justification of the applicable institutional scheme would ideally presuppose that the court is more likely to act on the basis of appropriate interpretations of the law under such scheme rather than if it were to proceed with an independent interpretation itself (or to reconsider the institutional aspects from the beginning). Yet, this would be too demanding as a criterion for applying an institutional norm already in place. It is often the case that a court, after exhausting any power of revision or interpretive reconstruction (section D, below), has most reason (under public reason and political justice) to apply the norm even if the above ideal criterion is not met and even if a better norm is conceivable.

The reason can be derivative, as an instantiation, say, of a general duty to comply with non-unreasonable laws of a legitimate constitutional system. Perhaps, we may also identify legitimacy as an independent quality of single norms. In this sense, we may say that, given the importance of some collective arrangement over the division of interpretive labour, the fact that there is reasonable disagreement about which institutional scheme is the better, the transition costs of shifting to a better scheme, the risks of affecting the stability and workability of the overall institutional frame, etc, the court has a general reason to adhere by an institutional scheme even if it is not the one more likely to lead to the more appropriate interpretations possible.[12] Nonetheless, sufficient conduciveness to the general aim is presupposed. If a norm fails substantially in its paradigmatic service, it is unclear why we shall acknowledge its independent legitimacy. At the very least, we would normally need an argument showing the practical infeasibility of obtaining such conduciveness coupled with persuasive arguments for the importance of retaining a stable norm.

D. The Interpretation of Institutional Norms

Now, courts do not face the task of designing schemes of judicial review from scratch. Nor do they merely have to apply them, assuming or upholding their legitimacy. Ever since *Marbury v Madison*, they have been engaged in a continuous process of specifying their proper mandate, through constructive interpretation of past judicial practice and with the aim of effectuating the constitutional scheme as a whole.

In this interpretive process, we are governed by the general structure developed in Part One. Thus, we have reason, among reasonable interpretive constructions of the applicable scheme of review, to select the one that establishes the institutional structure more likely to produce and implement appropriate interpretations of the law.

Interpretive tinkering with the judicial interpretive mandate, of course, is subject to practice-dependent constraints of constitutional legitimacy. For instance, even if we consider the *Marbury* rationale deeply flawed, we are substantially disbarred from radically shifting towards an across-the-board, highly deferential standard of review. And uncertainty about the performance of radically novel standards of review would counsel for caution whenever established standards operate satisfactorily.

Yet, these constraints should not be overemphasised. Standards of review are made by courts themselves without express basis on the constitutional text. Moreover, constitutional legitimacy particularly invites sensitivity to ideal design here, as the merit of standards of review is heavily implicated in argumentative judicial practice. Applicable standards of review are committed, one way or another, to the aims of appropriate constitutional implementation. And courts tinker with standards of review all the time, in response to actualised deficiencies.

[12] See also Christine Korsgaard, *Self-Constitution: Agency, Identity, and Integrity* (Oxford, Oxford University Press, 2009) 149–50 ('it is irrational to follow a procedure merely because it usually gets a good outcome, when you know that this time it will get a bad one. So perhaps we should say instead that the normativity of the procedures comes from the usual quality of their outcomes combined with the fact that we must have such procedures and we must stand by their results').

Thus, the normative engagement in this chapter is suitable for exploring the potential that existing doctrine and practices have for further internal reconstruction and interpretive improvement.

IV. The Substantive Basis of Paradigmatic Institutional Justification

The account defended so far is based on the idea that in principle we have an independent (though obviously very abstract) criterion for the justification of institutional norms. It relates to the pursuit of appropriate interpretative outcomes and is specified in the light of normative accounts of constitutional interpretation, like the one defended in Part One. The reverse does not hold. The justice of an interpretive outcome does not derive from the application of any institutional norm whatsoever. Institutional performance does not determine fair or appropriate interpretive outcomes. A court that has employed even an ideal standard of review may fail miserably in the interpretive outcome reached.

Now this idea might give the impression that we take the purpose of political and judicial institutions to be one of merely 'implementing' a pre-ordained substantive conception. This does not follow. I do not assume in Part One that there is any single interpretation proper so that we should orchestrate processes of review with the aim that they reach it. The paradigmatic justification of institutional design is to be understood in the light of the constructive nature and deliberative character of constitutional interpretation. A general substantive conception like the one defended in Part One frames the pursuit of the activity; it does not determine its applications. Accordingly, an appropriate interpretation does not implement a pre-ordained order; it simply exhibits features that enable us, on due reflection, to assess its quality, justice, appropriateness or legitimacy.

Still, we will certainly be reminded that in a free political community citizens would express uncertainty or reasonable disagreement over substantive principles of constitutional justice and their specification. Both the commitment to democracy, as well as appreciation of uncertainty over both process and substance raise significant challenges to outcome-oriented institutional design. For instance, as I will argue in chapters nine and ten, the democratic commitment emphasises that the interpretive activity shall, among other desiderata, be fairly responsive to the moral visions and deliberations of the citizenry. Accordingly, institutional design shall aim at processes well-suited to engage in a dialogue with the citizenry. This dialogue should be open and conducted on reasons that in good faith reach all citizens as free and equal. For present purposes, I note that the main idea is that considerations of this sort are to be built within this (paradigmatic) structure of justification, linked with substance-sensitive features of appropriate interpretive outcomes.[13] This structure of justification responds to fundamental commitments pertaining to judicial reasoning under public reason and political justice. And these commitments include the critical independence of public reason and political justice from actual institutional applications and the centrality of the rule of law.

Let us conclude this section emphasising that the paradigmatic thesis has—at least in principle—liberating potential. It is an unfortunate part of the public culture that distinct institutions are perceived as 'deserving' the normative power to perform certain tasks as of privilege, tradition or nature. Although we are willing to criticise the way in which officials perform their tasks, we are somehow culturally debarred from suspecting that a deeper inquiry into issues of institutional structure is apropos. On the face of such alienation, we should insist that public institutions are to be conceived as the collective arms of free and equal citizens and we should scrutinise whether the processes they employ serve this role.

We do not know in advance what the findings of our inquiries will be. For example, by exposing the complex policy arguments that constitutional interpretation often involves, we may conclude that the judicial process suffers from insurmountable limitations and decide to encourage the engagement of political institutions over issues that crucially matter to us all. Or, we may conclude that courts are well suited to ensure compliance with certain issues of principle and urge them to show less deference to state legislatures over a pertinent field of judgements. We have no way of knowing in advance whether we will not make grave mistakes in appraising institutional schemes. But it is of paramount importance that we be able to ask appropriate questions and expand our capacity for critical reflection and normative appraisal over the very institutions that guide our lives.

V. Systemic Considerations

Institutionalised interpretation is merely one operation that public bodies perform in the process of exercising public power. This has important implications for our project. First, in determining which interpretation is appropriate, we appeal to its fit to other normative operations. We mentioned earlier that the distinction between lawmaking and law-applying institutions reflects a division of normative labour between lawmaking and interpretation, in our case between constitutional drafting and constitutional interpretation. Performance of interpretive labour shall contribute to the justice and effectiveness of the overall scheme. Therefore, in

[13] As Rawls warns us, 'it is common oversight … to think that procedural legitimacy (or justice) … can stand on its own without substantive justice: it cannot'. John Rawls, *Political Liberalism* (New York, Columbia University Press, 1993, 1996) 425.

determining *ex ante* the virtues that constitutional interpretation may bring in the overall scheme, we need to consider the virtues and weaknesses linked to the drafting process. In this sense, an appropriate interpretation is supposed to preserve the *virtues* reflected in the constitution-making structure while softening *side effects* resulting from the structure's inherent limitations. Accordingly, the proper role of the judiciary in the interpretive stage is supposed to fit in an appropriate overall division of normative labour so that the end results are just and effective overall.

These observations specify the application of paradigmatic justification. For instance, assuming that constitutional interpretation properly implicates some interpretive update of the constitutional scheme—given the nature of the amendment process—we have reason to consider what assignment of this task to the judicial branch would better serve this function. However, these observations also suggest the limitations of the thesis. Since institutionalised interpretation is merely one operation that public institutions perform in the exercise of public power, we should also attend the implications that a structure of assigning interpretive labour has for *other* operations. An institutional structure that is likely to produce appropriate interpretations of the law may impede other processes that affect the way public power is exercised. But our overarching aspiration is the just and effective exercise of public power overall.

An obvious example is the cost and delay associated with a heightened standard of review over issues of social and economic fact; perhaps, more generally, the overall cost, friction and delay associated with litigation as an additional social process implicated in the settlement of issues of constitutional law subjected to reasonable diversity of opinion; of issues that would not routinely be litigated *but for* the heightened standard of review under consideration.

An even more fundamental issue relates to the constitutional *integrity of the office* of the implicated institutions. An across-the-board scheme of broad deference would not only make judicial review meaningless; it may also implicate the federal judiciary in performances of apparent dignity but actual deceptiveness.[14] Similarly, it may also fail to respect the rights of litigants to present arguments, to have them considered and to receive a reasoned explanation for the determinations of law involved in the resolution of the case.[15] It should be noted though

[14] Phillip Hamburger has powerfully argued that the office of the judge is an 'office of independent judgment'. *Is Administrative Law Unlawful?* (Chicago, University of Chicago Press, 2014) 148 ff. On this ground, he questions the legitimacy of deference altogether (at 316–17). Nonetheless, judicial integrity is not technically violated so long as the judge exercises independent judgement in crafting, recognising and interpreting legal norms allocating and regulating interpretive authority. In the case of constitutional interpretation, such norms have to be of a constitutional nature, anchored in text or precedent and developed for the purpose of effectuating the constitutional scheme. As to the underlying idea, the functional arguments discussed in the previous sections make it rather difficult to defend an absolutist claim equating independent assessment of constitutional substance with integrity of judicial duty. Having said all that, Hamburger's argument is a systemic argument, properly implicated in the justification of institutional norms.

[15] Harel and Kahana, above n 11.

that considerations of this sort cannot operate independently from the comparative and functional conduciveness of judicial review to appropriate outcomes. For example, litigants do not merely ask the judge to explain to them whatever reasons support the issue in dispute; they rather ask him to review and assess such reasons already examined (in fact or presumption) by another body. And such a process of review would not respond to the respective due process claims of all implicated parties unless presumed standing in a certain degree of conduciveness to appropriate outcomes. And this is turn shows why the paradigmatic justification thesis is not an opportunistic thesis, aiming to reach good results by any means, but brings forward the functional aspects of public institutions, as trustees of the people, with a mandate to uphold the Constitution and institutional capacity to exercise public reason.

Another example relates to the virtue of encouraging public deliberation over value issues of common concern. It is often argued that non-representative structures have debilitating effects on popular political engagement over issues of constitutional significance. And bold, non-dialogic judicial pronouncements may be more likely to provoke resistance and erode public trust and fidelity to the constitutional scheme. Similarly, we should consider whether a scheme of assigning interpretive labour radically alters or, more importantly, impedes other constitutional functions that the implicated institutions perform. For instance, a scheme assigning to the Supreme Court the primary role in the exposition of constitutional principles has to fit the function of courts in resolving concrete controversies.[16]

More generally, in assessing an institutional assignment of interpretive labour, we have reason to consider its fit to other features of the institutional environment, ranging from constitutional amendment rules to permissible judicial remedies. Some of these features may lie within the decision-making power of the very institution designing the applicable standard of review, so that the object of assessment may cover a wider scheme of interlocking features; for instance, the Supreme Court may adjust the remedial power of federal courts (say, over the non-retroactivity of remedies) with a view to ameliorating side-effects from schemes of judicial scrutiny. But in most cases, at least in the short run, these systemic features have to be taken as given.

At any rate, institutional judgement has to accommodate and even trade-off different virtues that pertain to different public tasks. Accordingly, we may be forced to prefer an overall institutional structure that is likely sometimes to reach second best interpretations of the law. However, such an eventuality is justified only to the extent required by public reason and principles of political justice. Such a scheme is preferable only to the extent it facilitates the exercise of public power *on the basis of appropriate reasons* overall.

[16] See Girardeau Spann, 'Expository Justice' (1983) 131 *U PA L Rev* 585.

VI. Uncertainty and the Limits of Instrumental Design

Instrumental justification of institutional norms suffers from an important limitation: uncertainty. We often do face deep uncertainties over the institutional capacities and likely outcomes of candidate institutional schemes. Relevant functional arguments often run out without a definite winner. The institutional world is non-ergodic and past performance of institutions sometimes provides very poor prognosis over their future one,[17] at least in the long run. Moreover, it is often the case that, no matter what we think at the time of original design, institutional schemes acquire a life of their own and radically fail to redeem the functional expectations of their designers.[18] In setting up a scheme of strict scrutiny for racial classifications on the face of racial prejudice, for instance, we cannot predict with reasonable confidence how such a scheme will approach affirmative action in public education a generation after.

One way to deal with this difficulty would be to bracket highly uncertain outcome-based assumptions and pay increasing attention to process-based arguments and systemic costs. Adrian Vermeule, for instance, has advanced a provocative argument to the effect that, while there is severe uncertainty over institutional capacities, there is certainty over the costs of various interpretive techniques and review processes, including decisional costs and indirect costs like loss of legal certainty.[19]

The argument is fair, but its force limited. It may provide, for instance, a reason for courts to be deferential in areas of radical uncertainty about the net benefits of judicial scrutiny so long as grave constitutional error is not an issue. But excessive bracketing leads to institutional blindness, to inability to redeem whatever potentiality functional institutional schemes may have or acquire. And utterly parsimonious methods of reasoning may fail to respond even to the very reasons behind the normativity of institutional rules themselves. If we have reasonable certainty only over considerations of minimal, peripheral importance, then anything goes. Is this our predicament?

I doubt it. First of all, institutional uncertainty is not uniform. For instance, if we believe that courts are more likely to detect a certain category of errors while

[17] The emphasis on uncertainty and perception of uncertainty in macroeconomic life was an important insight of Keynesianism. See Paul Davidson, 'Is Probability Theory Relevant for Uncertainty? A Post Keynesian Perspective' (1991) 5 *The Journal of Economic Perspectives* 129–43.

[18] Paul Pierson, *Politics in Time: History, Institutions, and Social Analysis* (Princeton, Princeton University Press, 2004) 103 ff. Pierson emphasises the limits of functional analysis in the course of institutional development as well. We will discuss them at ch 7, section III.

[19] Adrian Vermeule, *Judging under Uncertainty: an Institutional Theory of Legal Interpretation* (Cambridge, Harvard University Press, 2006). Vermeule's description and pro-deference institutional prescription have been criticised for overestimating both the importance of such systemic considerations and the degree of uncertainty. See Jonathan R Siegel, 'Judicial Interpretation in the Cost-Benefit Crucible' (2007) 92 *Minn L Rev* 387, 416.

we remain ignorant over the rest, we may have strong reason to devise a standard of review tailored to capture the former while being deferential over the rest and see how it goes. Even if that is not feasible, we may be able to single out the gravity of certain errors (say, violation of fundamental rights) and devise schemes tailored to minimise them without incurring *undue* systemic cost. Precautionary approaches of this latter form are in fact prevalent in institutional life. For instance, Richard Fallon's appealing defence of judicial review rests on the assumption that 'rights under-enforcement' is worse than 'rights over-enforcement'.[20] And I will argue in Part Three that this idea provides an element in explaining schemes of judicial scrutiny.

Secondly, institutional reasoning does not aim at perfection. In fact, it is hard to specify such perfection since the criteria for assessment are often fuzzy in their application. Institutional alternatives usually come in small sets and all we need is some warranted confidence in selecting one among them. Confidence does not need certainty; when justified, it is based on systematised institutional experience. And its sufficiency is assessed in the light of the practical purposes at issue and some understanding and management of the pertinent risks of error. Thirdly, even if we have no definite reason to select any of the alternatives, we may have reason to exclude some of them or, anyway, to engage in institutional experimentation and learn from it. All instances of constitutional design were experiments of sort.

Most importantly, we do not have to inaugurate an experiment from scratch and run the risk of irreversibility. Judicial practice operates under a dense network of judicial doctrine incorporating various institutional standards of review. It may very well be the case that such schemes do not redeem the institutional expectations of their designers. Yet, they do redeem their contemporaneous value and exhibit their actual limitations; in their current operation and in the light of their past trajectories. History and context largely limit institutional uncertainty. In fact, much of the uncertainty over the operation of institutional rules relates to path dependence and to the potentiality of multiple possible institutional equilibria that cannot be predicted before the institutional trajectory has taken shape. But once on the path, its shape reduces feasible institutional options (chapter seven, section III) and makes their assessment more informed.

The actual challenges before us do not implicate de novo institutional design, but institutional revision and specification. Incremental revisions, while capable of being informed from actual experience, do not carry with them significant systemic risks and risks of irreversibility. At the same time, considerations of legitimacy also restrict choice under institutional uncertainty and set burdens of persuasion in revising well-practised institutional schemes. At any rate, incremental processes sometimes prepare the background for considering more

[20] See Fallon, above n 9, at 1709.

fundamental ones, testing possible avenues and providing some of the demanding resources that the latter often require.[21]

We need to make peace with uncertainty; and to attend to an important principle of rational institutional design: the facilitation of institutional flexibility and adaptability in an uncertain world.[22] In instances of uncertainty, we have reason to avoid irreversible commitments and to devise schemes of internal criticism, learning and revision; schemes that remain resilient in the face of unexpected outcomes (shock-resilience) or perhaps even to encourage such outcomes in order to learn from them, as some imaginative thinkers suggest.[23]

In this regard, institutional openness and transparency, and various principles like the requirement that systems of review be based on dialogic, argumentative interaction, provide some minimal safeguards for efficient adaptability. Similarly, the legal formalisation of an institutional norm in the process of its enforcement, and subject to interpretive specification or even revision under the rules of precedent, is a significant way to provide for institutional flexibility. And it may be combined with various other techniques: deferral of design to a more appropriate time (coupled with the adoption, in the meanwhile of some tentative solution); adoption of a more open-textured scheme delegating its specification to the courts that would implement it, etc. The choice depends on many factors, including an assessment of the current situation, the expectations about the kind of information that will be available in some future time and the institution and people that would make the decisions both in the initial settings and in the future, etc. For example, deferral for future stipulation normally presupposes that we expect that institutional life is subject to patterns that may become more transparent to us in the meanwhile. And, the optimal degree of flexibility also depends upon the biases and shortcomings operating at the various stages of its exercise, and the implicated costs and uncertainty.

Uncertainty may well be endemic in institutional design. Yet, a combination of reasonably precautionary and flexible, adaptive schemes may quite well enable us to deal with such uncertainty, without treating it as a self-fulfilling impasse.

[21] See the seminal article of Amitai Etzioni, 'Mixed-Scanning: A "Third" Approach to Decision-Making' (1967) 12 *Public Administration Review* 385–92 (arguing for a third way between rationalist models of design and incrementalist strategies).

[22] On the rationality of incorporating the 'preference for flexibility' in individual choice under uncertainty as to future preferences, see the pathbreaking article of David Kreps, 'A Representation Theorem for "Preference for Flexibility"' (1979) 47 *Econometrica* 565–77. On the importance of institutional flexibility to 'adaptive efficiency' see Douglas North, *Institutions, Institutional Change and Economic Performance* (Cambridge, Cambridge University Press, 1990).

[23] Nassim Taleb, *Antifragile: Things that Gain from Disorder* (New York, Random House, 2012).

7

The Operation and the Dynamics of Institutional Norms

I. Operational Priority

A. Order of Reasons

I have argued that the justification of institutional norms depends on the substantive desiderata of constitutional interpretation. The critical inquiry now is on the way such norms operate so as to serve the reasons for having them and treating them as legitimate.

An institutional norm, once framed and its legitimacy accepted (or, anyhow, assumed), operates by supplying *higher-order* propositions with regard to substantive interpretive judgements. Such propositions specify the role of substantive determinations of different bodies in the formation of interpretive conclusions on which public officials, here courts of law in the exercise of judicial review, are supposed to rely. Before determining the governing interpretative conclusion, courts are supposed to consider the applicable institutional norm and to apply it by attaching the prescribed significance to judgements of other officials and by making requisite substantive judgements themselves.

Take for instance the case of intermediate standards of review. The determination of a political branch is provisionally authoritative over courts. The latter, under the pertinent institutional norm, have the power to review interpretations of the former on a limited set of grounds: for instance, by employing an intermediate standard of interpretive reasonableness over certain judgemental factors that pertain to the overall interpretation under review. In exercising their power of review and making the substantive value judgements needed for this assessment, courts do not balance substantive and institutional considerations; they follow their institutional mandate. Their institutional mandate is neither to fully substitute their own judgements, nor to perform a review of manifest unreasonableness, but to make certain, more nuanced judgements about the quality of the determinations under review.

B. The Salience of Outcome over Process

On this account, institutional considerations serve us in reaching appropriate substantive determinations by inviting us to join forces in this pursuit. Yet this runs contrary to the common wisdom that institutional considerations often compete with substantive ones and that we are invited to accept some trade-off between the two. The more unjust or seriously flawed a judgement appears to be, the less we should pay attention to the institutional reasons supporting deference to it. I think that this apparently commonsensical view is misleading.

The source of the difficulty here lies in the fact that when a case is presented for review the primary process has already worked out its own contribution towards reaching an appropriate resolution, and the outcome is before us. This gives the impression that institutional reasoning is applicable only before performance of an operation, as the quality of the outcome is transparent once the operation is completed. 'Referring to an operation as successful after the patient has died remains unsatisfactory for most laypersons'.[1] The less satisfactory the quality appears, the more tempted we are to balance our substantive assessment of the outcome with institutional reasons to pay attention to the judgement of others.

There are two fundamental misconceptions at play here, arising from failure to appreciate that the institutional norm is supposed to settle the respective role of both the primary decision maker and the reviewing court in an overall decision-making system with complementary parts. First, institutional reasoning has to factor in the fact that the reviewing court already has before it the reasoning process that led to the result under review. In fact, much of the rationale for standards of review focusing on the reasoning process of the primary decision maker depends on the idea that the judge does not have to devise and work out the implications of the applicable reasons de novo, but merely to review those reasons before him, their pertinence and their rational relation to the result.

Secondly, the trade-off idea fails to see that partial or complete substitution of judgement by the judge, even with regard to the specific case at hand, presupposes an *institutional* reason justifying such substitution, that is, a reason of a higher order with regard to the substantive judgements of the primary decision maker and the reviewing judge. Independent review is not a default position.

Consider the following two possibilities, where the judge considers that she has reason to ignore an institutional norm providing for deference over a critical issue: First, the institutional norm is justified under the paradigmatic justification thesis. Yet, the judge considers that she has access to the right substantive determination. She knows that institutional judgements are probabilistic judgements that abstract

[1] Gideon Keren and Wändi de Bruin, 'On the assessment of decision quality: Considerations regarding utility, conflict and accountability', in David Hardman & Laura Macchi (eds), *Thinking: Psychological Perspectives on Reasoning, Judgment and Decision Making* (Chichester, Wiley, 2003) 347–63, 349 (emphasising the salience of the outcome).

from the particularities of individual cases (because of the inaccessibility of such particularities or the impracticability of their institutionalisation). However, she claims that the otherwise applicable institutional determination does not apply to her in the particular case at issue. The case is exceptional in light of features that do not relate to ordinary institutional considerations. This scenario is fully compatible with the paradigmatic justification of the institutional norm. Second possibility: the institutional norm is problematic in itself, and this is revealed by its failure to deal adequately with this case. It does not reflect the institutional fact that courts are well equipped and justified in detecting a category of mistakes (say, plain injustice) with no further institutional repercussions. Thus, it cannot justifiably preempt consideration of such reasons by the judge.

In both cases, judicial objection has to be defended on an institutional explanation that accommodates the fact that judicial review is a complementary element in the overall decision-making process. For instance, in the second case, the *fact* that a judge independently considers a rule under review to exhibit, say, plain injustice cannot justify treating his opinion on the matter as dispositive for the exercise of public power; a legitimate institutional reason investing the judge's independent judgement with controlling force is also needed. In both scenarios, the judge may proceed with a corrective interpretation of the institutional norm (or with distinguishing or revising it) or, putting legitimacy constraints aside, simply refuse to follow it under institutional reasons justifying independent review. Either way, the reasons supposedly supporting her conduct do not contradict the idea that institutional norms supply higher-order propositions. They do so whenever applicable. The judge does not trade-off substantive considerations with institutional ones whenever the latter do not apply or need revision.

It should be emphasised that the judge is taking a chance whenever holding that the case is exceptional or that, in the light of the outcome, the institutional norm is not justified. Consider the previous examples. Let us suppose that the political branch is recognised as competent to make pertinent judgements of social fact. To make this vivid, suppose its frequency of successful assessments is 7/10 and that the most practical institutional norm precludes the judge from reviewing the pertinent judgement (sometimes called an issue of compounded law and fact) at all (in all 10 out of 10). The judge thinks that she has individuated one of the cases falling in the 3/10 category. And it may be reasonable for her to think so in light of the information available to her. But, of course, she may be wrong. All we can say is that we have before us a potential asymmetry that is so common in institutional life: the asymmetry between what one has most reason to do and what he may reasonably think he has most reason to do from her standpoint and in light of available information.

In fact, this asymmetry is rather typical in situations of individualised assessment throughout professional life. And the asymmetry between what one has most reason to do and what a knowledgeable person considers in good faith he has most reason to do is even more pronounced once we include the various non-deliberate biases and shortcomings affecting such assessments. Decision makers are particularly prone to overestimate their ability for individualised ('clinical') judgements as well as the significance of unique situation features. It is no surprise then that various studies reiterate that decision-making processes based on statistical generalisations from empirically established relations ('actuarial' judgements) outperform those based on clinical, situation-specific assessments.[2]

In our setting, such judgemental biases may be coupled with ideological or motivational ones, whether non-deliberate or opportunistic, especially whenever the issue in consideration is one of critical or contested moral or political value. Thus, the judge may be tempted to overestimate the legitimacy of intrusive review in such cases, subjecting the pertinent judgements to almost independent re-assessment; or simply to ignore the necessity of grounding such intrusive review on an institutional account about the appropriate division of labour between the political branch and the reviewing court.

Legal systems are thus faced with a dilemma: on the one hand, any institutional division of labour would be blind if it would not take into account the operation of such processes of individualised re-assessment. At the same time, we may not tame biases and reduce asymmetries of the sorts discussed here, without providing processes for transparent and reasoned institutional judgement. In the case of judicial review, the main mechanism in this pursuit is the formalisation of the standard of review in judicial doctrine. In this way, the design or revision of an institutional norm becomes a focused issue in the adjudicatory process. And once designed, these norms provide reasons of legitimacy for following them and public standards for detecting and assessing deviation; while at the same time allowing for interpretive tinkering, specification or even revision. We will discuss these features in the rest of this chapter. But first, we need we examine certain worries about the capacity of institutional norms to perform their distinctive function.

II. Circularity and Plasticity

A. Institutional Norms and Normative Distance

I have argued that the paradigmatic justification of institutional norms is dependent upon the substantive desiderata of constitutional interpretation, and that such norms have operational priority over the substantive judgements at issue in concrete cases. Is this scheme of consecutive dependence coherent? Do institutional norms and substantive determinations about the law serve distinctive functions, or do they collapse in an *omnium gatherum*.

[2] Robyn Dawes, David Faust & Paul Meehl, 'Clinical Versus Actuarial Judgment' (1989) 243 *Science* 1668–74.

To explain away this apparent difficulty, we need to attend to the constructive character of constitutional interpretation. The relation between a general theory of interpretive substance and a concrete constitutional judgement is not analytic, but involves the creative engagement with a variety of considerations. Normative distance of a similar kind applies also to the relation between various intermediate theories about constitutional themes and concrete interpretative conclusions.

In the paradigmatic case, and to the extent that an institutional norm does serve its paradigmatic function, that norm mediates between the general conceptions regarding the interpretive issues to be resolved (at any level of generality selected) and the institutional scheme determining specific interpretive outcomes. Thus, although institutional determinations are accountable to considerations of substance, they exercise a distinctive service in covering the relevant normative distance. And to the extent that the institutional norm is justified on considerations beyond its paradigmatic function this problématique does not arise. Hence, the coherence of the scheme is not at risk.

Concededly, this complex way in which institutional and substantive considerations interrelate contributes to many complications that affect institutional reasoning. Successful mediation requires knowledge of institutional facts (an institution's structure, stuffing and procedures, environment, etc) and substantive assessment of likely outcomes.

A more focused problem arises to the extent that institutional assessment requires generalisations from likely outcomes, normally drawn from past performance. Here, the coherence of the scheme depends on our ability to distinguish between a general substantive assessment of general performance and specific substantive conclusions. Again, there is normative distance, though of course, the distinctiveness of institutional reasoning largely depends on the ability and willingness of the institutional designer to keep these issues separate.

B. Institutional Plasticity

The worry about circularity sheds light on an important feature of institutional norms: their plasticity. This feature is largely due to the substantive basis of their justification. The adjudicatory community experiences reasonable disagreement over substantive assessment of appropriate performance and the linkage between institutional forms and performance is not tight. Thus, standards of review are subjected to re-assessment all the time. The main way the interpretive community has managed to uphold a core of stability in these norms is by attaching to them flexibility in content and specification. Furthermore, we have seen that flexibility and adaptability are ways of coping with an uncertain world (chapter six, section VI). And although much may be said about the virtues and vices of plasticity, substantive disagreement, institutional evolution and change, and the salience of outcome over process explain the fact that institutions applying institutional rules often interpret them in ways that further enhance their flexibility.

In the rest of this chapter, we will address some central elements in this dynamic process. We will see that critical issues relate to the institution charged with investing such norms with the force of law and the implications of the process of design over their future trajectories (section III); the issues that the institutional scheme should leave open for further specification in the future and the operation of such specification (section IV); and the ways disapproval of institutional performance or change in substantive visions of constitutional law lead courts to conclude that a legally binding institutional norm either needs revision or is inapplicable to the case at hand (section V). Finally, in chapters nine and ten, we will examine the normative implications introduced by the fundamental commitment to democratic decision making.

These complications explain why institutional norms, judicially crafted standards of review in particular, are not as robust in their operation as other, well structured, formal institutions, which paradigmatically enable actors to treat them as settled and theoreticians to recognise them as exogenous sources of, or strong constraints upon substantive outcomes. In a sense, they straddle the divide between formal institutions and more fluid institutional patterns in temporary equilibrium.[3] And this feature has led scholars to question whether standards of review fulfil their preemptive function in practice and to parallelise them with fluid institutional understandings.[4] Yet, the practical limits in their exogeneity do not imply conceptual circularity, as discussed in this section.

III. Formalisation of Institutional Norms in Judicial Doctrine

A. The Doctrinal Nature of Institutional Norms

Institutional norms are often formalised as legal norms. In this way, institutional norms, despite their inherent plasticity, may acquire relative stability and uniformity in their operation and opportunistic or myopic institutional determinations may be kept within limits. In constitutional adjudication, this normally takes the form of judicially crafted doctrine, invested with the force of precedent.

The power to formulate such rules enables the Supreme Court to somehow discipline itself and limit the discretion of lower courts over the applicable standard of review. It is also a way to deal with institutional uncertainty, facilitating incremental adaptability and reversibility, informed by the actual practice of the rule itself. At the same time, it has the obvious disadvantage that the Court setting or

3 On the distinction see Kenneth Shepsle, 'Rational Choice Institutionalism' in Sarah Binder, RAW Rhodes and Bert Rockman (eds), *Oxford Handbook of Political Institutions* (Oxford, Oxford University Press, 2006) 23, 27–32.

4 See, eg, Jeffrey Dobbins, 'Changing Standards of Review' (2016) 48 *Loyola U Chicago LJ* 205.

revising the standard suffers from its own institutional biases (sometimes of ideological origin) over the interpretive capacities and trustworthiness of political and judicial institutions; and, as we shall see in this section, its reasoning is affected by the decision-making process employed—as is the case, of course, with any institution having the power or opportunity for institutional design.[5]

Once formed, judicial doctrine acquires a life of its own, setting in motion path dependent processes and troubling future courts. Regardless of intent, judicially crafted standards of review are always up to interpretation themselves, even revision. In the process of applying a standard of review, courts acquire more information, perceive salient features and even reconsider their assessments over substantive desiderata and institutional details. This creates a strong tendency towards critical reappraisal of the standard. The jurisprudence on affirmative action in education is illustrative of this process. From the moment the Court decided to calibrate its strict scrutiny standard to the educational setting (*Grutter v Bollinger*, 2003) to the more recent *Fisher II* decision, the Court engaged in a continuous tinkering of the applicable standard in the light of more specific institutional considerations and qualified substantive predispositions (chapter twelve, section III(C)).

We will discuss doctrinal specification and revision in some detail in the following sections IV–V. Here, I emphasise that this process experiences all the benefits and drawbacks of path dependent common law making: flexible adaptability, limitations over the scope of functional design, sub-optimal standards, and a standing risk that courts of law make institutional determinations or refinements on regrettable moments or on considerations they are not best equipped to handle. In the rest of this section, we will attend two noteworthy features of common-law institutional design, specification and revision: path dependence and the proximity between design and application.

B. Path Dependence

The trajectories of judicial doctrine are paradigmatically characterised by path dependence: further specification and potential revision is heavily constrained by the paths already followed, and, in fact, events occurred early in path formation have a disproportionate effect on current potentialities.[6] For instance, the *Marbury* super-precedent is a clear instance of an early institutional commitment shaping the subsequent path of judicial review.

[5] See also Donald Horowitz, 'Constitutional Design: Proposals Versus Processes' in Andrew Reynolds (ed), *The Architecture of Democracy: Constitutional Design, Conflict Management, and Democracy* (Oxford, Oxford University Press, 2002) 15–36 and 'Constitution-Making: A Process Filled With Constraint' (2006) 12 *Review of Constitutional Studies* 1–17 (discussing systematic biases that lead constitutional reformers toward some comparative models and away from others and toward some interpretations of their historical experience and away from others).

[6] See the excellent analysis of Paul Pierson, *Politics in Time: History, Institutions, and Social Analysis* (Princeton, Princeton University Press, 2004) (in passim).

Indeed, a variety of factors heavily restrict our ability to deviate from early choice. They may well include considerations of legitimacy, incorporation of judicial doctrine in complex, mutually reinforcing doctrinal webs, institutional interdependence, policy complexity, expectations for continuity, high switching costs and related difficulties of coordination, learning effects, fear of the unknown, short memories and time horizons, and the like.

Such dependence sometimes leads to institutional schemes acquiring the status of what is called a deep equilibrium. This is precisely what has occurred with the process of judicial review itself. As Paul Pierson notes, once courts became sites of constitutional resolution, various actors adapted and obtained stake in preserving and expanding judicial review, including intellectual forces contributing to this process being surrounded with an aura of institutional naturalness.[7]

At the same time, path dependence is compatible with and in fact channels path-constrained processes of remedial, *incremental* amelioration, not least because the judicial process provides for internal criticism and because the judiciary is not a unitary actor (as new members enter all the time, bringing with them the culture prevailing at the time of their appointment). In fact, it is such incremental change of non-durable elements that enable the wider institutional scheme to persist.[8] Punctuated change is not foreclosed, yet it is normally the result either of long preparation or of persistent failures to accommodate new pressures, especially due to fundamental gridlock over constitutional substance.

It should be noted, in this regard, that common law interstitial specification largely draws its focal points for dealing with uncertainty from its own traditions, through analogies and doctrinal reasoning. This narrows down the comprehensiveness of the pertinent thought process and restricts the conceivability of radical change. Institutional path-dependence even cultivates a sense of naturalness that institutional structures often exhibit in collective imagination. This sense of institutional naturalness is reinforced by a perception of uncertainty over changes in the institutional world; leading to institutional schemes exhibiting formal stability, coupled with occasional opportunistic tinkering and incapacity for radical reconstruction.

C. Proximity between Doctrinal Specification and Application

Common law institutional design is performed in adjudicatory settings and with a view to the doctrine's applicability to the case at hand or to forthcoming dockets. Moreover, this process of design is 'self-referencing'[9] in the sense that those who

[7] Pierson, ibid, at 159.

[8] Paul David, 'Path Dependence: A Foundational Concept for Historical Social Science' (2007) 1 *Cliometrica* 91, 106 ff.

[9] On this concept see Gary Miller, 'Rational Choice and Dysfunctional Institutions' (2000) 13 *Governance: An International Journal of Policy and Administration* 535, 539.

control it are directly affected by the choices they make—the judges themselves. These features affect the operational reasoning in various positive and negative ways. Let us briefly mention a few problematic ones.

Decision makers, being able to measure the short-term substantive effects of their institutional choices, may focus upon them to the detriment of long-term non-opportunistic institutional reasoning. Even if they do not act strategically, they may still miss the long term perspective, exhibiting asymmetric responses after positive or negative single outcomes, after periods of stability or extraordinary events, etc. Most importantly, they often have the tendency to identify with the organisational means of judicial review, as opposed to more fundamental goals, taking the former for granted, as definite goals themselves.[10]

An institutional feature that may somehow ameliorate these deficiencies is the role of the Supreme Court. Precedent-setting by the Court is perceived as an event beyond ordinary adjudication and subject to a relatively more rational process of decision making. Ideally, it is informed by past experimentation, especially before the lower courts, over a number of different cases. And it is supposed to benefit from the contributions of various amici and from criticism in scholarship and public debate.

IV. The Endless Specification of Institutional Norms

Institutional norms are subject to continuous specification, performed in the process of their application. Such specification may exhibit all the limitations discussed in the previous section. Still, ideally, it is performed with a view to better effectuate their paradigmatic function.

Let us suppose that a court reviews a constitutional determination under an intermediate standard of reasonableness. The test has preemptive force in the sense that if the court concludes that the reviewed determination is reasonable, it is not supposed to inquire whether it is the best one on the balance of appropriate reasons. We say that a judgement is reasonable if it responds to reasons that apply in light of some presupposed general concerns—even if it is not the one that best complies with all applicable reasons. Of course, the aim is that public institutions (as a whole) act on the basis of the more appropriate reasons. But, assuming that the paradigmatic justification thesis is satisfied, we think that we better approach this aim in the long run if we do not allow courts to strike down a policy merely because it is based on a determination that is not what the court thinks to be the most rational one. Suppose, for example: (a) that the primary decision maker has the capacity for a higher frequency of appropriate determinations than courts,

[10] See Bryan Jones, 'Bounded Rationality' (1999) 2 *Annual Review of Political Science* 297, 307.

and (b) that we may not specify in advance the cases falling within that superior capacity. Yet, we may specify categories of mistakes that courts are equally or more competent in avoiding. And we fear that lack of meaningful judicial review will distort political or bureaucratic motivation. Then, we may have reason to set up a structure that aims at combining the advantages of both decision-making processes. We invite courts to review pertinent determinations on restricted grounds. The institutional employment of the distinction between a reasonable interpretation and the more appropriate one is supposed to capture this point.

Having conceded the preemptive force of the reasonableness test, I believe that employment of the test often entails further institutional reasoning. The test is not self-explanatory; it does not specify the exact intensity of review, the degree and kind of discrepancy falling outside the margin of reasonableness. Reasonableness is a substantive concept invested here with an institutional function. Its specification is supposed to serve this function, that is, to activate the kind and degree of judicial screening that makes it more likely that we end up with appropriate constitutional determinations. This would normally involve an understanding of the kinds of mistakes that it is more suitable for the court to address in light of this rationale. And this in turn may entail a more nuanced account of the pertinent reasons, as certain kinds of concerns (say, those arising out of stigma-conferring classifications in equal protection analysis) may necessitate judicial attendance. It may also implicate supplementary, or more focused institutional judgements about the comparative competency, legitimacy, etc. of courts and primary decision makers in engaging with these concerns.

Accordingly, institutional specification invites argument and disagreement, which may sometimes even ascend to fundamentals of institutional structure and constitutional principle. To paraphrase Ronald Dworkin, institutional accounts often struggle side by side with litigants before the bar.

This does not mean that such specification has to take place, and much less that it does take place, every time we apply the norm. Considerations of clarity, coordination, inter-temporal division of labour, economising on decision costs, avoidance of various biases, etc, indicate the advantages of somehow fixing the assumptions and prioritising rule-like approaches to applying institutional norms.[11] But these assumptions are in principle always open to contestation and elucidation and rule-like approaches are always open to criticism for over- or under-inclusiveness.

The pressure to go 'local' in institutional assumptions reflects a general tension between reasons for uniformity and formality, on the one hand, and the pursuit of institutional accuracy, on the other. For instance, generalised assumptions about the administration do not account for the degree of trustworthiness and hence

[11] For instance, Professor Sunstein has famously argued for applying deference to agency interpretations of statutory law in a rule-like fashion, claiming that interpretive casuistry carries with it important decision costs and uncertainty, without any significant increase in quality. Cass Sunstein, '*Chevron* Step Zero' (2006) 92 *Virginia L Rev* 187.

deference that each agency deserves. Each agency has its own record of success or failure, independence or capture, public acceptability or public dissatisfaction. Furthermore, the record changes over time. What appeared to be a trustworthy agency in the 1970s may now seem to suffer from impermissible goal displacement. It is therefore an open question whether courts may consider the agency's record, including its past interpretive practice,[12] or whether such engagement would overburden judicial reason and exacerbate uncertainty and opportunism. And, as we shall see in chapters nine and ten, this issue raises difficult issues of democratic theory as well, given that such determinations have to be informed by judgements of principle and policy.

What should be stressed before moving on, is that the Supreme Court has famously engaged in the task of fixing and indeed tailoring scrutiny and deference in a theme-specific, doctrinal mosaic extending throughout constitutional law (chapter twelve, sections I–III). These doctrinal tests aim to contextualise. Sometimes they rest on narrower, but more rigid distinctions. Even so, they do not foreclose further specification. As the argumentative interpretive community comes to terms with them, it engages with the institutional and substantive aspects behind their justification and tinkers with their reach.

Affirmative action jurisprudence illustrates this process rather well. While the Court had accepted in *Adarand* that the standard of review does not vary with the institution engaged in affirmative action measures, it decided in *Grutter* to adapt the generic strict scrutiny standard to the peculiarities of the educational setting. As Justice O'Connor, writing for the majority, announced, 'that inquiry must be calibrated to fit the distinct issues raised by the use of race to achieve student body diversity in public higher education'.[13] The Court specified the degree of deference recognised to Universities over distinct determinations material to the overall constitutional question, taking into account more local substantive assessments about the constitutional principles at stake and more local institutional assessments about the expertise of Universities in educational policy.[14] After Justice O'Connor retired, *Grutter* was thought not to have framed the applicable standard in a satisfactory manner. *Fisher I* assumed this task, and crafted a comprehensive standard, and *Fisher II* applied it. Yet, with Justice Kennedy now as the pivotal justice, both cases tinkered with the applicable standard of review in the light of shifting views concerning both the substantive aspects and the relevance of institutional good faith. But the underlying idea was the same: how to setup and specify an overall decision-making scheme likely to secure appropriate constitutional implementation, in the light of prevailing substantive desiderata and institutional assumptions.

[12] See ch 14, n 20.

[13] *Grutter v Bollinger*, 539 US 306, 333–34 (2003).

[14] *Grutter*, ibid, at 328 ('taking into account complex educational judgments in an area that lies primarily within the expertise of the university').

V. Institutional Revision

Institutional judgements change over time. This is due to change in the underlying substantive judgements about what constitutes an appropriate interpretation of the law, change in the perceptions about the behaviour of public institutions and change in the structure and performance of these institutions themselves. Institutional competency is not fixed but evolves informally over time. Institutions adapt to dynamic environments and often perform quite well tasks they were not initially designed to perform.[15] Or, they may be affected by a surrounding insensitivity to pertinent concerns and, despite arguments about institutional competency, expend part of their trustworthiness.

For example, much of the activism of the Warren Court resulted from the Court's lack of trust in the political branches over the specification of many constitutional principles. Consider, for example, the First Amendment jurisprudence of the Warren Court over issues of national security. In the 1950s and 60s, many academic scholars were concerned that Congress was consistently failing to engage in good faith constitutional deliberation when issues of national security, broadly understood, were implicated.[16] Members of Congress even rationalised neglect for First Amendment concerns by arguing that this task should best be left to the judiciary.[17]

Liberal members of the Court gradually recognised that even Congress could not be treated as a co-equal partner in accommodating First Amendment concerns. An attempt by McCarthyite legislators and Southern opponents of *Brown* in 1957 to curtail the Court's appellate jurisdiction formented the Court's lack of trust further.[18] As a result, the Court narrowed the degree of deference recognised by preexisting doctrine. For example, the Court developed the overbreadth and vagueness doctrines and applied them with real bite even in areas affecting national defence. In *United States v Robel*, the Court held that a federal statute prohibiting the employment of members of the Communist party in defence facilities was unconstitutionally overbroad.[19] In the same vein, the Court developed a tough standard for the regulation of political advocacy.

[15] Chayes' famous critique of the traditional model of adjudication is informative on this point. Abram Chayes, 'The Role of the Judge in Public Law Litigation' (1976) 89 *Harvard L Rev* 1281–1316.

[16] Donald Morgan, *Congress and the Constitution, A Study of Responsibility* (Cambridge, Harvard University Press, 1966) 246–68.

[17] ibid, at 255.

[18] Morton J Horwitz, *The Warren Court and the Pursuit of Justice* (New York, Hill & Wang, 1998) 65.

[19] *United States v Robel*, 389 US 258 (1967). Justice Brennan concurred in the judgment, adding vagueness concerns. In his opinion, the reviewed statute was devoid of adequate standards or procedural protections that would safeguard against arbitrary or indiscriminate application by the Secretary of Defense. ibid, at 282.

In *Brandenburg v Ohio*, the Court unanimously held a criminal syndicalism law invalid, ruling that advocacy of the use of force is constitutionally protected unless it is directed to inciting or producing imminent lawless action and it is likely to incite or produce such action.[20]

Compared with constitutional doctrine developed in other areas of the law, both doctrinal tests illustrate the willingness of the Court to assess at a high degree of specificity the appropriate accommodation between interests protected by the First Amendment and other legitimate interests, and to independently assess the necessity of measures for the protection of legitimate public interests. More restrained judges were eager to criticise the Court for 'arrogat[ing] to itself an independent judgment of the requirements of national security'. In their opinion, '[t]hese are matters about which judges should be wary'.[21] But the liberal wing of the Court knew quite well that political and bureaucratic institutions were not likely to align with what the judiciary considered an appropriate approach to First Amendment issues. Justice Douglas' concurring opinion in *Brandenburg* revealingly exhibits this institutional judgement, citing the 'deep seated fault in the infamous loyalty-security hearings which, since 1947 when President Truman launched them, have processed 20,000,000 men and women … They were the most blatant violations of the first amendment we have ever known'.[22]

That institutional judgement was grounded on deeper substantive disagreement over what constitutes an appropriate approach to First Amendment issues. As Chief Justice Warren emphasised in *Robel*, '[the Government's] concept of national defense cannot be deemed an end in itself … Implicit in the term national defense is the notion of defending those values and ideals which set this Nation apart … It would indeed be ironic if, in the name of national defense, we would sanction the subversion of one of these liberties—the freedom of association—which makes the defense of the Nation worthwhile'.[23] The message was rather clear: a department thought to be quite removed from this constitutional commitment of principle is not to be trusted over its specification.

[20] *Brandenburg v Ohio*, 395 US 444, 447 (1969).

[21] *Robel*, above n 19, at 289 (White, J, dissenting).

[22] *Brandenburg*, above n 20, at 456. Justice Douglas further explained that the specificity of the test was also justified in light of the unreliability of many judges who were 'so wedded to the status quo that critical analysis made them nervous'. ibid, at 454.

[23] *Robel*, above n 19, at 264. Similarly, the minority's institutional stance was developed against the backdrop of a free-floating, balance-of-interests understanding of the pertinent concerns. 'Having less confidence than the majority in the prescience of this remote body when dealing with threats to the security of the country, I much prefer the judgment of Congress and the Executive Branch that the interest of appellee in remaining a member of the Communist Party … is less substantial than the public interest in excluding him from employment in critical defense industries'. ibid, at 285 (White, J, dissenting).

8

Functional Analysis and Institutional Checks

I. Beyond the Walls of Separation

It is often assumed that there is a sharp distinction between the policy determinations that the political branches make within the boundaries of constitutional law and the interpretive determinations over applicable constitutional law. On the separation model, this distinction is coupled with a corresponding sharp division of normative labour between the lawmaking power of the political branches and the interpretive authority of courts.

In the history of legal culture these two distinctions stood in a relationship of mutual reinforcement. The supposedly sharp differentiation between the realms of political will and of interpretive judgement lent support to separate institutional assignments. Interestingly enough, the sharp institutional demarcation envisaged by the separation model also reinforced the fallacious idea behind the first distinction. The supposed necessity of the judiciary to interpret the Constitution on a fully independent basis legitimated arguments reducing the content of constitutional law to what is cognizable under judicially manageable standards. The result was a confused stance over the relation between substance and structure and erosion of the capacity for interpretive imagination.[1]

In the twentieth century both distinctions came under heavy attack. The institutional division has been challenged on the ground that the conduciveness of judicial review to the confinement of political and bureaucratic institutions within the boundaries of law does not entail that the judiciary exercise full interpretive independence. This was not perceived merely as a theoretical matter, but as one of grave practical significance, exemplified repeatedly in American political history; most clearly in the confrontation between the common law-inspired jurisprudence of the old Court and the world of the New Deal. Ever since, American legal

[1] Leftist theorists have pursued this criticism further. See, for instance, Duncan Kennedy, *A Critique of Adjudication {fin de siècle}* (Cambridge, Harvard University Press, 1997) 236 ('the practice of withdrawing a large part of the lawmaking function into a domain governed by the convention of legal correctness and the denial of ideological choice' makes 'the particular set of hierarchies that constitute our social arrangements look more natural, more necessary and more just than they "really" are').

culture has been sensitive to limitations of the judicial process as a social decision-making mechanism.

This sensitivity was reinforced by the blurring of the first distinction through the sometimes painful recognition that issues of principle and policy, along with assessments of social and economic fact, pertain to constitutional judgement. The net result was not across-the-board judicial restraint, as such recognition also facilitated arguments for an expansive conception of constitutional rights and for judicial scrutiny over issues of principle. But this cultural shift away from treating the separation model as the natural baseline had important repercussions in the discipline's imagination about the scheme of review. At a minimum, it made it easier to contemplate that schemes of review departing from the independent judgement rule may sometimes be more conducive to reaching appropriate constructions of the Constitution.[2] More fundamentally, it called on scholars and practitioners to appreciate that schemes of review need functional justification; and that this in turn entails functional institutional analysis. This transformation in mentality also instilled in constitutional culture a countervailing concern with limitations on functional reasoning arising out of the democratic commitment. We will discuss the first theme in this chapter, and the implications of the latter in chapters nine and ten.

II. Institutional Imperfection and Schemes of Review

A. The Mentality of the Office

Institutional analysis focuses on expected performance. The starting point in this regard is institutional competency, say the competency of the legislature to comprehend difficult regulatory problems, assess expected consequences, and devise optimal solutions. But institutional expertise is not directly transformed in firm expectation about performance.

The main concern for our purposes is that the set of reasons the political branches are moved by often diverge, in part, from some of the reasons that are appropriate in certain constitutional domains. This can occur *despite* fidelity to the duties of the office, since we are often moved by inclinations that are not transparent to us or, at least, we often fail to appreciate otherwise applicable concerns.

There are two main, interrelated reasons to this effect. The first is institutional culture. On the one hand, the continuous involvement with specific policy fields

[2] Even traditional elements of statutory interpretation have not escaped this challenge. See Peter Strauss, 'When the Judge is not the Primary Official with Responsibility to Read: Agency Interpretation and the Problem of Legislative History' (1990) 66 *Chicago-Kent L Rev* 321 (agencies are often more capable than courts of ascertaining the legislative intent behind the statutory schemes they are charged with implementing).

and engagement with interested constituencies makes an institution uniquely qualified to address relevant public concerns. At the same time, the developing culture in which it operates often reinforces debatable attitudes beyond full transparency. Electoral politics and consequent partisanship, for instance, often disable its agents from perceiving that the pursuit of constituency interests is not to be equated with the public interest as such. A variant of this concern applies with considerable force to the bureaucracy. Once agencies of government become specialised in one field, they acquire policy expertise and normally feel subjected to professional norms and expectations; at the same time, they also tend to get locked in conventional modes of operation and to fall into the so-called 'complacency trap';[3] moreover, the sense of identity and mission they form becomes narrow, often tailored along thematic policy expectations.

This risk is particularly troubling in the realm of public values, since we cannot often perceive and specify the moral reasons relevant to some field of constitutional concern without ourselves being sensitive[4] to these reasons in our official conduct. Despite intentions, the organisationally-induced lack of the requisite sensitivity affects the quality of our judgements.

Indeed, in reasoning about political justice, we do not separate between our belief, on the one hand, that political justice is valuable and that we should strive to live up to its standards and, on the other, our 'cognition' of its normative content.[5] We construct an account of what political justice requires in light of some deeper concerns that are driving us and that help us understand why one specification is more appropriate than another. In one prominent view, what is driving us is our concern with being able to justify to others the exercise of political power under conditions of reciprocity among free and equal citizens. In light of such a concern, political justice requires that public power be exercised on the basis of principles that rational citizens could reasonably endorse in approaching one another as free and co-equal members of the political community.[6] Quite evidently, the institutional specification of such principles requires institutional cultures that cultivate the sense of reciprocity among equals and remind partisan representatives about the polity's deepest moral commitments; including, in Mattias Kumm's vivid expression, cultures of Socratic contestation over the reasons driving public policies.[7]

[3] Barbara Levitt and James G March, 'Organizational Learning' (1988) 14 *Annual Review of Sociology* 319.

[4] See *Board of Trustees of Univ. of Alabama v Garrett*, 531 US 356, 374 (2001) (Kennedy, J, concurring) ('Prejudice, we are beginning to understand, rises not from malice or hostile animus alone. It may result as well from insensitivity …').

[5] See also John McDowell, 'Virtue and Reason' (1979) 62 *Monist* 331.

[6] See John Rawls, *Political Liberalism* (New York, Columbia University Press, 1993, 1996). See also Thomas Scanlon, *What we Owe to Each Other* (Cambridge, Harvard University Press, 1998) 156 (the ideal of justifiability to others does not figure merely as a 'sanction' that is triggered once we have concluded that an action is wrong).

[7] Mattias Kumm, 'The Idea of Socratic Contestation and the Right to Justification: The Point of Rights-Based Proportionality Review' (2010) 4 *Law & Ethics of Human Rights* 140, 157.

B. On the Justification of Judicial Review

Hence, the necessity for review over issues of constitutional law, including pertinent moral judgements. But the implications of this argument cut both ways. It has rightly been pointed out that any scheme of decision making that assigns final authority over a case is allowing its holder to act as a judge in its own case.[8] Given the inadequacy of formal political controls (like impeachment and constitutional amendment), the separation model is in fact empowering the judiciary to act as a judge in its own case. Accordingly, we also need to pay close attention to the kinds of judgemental deficiencies that the judiciary is less competent or trustworthy to handle, and to strategic considerations regarding the effects of the institutional scheme selected to the ex ante motivations of all institutional actors.

How are we to proceed? Let us first discuss the justification of the system of judicial review. This discussion will set the stage for addressing schemes of review.

Were we to adopt and adapt to our perspective the analytic turn that discussions of judicial review have taken recently, we may claim that the justification of judicial review would normally involve a set of assumptions: first, an assumption that the addition of judicial review would supply a distinctive (vis-à-vis the political branches) contribution in appropriate constitutional specification and implementation; secondly, an assumption that the risk of judicial overreach would be manageable in light of both the *reciprocal gravity* of error and the *reciprocal likelihood* of error;[9] and thirdly, an assumption that systemic considerations would supplement or at least not outbalance the expected benefits.

Accordingly, the justification of judicial review turns in part upon precautionary considerations about minimising risks of grave constitutional error. This might give the impression that such calculus can be performed without taking into account the degree of correct resolutions. Nonetheless, careful attendance to the matter shows that the pertinent assessment cannot be agnostic to the interpretive capacities and performance of the judiciary in reaching appropriate resolutions, as the latter clearly affect the degree of both rights under-enforcement and judicial over-enforcement. If the judiciary fails to capture a significant portion of truly deficient statutes, or if the judiciary has a strong proclivity to strike down unproblematic statutes, the calculus is seriously affected. Thus, precautionary approaches are justified only if there is confidence in the comparative ability of the judiciary to provide adequate protection over rights-violations without too much overreaching.

We do not face the herculean task of performing such a complex precautionary calculus since our perspective presupposes the institutional provision for judicial review. I do assume though that courts may reasonably be thought less likely to

[8] Jeremy Waldron, *Law and Disagreement* (Oxford, Oxford University Press, 1999) 297.

[9] The best defence of judicial review on precautionary calculus has been provided by Richard Fallon in 'The Core of an Uneasy Case for Judicial Review' (2008) 121 *Harv L Rev* 1693.

experience *some* of the failures discussed in the previous paragraphs. The selection process, institutional expectations, organisational culture,[10] and the duty to give reasons over focused issues arising within the context of concrete disputes about claims of right,[11] encourage appellate court judges to develop a distinct sensibility that bureaucrats and politicians often lack. Such sensibility perhaps enables its holders to appreciate certain commitments of free and equal citizenship and to attend to subtle vices and shortcomings in the efforts to remain faithful to them. Moreover, life tenure makes it more likely that judges will *in fact* rely on such reasons. Conversely, politicians and political appointees develop their sensibilities in a culture that values electorally promising compromises and polls, and electorally-conditioned time horizons often determine their official choices.

A few points of clarification. First, as the pertinent comparison is between a scheme of judicial review and a scheme lacking such review, it is of relevance to consider the effects the presence of judicial review has over the performance of the political branches. For instance, schemes of overlapping jurisdictions and argumentative interaction, as is the case with judicial review, enhance the free flow of ideas about constitutional issues, and potentially improve self-criticism and long-term adaptability of the overall institutional system. Moreover, the history of constitutional jurisprudence provides a background constitutional culture making certain political choices unintelligible.

More importantly, the very expectation of review has a restructuring effect on the motivational structure of politicians and bureaucrats. Critics of judicial review point out that the pillar of judicial review may have promoted legislative irresponsibility over constitutional matters.[12] Thus, we may not assume that the political branches would have behaved in the same manner in its absence. In fact, in polarised times, they could have performed even worse. After all, when outcome matters, judicial review provides public officials with a prudential reason to care about deficiencies in their performance—at least as assessed in the light of current judicial doctrine and expectations about judicial performance.

[10] Richard Posner, 'Pragmatic Adjudication' (1996) 18 *Cardozo L Rev* 1, 11–12 ('Judges are schooled in a profession that sets a high value on listening to both sides of an issue before making up one's mind, on sifting truth from falsehood, and on exercising a detached judgment. Their decisions are anchored in the facts of concrete disputes between real people. … Appellate judges in nonroutine cases are expected to express as best they can the reasons for their decision in signed, public documents (the published decisions of these courts); this practice creates accountability and fosters a certain reflectiveness and self-discipline. None of these things guarantees wisdom, especially since the reasons given for a decision are not always the real reasons behind it. But at their best, American appellate courts are councils of wise elders and it is not completely insane to entrust them with responsibility for deciding cases in a way that will produce the best results in the circumstances').

[11] See Jonathan Siegel, 'The Institutional Case for Judicial Review' (2012) 97 *Iowa L Rev* 1147. Siegel argues that such process-based features justify judicial review as an enforcement mechanism. I would add that these features also suggest its conduciveness to the cultivation of virtues that affect the deliberative quality of constitutional argument.

[12] See Mark Tushnet, *Taking the Constitution Away from the Courts* (Princeton, Princeton University Press, 1999) 57–65.

Concern with deterrence of unconstitutional conduct reaches its Madisonian peak in the anti-tyrannical prong of checks and balances; yet, it has force over more mundane failures as well; ranging from the short time-horizons of political decisions to the fact that the political branches are under no formal reason to explain the constitutionality of their decisions. And perhaps the argument has distinctive force to the executive branch, as bureaucrats have an institutional incentive to see their policies survive judicial attack. Thus, in *Grutter*, the affirmative action case, Justice Kennedy advocated strict scrutiny on this ground as well: 'By deferring to the law schools choice of minority admissions programs, the courts will lose the talents and resources of the faculties and administrators in devising new and fairer ways to ensure individual consideration. Constant and rigorous judicial review forces the law school faculties to undertake their responsibilities as state employees in this most sensitive of areas with utmost fidelity to the mandate of the Constitution'.[13]

Secondly, precautionary judgement about the optimal management of risk of error is not self-standing; it needs to be supplemented with argumentation about fairness in the allocation of such risk (chapter six, section III(B)). This in turn raises a host of thorny issues. How can judicial overreaching be justified to those harmed by judicial mistake (ie, to beneficiaries of the regulatory measures struck down in *Lochner*)? Is the argumentative and reason-giving nature of the judicial process an adequate mechanism in this regard? But be that as it may, I think that fairness is in principle respected when the institutional scheme aims at and turns out to be generally conducive to minimise grave error.

C. From the System of Judicial Review to the Optimal Standard of Review

It is crucially important to note that it is conceptually impossible to perform the calculus presented above without presupposing some scheme regarding the scope and intensity of review. Different standards of review would normally imply different results.

On this analytic basis, there is strong reason to doubt that the separation model would turn out optimal in such a calculus. No doubt, both instrumental and structural arguments for judicial review like those sketched above, imply *meaningful* review. Yet, this does not imply full substitution of judgement. First, the judiciary cannot claim comparative competency over all considerations that pertain to an overall interpretive judgement. Thus, to the extent that implementation costs are manageable, optimality may require tailoring the standard of review to category-specific considerations. Secondly, judges are drawn from a narrow

[13] *Grutter v Bollinger*, 539 US, 306, 393 (2003) (Kennedy, J, dissenting).

social segment that is perhaps subject to distinct social biases.[14] Judicial culture preserves an aura of political neutrality that affects the deliberation that takes place in judicial fora. And even if the judicial process exhibits more sensitivity to certain virtues of judgement, it is also subject to more subtle weaknesses; for instance, it may turn out to exhibit a reciprocal lack of sensitivity to legitimate policy concerns or, under the independent judgement rule, to get drifted into a culture of judicial indifference to public debate. Furthermore, it is likely that in certain areas, say economic regulation, the harm from judicial overreach to the implementation of legitimate state policies may be more significant, whereas in other areas, say personal autonomy, the harm from judicial under-enforcement may be quite grave. Finally, across-the-board schemes of judicial activism and supremacy seem likely to trigger unintended structural consequences, including reinforcement of public intolerance over issues of principle.

By adopting a model of separation, we would in fact create two princedoms ruled by different institutions. We may obtain simplicity but lack both in synergy and mutual criticism and learning. And subject to instances of encroachment, each institution would feel safe from control within its own princedom. No doubt, political and bureaucratic institutions would be held accountable by their 'constituencies'. But courts would not. Far from resolving problems of abuse, the model of separation often multiplies them in various subtler ways.

These casual comments may not establish that either a multiplicity of standards or intermediate standards of review are optimal. Personally, I believe that in certain areas we may only get the distinctive contribution of judicial review and avoid grave injustice with standards calling for focused, issue-sensitive judicial scrutiny. But arguably these comments do cast serious doubt over the separation model as an across-the-board solution. As we will see in part three, they cast doubt over full substitution of judgement even in areas where strict judicial scrutiny is in principle justified (chapter twelve, section IV). And this conclusion is reinforced if we retain a more uncertain standpoint: perhaps we cannot confidently determine which scheme of review is superior—at least in the long run. We still have reason to avoid rigid and irreversible institutional commitments and to employ standards that facilitate argumentative interaction and exhibit the virtue of correctability that characterises open and efficient democracies.

III. Interpretive Consistency

There is reason to value interpretive consistency. First and most importantly, interpretive consistency enhances legal certainty. Practised interpretations of the law provide social loci for the formation of reasonable expectations about how public

[14] Cass Sunstein, *Legal Reasoning and Political Conflict* (Oxford, Oxford University Press, 1996) 177.

institutions will resolve similar or related issues. Protection of such expectations is of paramount importance in enabling individuals to determine and implement arrangements that they consider efficacious for their own projects, commitments and plans. Secondly, interpretive consistency enables public institutions to apply public law in an efficacious and efficient manner. Regulatory agencies, for example, effectuate a legislative scheme more efficiently if they adopt one single and coherent interpretation of the whole scheme in all judicial circuits. Thirdly, in a scheme that values interpretive stability people feel little incentive to waste resources in re-litigating issues settled in the past. Finally, legal stability reduces transition costs. Accordingly, we have a *pro tanto* reason to adopt a scheme of assigning interpretive labour that will produce and rely upon interpretations exemplifying the requisite horizontal and temporal consistency. The reason is obviously conditional upon the interpretations falling within a range of reasonableness.

Alexander and Schauer have employed this argument to defend a defeasible duty of non-judicial officials to follow the interpretations of the law adopted by a single decision-making institution with sensitivity to interpretive consistency, most preferably the Supreme Court.[15] It is tempting to examine whether this same argument provides a defence of judicial non-deference to political and bureaucratic bodies:[16] the judiciary structures doctrine on an independent basis and applies it without deferring to pertinent judgements of the political branches. The underlying assumption is that the judicial department is quite respectful of well-articulated rules and standards of its own making. Political institutions, on the other hand, are taken not to focus on the constitutional dimension of their policy choices and, at any rate, to be driven by short political horizons, political bargaining, volatile public opinion and priorities of the day. If so, the separation model may be thought capable of providing the requisite legal stability.

This argument dovetails a more fundamental insight, that functional democracies shall combine both majoritarian institutions and institutions partly insulated from majoritarian pressures of the day;[17] the latter bind the polity on the time-consistent observation of certain commitments of principle or policy.

[15] Larry Alexander & Frederick Schauer, 'On Extrajudicial Constitutional Interpretation' (1997) 110 *Harv L Rev* 1359. Mark Tushnet has conceded that legal stability requires an institutional scheme that provides authoritative settlement, but has also argued that the decision maker may be a combination of more than one institution. See above, n 12, at 29. This in principle is correct. However, it matters whether the interaction between different institutions is very complex and time consuming. If so, we need to examine whether an institutional scheme with one supreme decision-making institution could better serve the concerns discussed in this section.

[16] See in this regard Jonathan Molot, 'Re-examining *Marbury* in the Administrative State: A Structural and Institutional Defense of Judicial Power over Statutory Interpretation' (2002) 96 *NW U L Rev* 1239, 1298 (emphasising the institutional determinants of consistency in judicial interpretive reasoning). See also Tribe, *American Constitutional Law*, 3rd edn, vol I (New York, Foundation Press, 2000) 998, explaining perceptions about agency interpretive flexibility ('the agency's act isn't really understood as an interpretation at all but is recognized, however silently, as an exercise in lawmaking').

[17] For a recent exposition of this argument, see Gary Miller & Andrew Whitford, *Above Politics, Bureaucratic Discretion and Credible Commitment* (New York, Cambridge University Press, 2016), chs 3–4.

The argument makes sense. For instance, a society in which the legal capacity of same sex couples to marry varies from one state, or from one referendum, to the next does lack in justice. At the same time, there are considerable difficulties with endorsing the argument as an across-the-board defence of judicial non-deference. I will focus on difficulties of three kinds: the difficulty of correlating separate institutions with constant degrees of consistency in performance, the multidimensional character of consistency and the fact that consistency is not an independent virtue but operates within the framework of political justice.

First, we need to attend to the factors affecting the consistency of judicial judgement. It matters whether courts are less prone to reverse their previous judgements (inter-temporal inconsistency), or to make disharmonious judgements over related areas of the law (horizontal inconsistency and incoherence). Consider the recent Supreme Court revisionism over federalism, its implications for the validity of large pieces of federal legislation, and the determination of the minority to reverse current doctrines as soon as it gets the fifth vote.[18] In addition, notice the fact that circuit courts are quite politicised and often unwilling to show deference to determinations made by other circuits. As public law scholars point out, given that the vast majority of public law cases decided by circuit courts are not arbitered by the Supreme Court, more deference to interpretations made by agencies enhances the consistency and coherence of legislative schemes.[19] And keep in mind the various ways of interstitial disagreement in common law adjudication, that turn out to be dispositive in the resolution of actual disputes.

On the other hand, the federal legislative process is geared towards policy stability by the scheme of checks and balances.[20] And in exercising legislative and rulemaking power, political and bureaucratic institutions have structural capacities conducive to grasping and respecting overall expectations of the affected public (often of a dynamic nature), as well as to providing stable ex ante rules of conduct.

Furthermore, there is quite a variety here. It may matter, for example, whether there is an expert body dedicated to protecting certain interests of constitutional significance, whether such a body operates through rulemaking or adjudication, whether it has shaped a culture favouring consistency in the constitutional policies

[18] *Alden v Maine*, 527 US 706, 814 (1999) (Souter, J, dissenting) ('I expect the Court's late essay into immunity doctrine will prove the equal of its earlier experiment in laissez-faire, the one being as unrealistic as the other, as indefensible, and probably as fleeting'), *Kimel v Florida Bd. of Regents*, 528 US 62, 98–99 (2000) (Stevens, J, dissenting in part and concurring in part) ('I remain convinced that *Union Gas* was correctly decided and that the decision of five Justices in *Seminole Tribe* to overrule that case was profoundly misguided. Despite my respect for *stare decisis*, I am unwilling to accept *Seminole Tribe* as controlling precedent .... The kind of judicial activism manifested in cases like *Seminole Tribe* ... represents such a radical departure from the proper role of this Court that it should be opposed whenever the opportunity arises').

[19] See Kenneth Culp Davis & Richard Pierce, *Administrative Law Treatise*, 3rd edn, vol I (Boston, Little, Brown & Co, 1994) 116–19.

[20] Tushnet, above n 12, at 28.

it administers, etc. One may not sidestep, for example, the sense of constitutional mission that Congress has showed in passing and sustaining civil rights legislation, often against judicial resistance. Casual generalisation from remarks of this sort suggests that each institution has (or suffers from) its own ways to blend stability and change and shape human and social interactions around them.

If this is so, then it is doubtful whether judicial scrutiny across the board would improve overall consistency. By adding one further decision maker (that is, the reviewing court—in fact the scheme of reviewing courts), we end up with a more complex scheme of combining stability with change. And, as Adrian Vermeule has emphasised, with significant uncertainty as to the decisions that would eventually survive attack and regulate our lives.[21]

This last point brings us to the second difficulty. Consistency is a multidimensional concept. There are various sets of expectations at play and different levels of analysis. For instance, we need to distinguish, say, between the expectation that the promulgated policy will be enforced in a uniform and enduring manner and the expectation that interpretations of the law applied in one policy issue will remain stable with regard to other related or subsequent policy issues. Similarly, even if we assume that the (often unarticulated) constitutional assumptions of legislatures are more likely to fluctuate over time or context, it remains the case that the coherence of the policies they enact would suffer if they are subjected to heightened judicial scrutiny. And such policy coherence and stability may be critical in the way people arrange their lives. Thus, a task for institutional design is to individuate various aspects of consistency and consider institutional schemes capable of combining relevant pursuits—say, multifaceted schemes of review sensitive to the fact that there are areas where the virtues of policy coherence and policy stability are critical.

Finally, consistency is merely one of the virtues that interpretations of law are to exemplify. We also care that the account of law we come up with be just, effective, faithful to the authoritative text, responsive to changing patterns of public culture, etc. We may have most reason to adopt an interpretation that is disharmonious with past interpretations in the name of these very reasons. If an established doctrinal line is questionable, it does not make sense to seek integrity in extension.[22] In such cases, 'even a modest extension is still an extension'.[23] And when the Supreme Court overrules a morally deficient precedent, or a precedent that fails to serve implicated interests, this hardly compromises some consistency-related value we care about (ie, it does not affect expectations we would call 'reasonable', or there

[21] Adrian Vermeule, *Judging under Uncertainty: an Institutional Theory of Legal Interpretation* (Cambridge, Harvard University Press, 2006) 261.

[22] Ronald Dworkin distinguishes between consistency and integrity (consistency of principle). 'An institution that accepts [the ideal of integrity] will sometimes, for that reason, depart from a narrow line of past decisions in search of fidelity to principles conceived as more fundamental to the scheme as a whole'. *Law's Empire* (Cambridge, Harvard University Press, 1986) 219.

[23] *Ziglar v Abbasi*, 582 US __ (2017) (slip op, at 24).

may be a clash of expectations as dynamic patterns of social judgement develop in the opposite direction, etc).

The critical issue, hence, is how to structure institutional arrangements so as to blend consistency and change in an appropriate manner. This task involves an examination and, perhaps thematic, assessment of the independent performance of each institution, and of the interactions generated by various (especially intermediate) schemes of review.

In this regard, the discussion so far shows that we have no a priori reason to expect that the separation model would serve as the appropriate default rule. In fact, it provides us with conjectural ground to consider more complex schemes of review that combine, say, judicial safeguarding of a framework of protective considerations with update, policy coherence and policy expansion driven by the political branches; and to incorporate direct concern with consistency within schemes of deference, tying for instance deference to the presence of interpretive consistency over issues where such consistency is of particular value.

The functionality of such complex schemes presupposes that the judiciary can operationalise applicable classifications and keep the risk of decisional casuistry at tolerable levels. Is this feasible? To this issue we now turn.

IV. Classificatory Rigidity

One practical way to proceed would be to divide interpretive reasoning into its component parts and assign primary responsibility over them to different institutions. This for instance, is the current, official doctrine in agency-administered statutory law. Courts have primary responsibility in determining genuine ambiguity in agency-administered statutes and agencies in specifying the applicable interpretation once such ambiguity is affirmed (chapter fourteen, section I).

There are important advantages in this approach as, for instance, courts are more capable of handling issues of narrow doctrine than issues of social or economic fact. So long as the judiciary lacks—on average—institutional capacity to improve on the reasoning of the reviewed body over certain classes of judgements, it is arguable that any kind of substantive judicial review over them (other than, say, review of reasonableness, aiming to capture motivating failures) would be expected to make things worse. We may be warned that it is not easy to distinguish assessments of social fact from judgements of value. Yet, we might insist on strong systemic reasons for employing distinctions of this kind. We live in a world of bounded rationality. Drawing sharp lines often helps us to avoid uncertainty and confusion and save decision costs and litigation time. And we might conclude that we have reason to adopt a rather rigid demarcation disallowing judicial scrutiny over judgements of social or economic fact: overall, we would be better off if these judgements are not subjected to any 'hard judicial look'.

The general idea is to obtain the benefits of complementarity without its weaknesses, to combine distinctive perspectives without inviting gridlock. Within reason, this approach is of use. In fact, courts often employ distinct standards of review over complementary parts of a constitutional judgement.

Yet, we shall not overemphasise the advantages of this approach, especially if pushed to the limit—if invoked to support rigid schemes of dividing interpretive authority. There are significant difficulties in associating a set of judgements to one corresponding skill only. Technical doctrinal reasoning, for instance, is notorious for having latent policy implications. In this light, it is by no means indisputable that judicial expertise should be dispositive over such reasoning.

To make this point vivid, we may move to another area where classifications appear well-settled: institutional expertise in addressing issues of science and, in particular, environmental health. Although the issue is quite removed from ordinary constitutional concerns, it is quite illuminating for our purposes.

We want to find out whether courts have reason to subject an agency's assessments of fact to a radically different standard of review from its statements of policy, on the idea that they involve a radically different kind of expertise. Regulation of toxic substances involves two different analytic stages, risk assessment and risk management. The common wisdom has it that risk assessment involves the resolution of complex issues of fact, while risk management involves the resolution of difficult issues of policy. Accordingly, risk assessment is often conducted by scientists and risk management by 'policy experts'. This example seems to be our perfect candidate for rigid institutional division of labour.

A more careful look at the problem is disappointing. Our operating assumptions are open to challenge. Risk assessment turns out to be policy laden and risk management is not detached from scientific considerations. Here is an argument against the first of these two assumptions.

In the process of assessing risk,[24] risk analysts evaluate the hazard potency of different dozes of a toxic agent on the basis of epidemiological studies on human population and toxicological studies on animals. This process suffers from great scientific uncertainty. Epidemiological studies are very difficult to conduct, the data are difficult to interpret and the results are available after the harm has occurred. Toxicological studies on animals involve highly contestable extrapolations to humans, including extrapolations from the biological effects of high dose animal exposure to effects on humans from longer duration exposure to smaller doses. After preparing the dose-response evaluation, risk analysts have to prepare an exposure assessment that includes both the probability of exposure and the magnitude of the toxic release. This assessment employs the concept of a model person. Since separate individuals face different exposure levels, analysts often study exposure to the maximally exposed person. But the pathways of exposure

[24] I rely here on Dade Moeller, *Environmental Health*, rev edn (Cambridge, Harvard University Press, 1997) 349–52.

are largely unknown. Exposure assessments are highly uncertain since they depend upon many variables including lifestyle and physical characteristics.

The main problem in this process is the lack of certainty. Our knowledge of all relevant factors is so fragmented that risk analysts resort to assumptions with limited factual support. Accordingly, these assumptions often rely upon policy judgements about the appropriate degree of conservatism. This in turn depends on considerations of risk management that include difficult value judgements, assessments of economic consequence resulting from alternative regulatory choices, etc. We may also have reason to employ different models in light of the policy problems we face. For example, we may have reason to use more conservative assumptions in assessing the risk of toxic agents that affect sensitive classes of people than we do when we address policy measures that threaten industries.

It is often proposed that risk analysts use 'best estimates' regarding the risks posed. But there are limits here as well. First, the level of uncertainty is often so great that no meaningful sense of best estimate could be made. Secondly, in case of uncertainty, employing a single best estimate may not be a value-neutral default position. It often turns out that our current state of knowledge grossly underestimates the risk. The assumption to employ depends upon whether we wish to err on the side of caution or not. Thirdly, before we decide what the single best estimate is we have to decide who the model person is supposed to be. But assessments made on the basis of a model person might prevent us from addressing the distributional implications of public policy. For example, a decision to examine the risk posed to the average worker might turn out prejudicial to discrete classes of people that are maximally exposed. Thus, considerations of distributive justice are implicated even in the very decision whether and how to employ the 'model person' approach.

In pressing these points, I do not claim that it is impossible to exhaustively describe our reasoning and to distinguish among its various aspects. But such exhaustive descriptions cannot substitute for operational judgements. We need to reach operational judgements and, in this regard, we have good reason to separate, say, risk assessment from risk management. Yet, even in this highly technical field, both operations rely upon considerations that require multiple skills. Even in the case of an assessment about the carcinogenicity of a substance, officials rely on both technical expertise and value judgements. But if different sets of considerations interrelate in the process of reaching such an assessment, and we do not trust all the relevant skills of the institution primarily charged with making it, we may have reason to provide for a review process—with full appreciation of the reviewer's own deficiencies and the systemic costs of such multiplicity of examination, including reciprocal risk of error. This is particularly so once we broaden our conception of institutional capacity to incorporate biases—say, the professional and cultural biases of experts, or their strategic conduct in intermediating between knowledge and power.[25]

[25] For an illuminating account of the role of expertise in law and governance, see David Kennedy, *A World of Struggle, How Power, Law and Expertise Shape Global Political Economy* (Princeton, Princeton University Press, 2016) part two.

To conclude: Classificatory distinctions, like the one between risk assessment and risk management, may provide us with prima facie institutional directions, but they often fail to support rigid institutional divisions.

We encounter this same pattern in constitutional law, say, in reviewing policy measures affecting protected personal liberties like abortion. Under applicable doctrine, regulations governing abortion processes and procedures shall not impose an 'undue burden' on women's constitutionally protected interests. In this regard, it is of particular relevance whether challenged processes and procedures endanger women's health or whether, as the case may be, they are 'necessary' to cure 'significant' health related problems. Nonetheless, whether this is so is a matter of scientific debate and possible uncertainty. For reasons quite similar to those discussed above, differences of opinion affect both the assessment of 'necessity' and the determination of the reasonableness ('undue') of the policy under review. And the formation of opinion in both areas is subject to biases of various sorts. It is therefore not surprising that courts do not employ radically different standards of review over the implicated issues of social fact and the policy management of the factual uncertainties. They may even take a closer look to ensure whether there is genuine uncertainty over the implicated scientific issue (endangerment to health, or necessity to cure significant health related problems).[26] Once satisfied on the existence and scope of genuine uncertainty, they supervise in its light the reasonableness of the governmental assessment of marginal safety and balance of risks, to conclude whether the burdens imposed are 'undue'.[27]

Our focus in this section has been on distinctions between issues of different nature (ie, fact and value). We may extend the argument to distinctions of different content. For instance, a similar pattern is seen in the *Fisher* jurisprudence with regard to affirmative action in educational settings. *Fisher I* ambitiously distinguished between judgements about the educational benefits from student body diversity and determinations concerning the necessity and narrow tailoring of racial classifications in this pursuit. Justice Kennedy granted some deference to Universities over the former, but none over the latter. In *Fisher II*, he imperceptibly moved towards a 'rational explanation' standard of review over determinations of necessity. Considerations of educational policy affect the resolution of both

[26] See *Stenberg v Carhart* 530 US 914, 937 (2000) ('The word "necessary" in *Casey's* phrase "necessary, in appropriate medical judgment, for the preservation of the life or health of the mother," … cannot refer to an absolute necessity or to absolute proof. Medical treatments and procedures are often considered appropriate (or inappropriate) in light of estimated comparative health risks (and health benefits) in particular cases').

[27] See *Gonzales v Carhart,* 550 US 124, 165, 166–67 (2007) (the 'Court retains an independent constitutional duty to review factual findings where constitutional rights are at stake'; yet, after confirming medical uncertainty, concluding on a deferential standard that 'the Act is not invalid on its face where there is uncertainty over whether the barred procedure is ever necessary to preserve a woman's health, given the availability of other abortion procedures that are considered to be safe alternatives'), and *Whole Woman's Health v Hellerstedt*, 579 US ___ (2016) (giving significant weight to evidence in the judicial record and, after refuting the argument for genuine medical uncertainty, weighing the asserted statutory benefits against the burdens).

issues and sharp institutional differentiation was ultimately thought unwarranted (chapter twelve, section III(C)).

We have examined the benefits and limitations in tailoring the standard of review along classifications of expected institutional significance. Let us conclude by addressing the ultimate checkpoints of our institutional conjectures.

V. The Olympian Point of View

The realist lesson that interpretation involves policy judgements invited immediate attention to the institutional locus where these judgements are made. The *legal process* school made a serious attempt in the 1950s and 1960s to rationalise the institutional landscape. The advocates of the school proposed an account of the distinctive function of the judicial process within society-wide schemes of policy making.

An understanding of that role requires elevation at a higher vista to comprehend how different elements of the institutional puzzle stick together. Accordingly, the aim of the legal process school was to capture the 'Olympian point of view'. From that perspective one could design and assess an overall scheme 'giving each agency of decision or action the opportunity to decide and to act in the fashion in which it is best equipped to do'. Once such a system is structured, 'decisions which are the duly arrived result of duly established procedures [for making decisions] of this kind ought to be accepted as binding upon the whole society unless and until they are changed'.[28]

The legal process school assumed that institutional design cannot sensibly be based on *ex ante* assessments of what the right outcomes are supposed to be in myriad cases to come. It conceded that public institutions are supposed to aim at 'maximizing human satisfaction without undue sacrifice of other satisfactions'.[29] Yet, it refused to incorporate any thick normative theory as the basis for assessing competing institutional schemes. Rather, it emphasised formal organisational features and, in particular, procedures, and tried to explain the distinct institutional processes in light of the separate function that each institution serves. 'The criterion of sound legislation is the test of whether it is the product of a sound process of enactment'.[30] The association of particular processes with distinct functions led process theorists to advance a relatively rigid institutional scheme. In juxtaposition to courts, legislatures were portrayed as the most competent mechanisms for collective choice and agencies as the most effective mechanisms for implementing public-regarding values. The scheme would work at its best if each institution

[28] Henry Hart & Albert Sacks, *The Legal Process: Basic Problems in the Making and Application of Law* (ed William Eskridge & Philip Frickey, Westbury NY, The Foundation Press, 1994) 67, 4.

[29] ibid, at 67.

[30] ibid, at 695.

performed the task it was equipped to perform, without encroaching upon the role of other institutions. The idea was that there 'could be a natural, functional correlation between different kinds of disputes and different kinds of institutions, so that the category of dispute could be matched up with the kinds of institutional procedures corresponding to them'.[31]

These core positions of the legal process school were crafted in the 1950s, a period of value consensus within the legal academia and satisfaction with the workings of the regulatory state. Given this stable background, the proponents of the school thought that they could justify institutional structures without committing themselves to contested arguments about political justice. As a result, some proponents of the school were unable to explain why innovative judicial practices were needed to review political institutions producing unjust legislation. In fact, they were even unable to distinguish between contested principles of political morality that may legitimately be pursued in constitutional litigation and mere politics. The most telling example was perhaps Wechsler's explicit questioning of *Brown v Board of Education* itself for not following neutral principle.[32]

Erosion of satisfaction with the workings of the regulatory state also helped reveal the thinness of the institutional theory employed by the process school. The school focused exclusively on one variable of institutional behaviour—process—and aimed to justify the competency of different institutions in light of the different processes they employed. But an abstract account of procedures tells us little about the way institutions employ them and the outcomes they produce. Institutions are not merely sets of rules and procedures. They are stuffed with individuals pursuing a variety of interests[33] and are loci of distinct institutional and organisational cultures. They are often moved by distinct commitments and care most about particular policy goals that do not exhaust the rationale behind the legal scheme they administer. Organisational interaction affects cultural attitudes, sharpens, softens or reinforces group identities, differences and stereotypes. In fact, the vigilance of the Warren Court was not premised on competency, but on a sense of duty. As the Court acknowledged in a seminal case of the forties, hinting at the jurisprudential revolution that was to follow in the 1950s and 1960s,

[31] Gary Peller, 'Neutral Principles in the 50's' (1988) 21 *U Mich JL* 561, 594.

[32] Herbert Wechsler, 'Toward Neutral Principles of Constitutional Law' (1959) 73 *Harvard L Rev* 1, 32–33. On the other hand, Sacks praised *Brown* as illustrating 'the functioning of the judicial process at its best ... the triumph of principle ... [by] a politically sheltered institution whose function it is to seek to reflect the sober second thought of the community'. See Albert M Sacks, 'The Supreme Court, 1953 Term- Foreword' (1954) 68 *Harvard L Rev* 96, 96. The ambivalence of process theorists toward constitutional review is also reflected in much of the criticism against *Roe v Wade*. See John Hart Ely, 'The Wages of Crying Wolf: A Comment on *Roe v. Wade*' (1973) 82 *Yale L J* 920.

[33] Thomas Hammond & Christopher Butler, 'Some Complex Answers to the Simple Question 'Do Institutions Matter': Policy Choice and Policy Change in Presidential and Parliamentary Systems' (2003) 15 *Journal of Theoretical Politics* 145 (one cannot draw inferences about the nature of policy choice and policy change in different kinds of institutional systems just by considering the institutional rules alone, and without considering the interaction between such rules and the policy preferences of the individual officeholders).

'we act in these matters not by authority of our competence, but by force of our commissions'.[34]

And finally, institutions evolve. Institutional competency acquired from engagement in one task may appear of relevance in resolving problems that other institutions have failed to deal with.[35] What ultimately matters is an account of how institutions perform *in time* and *in fact*.

This leads to the third problem of the process school. Once we get a more realistic and history-sensitive picture of human and institutional behaviour, we can appreciate the importance of institutional overlap and checks. Indeed, as the country moved into the 1960s and 1970s, the sense of trust to the regulatory state began to evaporate. This led to institutional friction, and multiplication of checks, including 'hard look' approaches in judicial review of agency conduct. Descending from Olympus, we can better see the vitality of *sophisticated institutional analysis*, the indispensability of *contestable moral reasoning* and the *imperfection* of public institutions.

It may be argued that the simplicity of the process school analysis is also a virtue. We live in a world of limited time and resources. Institutional assignments are made by institutions stuffed with humans and subject to limitations and biases, and the empirical workings of institutions are often clouded with uncertainty and volatility. Why shall we invest extra resources to pursue more subtle information that might end up being inconclusive and malleable? Indeed, there is truth in these concerns. The relevance of some institutional considerations may be minimal when compared with the difficulty in operationalising them. In theory, we can even talk about an optimal level of complexity. Beyond a certain point, complexity becomes too costly and unmanageable. And this is particularly so with regard to rules designed by the judiciary in the adjudicatory process. At the same time, it is doubtful whether these grounds for concern support parsimony in institutional reasoning—either in theory or in practice.

First, one cannot assume that by avoiding some institutional considerations that truly apply to the issue at hand, one errs on the side of 'safety'. It is likely that options of avoidance—like restricting ourselves to some aspects only (say, formal process), or simply assuming full or minimal judicial interpretive authority and putting institutional analysis at rest, would end up being the worst ones. For example, it is not clear whether adopting an institutional solution on the basis of some relevant considerations is better than adopting one on a less than thorough understanding of all relevant considerations.

Secondly, the difficulty of institutional analysis shall not be exaggerated. The discipline is still nascent. As it grows, we learn more about public institutions and

[34] *West Virginia State Bd. of Educ. v Barnette*, 319 US 624, 640 (1943) (State action making it compulsory for children in the public schools to salute the flag and pledge allegiance is unconstitutional).

[35] James G March & Johan P Olsen, 'The Institutional Dynamic of International Political Orders', in Peter Katzenstein, Robert Keohane, and Stephen Krasner (eds), *Exploration and Contestation in the Study of World Politics* 303, 326–28 (Cambridge, The MIT Press, 1999).

about how to operationalise institutional analysis. The marginal improvement we get by introducing rough comparative assessments about under-examined institutional aspects may be worth the try. Even today, available information does illuminate the way institutions respond to the legal schemes they administer and explains why simple process-based models offer a distorting picture. Most importantly, local experimentalism is performed all around, in the common law methods of expounding and applying standards of review. It is important, no doubt, that we keep in mind the various tensions between complexity and simplicity, and the related tensions between formality and plasticity discussed in the previous chapter; but ultimately, the results of institutional design and tinkering, successes, shortcomings and big disappointments, are out there to assess, standing as the ultimate checkpoints of our theoretical conjectures.

9

Democracy and Institutional Design

I. The Charge of Instrumentalism

The account of paradigmatic justification I defended was stated at a very general level, employing relatively formal accounts of political rationality. Yet, in making operational use of the idea, one needs to thicken the operative accounts of public reason and political justice. We were quite agnostic on the content of political justice in Part One. But if we are to be more informative on the fundamental tensions of institutional reasoning, we have to become more specific.

There is a fundamental idea, already presented in Part One, that is both normatively appealing and based on ideals that the American polity and its constitutional structure are said to be committed to: that public institutions are to be understood, normatively speaking, as the collective arms of free and equal citizens, constituting as a whole the inclusive category of 'We, the People'. As Chief Justice Jay emphasised in *Chisholm v Georgia* (1793), 'at the Revolution, the sovereignty devolved on the people; the citizens of America are equal as fellow citizens, and as joint tenants in the sovereignty'.[1]

We may expand upon this idea, as reflecting two fundamental normative commitments: first, the idea that the ultimate locus of political value lies in each citizen. Respect and care for the interests of each citizen is the ultimate concern of political institutions. Political institutions do not have legitimate interests of their own. Accordingly, they do not have any inherent claim of authority detached from their ability to respond to reasons that apply to the citizens in light of their fundamental interests. Secondly, we are supposed to recognise one another as having an interest in participating in and influencing the collective governance of public affairs and an interest in recognising ourselves and being treated as co-equal members of the political community. In light of these two fundamental commitments, we have reason to conceive political power as the collective power of free and equal citizens.[2]

Once we endorse this conception of public institutions, we are faced with a very serious challenge. If public institutions are to be treated as the collective arms of

[1] 2 US (2 Dall) 419, 454 (1793).

[2] See John Rawls, *Political Liberalism* (New York, Columbia University Press, 1993, 1996) 136.

free and equal citizens, there is something disturbing about also treating them as instruments of one's own policy views and seeking the most effective structure in concretising such views. It is rather *their* task to define the applicable conceptions of justice and legitimacy and accordingly to give interpretive content to constitutional laws. No doubt, we need some idea on how to structure such institutions. But, and here the critique sharpens its focus, the pertinent argumentation has to be neutral with regard to substance. We are not supposed to bootleg our own particular judgements about what substantive justice requires by orchestrating an institutional structure best calculated to realise them. On a more 'democratic' variant of this argument, associated with the views of Jeremy Waldron, in a political community where people disagree about public policy in general and political justice in particular, we need neutral procedures for the people, treated as free and equal, to select for themselves what they take to be just public policy.[3] We may call this charge the charge of *instrumentalism*.

The charge of instrumentalism is usually associated with a parallel critique addressed against academic lawyers or philosophers who advance particular substantive conceptions of justice.[4] But such narrow focus is arbitrary. Institutional structures are not selected at a pre-political stage. They are the products of public conventions or public institutions whose legitimacy to make substantive policy decisions Waldron does not (necessarily) challenge. The appropriate design of these institutions and the appropriate timing of design are separate institutional issues themselves. But given their authority, the role of academic lawyers or philosophers in this process does not differ from the role of other citizens.[5] They all appeal before supposedly legitimate institutional processes and argue what, in their opinion, the best ways to design new or specify existing institutional norms are. The charge of instrumentalism, if valid, applies to everybody. In our case, it allegedly applies to the employment of substantive considerations of justice in institutional reasoning.

Is it valid? What is its real bite? Let us first clarify that it would be unreasonable to claim that we shall not design and interpret an institutional structure on the basis of (unavoidably contested) conceptions of political justice. Constitutional theorists have long insisted that we cannot assess any process unless we make judgements about what is of (intrinsic or instrumental) value about the process. This evaluative issue cannot be settled by mere reference to the process itself.[6]

[3] See Jeremy Waldron, *Law and Disagreement* (Oxford, Oxford University Press, 1999) 295–96 and 300. See also Stuart Hampshire, *Innocence and Experience* (Cambridge, Harvard University Press, 1989) (minimum procedural justice provides the shared basis that humans need to defend their conceptions of the good and the substantive conceptions of justice that derive from them).

[4] Most notably, Habermas criticises Rawls (and Kant) for offering 'monological' theories. See Jürgen Habermas, 'Reconciliation through the Use of Public Reason: Remarks on John Rawls' Political Liberalism' (1995) 92 *Journal of Philosophy* 109.

[5] Rawls, above n 2, at 426–27.

[6] See Laurence Tribe, *Constitutinal Choices* (Cambridge, Harvard University Press, 1985) 13, and Frank Michelman, 'Must Constitutional Democracy be "Responsive"?' (1997) 107 *Ethics* 706.

This applies to Waldron as well. His position on process is informed by his ideas about political justice. It is dependent, in particular, upon a specific understanding of what due respect to the citizens' sense of justice and political capacity requires and upon a subsequent, highly contested argument that considerations of political fairness only (as a sub-set of political justice) provide us with second-order reasons that determine whose judgements about substantive justice would be authoritative in a political community.[7] But this account about the structure of political values is a conception of political justice to be defended on its merits—discussed and questioned in the next section.

In assessing institutional structures, we appeal to what we take to be the best conception of political justice. We do not appeal to the force of some procedure, but to what we take to be right reason. In fact, it is precisely ideas of political justice that disallow the kind of instrumentalism that troubles us here.

The charge of instrumentalism points out, rightly I think, that if public institutions are treated as mere instruments of one's policy views, they cannot serve as the collective arms of free and equal citizens with a genuine interest in governing themselves. In particular, it emphasises that important elements of political justice disallow treating public institutions as mere instruments of the designers' policy views. We now need to clarify these elements and their implications for the design of public institutions.

II. Equal Political Liberty does not Require Indifference to Outcomes

A. The Principle of Equal Political Liberty

If public power is to be understood as the collective power of free and equal citizens, its exercise should be based on reasons that reflect the relation to one another as co-equal and free members of the political community.

Citizens have a fundamental interest in being recognised as the fundamental loci of political value, conferring legitimacy to structures of government and having a claim that public power is conceived and is exercised as their collective power. Refusal of such status carries a strong sense of domination by alien and arbitrary forces and is incompatible with any reasonable conception of democratic ideals. At the same time, this status implies the active liberty to participate in politics and, through the exercise of deliberative responsibility, to affect the exercise of public policy.[8] Recognition of this active liberty (political liberty) is also of fundamental

[7] Waldron, above n 3, at 295–96 and 196–97.

[8] See Rawls, above n 2, at 205–06 and Rawls, *A Theory of Justice*, rev edn (Cambridge, Harvard University Press, 1999) 404 (fn 39).

importance for their sense of self-respect; it enables them to develop and exercise their sense of justice, and to strive for the public endorsement of political ideas they deem appropriate.

Moreover, recognition of political liberty lays the foundations for the development of the virtue of civic friendship and the commitment to civic reciprocity that are important elements in a stable political community aspiring to political justice; it also enables individuals to protect themselves from political measures that would unfairly limit their ability to consider, revise and pursue their conception of good life[9] and to ensure that public policies take the welfare of their various groups into account. The exercise of political liberty provides information to decision makers about the people's interests and incentives to be responsive to them.[10]

Furthermore, an active political culture provides stimuli and information that enable citizens to exercise their fundamental interests in informed and reflective manner.[11] More fundamentally, as a strong tradition going back to Aristotle[12] affirms, participation in the practical reason that develops in political communities enables citizens to cultivate their rational abilities and realise their conception of the good. Finally, the recognition of political liberties accommodates the fact that for many people the exercise of such liberties is an important aspect of good life itself. One should not forget the multiplicity of ways in which we exercise political liberty, including speech and communication over issues of political concern. For these reasons, we may say that, in Rawls's phraseology, the recognition of an adequate scheme of political liberties provides necessary institutional means for or constitutive elements of the free, full, and informed exercise of the citizens' sense of justice and their power of forming, assessing and living by a conception of good life.[13]

All these considerations support the establishment of a fully adequate scheme of political liberties. But the adequacy of the scheme and the distribution of rights under it may not be settled without introducing the idea of equal citizenship. A fundamental aspect of the democratic commitment is the conception of citizens as equal in the sense of having the capacity for a sense of justice and for a conception of the good that enables them to be fully cooperative members of the

[9] See *Katzenbach v Morgan* 384 US 641, 652–53 (1966) (Congress may permissibly lax state law voting qualifications with a view to securing for the Puerto Rican community residing in New York nondiscriminatory treatment in the provision of public services—citing *Yick Wo v Hopkins*, 118 US 356, 370 (1886) for the proposition that the political franchise of voting is 'preservative of all rights'). See also Rebecca I Brown, 'Accountability, Liberty and the Constitution' (1998) 98 *Colum L R* 531, 570 (political accountability serves the interest of citizens to secure state respect of their liberty).

[10] See also Amartya Sen, *Development as Freedom* (New York, Knopf, 1999) 5–6, 51–53 and 152–53.

[11] ibid, at 153–54.

[12] *Politics*, 1253^{a}33–34 (participation in the activities of the polis plays a vital role in the acquisition of practical wisdom and unqualified virtue).

[13] John Rawls, above n 2, at 310–24.

political community on terms of reciprocity.[14] Accordingly, the extent and distribution of political rights should reflect the fact that all citizens are to be treated as co-equal members of the political community. In fact, institutional structures that fail to keep up to this requirement would harm the self-respect of many individuals, disable them from protecting their non-political liberties, create conditions in which the commitment of others to the virtue of civic friendship would be jeopardised, and undermine political stability. More fundamentally, they would signify subjugation by the more powerful. Thus, the principle of *equal* and *fully adequate* political liberty stands as a basic tenet of any reasonable conception of political justice.

B. The Limitations of Aggregative Conceptions of Democracy

Now, I believe that a close examination of the reasons supporting the principle of equal political liberty helps us refute the argument that the design of public institutions in a democracy shall be based on strict *indifference to the substantive justice of expected outcomes*. The charge assumes that by prejudging what a just outcome is, we violate people's political equality. On certain demanding variants of this claim, political equality requires that public institutions aggregate the political preferences of each citizen valued equally. In designing public institutions we have reason to select the structure that will more likely perform this task accurately. On the contrary, I wish to claim that, in designing the institutions that will exercise public policy, political equality does not require treating each person's political preferences equally; and, in fact, that it permits making certain ex ante substantive determinations about the justice of the policies competing structures are likely to produce.

Does political equality require that public institutions make public policy, especially over issues of political justice, by aggregating the political preferences of the people valued equally—regardless of their content? We argued that political liberty primarily covers the fundamental interest of a free citizen to participate in politics and affect the formation of public policy through the exercise of deliberative responsibility. But public policy is the policy produced in the name of the political community as a whole. And as Ronald Dworkin has argued, the individual liberty to affect such formation does not necessarily extend to actual impact of each individual in the policies formed. What is important is that decision-making processes are not closed, but leave adequate room for meaningful deliberation and influence mainly—though not exclusively—through structures of political representation and accountability and the operation of uninhibited public debate, criticism and association. Such structures are not supposed merely to process citizens' unfiltered political judgements. What each citizen may demand is, first, that

[14] John Rawls (1999), above n 8, at 441–49.

there is adequate openness of the requisite kind and, secondly, that the choices ultimately made are supported by good reasons and that they can reasonably be addressed—and are in principle addressed—to the dissenter in light of all citizens' fundamental interests.[15]

But what about *equal* citizenship? Does the fact that an institutional structure has a built-in substantive predisposition imply that one's status as a co-equal member of the political community is disrespected? Not necessarily. Showing equal respect for each citizen does not imply institutional acceptance that any political preference actually defended is as effective or as permissible, as any other. For example, most of us would agree that, with regard to some issues, informed and reflected public policy is more appropriate than uninformed responses that just capture the spirit of the moment. Accordingly, we set up structures that are more likely to produce adequately deliberated outcomes. If our only concern were to secure for each individual an equal chance to see her political preferences fulfilled, we would have to reject any preference for deliberative structures. Such structures, for example, have disparate impact upon the political influence of those who do not have political charisma or ability to articulate their preferences in a sophisticated manner. And the same applies to many other virtues of public policy, from monetary stability to responsible foreign relations.

At the same time, political equality does set important limits to the scope of substantive judgements that may permissibly be employed in the process of institutional design. For example, if institutional reasoning were to prejudge most contested issues of political principle, future collective political engagement would be unworthy for those that do not share the judgements preferred. Similarly, exclusions from the process of otherwise open public deliberation and collective choice would impermissibly disrespect the excluded person's individual worth and her capacity to form a sense of justice that is worthy of respect. The same may be said about schemes that confer superior or inferior status, like schemes of multiple voting that award more votes to some members of the electorate, etc.

C. Political Equality and Political Justice

Discrediting the aggregative conception of political equality does not establish the permissibility of employing substantive ex ante judgements in the process of institutional design. Waldron, for example, would argue that what is at stake is not the positive employment of a particular theory about aggregating political preferences, but merely the negative claim that ex ante judgements about the substantive justice of expected outcomes may not permissibly be employed in the process of

[15] See Ronald Dworkin, 'What is Equality? Part 4: Political Equality' (1987) 22 *U San Fran L Rev* 1–30 and Charles Beitz, *Political Equality: An Essay in Democratic Theory* (Princeton, Princeton University Press, 1989) ch 3.

selecting an institutional structure. Considerations of equal political liberty are legitimate, but considerations about just outcomes are not. And the stakes of this argument are important in that considerations of the former kind are normally held to justify the plenary powers of the political process operating under majority rule and to question elitist schemes like judicial review.[16]

We have multiple reasons to doubt this negative claim. First, no matter how important political equality is, it is a sub-part of political justice. We have as much reason to care about other aspects of the encompassing principle of equal liberty (and, more generally, other aspects of political justice) as we have about political equality. We cannot accept that political equality gives us second order reasons about which conception and implementation of those other aspects is more appropriate because we know that political decisions that are responsive to the political preferences of many citizens may sometimes be strikingly unjust. In fact, people often participate in the political process with little regard for the interests of others and the overall justice of public policy.[17] We do not disrespect them when we base our judgements on solid knowledge gained through empirical political science and confirmed in history. Even when citizens are concerned about justice, one's view about political justice is not equated with the requirements of political justice themselves. Therefore, other aspects of the commitment to political justice support the conclusion that it is not in principle impermissible to consider the substantive quality of expected outcomes at the level of institutional design.

Secondly, public policy includes the regulation of the exercise of political rights. But the political process is not always trustworthy in respecting the political rights of all citizens. In response to the political preferences of large segments of the citizenry, it has repeatedly attempted to limit the political power of insular minorities. In such and many other related cases, tension between different aspects of political equality occurs.[18] The popular appeal of the policy outcomes cannot conceal the substantive violation of the requirements of political equality.

Thirdly, outcomes whose substantive content violates the requirements of political justice also violate (at least an aspect of) equal political liberty and compromise the democratic commitment. We can approach this interconnection in three complementary ways. First, equal political liberty and the rest of equal liberty stand in a relation of *practical mutual presupposition*. We have already discussed

[16] See, eg, Richard Bellamy, *Political Constitutionalism: A Republican Defense of the Constitutionality of Democracy* (Cambridge, Cambridge University Press, 2007).

[17] In fact, the giants of democratic theorising, Rousseau in particular, emphasised that the general will is to be understood as the common will of members of the community in the light of their common fundamental interests. See John Rawls, *Lectures on the History of Political Philosophy* (ed S Freeman, Cambridge, Harvard University Press, 2007) 224.

[18] This realisation underlies much of the jurisprudence of the Warren Court. It is also the official emblem of Ely's theory of judicial review. John Hart Ely, *Democracy and Distrust: A Theory of Judicial Review* (Cambridge, Harvard University Press, 1980) 15.

the role of political liberties in the free and informed exercise of one's conception of good life. We may add here that an adequate scheme of basic liberties is a practical precondition for the free and informed exercise of political liberties. We may not expect citizens to freely participate in public deliberation unless, for example, certain safeguards for their security are in place. A conscription of their sphere of autonomy is likely to harm the freedom and robustness of political life as well.

Secondly, all the reasons I discussed above supporting political equality are ultimately based on some more fundamental principle of equal liberty. We care about the equal political liberty of citizens because we care about their status as free and equal citizens. As both Jürgen Habermas and John Rawls have asserted in their noted debate, equal political liberty and other aspects of equal liberty are co-original.[19] We would lack in *integrity* were we to invoke the political liberty of a majority of the citizens to unjustly harm the substantive liberty of others.

In fact, thirdly, there is a sense in which the full breadth of equal liberty is not merely co-original with but *constitutive* of the democratic commitment.[20] This can be established by reflecting upon the idea of democracy. The mere existence of some scheme of representation and collective choice, though indispensable, is insufficient for a regime to qualify as truly democratic. To assess different schemes of this kind, we need to appeal to what is of value in a democracy as an important element of a just regime. In this pursuit, we may argue that what drives us in affirming the principles of democratic governance is the commitment that each of us is to be conceived as a free and co-equal member of the political community. Without a commitment of this sort, it is hard to see why schemes of representation deserve general allegiance. Accordingly, democracy may be understood as the political regime where public power is exercised in the name of free and equal citizens. Yet, this presupposes, for reasons going back to the formation of the very notion of the general will,[21] that such power is exercised on the basis of reasons that reach each and every citizen as free and equal and as a joint-tenant in sovereignty, and therefore on reasons that such citizens could in principle endorse. In this sense, a worthwhile conception of democracy has a built-in substantive conception of public reason. In conceiving public power as the collective power of free and equal citizens, we are committed to exercise such power on the basis of reasons that treat all citizens as free and equal.

[19] Jürgen Habermas, 'Constitutional Democracy: a Paradoxical Union of Contradictory Principles?' (2001) 29 *Political Theory* 766, and Rawls, above n 2, at 409 ff. The two authors talk about the co-originality of private and public autonomy.

[20] I largely draw upon arguments to this conclusion by Dworkin, *Freedom's Law: The Moral Reading of the American Constitution* (Cambridge, Harvard University Press, 1996) 15–31, and Joshua Cohen, 'Procedure and Substance in Deliberative Democracy' in Jon Elster (ed), *Deliberative Democracy* 185–231 (Cambridge, Cambridge University Press, 1998). For some important qualifications I would propose, see ch 10, section IV.

[21] See above n 17.

III. Equal Political Liberty does Guide and Limit Instrumental Institutional Reasoning

At the same time, this conclusion confirms that political equality does set important limits to the scope of substantive judgements employed in institutional design. In deliberating about appropriate institutional process, we shall appeal to reasons that reflect the bonds of reciprocity among co-equal and free members of a political community with diverging views about political justice. And this implies, among others, that we respond to the fundamental interest of each citizen to participate in public life and through the exercise of deliberative responsibility affect the formation of public policy, and to be treated as having the capacity for a sense of justice that is worthy of equal respect.[22]

On this ground, we may single out three main implications for institutional reasoning. First, the institutional structure selected shall reflect, in its form, the nature of public power as the collective power of a political community of equal members and shall not deny any citizen her status as a co-equal member with a sense of justice worthy of equal respect. Appropriate formation largely depends upon history and prevailing cultural and political understandings. Given the history of democratic progress, this normally implies a system of representative institutions having plenary powers over ordinary lawmaking and principles of equal political rights.

This does not in principle preclude investing non-representative institutions with specific functions, like judicial review. The justification of such assignment depends on various factors, including the kind of instrumental reasoning discussed in chapter eight, section II(B), systemic considerations, and various other considerations of strategy, constitutional continuity, social acceptance, etc. The main idea is that the overall institutional structure is well-suited to uphold and implement principles of political justice in a political community of free and equal citizens. Such a structure recognises and secures a fully adequate scheme of equal liberty in which the political and the non-political dimension are mutually adjusted.

Secondly, the content of public policy shall be *responsive* to the citizens in a manner that is requisite under the principle of equal political liberty. Institutional design shall aim at structures likely to produce, as a whole, policies responsive to the political judgements and deliberation of the citizenry. This idea applies to the complete system of public institutions, representative or otherwise, demanding that an adequate degree of political responsiveness applies to institutionalised policy-making, while accepting intra-systemic differentiations to secure other virtues of just and effective public policy under the general aim of better compliance with public reason.

[22] *cf* Rawls, above n 2, at 205–06 and Rawls (1999), above n 9, at 310–24 and 404 (fn 39).

This second implication limits the permissible employment of considerations about the substantive justice of expected policy outcomes both in terms of scope and content. For instance, it supports a requirement of *appropriate generality*. Suppose that a duly authorised institutional designer is reasonably confident about the specifics of many normative issues that may have to be decided in the future. He has a clear idea, for example, about reproductive freedom, the trimester system and the moral status of the fetus. However, he does not want—or does not have the power—to institute a substantive determination as law. In designing the institutional structure to handle such issues, I suggest, he is disbarred from considering some of these specifics. The criterion guiding the appropriate standard of specificity relates, among other considerations, to the interest of participants in the selected structure to have reasonable opportunity to affect the decision-making process by exercising deliberative responsibility. The permissible level of specificity varies among categories of issues and institutional settings, and the variation relates to the relative role of political responsiveness (vis-à-vis other criteria). Thus, the degree of permissible instrumentality largely depends on the political legitimacy of the structures implicated in designing and applying the pertinent institutional scheme and the scope the scheme allows for the exercise of deliberative responsibility and public responsiveness.

Thirdly, institutional structures shall also be assessed in light of their side effects to the vigor of the broader political culture. Viable democracies and open societies largely depend on open electoral contestation, uninhibited public debate and institutional accountability. On the specifics, it is pertinent whether, for example, an extensive judicial role over constitutional implementation debilitates democratic politics (say, by giving the impression that popular engagement is futile, or by giving a misleading aura of moral correctness to judicial doctrine), or whether, on the contrary, it improves the quality of public debate (say, by encouraging the framing of contesting viewpoints in the language of political justice and principle).[23] These are difficult institutional issues under public reason, guided by the overall commitment to political justice.

IV. Uncertainty Distinguished

Limitations in instrumental institutional reasoning arising out of the democratic commitment need to be distinguished from limitations arising out of uncertainty. In the former case, we are disbarred on considerations of political fairness from

[23] See Rawls, above n 2, at 237–38 (the Court's role as exemplar of public reason gives public reason vividness and vitality in the public forum). See also Dworkin, above n 20, at 344–45 (ordinary politics generally aims at political compromise—the great moral debate never begins).

performing instrumental institutional reasoning on the basis of certain substantive desiderata. In the latter case, we cannot confidently form a judgement about which institutional structure is more efficacious in reaching appropriate outcomes—either because of uncertainty as to institutional performance or because of substantive uncertainty about what a right outcome is like.

In cases of uncertainty, institutional design is supposed to proceed on the basis of those aspects of the problem that we have some confidence about, while also taking into account precautionary considerations and providing for discursive openness and adaptability (chapter six, section VI). A minimal understanding of the substantive virtues at play is always important to avoid blind institutional choice. For example, the more we consider stability and uniformity to be essential, the more reason we have to select processes highly correlated with stable outcomes. The more we deem the consequences of a substantive mistake morally frustrating, the more we seek structures facilitating reversibility, quality of deliberation, transparency and free flow of information, dialogic interaction and the operation of institutionalised devil's advocates. It is apparent, I think, that these virtues are particularly pertinent in judicial review involving issues of moral significance.

Discursive openness, adaptability and reversibility are virtues that find support both on cognitive uncertainty and on political fairness. Yet, given the necessity for interim choice, they are not enough to prevent mistake. And persons are harmed while discursive processes take their time.[24] Precautionary frames provide some comfort. But error is always to transpire.

In chapter six, section III(B), I endorsed the argument that process shall reconcile us with the possibility of error. Employment of this idea in democratic theory turns out to be a very complex issue, as we have to distinguish error from reasonable disagreement, and further clarify whether we have in mind error in design, error in implementation or plain violations. But it is essential to emphasise that fairness is implicated in all such cases: the person on the losing side, whether citizen whose reasonable political preferences were denied or litigant whose substantive right was violated, should not be able to claim that the design aimed at such loss or error, or that she was denied a process that respected her status as a free and equal citizen with a sense of justice worthy of respect; and, in the likelihood of such error, she should not be able to claim that the process was indifferent to considerations about the fair allocation of the pertinent risks and the feasibility of remediation. Finally, since dysfunctional outcome-oriented institutional structures are particularly likely to cause public distrust and discontent, it is important that the scheme selected be responsive to and do not disrespect the self-esteem and the equal political liberty of all citizens as joint holders of public power.

[24] *Obergefell v Hodges*, 576 US __ (2015) (slip op, at 25) ('In *Bowers*, a bare majority upheld a law criminalizing same-sex intimacy … That approach might have been viewed as a cautious endorsement of the democratic process, which had only just begun to consider the rights of gays and lesbians … Although *Bowers* was eventually repudiated in *Lawrence*, men and women were harmed in the interim, and the substantial effects of these injuries no doubt lingered long after *Bowers* was overruled.').

Let us conclude. The commitment to democracy does not disbar us from employing substantive judgements about just public policy in the process of institutional design. But we have to make sure that our substantive judgements and the structures we design respect the status of each citizen as a free and co-equal member of the political community, and that our institutional choices create adequate room for future political reflection and remain open to revision themselves. While faithful to these commitments, we have most reason to select the institutional structure that will more likely uphold and secure principles of political justice in a political community of free and equal citizens. Such a structure recognises and secures a fully adequate scheme of equal liberty in which the political and the non-political dimension are mutually adjusted.

Pursuing this general idea, I discuss in chapter ten how, in the realm of constitutional interpretation, considerations of equal political liberty may become operationalised in arrangement with other aspects of political justice, through the notion of fair public responsiveness.

10

Democracy and Judicial Review

The previous chapter discussed how the democratic commitment affects institutional design over the exercise of public power in general. Let us now focus on the particularities of constitutional interpretation in the process of American-style judicial review.

I. The Responsiveness of Interpretive Judgement to the Citizenry

The general idea is to single out those features of constitutional interpretation that ground as well as qualify the relevance of public responsiveness and then examine the institutional implications for the process of judicial review. In this course, we shall first return to the main ideas discussed in Part One about the substantive structure of constitutional interpretation.

A. Qualifying the Domain of Public Responsiveness

The main argument in Part One (chapter five) rested on the idea that constitutional interpretation has a conservative and an innovative component and that both components are supposed to contribute to the same general aim: the construction of such an account of the Constitution and surrounding constitutional practice that by following it public power is exercised in better compliance with public reason and political justice. They are complementary dimensions of complex judgements of public reason about the normative significance of constitutional practices, with a view to presenting such significance in ways that better serve compliance with political justice. The conservative element serves the pursuit of political justice in an indirect manner—through the commitment to the practice-dependent reasons for endorsing the status of constitutional text and precedent. Considerations of just content serve this pursuit in a direct manner—as the former reasons are properly adjusted with virtues of substantive content under an inclusive account of constitutional legitimacy.

Respect and response to the practice-dependent reasons for endorsing the authoritative status of text and precedent normally imply the employment of various partly content-independent modes of argumentation. To a certain extent, such modes disbar us from considering the substantive justice of constitutional content and, accordingly, limit the appeal of responsiveness to the substantive judgements of the citizenry of today. For instance, the coordinative function of language or the convergence-seeking and stability-promoting function of judicial doctrine could be jeopardised where we to appeal, at least in indiscriminate manner, to popular constitutionalism.

Moreover, text and history already exhibit some responsiveness to the political judgements of the people, especially to judgements formed under conditions of extended and widespread popular mobilisation during transformative moments in the history of the Nation.[1] Respect to such responsiveness may better be protected by insulating, in part, constitutional interpretation from the uncritical injection of current political preferences and by opting for relatively formal interpretive techniques.

B. The Relevance of Public Responsiveness

Having made these qualifications, we need to be sensitive to two fundamental reasons for holding interpretive judgement responsive to the citizenry.

First, current political endorsement is a fundamental feature underlying, in and of itself, the legitimacy of constitutional practices. Accordingly, upholding the reasons behind constitutional legitimacy would strongly support a significant degree of interpretive alignment with fundamental values of the nation and avoidance of deeply traumatic confrontations with considered judgements of the citizenry.

Secondly, interpretive judgement implicates appeal to the substantive justice of competing interpretations. As Frank Michelman has rightly insisted, arguments about just content are subject to reasonable disagreement among free and equal citizens. And democratic constitutionalists have emphasised the disingenuity of a scheme of public reason divorced from the actual reasons endorsed by the public.[2] In the previous chapter, from our part, we emphasised that both the content of public reason and the process of its institutional elaboration shall ideally reflect the bonds of reciprocity among co-equal and free members of the political community with diverging views about political justice.

These two fundamental reasons justify, I would argue, the responsiveness of interpretive judgement—and, especially, of its innovative component—to the political culture and the deliberations of the political community; in a manner

[1] On transformative constitutional moments, see the trilogy of Bruce Ackerman, *We The People (Volume 1, Foundations* (Cambridge, Harvard University Press, 1991), *Volume 2, Transformations* (Cambridge, Harvard University Press, 1998), *Volume 3: The Civil Rights Revolution* (Cambridge, Harvard University Press, 2014)).

[2] Richard Bellamy, *Political Constitutionalism: A Republican Defense of the Constitutionality of Democracy* (Cambridge, Cambridge University Press, 2007).

that is requisite under the principle of equal political liberty.[3] Failure of responsiveness to the citizenry over issues of this subject matter would imply disrespect to fundamental principles of equal citizenship, like the conception of citizens as joint holders of public power and the commitment that all public institutions treat each citizen as possessing a sense of justice worthy of equal respect.

Accordingly, we have reason to select standards of judicial review likely to produce appropriate interpretations of the law so understood; subject of course to systemic considerations about the positive and negative side effects that different institutional assignments have in the wider scheme of policy making and the political culture in general.

C. The Requirements of Public Responsiveness

Public institutions are supposed to be sensitive to both public culture and to the feedback they get from the citizenry. Public culture is evidently an amorphous concept. It ranges from deep-seated, valued institutions, practices and commitments of the nation to the diverse ideas and evaluations, claims of right and recognitions of wrongness, and senses of progress or disenchantment that make the social world morally intelligible. Moreover, public deliberation about constitutional justice is often conducted within the institutional processes of decision making or in dialogue with such processes. It does not occur at a separate space that officials simply take note of. Thus, responsiveness implies constructive engagement. And fairness in such responsiveness is even harder to specify. In the rest of this section I attempt a preliminary discussion and in section II, below, I will discuss some theoretical conclusions.

Let us recall the two main inquiries pertaining to constitutional interpretation and to constitutional adjudication. How are public institutions to engage with the citizenry and with public culture in constructing and settling upon appropriate interpretations of the Constitution, of giving shape to the constitutional principles of equal citizenship and of equal liberty? And what, in particular, is the proper role of the political and the judicial branches in this regard?

Our approach to the former question depends upon both subject matter and features of public culture. For instance, it is relevant to consider whether the issue in question is one calling for local experimentation, in light of the fluctuations of public perception, or whether it calls for a consistent commitment of principle. A different kind of responsiveness is apposite when we inquire into the rationality of regulating the production of milk, as contrasted with our inquiry into the permissibility of controversial kinds of punishment. Changing public judgement is relevant in both cases, but in a palpably different way. In the former case, we would

[3] See Frank Michelman, *Brennan and Democracy* (Princeton, Princeton University Press, 1999) 59–60.

expect prevailing policy consensus to affect interpretive attitude; in the latter, we would normally seek for more. We would honour current judgement aligning with the nation's efforts to overcome prejudice and to improve its commitments of principle. But we would be hesitant to confirm return to practices of exclusion.

Similarly, public responsiveness is more demanding with regard to ideas that have gained the wide and persistent endorsement of the people under conditions of due deliberation and energetic mobilisation. In other circumstances, a more relaxed alignment may be permissible; its realisation may be satisfied if the moral judgements employed are among those defended by large segments of the citizenry under conditions of due deliberation—while citizens defending other options have their views seriously considered and retain a reasonable opportunity to organise for policy reversal.

I have drawn these distinctions in an intuitive manner. The important point for us is to single out the generic function at issue. The fundamental idea is that public decision makers engage in a dialogue with the citizenry,[4] a dialogue that is open and conducted on reasons that in good faith reach all citizens as free and equal. The purpose of the dialogue is to construct accounts of constitutional justice for a community committed to equal citizenship, and a polity committed to treating its citizens as joint holders of public power and as possessing a sense of justice worthy of equal respect.

Now, it is readily apparent that such a dialogue is a constructive one, as it is the task of public institutions to settle and act upon appropriate interpretive accounts. This constructive engagement is pertinent to both the legislative and the judicial enterprise. Yet, its very nature affects institutional architecture as courts and the political branches respond to public culture and to the citizenry in their own distinctive ways. Obviously, legislatures are subject to electoral selection and accountability in the overall way they exercise their plenary powers. Thus, their choices already reflect responsiveness of a kind. At the same time, we need to be sensitive to the distinctive input expected from each branch. Courts, for instance, appear to have certain institutional advantages in engaging with fundamental commitments of the community and with macroscopic features of public culture, while legislatures appear particularly competent in capturing the pulse of social and economic life. And such capacities are reinforced by features of the processes they employ and of their operating environment. Judicial holdings, for example, are not subject to easy reversal by the political branches, while considerations of constitutional legitimacy impose a heavy burden on the side advocating doctrinal change.

This brings us to the most delicate aspect of constitutional dialogue: the self-critical and educative role of the judiciary in the process of constitutional implementation. Courts have a certain degree of detachment from partisanship and passions of the moment. And sometimes (though not always) they may be

[4] See also L Tribe, *American Constitutional Law*, 3rd edn, vol I (New York, Foundation Press, 2000) 310.

well situated to develop an emerging principle and speed up its endorsement by the public community at large. As Alexander Bickel has famously noted, 'the Court is a leader of opinion, not a mere register of it'.[5] In this sense, courts, deliberating on macroscopic commitments of the community, are perhaps well-suited to further refine the responses they get and to bring forward principled ways to structure the deepest commitments of the citizenry. And although much may be said about the conservative effects of the juridicalisation of politics in our social imagination and about the backlash judicial activism may provoke, a fair argument may be made that the Supreme Court has managed to transform many issues of initially marginal significance to the political establishment, into issues of principle, and to engage society in wide deliberation. This is a public good in itself and sometimes, as in the case of racial segregation, with good endings under political justice.

D. Judicial Duty at the Margins of the Reasonable

Bickel adds that the Court 'must lead opinion, not merely impose its own.'[6] His main concern was preservation of the Court's social capital. Yet, the point has an obvious bearing on issues of democratic theory as well. It is of special relevance whenever a transformative moment of constitutional significance has occurred and the people have formed a judgement contrary to the judgement of the interpreter in question. It cannot be dismissed in less extraordinary times either. And it reveals the tensions and dilemmas that the Court faces in performing its judicial duty. We had the opportunity in chapter five, section III(B) to address in brief how the death penalty jurisprudence had to grapple with social conviction in the 1970s; and how it still has to assemble in a coherent scheme the commitment to contemporary standards of justice and the necessity for independent judicial judgement to ensure that such standards respect the dignity of the person.

The prime goal is one of dovetailing self-critical constitutional reasoning to values deeply embedded and proudly cherished in public culture; and of engaging in sincere dialogue about the particulars of constitutional justice, reaching all citizens as free and equal, with a sense of justice worthy of equal respect. But our analysis of equal political liberty in the previous chapter suggests that there are instances when fair responsiveness cannot extend beyond paying due attention to certain dominant ideas, listening to the arguments and explaining in good faith why they are far removed from the principles underlying fundamental constitutional commitments, and in particular the very commitments that exhibit our

[5] Alexander Bickel, *The Least Dangerous Branch: The Supreme Court at the Bar of Politics* (Indianapolis, Bobbs-Merrill, 1962) 239.

[6] Bickel, ibid, at 239. For an argument that the Supreme Court, with lags and hesitations, indeed adapts to ever-changing political culture see Barry Friedman, *The Will of the People: How Public Opinion Has Influenced the Supreme Court and Shaped the Meaning of the Constitution* (New York, Farrar, Straus & Giroux, 2009).

respect for others as free and equal. Political responsiveness is part of the wider principle of equal liberty and the very integrity of this principle is compromised when political responsiveness is invoked as a ground to violate the rest of political justice. In such cases, we are plainly outside the realm of reasonable disagreement. And one should not forget that public law does not merely have an empowering function; it also has a restrictive function in the pursuit of political justice.

Fortunately enough, outright rejection of public reason does not occur often. Far more familiar are cases involving the arbitrary application of a principle people are supposedly committed to. We have seen this in famous cases at the crossings of liberty and equal protection, like *Obergefell,* as well as in the line of equal protection jurisprudence involving social regulation held to fail rationality review.[7] In such cases, it is incumbent upon a deliberative institution charged with interpreting the Constitution to indicate the principled ways in which citizens may pursue the very commitments they purport to have in a process of open dialogue.

We may be reminded at this point that the distinction between imposing an 'alien' scheme of justice and securing the principled application of fundamental constitutional commitments is a context-sensitive one. What appears from a certain perspective as a specification of equal protection turns out, from a different one, to raise a disagreement over fundamentals. Still, keeping the distinction in mind is helpful even as regards cases of more radical content. For instance, to return to *Obergefell*, it is one thing to defend the right of same sex couples to marry as a right to a new social institution, and an altogether different thing to argue that state exclusion of same sex couples from enjoyment of a valued social institution is unprincipled and arbitrary. It is important to be able to identify the salient features in each argument and to situate them under the overall principle of equal liberty and the way this principle has been understood in well-respected applications. No doubt, the proper way of framing the issue is a contested, non-neutral matter of substance. But we shall pause for a moment and wonder whether the same can be said about *Brown* itself on school segregation. Did the Court there impose upon the South an alien conception of justice, or did it declare what adherence to the commitments to equal citizenship implies?

I have sketched a rudimentary account of public responsiveness and of its institutional implications. One may disagree on the details. For instance, a critical issue is whether common-law modes of reasoning facilitate or inhibit judicial engagement in a wider constitutional dialogue. Such modes have obvious advantages in facilitating tentative approaches and flexibility, but they are often associated with lack of transparency or even of underlying principle. There is also some concern about the role of pivotal judges, ultimately charged with umpiring the deliberative contest: Justice Kennedy in *Obergefell* and *Fisher*. There is a sense

[7] *Romer v Evans*, 517 US 620 (1996), *Cleburne v Cleburne Living Ctr.*, 473 US 432 (1985), *Plyler v Doe*, 457 US 202 (1982), *U.S. Dep't of Agric. v Moreno*, 413 US 528, 534 (1973) and, with the liberty prong already emerging, *United States v Windsor*, 570 US __ (2013).

of privileging the policy space that pivotal judges happen to occupy. But we shall not forget that a judge acquires such a role, as to substance, by virtue of the placement of judgement in the rest of the Court and, as to process, by virtue of fair decision-making rules; and that normally such judges exhibit a degree of sensitivity to the pursuit of reasonable common ground—no doubt a pursuit of contingent and questionable quality, for radical minds. Finally, it matters whether the citizenry or the political branches have reasonable opportunities to respond to a questionable judicial holding. In some common law jurisdictions, judicial decisions are subject to reversal by the political branches.[8] In the United States, the critical issue relates to the contours of judicial supremacy and to the availability and scope of concurrent, nonjudicial processes of constitutional enforcement—an issue to be discussed in chapter thirteen.

The important point though is that once we have a conception of political responsiveness under political justice, we may then examine the capacities of the political branches and the judiciary to engage with the citizenry over issues of constitutional principle. Once we form an idea about the distinctive input expected from each branch, and after taking into account synergistic and interactive effects, we may then approach the appropriate standard of review with a view that judicial involvement does not betray, but rather upholds the relevant requirements. Similarly, by appreciating the force of political responsiveness in different constitutional domains, we may be able to justify more context-sensitive standards of review.

We will discuss this point in more detail in chapter fourteen (sections IV–V), after sharpening our intuitive distinction between issues of principle and issues of policy. But what becomes evident from our discussion so far is that courts need to appreciate that there is a genuine issue about public discursiveness and about the contribution from the political branches; and a countervailing ground for safeguarding the scope of reasonableness, the very idea of ensuring that the pertinent reasons reach all citizens as free and equals.

II. The Chimera of Pure Procedural Justice

A. The Non-reducibility of Substance to Process

On the account defended here, the justice of the process of judicial review, and in particular of the applicable standard of review, is *not* an instance of what Rawls calls *pure or quasi-pure procedural justice.* And political responsiveness cannot

[8] See Mark Tushnet, 'The Rise of Weak Form Judicial Review' in Tom Ginsburg & Rosalind Dixon (eds), *Comparative Constitutional Law* 321 (Cheltenham, Edward Elgar, 2011).

provide us with an independent procedural criterion, so that performance of the procedure constituted thereunder would guarantee the justice or appropriateness of the results produced.

We employ the notion of pure procedural justice when we lack an independent criterion for the right outcome while having an independent criterion for judging the fairness of the procedure. In such a case, the justice of the outcome is guaranteed by the fact that it is the result of a fair procedure under conditions of procedural regularity. Similarly, we talk about quasi-pure procedural justice when we independently define a range of equally appropriate outcomes and we have an independent criterion to judge the fairness of the procedure.[9] The justice of the outcome, in such cases, is determined by the fact that the outcome is produced by the fair procedures under conditions of procedural regularity and the fact that it is within the acceptable range.

Pure procedural justice is inapplicable to humanly staffed institutions charged with making decisions about just policy. To come back to a point made in chapter six, section IV, it would be absurd to define the justice of a policy outcome by reference to an independent criterion for judging institutional process. We cannot define what justice requires from what some people happen to think that justice requires after following some independently evaluated institutional process. Justice is the quintessential action-guiding concept we have in public affairs and its requirements cannot be reduced to facts like the beliefs office-holders assert within certain institutional structures. Moreover, cognitive uncertainty and motivational imperfection make it impossible to guarantee that some process will not produce unjust outcomes. As John Rawls forcefully argues, public decision-making processes are almost always imperfect.[10]

In our case, of course, we do not pursue political justice itself, but appropriate interpretations of the Constitution under public reason and political justice. But the point is the same. We do not have an independent criterion to assess the fairness of the standard of review so that its operation would guarantee just or appropriate interpretations. Furthermore, we do not normally treat interpretive outcomes as equally acceptable, but assume that we can in principle subject them to comparative assessment.

What about political responsiveness in particular, as a component of interpretive appropriateness? Can we have an independent procedural criterion establishing satisfaction at least with this requirement? I doubt. The performance of some procedure is not constitutive of *fair* responsiveness with regards to issues of constitutional principle. In assessing whether an interpretation of the law satisfies public responsiveness, we are supposed to make a variety of substantive value judgements that go far beyond the process leading to this determination. We may

[9] See John Rawls, *A Theory of Justice*, rev edn (Cambridge, Harvard University Press, 1999) 75 and 176.

[10] Rawls, ibid, at 173 and 311, and *Political Liberalism* (New York, Columbia University Press, 1993, 1996) 421–32.

need, for example, to assess the deliberative quality of the public culture and of processes of institutional engagement, the absence of exclusionary or silencing practices, etc. Therefore, the justice of the process of judicial review, and of the applicable standard of review, cannot be an instance of pure procedural justice even with regard to the requirement of public responsiveness.

B. Political Discourse and Constitutional Dialogue

This conclusion may appear puzzling to those who assume that endorsement of a constitutional argument in the political process is supposed to settle, at the very least, the political pedigree of that argument. Unless the political procedure in itself is flawed or a procedural defect has occurred, one could argue, non-representative institutions shall be barred from questioning the political responsiveness of the procedure's results. Whether the constitutional ideas surrounding a statutory settlement reflect the principles of constitutional justice endorsed by the citizenry depends, on this idea, on the enacting political process.

Now, there may be a variety of reasons for accepting the provisional authority of the political process: considerations of institutional settlement and political closure, provision of incentives for political mobilisation under settled rules of collective decision making, public transparency, etc. Considerations of this nature, coupled with the value of political accountability and the symbolic function of giving expression, through representation, to equal political standing may appear dispositive over ordinary issues of statutory policy.[11] But the requirement of fair responsiveness in constitutional matters serves a variety of purposes that may include but cannot be *reduced* to the representative function of political institutions and to the necessities of political settlement. It involves engagement with public debate in the process of constructing appropriate judgements of constitutional justice that give shape to the values of equal citizenship and equal liberty; a kind of engagement ideally conducted on reasons that in good faith reach all citizens as free and equal.

Is this debate fundamentally different from ordinary political discourse? The traditional reply from constitutionalists is in the affirmative. The distinctive nature of the debate is settled by the constitutional nature of the relevant domain.

[11] John Rawls thinks in a *Theory of Justice* that in certain circumstances the procedure of majority rule is an instance of quasi-pure procedural justice. Rawls, above n 9, at 318. Evidently, he has in mind ordinary policy making, not issues of constitutional principle. At any rate, I think that it is appropriate to employ here the distinction between the justice of an outcome and its legitimacy. The performance of some fair procedure may render the outcome legitimate (provided that some substantive minima are secured), but not fully just. May be this is what Rawls implies in adding that under certain conditions the decisions of the majority rule are 'practically authoritative'. ibid, at 318. And in his reply to Habermas he clarifies that there are serious doubts about a procedural concept of legitimacy since 'legitimacy of legislative enactments depends on the justice of the constitution'. Rawls (1996), above n 10, at 429.

The constitutional domain is curved from ordinary lawmaking and lies, having the status of supreme law of the land, beyond the ordinary settlement function of legislatures. 'The very purpose of a Bill of Rights', we are reminded, 'was to withdraw certain subjects from the vicissitudes of political controversy'.[12]

Constitutional discourse is in fact distinctive, even when it does not address narrow issues of text, doctrine or operational efficacy, but reaches the high level of constitutional justice. Yet, this is so on more nuanced grounds. The starting point is that constitutional justice operates in the context on policy contest. This is the domain of ordinary political discourse about fair and operational policies. Constitutional principles reflect bonds of reciprocity among free and equal members, as joint holders of public power. These bonds work out their implications in the daily business of the political branches. And benign arrangements settled in the political process normally both give content to and secure proper bonds among citizens.

Now, policies often fail. They may turn out to be dysfunctional or to distribute burdens in undue way. What imperiled constitutional principle normally signifies is a particular, morally alarming failure of ordinary policy discourse. Constitutional injustice normally implicates violation of the fundamental terms of reciprocity among free and equal citizens and possible fractures in the very nature of public power as their collective power. Accordingly, explicit reasoning about constitutional justice aims to unearth the very substantive preconditions that enable the policies public institutions select to be understood as 'public' policies, policies that may legitimately be enforced in the name of a political community of free and equal citizens.

This distinctive failure of policy discourse is often tied to occasional shortcomings of actualised public reasoning. Some may suggest that the problem lies in the engaging and conflictual nature of constitutional politics. But this is rather hasty. At a minimum, 'democracy does not presume that some subjects are either too divisive or too profound for public debate'.[13] And as a matter of fact, values of equal citizenship have historically become part of public consciousness by inspiring political contestation. This was particularly so in formative moments of constitutional history, as the American Civil War testifies. The roots of the problem rather lie in the lack of proper sensitivity and focus and, exceptionally, in improper animus. Indeed, we cannot equate the political engagement involved in the historical pursuit of equal liberty, with the predicament of certain polarised debates about the content of fundamental rights—debates conducted under prejudice and zealotry. Consider the intolerance in the public debate over abortion in the years between *Roe* (1971) and *Casey* (1992), presumably provoking the plurality of *Casey* to exhibit an equally troubling, self-regarding obsession with the Court's finality over constitutional issues.[14] And a similar argument can be

[12] *West Virginia State Bd. of Educ. v Barnette*, 319 US 624, 638 (1943).

[13] *Schuette v Coalition to Defend Affirmative Action*, 572 US __ (2014) (slip op, at 18).

[14] *Planned Parenthood of Southeastern Pa. v Casey*, 505 US 833, 869 (1992) (joint opinion of O'Connor, Kennedy, and Souter, JJ).

made with regard to more mundane matters, sometimes debated in a climate of gross indifference about equal citizenship and with a winner-takes-all attitude.

This way of framing the matter explains both why constitutional interpretation normally implicates intertwined issues of principle and policy and why, at the same time, constitutional challenge and failure are distinctive from ordinary policy challenge and failure. Similarly, it clarifies how constitutional discourse does not have to be elitist. Constitutional deliberation does not require intellectual distance and public disengagement, but a proper kind of engagement and empathy.

Of course, the adjudicatory context colours constitutional discourse in various distinctive ways, ranging from common-law modes of reasoning to the indispensability of standards for effective and uniform judicial implementation. Still, considerations of this sort do not alter the nature of substantive constitutional argument and, at any rate, shall accommodate the central role for deliberative engagement advanced here.

Finally, I understand that even this more moderate argument for the distinctive nature of constitutional discourse may be contested from a line of thought emphasising the unitary claims of political will. On this idea, representative institutions somehow construct such will, the will of the nation. This, I claim, is an indefensible position. Diverse societies experience pluralism over political justice. In fact, the political community is more-or-less evenly divided over many hotly contested issues of American constitutional law. And although such pluralism suffices to refute visions of judicial elitism, it also discredits the idea that the results of majoritarian politics are to be treated as representative of 'the' moral vision of the nation.[15] Such a conception of public institutions, representative or otherwise, would cry out institutional fetishism and be inconsistent with the fundamental democratic idea that public institutions are not sovereign bodies, but exercise functions in the name of thoroughly pluralistic societies. And they do so in inescapably imperfect ways.

C. Imperfect Structures of Constitutional Dialogue

Recognising that both the political and the judicial process are imperfect structures of constitutional dialogue, we shall be open to the virtues of institutional synergy. Considerations of political accountability, coupled with the symbolic and systemic arguments mentioned above, strongly favour the primary role of political institutions as to matters where ordinary political responsiveness is of utmost

[15] On related reasoning, Christopher Eisgruber has argued that both political and judicial institutions are imperfect reflectors of the people's views over constitutional essentials. Distinguishing between different dimensions of democracy, he argues for schemes of engaging majoritarian and non-majoritarian institutions in the aim of rendering self-government meaningful for a large and diverse people. Christopher Eisgruber, *Constitutional Self-Government* (Cambridge, Harvard University Press, 2001).

importance. Indeed, I will argue near the end of this book (chapter fourteen, section V(A)) that judicial passivity over economic regulation is largely explained (though not justified in its extremity) by an underlying sensibility that the field is governed by competing policy claims. Policy delivery and balance among competing policy elements are considered interdependent with responsiveness and accountability to the policy judgements of the public. And politics, coupled with a reasoned administrative process, is firmly thought more likely to secure these desiderata, than a judiciary invested with the power to scrutinise legislation for policy rationality or policy equity on constitutional grounds.

But even as regards constitutional principles reflecting fundamental commitments of political justice, courts shall always consider the value of institutional synergy and reciprocity with the political branches. The aim is that institutional reciprocity honours the fundamental interest of each citizen to participate in public life and, through the exercise of deliberative responsibility, to affect the formation and specification of such commitments; and that it acknowledges each citizen as having the capacity for a sense of justice that is worthy of equal respect. This aim also implies willingness by the judiciary to seek out for and to reconstruct the unarticulated constitutional ideas behind benign arrangements reached in the political process; and to show due respect to the efforts of deliberative structures accountable to the nation in promoting complementary visions of constitutional justice in the joint task of constitutional implementation. At the same time, this very aim also underscores the importance that the dialogue is genuine and constructive and that it is conducted on reasons that in good faith reach all citizens as free and equal.

But as biases and shortcomings affect the commitment to equal citizenship, we also have to be sceptical with regard to the claim that political equality is *necessarily* compromised whenever a court refuses to uphold a legislative determination[16]—even if the court properly implements substantive principles of constitutional justice silenced by exclusionary practices or by a culture of indifference in the political process. As I will argue, such instances may best be seen as sources for regret—regret for the fact that public autonomy and genuine self-government is not realised (section IV, below).

III. Non-Ideal Theory

Let us wrap up. Structures of constitutional implementation shall be compatible with and give effect to fundamental commitments of political justice: to the fundamental interests of free and equal citizens in living in a just political community and in participating and, through the exercise of deliberative

[16] See Jeremy Waldron, *Law and Disagreement* (Oxford, Oxford University Press, 1999) 293–94.

responsibility, influencing the specification of the requirements of political justice. This implies, among others, due attention to one desideratum of constitutional interpretation, namely that applicable judgements of substance be fairly responsive to the deliberation of the citizenry. However, in this pursuit considerations of pure procedural legitimacy are of doubtful use and ideal institutional conditions may not be assumed. This realisation invites us to adjust our approach to the fact that we live in a non-ideal world.

In this pursuit, we need to be cognizant of the fact that non-ideal theory is particularly vulnerable to rationalising abuse and reinforcing complacency to institutional deficiencies. This has two important implications for our task. First, it invites us to pay due attention to what we demand from institutions, to take care that non-ideal structures of review do not debilitate the capacity of political institutions and courts to live up to such demands, and to stand alert to criticise their eventual shortcomings. Secondly, it warns us to avoid coupling institutional with substantive complacency;[17] and not to abandon as futile the paradigmatic pursuit of institutional design: the selection of schemes of review that are more likely to contribute to the establishment and reliance upon appropriate interpretations of the Constitution under political justice.

The first of these two considerations suggests that institutional analysis commences with the constitutionally designed function of an institution and then adjusts to the facts we know about institutional behaviour. Political institutions are supposed to represent the citizens exercising their political liberty under conditions of political equality. In such a world, the task of judicial review is arguably to secure that judgements of the political branches fit under a plausible reading of the relevant textual and doctrinal materials in the light of a reasonable conception of political justice. The pertinent standard of reasonableness would vary according to pertinent judicial virtues. Let us assume that the judiciary is expected to exercise reasoned judgement, showing particular sensitivity to certain concerns of principle and developing rigorous institutional expectations and culture. This would justify standards of intensive review over those issues of principle whose adequate treatment calls for the kind of sensibility the judiciary is particularly expected to possess (say, considerations of fairness and impartiality and considerations of interpretive stability). On the other hand, more deferential review would be appropriate with regard to issues that are largely sensitive to the political judgements of the citizenry under conditions of fair electoral competition.

Now, it is pretty clear that public institutions approximate such assumptions only to some extent. This invites adjustment of the contemplated standards of review in the light of experienced or expected shortcomings and legitimate institutional concern. For instance, with regard to the issue of public responsiveness,

[17] Rawls relatedly warns us that abandoning the pursuit of justice for procedural legitimacy may ultimately weaken even the very requirement of legitimacy. Rawls (1996) above n 10, at 429.

we examine how different institutions may operate as *complementary* structures of public deliberation over issues of constitutional principle and over compliance therewith. So long as we really care about the realisation of equal political liberty, we examine whatever virtues each institution—including courts—may bring into the picture in the light of systemic failures of process. We pay attention to the role of the judiciary in the overall system of constitutional implementation. Which views are likely to be excluded or silenced in the operation of the political process? Does judicial involvement re-describe contested issues in a manner that makes it more likely that politically-engaged citizens would exercise deliberative responsibility? Does judicial involvement debilitate popular participation and form a culture of alienation from political justice? In this process, we do not consider the political responsiveness of each institution independently. Focused on the *system* of constitutional implementation, we attend to strategic and interactive considerations,[18] systemic tendencies and side effects.

In adjusting to the non-ideal, we need a theory of error. We have already discussed this matter (chapter six, section III(B); chapter nine, section IV) and I will simply repeat here that it involves precautionary adjustment of the standards of review in the light of assumptions regarding the gravity of error. It also entails procedural safeguards so that the person on the losing side, whether a citizen whose reasonable political preferences were denied or a litigant whose substantive right was violated, would not be able to claim that the design aimed at such loss or error, or that she was denied a process that respected her status as a free and equal citizen with a sense of justice worthy of respect.

IV. Public Autonomy and Judicial Review

A. The Notion of Public Autonomy

Much of the argumentation so far has focused on the principle of equal political liberty as a fundamental commitment of a democratic polity. At the same time, academic discourse has entertained the further idea that a democratic system is supposed to pursue public autonomy as an ultimate political ideal. On this basis, academic scholars have preoccupied themselves with whether the (partial) exclusion of contested interpretive issues of constitutional law from the scheme of equal participation and political representation contradicts the pursuit of public autonomy.

One's autonomy consists in his ability to be sovereign over the employment of his rational capacities, in control of desires of the moment and uncritical

[18] See Lawrence Baum, *The Puzzle of Judicial Behavior* (Ann Arbor, The University of Michigan Press, 1997) 89–124 (even ideologically committed judges have reason to accommodate public opinion in order to avoid backlash from the political branches or corrosion of their institutional legitimacy).

inclinations. The realisation of autonomy consists in one's engagement in rational deliberation and conduct in a way that is not dictated by such external causes. An important aspect of one's deliberation and conduct is the assessment and compliance with principles of justice. A citizen's political autonomy consists in his ability to publicly recognise, endorse and act by principles of justice.[19] The realisation of his political autonomy consists in the fact that his social conduct is governed by principles of justice that he would give himself upon appropriate reflection.

By extension, we may introduce the concept of public autonomy. Reasonable members of the political community are exercising public autonomy when they all recognise and affirm principles of political justice, and act by legally instituted specifications of these principles that each of them would uphold as reasonable, or at least not reject as unreasonable. In this sense, all reasonable citizens are governed by laws they would give themselves. This does not require that all reasonable citizens actively participate in the formation of the laws. It is enough that they recognise that the laws are reasonable under principles of justice, affirm their legitimacy, and comply with them in their conduct.[20] At the same time, the making of laws would have to be responsive to the political judgements of the citizens under the principle of equal political liberty.

This account of political and public autonomy also applies to deliberation about political justice that pertains to interpretive reasoning about constitutional law. Given the fact that the realisation of public autonomy is a public good, academic scholars have examined whether the assignment of extensive interpretive power to the judiciary makes this realisation more difficult.

B. Does Judicial Review Compromise Public Autonomy?

The conventional wisdom has it that the institutionalisation of judicial review burdens the pursuit of public autonomy in limiting the scope of the scheme of equal political participation and political representation. Similarly, the exercise of judicial power to hold a statute unconstitutional is understood as a compromise to the pursuit of public autonomy. Such compromise may of course be necessary to secure some other aspect of political justice. In such a case, judicial review is said to secure liberty at the cost of democracy.

This conventional line of reasoning has been attacked for uncritically juxtaposing the democratic with the liberal strand of political justice. We have argued that, in pain of inconsistency, the commitment to the principle of equal political liberty and, more generally, to the principles of democratic governance implies commitment to the rest of political justice and, in particular, to the broader principle of equal

[19] See Rawls (1996), above n 10, at 77–78.

[20] See Rawls (1996), above n 10 at 403 ('those already living in a just constitutional regime cannot found a just constitution, but they can fully reflect on it, endorse it, and so freely execute it in all ways necessary').

liberty (chapter nine, section II(C)). We even went further to suggest that the principle of equal liberty is constitutive of the democratic commitment. If that is so, one may suggest that judicial decisions that 'correctly' specify and uphold such substantive principles of democratic governance strengthen public autonomy. Accordingly, our assessment about whether judicial review compromises or strengthens public autonomy depends upon the comparative conformity of judicial decisions to the substantive principles of democratic governance. In fact, Ronald Dworkin has argued that when a court correctly specifies the substantive requirements of democracy to hold a statute unconstitutional, political equality is enhanced rather than compromised and citizens' power to participate in a self-governing community is improved.[21]

Along with Ronald Dworkin, Frank Michelman rejects the conventional wisdom and affirms that a scheme of governance may not be considered democratic unless certain aspects of the wider principle of equal liberty are secured. Nevertheless, he claims that while such security is a constituent feature of a democratic polity, it is not a sufficient one. It also matters whether such security is the result of imposition by some authorised institution or the product of endorsement by the citizenry. In the former case, perhaps dissenting citizens have reason to respect and comply with the decision. Nevertheless, they may not identify themselves with those who authored the decision and, hence, they may not claim that they are *pro tanto* governed by principles they would give themselves.[22]

C. Public Autonomy and Public Affirmation of the Reasonable

In the process of assessing the exchange between Ronald Dworkin and Frank Michelman, we should recognise two competing pressures. On the one hand, as both scholars emphasise, the security of certain substantive principles of justice strengthens the pursuit of public autonomy. Certain ways of political reasoning are violative of the very possibility of pursuing public autonomy. Public autonomy consists in the political autonomy of all *reasonable* members of the political community who participate in and constitute a community valuing this ideal. On the other hand, an important aspect of our deliberation consists in the assessment of competing accounts and specifications of principles of justice. And under the account of political autonomy employed here, the realisation of political autonomy includes the deliberative affirmation of the specifications selected as reasonable, or at least as not unreasonable.

An ideal solution to this tension would identify a principle of public reasoning that is not an external dictate to our will, but a necessary condition for the realisation of public autonomy. Its judicial imposition would not constitute an

[21] See Dworkin, *Freedom's Law: The Moral Reading of the American Constitution* (Cambridge, Harvard University Press, 1996) 32.

[22] Michelman, above n 3, at 30–34.

impediment in the pursuit of public autonomy. Such a principle, like, say, the rules of grammar and syntax, would rather structure our very activity of reasoning in the relevant manner and of exercising our autonomy.[23] Yet, this solution has a significant, potentially fatal defect. In contradistinction to the rules of grammar, such a principle would have to be a substantive principle of practical reason upheld in light of a (contestable) practical conception of public power. Some citizens would reject it without being irrational. And social disagreement precludes us from saying that its validity is assessed at a pre-deliberative stage. Even so, the question is whether social disagreement also implies that judicial imposition of the principle is an external constraint upon our deliberative autonomy.

It is hard to answer, but I will state some tentative thoughts that may help us make progress. Let us suppose that we identify such a principle so that compliance therewith would be a necessary condition for the realisation of public autonomy. Its violation would not merely reflect another political disagreement; it would undermine the very project of pursuing public autonomy. Since public autonomy is understood as the political autonomy of all reasonable citizens, any complaint to the effect that the imposition of our principle violates one's political autonomy may be rejected as unreasonable.

Is there a candidate for the principle we search for? A fundamental principle of public reason in a political community of free and equal citizens requires that the exercise of public power be based on reasons that free and equal citizens can reasonably endorse. If the laws do not satisfy this requirement, public autonomy cannot be realised. Accordingly, supporters of such laws cannot reasonably claim that the imposition of this principle upon them *pro tanto* excludes them from the pursuit of public autonomy. In doing so, they would be denying the very pursuit of public autonomy.

Nonetheless, the fact that such complaint may be dismissed as unreasonable, that they have not been *unfairly* excluded from the pursuit of political autonomy, does not imply that they also partake in the community's public autonomy, or that the community itself has attained such a public good. Perhaps the latter could be the case if judicial involvement is reserved for truly aberrational cases, allowing for a genuine community to pursue public autonomy over myriad other issues of policy making. Or perhaps we might be willing to claim that, given the rejection of the fundamental principles of public reason itself, there is nothing to regret as far as public autonomy is concerned.

Yet, this last point—making an exception for the aberrational case of outright rejection of public reason—cannot be generalised. We need to distinguish between the fundamental principle that supposedly structures the activity of public reasoning and the activity of public reasoning itself. A wide range of disagreement over the requirements of justice (covering the majority of the cases litigated

[23] See Andrews Reath, 'Legislating for a Realm of Ends: The Social Dimension of Autonomy', in Christine Korsgaard (ed), *Reclaiming the History of Ethics: Essays for John Rawls* (Cambridge, Cambridge University Press, 1997).

under constitutional law) cannot be understood as a rejection of the fundamental principle itself. People who are not insensitive to the fundamental principle would disagree about its appropriate specification. Many instances of such disagreement would differ from instances of outright rejection of the fundamental principle itself. So how are we to approach the more mundane cases?

I believe that we can make progress by treating public autonomy as a multidimensional ideal we have reason to pursue, rather than as a principle of strict binary application. If this is sound, public autonomy may *fail to redeem* its potential when a duly authorised institution (say, the Supreme Court), faced with the need to settle an issue, correctly selects the more appropriate specification of the requirements of justice and holds that the confident and considered determinations of the legislature to the contrary violate such requirements and 'wrong' the party making the relevant assertion of right. No doubt, in one sense, the appropriate resolution may strengthen democracy and be overall an achievement. At the same time, public autonomy may not have been realised in the sense that many citizens who are not outright unreasonable strongly disagree with this resolution and are *pro tanto* not governed by laws they would give themselves.

Of course, the realisation of public autonomy does not require consensus about every specification of principles of justice. What is minimally required is that reasonable members forming a political community acknowledge that the specification instituted is not unreasonable even though it diverges from the specification they prefer, given the necessity for settlement in a political community of free and equal citizens. If that is so, they may claim that they partake in the exercise of public autonomy by recognition and mutual compliance. But when they stand in deep disagreement with the decision reached and they feel discontent about the workings of public institutions, especially of structures outside the scheme of equal participation and political representation, it is ironic to say that the community is realising public autonomy or, anyway, that there is nothing to regret about the necessity for judicial intervention. Even if they are mistaken about the substantive issue in dispute, and even if the judicial decision actually strengthens their ability to participate in public decision making in the future, their compliance with the decision may *pro tanto* be a case of, perhaps unavoidable, heteronomy.

D. The Ideal of Public Autonomy and the Principle of Equal Political Liberty

The limitations in the ability to realise public autonomy relate to fundamental features of social organisation and human psychology. Under any scheme of collective decision making (whether based on the principle of equal participation or not), some people would feel betrayed and unable to realise political autonomy.

No doubt, we have strong reason to facilitate institutional synergy and to encourage mutual understandings and genuine reciprocity, with a view to the widest and deepest endorsement of commitments of principle. But at the end of the day, a genuine political community presupposes the willingness of its members to affirm that there is place for reasonable disagreement. Institutional design shall attend the capacities of public institutions to engage in dialogue and address the concerns of the dissenters. Indeed, it becomes relevant here to examine whether decisions of political institutions are more likely to rest on reasoning that is not intended to extend to opposing coalitions. Similarly, it is helpful to know more about the willingness of the judiciary to reconsider its decisions by paying attention to the substantive arguments of the dissenters. But evidently popularity is not the criterion of choice. The fact that in one situation a tiny portion of the citizenry feels that public institutions have betrayed their commitment to political justice is as worrisome as the fact that in another case a sizable segment has the same concern.

Having said all that, I wish to defend the emphasis attached throughout this chapter on the principle of equal political liberty. Given the inherent limitations in the pursuit of public autonomy, I think that we are justified in focusing upon the principle of political equality as an attainable and worth pursuing principle that embodies the commitment to democratic governance.

First, compliance with the requirements of political equality is more feasible. The fact that the *ideal* of public autonomy is often not achieved does not in itself imply that the *principle* of equal political liberty is violated. Despite the persistence of strong contestation and bitter dissent, we often need institutional settlement over the requirements of basic justice. So long as the reasoning duly engages with public deliberation on the basis of reasons that reach all citizens as free and equal and the decision process respects the status of all citizens as co-equal participants in exercise of their deliberative responsibility, the requirements of political equality can be satisfied—even if public autonomy is not realised. Dissenting citizens have not been denied a reasonable chance to influence public policy through the exercise of deliberative responsibility, nor have they been denied their status as citizens with a sense of justice worthy of equal respect, and the political system has reasonable operating procedures that allow for reversibility of the decision made.

Secondly, compliance with the principle of political equality is crucial for the legitimate exercise of public power. Its violation signifies that the political community incurs some special moral loss. While failure to achieve public autonomy is to be regretted, denial of one's status as a co-equal member of the political community compromises the commitment to political justice.

V. Judicial Reasoning and Objectivity

In legal and political discourse, judicial decisions are often criticised as products of crude voluntarism or defended as expressions of objective human reason. Some commentators assume that, in contradistinction to the subjectivity that rules the political realm, the identification and application of principles of law is subject to objective reasoning. Others strongly contest this assumption as unrealistic.[24] They often invoke the realist lesson that the relation between an abstract legal principle and an application is not one of conceptual containment, but one of substantive normative support. And they hold that substantive arguments about just policy are incapable of objective assessment; they are choice-sensitive in the sense that their validity largely derives from the fact that citizens have approved them in exercising their equal political liberty after due deliberation.

The contestation over the objectivity of legal reasoning is traditionally related to the debate over the legitimacy of judicial review. The conventional wisdom has it that choice-sensitive issues should be handled by the political process only. Once New Dealers grasped the realist lesson, they doubted the capacity and legitimacy of courts to perform much of the interpretive task on independent basis. Deference to political and bureaucratic bodies was the recipe they proposed. Herbert Wechsler, in his famous counter-attack, conceded that judicial reasoning includes value judgements, but insisted that they are subject to the guidance of reason through the employment of neutral principles, fairly susceptible of general application.[25]

Wechsler's account of reason was an impoverished one. The significance he attached to formal neutrality disabled him from making qualitative distinctions that matter to any decent account of political justice. Thus, he notoriously concluded that neutral principles could not bridge the gap between racial equality and racial inclusion and could not justify even *Brown*.[26] Still, the same point is repeatedly brought back to the surface; more recently by Chief Justice Roberts, arguing that a constitutional right of same sex couples to marry cannot be grounded upon neutral principles. Accordingly, the majority's reasoning in *Obergefell* was decried as 'an act of will'.[27]

In this section, I revisit the idea that constitutional reasoning is incapable of objective assessment by relaxing objectivity's requirements and by indicating that argumentative constitutional practices rest on the supposition of the objectivity of their subject matter. I argue that neither value-sensitivity nor sensitivity to public discourse threaten this conclusion. Accordingly, the debate over objectivity, though informative, is not determinative over issues of institutional allocation. But first we need a working conception of objectivity.

A successful account of objectivity captures the distinction between the personal and the objective point of view. Wherever an objective point of view is available, it makes sense to distinguish between the claim that a proposition is valid and the claim that it is thought by an agent to be valid. Influenced by John Rawls, we may accept that a normative proposition is objectively valid if and

[24] For a discussion of this theme from the standpoint of critical legal studies see Duncan Kennedy, *A Critique of Adjudication {fin de siècle}* (Cambridge, Harvard University Press, 1997) ch 5.

[25] Herbert Wechsler, 'Toward Neutral Principles of Constitutional Law' (1959) 73 *Harvard L Rev* 1.

[26] ibid, at 31–34.

[27] *Obergefell v Hodges*, 576 US __ (2015) (slip op, at 3) (Roberts CJ, dissenting) (distinguishing between neutral principles and the majority's understanding of freedom).

only if its validity is determined by considerations that rational individuals could reasonably endorse if motivated by a sincere interest in ascertaining the validity of the proposition at issue.[28] This general account includes two normative concepts, namely the concepts of rationality and reasonableness. However, it leaves their specification to theories of the particular subject matter in question. It is the task of a theory of constitutional law, for example, to specify the requisite notion of reasonableness and to explain, first, how it is that others could reasonably endorse the relevant considerations and, secondly, what failings they exhibit if they do not actually endorse them. In this sense, a theory defending the objectivity of a field of inquiry is also a substantive account about the kinds of reasons applicable within its domain.

Constitutional interpretation involves judgements about political justice and political legitimacy, including judgements about fair responsiveness to the citizenry. In making these judgements, we are supposed to ask what principles rational citizens could reasonably endorse if motivated by a sincere interest in responding to the fundamental desiderata of constitutional interpretation. Under political justice, the pertinent notion of *reasonableness* is specified by a conception of *free and equal citizenship*. Under the commitment to constitutional legitimacy, the pertinent notion is further specified by an assumption that constitutional law is legitimate, which implies that such law, even though non-ideal, is capable of reasonable acceptance by citizens conceiving of one another as free and equal.

Now, constitutional practice by and large rests on the assumption that such objective reasons exist and suffice to resolve even the thorniest of constitutional disputes. Regardless of what position one adopts on the merits, one has to acknowledge that this perspective was paradigmatically employed by Justice Kennedy in *Obergefell*, distinguishing between metaphysical theories of the good and considerations of liberty and exclusion: 'Many who deem same-sex marriage to be wrong reach that conclusion based on decent and honorable religious or philosophical premises, and neither they nor their beliefs are disparaged here. But when that sincere, personal opposition becomes enacted law and public policy, the necessary consequence is to put the imprimatur of the State itself on an exclusion that soon demeans or stigmatizes those whose own liberty is then denied'.[29]

Of course, it remains to be seen whether such objective reasons do exist and suffice to direct the resolution of interpretive problems. This is a substantive problem. Its resolution depends on whether the considerations we employ in defending interpretive propositions could reasonably be endorsed by others, if motivated by the commitment to free and equal citizenship. And, as Ronald Dworkin would argue, we have no demonstrative argument to a positive conclusion, other than the interpretive propositions we would confidently assert in the practice itself. Since actual endorsement is not required, each of us has to consider whether, in his

[28] See Rawls (1996), above n 10, at 112–18.

[29] *Obergefell*, above n 27 (slip op, at 19).

judgement, there is a sufficient range of reasons that are capable of reasonable endorsement; whether the arguments offered by Justice Kennedy in *Obergefell*, for instance, are capable of endorsement by citizens who approach one another as free and equal, or whether they merely represent the majority's will.

But we shall emphasise that an across-the-board rejection of objectivity is inconsistent with much of argumentative discourse, that is based on the idea that sufficient objective reasons do exist. In criticising or applauding a judicial opinion on a contested issue of constitutional law, we normally imply that the members of the Court had reason to endorse or reject the opinion given. In engaging in such argumentation we normally imply that ourselves, as well as the addressees of our claims, stand correctible to standards partly independent from each individual standpoint. Even when we are uncertain about some issue, we often think that the pertinent considerations are subject to reasonable endorsement, although we are uncertain about how to specify them.[30]

And this feature of constitutional discourse is strengthened by two further features peculiar to the legal character of the discourse. First, the very nature of constitutional interpretation as an inquiry aiming to carry out the normative import of the Constitution, and of the practice of its authoritative exposition, frames the interpretive activity and narrows (as compared with more open-ended moral inquiries) the scope of permissible argument. Secondly, as a practical matter, institutional culture and expectations, precedent, and various other practice-dependent or convergence seeking features of constitutional argumentation (chapter four, section IV) enable us to anchor our determinations on ideas seeking wider endorsement, rather than on quixotic pursuits.

This approach to the problem of objectivity can accommodate the fact that there is reasonable *disagreement* about both public reason and the law. The objectivity of a subject matter does not imply that there is no scope for reasonable disagreement about what we have most reason to believe or do. One may consistently hold that a practical proposition he asserts is supported by reasons that all others could reasonably endorse, while conceding that rational individuals could reasonably conclude that these very reasons support some other proposition as the better one.

But what about radical disagreement over the underlying reasons? What about the claim that *Brown* rested upon shaky moral grounds, a claim that presumably many Americans in the South endorsed in the 1950s and 1960s? Radical disagreement does not disable us from holding that the applicable reasons are still capable of endorsement by rational citizens appropriately motivated. Of course, in asserting our confidence against unreasonable disputation, we may have to explain the failure of the radical other to endorse the applicable reasons. We may appeal to cultural or ideological over-determination, argue that they are unwilling to

[30] Note that faith in the existence of objective reasons is compatible with local uncertainty about their content and force. See R Dworkin, 'Truth and Objectivity: You'd better Believe it' (1996) 25 *Philosophy and Public Affairs* 87 and Nicos Stavropoulos, *Objectivity in Law* (Oxford, Oxford University Press, 1996) (passim).

consider a relevant standpoint, or indicate that they have not exposed themselves to some pertinent experience or developed a requisite sensibility.[31]

What about political responsiveness? The validity of an interpretive proposition is affected (in a value-laden and conditional way) by the political judgements of the citizenry. Does this unsettle the objectivity of constitutional discourse? I think not. The existence or non-existence of certain judgements is a fact capable of objective assessment. We often assess a practical proposition on the basis of considerations that relate to subjective responses that agents form (after following a rational deliberative route and so long as such responses lie within certain substantive limits).[32] And constitutional judgement, whether performed by the legislature assessing rational means to pursue a synthesis of legitimate policy interests, or by a court of law assessing the requisite rationality of the policy selected, is supposed to engage with the pertinent considerations, rather than substitute them with subjective volition.

Therefore, the fact that constitutional interpretation engages with judgements of others does not demonstrate that such engagement is incapable of objective assessment. The relevancy and force of citizens' judgements is to be determined on the basis of principles of political justice and political legitimacy that seek reasonable endorsement. Objective reasons specify the conditions under which subjective responses matter: what kind of deliberative route has been followed, how responses are aggregated under the principle of equal political liberty and what the limits of acceptable judgement are.

We may now conclude on the *institutional implications* of this account. The lesson is rather deflationary: it dissolves the idea that the legitimacy of non-deferential judicial review turns upon a thick sense of objectivity of constitutional judgements. We may rest content with an account like the one employed here and seek institutional structures likely to produce and enforce interpretations grounded on reasons that citizens could reasonably endorse, if motivated by the commitment to equal citizenship and the commitment to constitutional legitimacy. Much of argumentative practice rests upon the feasibility of this pursuit. And neither the relevance of the judgements of the citizenry, nor the contestability of arguments about political justice and political legitimacy show otherwise.

[31] See Thomas Scanlon, *What we Owe to Each Other* (Cambridge, Harvard University Press, 1998) 357–59.

[32] In the terminology of Thomas Scanlon, objective reasons may include subjective conditions. See Scanlon, ibid, at 41–49. That is the case, for instance, with many propositions about the reasons that each of us has in conducting his personal affairs. We may not assess whether Joe has reason to pursue a particular career unless we take into account what his considered preference is. Such subjective responses are facts that become relevant, and sometimes conclusive, for an objective assessment of these reasons.

Part 3

Constitutional Doctrine

In one of the most famous dicta ever pronounced by a judge, Chief Justice Marshall stated that 'it is emphatically the province and duty of the judicial department to say what the law is. Those who apply the rule to particular cases, must of necessity expound and interpret that rule'.[1] This opinion followed Hamilton's position in the Federalist Papers that 'the interpretation of the laws is the proper and peculiar province of the courts. A constitution is in fact and must be regarded by the judges as a fundamental law. It therefore belongs to them to ascertain its meaning as well as the meaning of any particular act proceeding from the legislative body'.[2] These important pieces in American legal history are often said to support the view that as a matter of federal law the judiciary is supposed to resolve cases within its jurisdiction on the basis of fully independent interpretive reasoning. If that were true, American law would have adopted the separation model and the normative account I offered in Part Two would primarily be a revisionist one. In this part, I argue that much of judicial practice in public law litigation is incompatible with the separation model. Judicial doctrine institutionalises a complex scheme of regulating the interpretive responsibilities of the judiciary in the process of judicial review. Moreover, as judicial precedent underdetermines the institutional division of interpretive labour, the account presented in this book may, beyond its explanatory potential, provide guidance over the interpretive reconstruction of this area of the law.

[1] *Marbury v Madison*, 5 US 137, 177 (1803).

[2] *The Federalist*, No 78 (Alexander Hamilton).

11

The Province and Duty of the Judicial Department

I. From *Marbury* to the Clear Mistake Rule

In *Marbury v Madison*, the Supreme Court is understood to have held that federal courts are supposed to resolve disputes within their jurisdiction on the basis of an independent judicial interpretation of the Constitution and assessment as to the constitutionality of laws. The Court reasoned first that unconstitutional statutes lack legal validity. If the Constitution is paramount law, 'an act of the legislature repugnant to the constitution is void'.[1] The Court then proclaimed that it has the power to review the constitutionality of laws on independent judgement. It settled the principle that, in case of conflict as to the applicable law, it is 'of the very essence of judicial duty' to apply the Constitution since 'the constitution, and not such ordinary act, must govern the case to which they both apply'; and claimed judicial independence over this syllogism of conflict and inapplicability on the generic idea that it is 'emphatically the province and duty of the judicial department to say what the law is. Those who apply the rule to particular cases must, of necessity, expound and interpret that rule'.[2]

This latter claim does not address the creative character of constitutional interpretation. *Marbury* invokes traditional understandings about judicial duty and, strictly speaking, its independent judgement assumption relates to the resolution of the issue of constitutionality, a collateral finding of law that is necessary for determining the applicable rule of decision. Of course, the Federalist had also employed a functional argument: courts are supposed to act as 'an intermediate body between the people and the legislature in order … to keep the latter within the limits assigned to their authority'.[3] Still, the Hamiltonian reasoning assumes that constitutional interpretation explains the will of the people (formed in their capacity as exercising constituent power) that is superior to the will of the

[1] *Marbury*, 5 US, at 177.
[2] ibid, at 178, 177.
[3] *The Federalist*, No 78 (Alexander Hamilton).

legislature. In this regard, it is doubtful whether and how it is supposed to apply to norms that do not exhibit volitional transparency. Thus, a fair argument may be made that neither *Marbury*, nor the Federalist addressed the interpretive mandate of courts in constitutional issues of contested moral principle.

In fact, constitutional scholars and practitioners have always felt some uneasiness about the justification of *Marbury* as applied to the judicial resolution of highly contested issues of constitutional law. Some have pressed for a sharp limitation of *Marbury*. And many others argue that considerations of institutional role affect judicial reasoning. On related grounds, Professor Ely has famously claimed that Chief Justice Marshall's justification of judicial review does not fit ambitious conceptions of judicial reasoning; it better dovetails with what he calls the 'interpretivist' mode.[4]

Long before Ely's position, there had developed a respected line of jurisprudence arguing for a significantly limited judicial role in the exposition and enforcement of constitutional law. In a famous article written in 1893,[5] James Thayer claimed that it is 'the legislature to whom this power is given- this power … of putting an interpretation on the constitution which shall deeply affect the whole country … except as some individuals may find it for his private interest to carry the matter into court'.[6] In such a case, '[the Court] can only disregard the Act when those who have the right to make laws *have not merely made a mistake, but have made a very clear one*, so clear that it is not open to rational question'.[7] His position was based on a pragmatic understanding of constitutional interpretation in light of the comparative institutional position of courts and legislatures. The constitution admits of different reasonable interpretations; in many cases, we are told, there is no one right interpretation. Consequently, 'the ultimate question is not what is the true meaning of the constitution, but whether legislation is sustainable or not';[8] 'in such cases the constitution does not impose upon the legislature any one specific opinion but leaves open this range of choice'.[9] Since constitutional review is necessarily of a political function, courts should employ methods that 'befit their task'; this is so when courts examine merely the rationality of the legislative interpretation. Otherwise, by 'import[ing] their own opinion of the true construction',[10] they are stepping 'into the shoes of the law-maker'.[11] This argument is

[4] See John Hart Ely, *Democracy and Distrust: A Theory of Judicial Review* (Cambridge, Harvard University Press, 1980) 186 (fn 11).

[5] James Thayer, 'The Origin and Scope of the American Doctrine of Constitutional Law' (25 October 1893) 7 *Harv L Rev* 129.

[6] ibid, at 136 (since the court's role is incidental and postponed).

[7] ibid, at 144. See also *Sturges v Crowninshield*, 17 US (4 Wheat.) 122, 202–3 (1819) (a challenge can succeed only if 'the absurdity and injustice of applying the provision to the case would be so monstrous that all mankind would, without hesitation, unite in rejecting the application').

[8] Thayer, ibid, at 150.

[9] ibid, at 144.

[10] ibid, at 151.

[11] ibid, at 152 with references to Holmes.

ultimately rooted in a belief in the advantages of democratic governance and civic discourse: 'under no system can the power of courts go far to save a people from ruin; our chief protection lies elsewhere'.[12]

In approaching the force of Thayer's argument, we shall note that he does not confuse issues of judicial reach with the substance of constitutional construction. His argument, by and large, does not trivialise constitutional law, nor does he deny that legislators shall strive for the better construction of the Constitution.

The position he was advocating was not a lonely one. In fact it dovetails much of constitutional practice before the development of the economic due process jurisprudence.[13] And there have been voices in the Supreme Court in the twentieth century defending variants of the 'clear mistake' standard. One of them was, of course, Justice Frankfurter. In his view, 'matters of policy … are by definition matters which demand the resolution of conflicts of values and the elements of conflicting values are largely imponderable … The proper forum … is the body chosen for those purposes by the people'.[14]

In exhuming these arguments of the past, I do not intend to deny the primary role that the Supreme Court exercises in the exposition of constitutional law. Rather, I wish to sensitise the reader to the fact that the apparent transparency and deductive logic of *Marbury* is misleading and that subsequent American constitutional practice has also flirted with diametrically opposed views.

Having said that, one needs also to emphasise that the extreme positions of Professor Thayer and Justice Frankfurter finally came to be the dissenting view in the Court, and ultimately disappeared from the case law. This is nicely exhibited in one of the first liberal decisions of the Court in the post-New Deal era, *Board of Education v Barnette.* Justice Frankfurter argued forcefully against judicial activism, quoting Thayer for the proposition that '[the legislature] is entitled … as among all rationally permissible opinions as to what the constitution allows, to its own choice'.[15] He was committed to the view that this is the only way to bring the people to a sense of collective responsibility. His argument was the minority argument though. Both Justices Douglas and Black, who clashed later in *Griswold*, responded emphatically that 'decisions as to the constitutionality of particular laws which strike the substance of religious tenets and practices must be made by the Court'. The two judges went on to determine that 'these laws must, to be consistent with the first amendment, permit the widest toleration of conflicting viewpoints consistent with a society of free men'.[16]

[12] ibid, at 156.

[13] See, eg, *Adm'rs of Byrne v Adm'rs of Stewart*, 3 Des 466 (S Car 1812) ('it should be presumed that all [legislative] acts conform to [the Constitution] unless the contrary is manifest').

[14] *A.F. of L. v American Sash Co.* 355 U.S. 538, 557 (1949) (Frankfurter, J, concurring).

[15] *West Virginia State Board of Education v Barnette*, 319 US 624, 669 (1943) (Frankfurter, J, dissenting).

[16] ibid, at 644 (Black and Douglas, JJ, concurring).

It is fair to say that since *Marbury* the Court has been engaged in a neverending process of interpreting its institutional mandate. Operating within the frame of *Marbury*, it strives to structure and specify what it considers an appropriate institutional scheme to effectuate the Constitution and its underlying principles. And as institutional perceptions and choices are contested and change over time, so do the applicable standards of review.

It now appears well established that the Court has rejected the 'clear mistake' principle. More generally, the Court does not recognise authoritative force to constitutional determinations made by the political branches. In the process of judicial review the Court does not examine whether a *determination* as to the constitutionality of a statute[17] or an *abstract* interpretation of the Constitution offered by another body *itself* deserves deference. Furthermore, the Court assumes primary responsibility for many component judgements employed in the process of a constitutional determination. For example, the Court relied on independent moral reasoning in determining that the right of privacy is constitutionally protected and that it includes the right to abortion: 'We, therefore, conclude that the right of personal privacy includes the abortion decision', the *Roe v Wade* Court tells us.[18] But beyond such elementary findings, there is a complex doctrinal landscape in need of understanding and rationalisation.

It is the task of this Part Three to shed some light on the institutional topography of current doctrine. But first, we need to approach the outer contours of this project, areas excluded from the *Marbury* landscape on the so-called political question doctrine—with particular emphasis on the lack of judicially manageable standards for performing constitutional review.

II. The Interplay between Scope and Intensity of Review

A. The Political Question Doctrine and the Separation Model

A proper place to commence is a field of the law where the *Marbury* doctrine is inapplicable under principles precluding judicial review. The main example is the political question doctrine, covering non-reviewable ('non-justiciable') political questions whose resolution does not lie within the constitutional reach of the judicial power.

17 *INS v Chadha*, 362 US 919, 941–42 (1983) ('No policy underlying the political question doctrine suggests that Congress or the Executive, or both acting in concert and in compliance with Art. I, can decide the constitutionality of a statute; that is a decision for the courts'). See also *Zivotofsky v Clinton*, 566 US __ (2012) (slip op, at 8).

18 *Roe v Wade*, 410 US 113, 154 (1973).

As framed, the political question doctrine involves jurisdictional limitations. The Court lacks power to expound and interpret the rule simply because the matter in controversy is not subject to judicial resolution, while the pertinent dispositions of the political branch are to be taken as authoritative to the extent needed for issuance of decision. Norms governing the jurisdiction of the judicial branch differ from norms regulating the interpretive power of the judiciary in resolving cases and controversies lying within judicial jurisdiction.

This classificatory scheme does not correspond to the separation model, that is to say, the institutional alignment of judicial power along the distinction between issues of law and issues of policy within the boundaries of law. True, almost by definition, constitutional review does not extend to policy conduct within the boundaries of constitutional law. Indeed, in *Marbury* the political question doctrine was understood to preclude review of purely discretionary conduct, like the presidential decision to veto a bill.[19] However, much of the debate over the scope of the political question doctrine ever since has involved considerations about constitutional implementation and compliance; about whether, in narrowly defined areas, the political branches should have exclusive authority over the specification and enforcement of the pertinent *law*. And its interpretive limitation in recent times is best understood as an interpretive reconstruction of the applicable institutional structure, with a view to improving the collective effort to construct the more appropriate interpretations of the law. Understanding this will set the ground to move on and examine how institutional concerns of the very same nature are present in many other disputed issues of constitutional law—even though they do not justify judicial abstinence.

B. The Political Question Doctrine in the Architecture of Constitutional Implementation

The Supreme Court traditionally exercised an eclectic stance in deciding when not to review the constitutional judgements of its co-equal branches of government. The content of that stance varied during the history of the Court, reflecting the prevailing views of the time about the role of the judicial branch in the exposition and implementation of the law of the Constitution.

An exemplar of times past is *Colegrove v Green*, a case in which the Court refused to examine the constitutionality of a districting scheme on the grounds that the Constitution confers upon Congress the exclusive power to ensure compliance with the Constitution[20] in the litigated issue. The Court was primarily

[19] *Marbury*, above n 1, at 165–70.

[20] 328 US 549 (1946).

concerned that involvement with politically contested issues would undermine its institutional legitimacy. Writing for the majority, Justice Frankfurter stressed that the controversy before his colleagues 'concerns matters that bring courts into immediate and active relations with party contests. From the determination of such issues this Court has traditionally remained aloof … Courts ought not to enter this political thicket.'[21] That was the time when the Court was particularly sensitive to its perceived legitimacy in the eyes of the political branches. And he was the judge who so consistently personified that concern. Fearing that the institutional legitimacy of the Court was fragile, President's Roosevelt's appointee was exceedingly preoccupied with the tactics that the Court is supposed to employ to preserve its political capital.[22]

As we move into the 1950s and 1960s, this conservative view about the role of the Court in constitutional implementation eroded. The wide-ranging prudential concerns of Justice Frankfurter were considered to lack both firm legal foundation and normative appeal. It became more and more evident that respect for the constitutional role of a political department does not entail yielding to the latter's constitutional judgements.[23] To the extent that the political question doctrine were to survive, it could no longer be understood as an expression of judicial humility, or a symbol of good standing in the Washington establishment. Rather, it needed a functional account that would explain when judicial abstinence is justified in light of the Court's distinct function in a well-ordered polity, and, in particular, of the fact that the Court is especially needed to end those injustices that the political process fails to redress or even address.

Justice Frankfurter had not appreciated the fact that the shameful malapportionment of state legislatures was such a case of political gridlock. His colleagues reconsidered the issue in the seminal case of *Baker v Carr* and held that the apportionment issue before them did not raise a non-justiciable political question under the Equal Protection Clause. Writing for the majority, Justice Brennan argued that the basis and specification of the doctrine 'is itself a delicate exercise in constitutional interpretation [lying within] the responsibility of this Court as ultimate interpreter of the [Constitution].'[24] This would appear perplexing, but the most appropriate understanding is that under *Marbury* the Court has ultimate responsibility to interpret the law governing the Court's interpretive assignment.

The Court's reasoning—as I would interpret it—proceeded as follows: Any interpretation of the law (including jurisdictional law) is supposed to make sense of textual and doctrinal considerations. Accordingly, courts first examine whether

[21] ibid, at 553, 556.

[22] The best defence of that concern was given by Justice Frankfurter's clerk Alexander Bickel in 'The Supreme Court, 1960 Term: Forward: The Passive Virtues' (1961) 75 *Harv L Rev* 40.

[23] 'Interpretation of the Constitution does not imply a lack of respect for a coordinate [branch]', *Goldwater v Carter*, 444 US 996, 1001 (1979) (Powell, J, concurring).

[24] 369 US 186, 211 (1962).

there is a textually demonstrable commitment of the interpretive issue to a coordinate political department. If not, courts are supposed to consider the appropriateness of attributing finality to an action of a political department and the availability of satisfactory standards for judicial determination. By applying these criteria, the Court determined that resolving the question at issue would not 'risk embarrassment of our Government abroad or grave disturbance at home', nor would it involve 'policy determinations for which judicially manageable standards are lacking'.

The political question doctrine is to be understood within a wider account of the role of each branch in specifying and enforcing the Constitution. It shall best be construed as part of a structural scheme aiming at satisfactory constitutional implementation, by singling out those issues of constitutional construction and, in particular, implementation that should be assigned to the conclusive authority of another co-equal branch of government. This understanding of the doctrine illuminates its legal basis. As Justice Brennan emphasised, the doctrine rests on an appropriate interpretation of constitutional law that the Court performs on independent basis.[25] Constitutional law settles issues of institutional assignment either through explicit textual delegation, or, on more constructive reasoning, by setting up structures that effectuate the constitutional scheme[26] (as is the case with *Marbury* itself as well). Relevant considerations in interpreting such assignments include whether 'judicial reason' cannot adequately resolve the substantive issue in dispute and whether there is strong ground to insist on the finality of the decisions of another branch.

The first of these considerations invites us to construct an account of judicial reason under the paradigmatic justification thesis; and, in particular cases, to examine whether we can articulate appropriate standards for judicial review, doctrinal tests that mediate between abstract accounts of the constitutional norm and the resolution of the issue in controversy. The main difficulty in this enterprise lies in the fact, illuminated by the paradigmatic justification thesis, that such standards of judicial implementation are accountable to the applicable substantive constitutional principles—principles to be effectuated by the synergy of political and judicial constitutional implementation.

[25] For this very reason, the doctrine does not contradict *Marbury.* See Gerald Gunther, 'Judicial Hegemony and Legislative Autonomy: The *Nixon* Case and the Impeachment Process' (1974) 22 *UCLA L Rev* 30, 33–34, ('there is nothing in *Marbury v Madison* that precludes a constitutional interpretation which gives final authority in another branch').

[26] See *Gilligan v Morgan*, 413 US 1, 10 (1973) ('[i]t would be difficult to think of a clearer example of the type of governmental action that was intended by the Constitution to be left to the political branches directly responsible … It is this power of oversight and control of military force by elected representatives and officials which underlies our entire constitutional system'). Note that for the purpose of my argument it is not relevant whether in some circumstances 'prudential considerations' may be most relevant. Yet, I am inclined to think that even such considerations are best to be understood through constitutional lenses.

Indeed, as Justice Frankfurter accurately noted in dissent, the *Baker* Court was actually asked 'to choose among competing bases of representation-ultimately, really, among competing theories of political philosophy'.[27] And its decision is important in this respect because it acknowledged that the judiciary is not ill-equipped in principle to consider issues of political justice pertaining to constitutional interpretation. In the years that followed *Baker*, the Court would not normally acquiesce in violations of the Constitution on the mere basis that the issues involved are being contested in the political arena or that they raise difficult judgements of political philosophy. It would rather address them, inviting constitutional scholars to envisage, and sometimes to idealise the Court as a forum of principle, in Dworkin's famous metaphor.

Controversies do remain, as does the occasional, yet futile pursuit of 'comprehensive and neutral principles' and 'agreed upon model[s] of fair and effective representation',[28] but they reflect competing conceptions of institutional legitimacy in the light of competing visions of public reason and constitutional justice. This is apparent in the deadlock over justiciability in partisan (as opposed to racial—see section C, below) gerrymandering cases. The inability of the Court to conclude, one way or another, shows that the articulation and endorsement of judicially manageable standards presupposes some solid understanding by a majority of the Court of the applicable substantive principles.[29] Once such an understanding is available, it is then possible, on institutional grounds, to consider the proper role of the judiciary in supervising the enforcement of the applicable principles. Indeed, consideration of pertinent institutional grounds normally presupposes a confident position over what principled resolution entails.[30]

A disturbing complication in this regard arises when uncritical invocation of institutional grounds has the effect of silencing the applicable substantive principles. For instance, the non-justiciability of partisan gerrymandering cases was defended by Justice O'Connor on the fact that 'members of the Democratic and Republican Parties cannot claim that they are a discrete and insular group vulnerable to exclusion from the political process' and, at any rate, that there was 'no proof' that political gerrymandering cannot be cured by the

[27] 369 US 189, 300 (1962) (Frankfurter, J, dissenting).

[28] *Vieth v Jubelirer*, 541 US 267, 306–07 (2004) (Kennedy, J, concurring in the judgment).

[29] Justice Kennedy's concurrence in *Vieth* is an excellent statement of the accountability of judicial standards to applicable substantive principles. Yet, it frames the matter in a mentality reminiscent of past preoccupation with neutral principles: 'Because there are yet no agreed upon substantive principles of fairness in districting, we have no basis on which to define clear, manageable, and politically neutral standards for measuring the particular burden a given partisan classification imposes on representational rights (Kennedy, J, concurring in the judgment)'. ibid, at 307–8.

[30] Bickel has famously argued that an important ground for lack of judicial capacity is the intractability of the issue to principled resolution. Alexander Bickel, *The Least Dangerous Branch: The Supreme Court at the Bar of Politics* (Indianapolis, Bobbs-Merrill, 1962) 184. On the misconceived tendency to collapse principle to neutrality see ch 8, n 32 and ch 10, n 25, above.

political process.[31] Justice O'Connor offered further arguments and I do not wish to diminish the coherence of her position. But it is important to see that this line of argumentation, which surfaces also in areas of nominal, highly deferential review, cannot by any means be dispositive; most importantly it fails to deal with the magnitude of the constitutional wrong whenever the political process is in fact dominated by invidious partisan factors, and with the appropriate institutional inquiry on the role of the judiciary in detecting such instances—without, of course, incurring undue repercussions and running a high risk of error (false detections).

Justification of the scope of review is also subject to various systemic considerations. The second set of criteria (the need for swiftness and finality, and structural issues) points to such concerns. For example, as Professor Tribe has argued, the elaboration of substantive criteria for amendment appropriateness should be considered a political question and Congressional determinations as to procedural conformity to article V should be treated with substantial deference given that amendments are the only way for the political branches to overturn judicial interpretations of the Constitution.[32] Similarly, Justice Rehnquist has noted that preclusion of judicial review for impeachments is justified in light of the fact that 'impeachment was designed to be the only check on the judicial branch by the legislature'.[33] What is important, from our viewpoint, is that the employment of such considerations is to be justified under constitutional justice, given the overall tasks of public institutions, and not offered as a pretence rationalising schemes of privilege.

This understanding of the political question doctrine enables the operation of the doctrine in ways that do not betray the commitment to constitutional justice. In applying it, courts are not necessarily supposed to hold that there is no law to apply, or to imply that the political branches are under no legal duty to enforce the applicable law of the Constitution. The non-justiciability of a claim is fully compatible with the recognition of both textual legal basis and applicable intermediate norms that do not nonetheless contain administrable standards to review certain issues of implementation and enforcement.[34]

31 *Davis v Bandemer*, 478 US 109, 152 (1986) (O'Connor, J, concurring in the judgment). The plurality in *Vieth*, joined by Justice O'Connor, was more transparent on the underlying substantive conception, considering that partisan gerrymandering involves merely an 'excessive injection' of otherwise legitimate political considerations. Above n 28, at 293.

32 Laurence Tribe, 'A Constitution We Are Amending: In Defense of a Restrained Judicial Role' (1983) 97 *Harvard L Rev* 433–45.

33 *Nixon v United States*, 506 US 224 (1993).

34 *Vieth*, above n 28, at 313–14, 316 (Kennedy, J, concurring in the judgment) ('The Fourteenth Amendment standard governs; and there is no doubt of that. My analysis only notes that if a subsidiary standard could show how an otherwise permissible classification, as applied, burdens representational rights, we could conclude that appellants' evidence states a provable claim under the Fourteenth Amendment standard … Finally, I do not understand the plurality to conclude that partisan gerrymandering that disfavors one party is permissible. Indeed, the Court seems to acknowledge it is not … That said, courts must be cautious about adopting a standard that turns on whether the partisan interests in the redistricting process were excessive').

C. The Continuity between Scope and Intensity of Review

Putting aside systemic considerations, it is an open question whether complete preclusion of review may ever be justified under the paradigmatic justification thesis, in light of the arguments against institutional rigidity presented in chapter eight (sections II and IV). For example, many foreign policy questions have been held to be unreviewable political questions given the expertise needed for appropriate resolution.[35] But it has been pointed out that the judiciary is institutionally competent to provide some principled guidance on constitutional questions even in the field of foreign policy. In refusing to do so, the argument goes, the Court is confusing deference to judgements made by expert bodies with abdication of its role.[36] Alternatively, the Court could encourage responsible performance of executive constitutional duties by establishing a heavy presumption of non-reviewability.[37] Such a test would not be too malleable and a court would have a real burden to justify a decision to exercise review.

At any rate, the trend to limit the operation of the political question doctrine has been coupled with an effort to tailor the applicable standards of review so that they take account of the institutional concerns at play. For instance, after *Baker v Carr*, courts have been cognizant (at least in theory) of the fact that 'federal-court review of districting legislation represents a serious intrusion on the most vital of local functions. … The courts, in assessing the sufficiency of a challenge to a districting plan, must be sensitive to the complex interplay of forces that enter a legislature's redistricting calculus'.[38] In racial gerrymandering, this principle of caution has been held to require 'courts to exercise extraordinary caution in adjudicating claims that a State has drawn district lines on the basis of race. The plaintiff's burden is to show … that race was the predominant factor motivating the legislature's decision to place a significant number of voters within or without a particular district'.[39] In the area of political gerrymandering, a plurality

[35] See Fritz Scharpf, 'Judicial Review and the Political Question: A Functional Analysis' (1966) 75 *Yale L J* 517, 567.

[36] See the discussion in Erwin Chemerinsky, *Constitutional Law: Principles and Policies*, 5th edn (New York, Wolters Kluwer, 2016) 139.

[37] Justice Souter noted in *Nixon v United States* (above n 33, at 253) (Souter, J, concurring) that 'if the Senate were to act in a manner seriously undermining the integrity of its results … judicial interference might well be appropriate'. And Justice Kennedy hinted in *Vieth* (above n 28, at 312) (Kennedy, J, concurring in the judgment) that 'if courts refuse to entertain any claims of partisan gerrymandering, the temptation to use partisan favoritism in districting in an unconstitutional manner will grow', leaving the issue over the existence of manageable standards open for future reexamination.

[38] *Miller v Johnson*, 515 US 900, 915–16 (1995).

[39] ibid, at 916. The Court clarified that a determination that race was 'the predominant, overriding factor' is a prerequisite for subjecting the plan to strict scrutiny (at 920). The minority, while offering a different standard and emphasising that judicial intervention is mainly needed to prevent dilution of 'minority voting strength', was in agreement that 'federalism and the slim judicial competence to draw district lines weigh heavily against judicial intervention in apportionment decisions; as a rule, the task should remain within the domain of state legislatures'. ibid, at 936–37 (Ginsburg, J, dissenting).

of the Court retreated back to non-justiciability, while Justice Stevens in dissent forcefully accused the plurality of collapsing arguments for deferential review to a rule of non-justiciability, and proposed a 'narrow' standard of review that 'would cover only a few meritorious claims, but it would preclude extreme abuses'.[40] In between, Justice Kennedy delivered his pivotal concurring opinion, accepting that the claimants had stated no valid claim under the equal protection clause as no manageable standard was available for determining their specific allegations for impermissible gerrymandering; yet, he explicitly refused to 'foreclose all possibility of judicial relief if some limited and precise rationale were found to correct an established violation of the Constitution in some redistricting cases'.[41]

This interplay between non-justiciability and narrow review helps us see why the political question doctrine is not to be treated as an isolated, anomalous feature of constitutional adjudication. It is extreme in its effect since it blocks judicial review. However, it is inspired by considerations that apply with lesser force to many other cases of constitutional adjudication. Indeed, I argue that it is the limiting case of a phenomenon that is prevalent in public law adjudication. Many constitutional disputes raise issues that cannot be fully resolved by independent judicial reason alone. In such cases, the judiciary performs the judgements it considers appropriate for independent judicial resolution and defers to and incorporates in its reasoning the relevant judgements of the political branches of government (normally subjecting them to review of varying intensity). This will be the main topic of the following chapter. At this point, I emphasise that the underlying institutional concerns are not restricted to so-called political questions. Rather, they operate there in an extreme fashion, by justifying the assignment of final interpretive authority to another branch. But there is a whole spectrum of cases that require a more sophisticated assignment of interpretive labour—usually incorporated in a variety of standards for review. And the way one understands the role of institutional considerations in the limiting case (where no judicially manageable standard is available) has evident implications for the way one understands their role in ordinary ones. In fact, Justice Frankfurter and Justice Brennan, the two judges mainly associated with the preservation and the constriction of the political question doctrine, are perfect examples of across-the-board judicial passivity and activism respectively.

[40] *Vieth*, above n 28, at 339 (Stevens, J, dissenting).

[41] ibid, at 306 (Kennedy, J, concurring in the judgment).

12

The Subtlety of Constitutional Doctrine

I. Constitutional Doctrine and Schemes of Deference

A. Introduction

Constitutional scholars have emphasised that in the process of applying constitutional law, the Supreme Court crafts 'doctrine'.[1] The term constitutional doctrine refers to intermediate norms that interpretively reformulate a broad constitutional norm and structure its application to varying sets of facts.

Constitutional doctrine serves various functions. It enables the Court to discipline itself and limit the discretion of lower courts; it facilitates interpretive convergence and stability while channeling further constitutional specification. I wish to emphasise here that constitutional doctrine also serves an important institutional purpose: to set up and operationalise the applicable standard of judicial review and, in particular, the scope and intensity of review over the various considerations implicated in a complete constitutional determination. In this sense, it provides an institutional structure for organising the substantive judgements of the reviewing court and the reviewed body in the constitutional determination at issue. Such a structure provides relative institutional formality, limiting the kind of opportunistic or myopic institutional casuistry that flourishes in the absence of applicable institutional norms; at the same time, it sets in motion path-dependent trajectories of institutional elaboration, allowing for occasional contest and path-constrained revision.

In operationalising the scope of review, constitutional doctrine does not necessarily exhaust applicable constitutional law. It rather captures judicially cognizable categories of constitutional violation. The task of specifying and applying the pertinent law not captured by the doctrine is left to the political branches. In operationalising the intensity of review, constitutional doctrine performs a similar function, distinguished from the former case only by degree. The substantive judgements built into the doctrine or performed under the doctrine by the court

[1] See Charles Fried, 'Constitutional Doctrine' (1994) 107 *Harvard L Rev* 1140 and Richard Fallon, *Implementing the Constitution* (Cambridge, Harvard University Press, 2000).

itself do not exhaust the overall interpretive judgement needed for the resolution of the case. They do so only when combined with the pertinent substantive judgements of the reviewed body under the structure provided by the doctrine. In this sense, the doctrine has both a substantive and an institutional function.

B. The Issue of Judicial Under-enforcement

Let me elaborate on this scheme by way of example. The law of the Constitution includes a norm of substantive due process. There is no canonical formulation of that norm partly because there is no firm textual provision to support it. The Fifth and the Fourteenth Amendments merely provide that government shall not deprive any person of liberty without due process of law and that no state shall abridge the privileges or immunities of citizens of the United States. On one interpretive formulation of the pertinent norm, assumed in much of academic literature and case law, individuals have a general constitutional right to liberty that is compatible with the recognition of an equivalent right for all. This right includes the right that the government does not restrict the claims, privileges and powers associated with liberty without due justification. No doubt, liberty is not to be equated with plenary freedom from any kind of restraint, but at least it does include a significant protected scope, valuable for the expression and development of one's autonomy, authenticity and dignity.

Anyone associated with constitutional practice will readily remind us that existing judicial doctrine does not embody the above-mentioned norm or a variant of it. The Court has rather constructed a doctrinal web that is supposed to capture many, but not all violations of the norm. For example, the Court has distinguished between fundamental liberty interests and other legitimate interests, and subjects interference with each category of interests to a different standard of review. Non-marginal interference with a fundamental liberty interest is normally appropriate if and only if it is the least restrictive alternative for the protection of a compelling state interest. On the other hand, interference with other legitimate interests is appropriate if it is rationally related to a legitimate state goal. In applying this doctrinal test (in a simplified version; details are not relevant), the Court upholds statutes interfering with economic liberty (other than existing proprietary or contractual interests) so long as: (a) under any reasonable assumption of facts, (b) it might be thought that the measures adopted would be a rational way to serve (c) any hypothesised public-regarding value, (d) while allowing for both under and over-inclusiveness. For instance, in *Williamson v Lee Optical Co.*,[2] the Court upheld an Oklahoma law prescribing that only a limited category of licensed professionals could fit lenses (including changing broken ones) without prescription! The Court assumed that the statute aimed at the protection of public health and reasoned that the legislature might have thought that a prescription may often be necessary.

[2] 348 US 483 (1955).

What sense are we to make of such doctrinal tests? Two possibilities have received attention in the literature. The first is to say that doctrinal tests exhaust constitutional law. We can call this the *reduction* thesis. Justice Holmes, for example, has famously argued that 'a constitution is not intended to embody a particular economic theory'. In his view, since the Constitution 'is made for people of fundamentally different views', the liberty clause in the Fourteenth Amendment protects individuals only against measures that 'a rational and fair man necessarily would admit that [they] would infringe fundamental principles as they have been understood by the traditions of our people or our law'.[3] On this account, the law does not recognise a general right to life and liberty.

I suppose that most practitioners would not subscribe to such a view. They would argue, for example, that 'the Constitution protects "ordered liberty" including a continuum of rights to be free from arbitrary impositions and purposeless restraints'. At the same time, they would insist, judicial review 'has no warrant to substitute one reasonable resolution of the contending positions for another, but authority to supplant the balance already struck ... only when it falls outside the realm of the reasonable'.[4] Doctrinal tests formalise this general, yet vague pursuit on the basis of the liberty interest affected and other relevant considerations.

How are we to rationalise this understanding? And what are the relevant considerations? In a seminal article, Lawrence Sager invoked the distinction between the content of a constitutional provision, as best understood, and the scope and depth of its *judicial enforceability*. On this distinction, he argued that constitutional doctrine often does not exhaust the underlying constitutional norm. There is normative space between the two that reflects the Court's understanding of judicial institutional role and other strategic concerns.[5]

Along with Professor Sager, I believe that the reduction thesis must be rejected. The case study is economic liberty. The constitutional status of economic liberty cannot reasonably be considered as infirm as current judicial doctrine implies. In market-based societies, certain aspects of economic liberty are necessary for the development and full and informed exercise of our capacity to pursue our conception of good life. Consider, for example, occupational liberty.[6] While the right to access to a common occupation may require a regulatory framework to become operational, its exercise

[3] *Lochner v New York*, 198 US 45, 75–76 (1905) (Holmes, J, dissenting).

[4] *Washington v Glucksberg*, 117 S Ct 2258, 2281 (1997) (Souter, J, concurring). Justice Souter considered the legislation challenged in *Glucksberg* reasonable after acknowledging 'the legislative institutional competence as the better one to deal with that claim at this time'.

[5] Lawrence Sager, Fair Measure: 'The Legal Status of Underenforced Constitutional Norms' (1978) 91 *Harvard L Rev* 1212 and *Justice in Plainclothes, A Theory of American Constitutional Practice* (New Haven, Yale University Press, 2004) 84–128.

[6] In California, for instance, the interest to engage in a common and otherwise lawful occupation is a constitutionally protected liberty interest. State interference with its exercise is constitutional if it is reasonably related to a valid public interest. In *Perrine v Municipal Court of East L.A. Judicial District*, the Supreme Court of California held that an ordinance excluding individuals with past criminal convictions from operating bookstores is unconstitutional because the requirement imposed is not a permissible occupational qualification. 97 Cal Rptr 320, 324 (1971).

is no less of a 'personal choice central to individual dignity and autonomy'[7] than many of the non-enumerated fundamental liberty interests recognised by the Court. Furthermore, it is implicit in the American constitutional tradition, whether liberal or republican, that governmental conduct is supposed to serve the public interest. Public institutions are supposed to act as the collective arms of free and equal citizens rather than as the instruments of particular groups and individuals. The republican character of the constitutional structure does not tolerate the enactment of private-regarding statutes;[8] rather, it requires that representatives of the people aim at specifying and pursuing the public interest. These considerations would normally suggest that economic liberty does restrict legislative omnipotence in the field. If so, one needs an institutional explanation of existing judicial doctrine, along the lines of Sager's distinction and of the theoretical framework presented here.

A similar pattern applies to equal protection claims not implicating suspect classifications or fundamental rights. The Court has proclaimed that 'the Equal Protection Clause of the Fourteenth Amendment commands that no State shall "deny to any person within its jurisdiction the equal protection of the laws," which is essentially a direction that all persons similarly situated should be treated alike. … [Yet] the general rule is that legislation is presumed to be valid, and will be sustained if the classification drawn by the statute is rationally related to a legitimate state interest. When social or economic legislation is at issue, the Equal Protection Clause allows the States wide latitude …'[9] The normative space between the two propositions is here more straightforward, given the constitutional text. At the same time, the Court has appreciated that the extremely passive institutional role reserved for courts under the rational basis test may fail to capture socio-economic classifications well outside the realm of the reasonable. Thus, given the occasional salience of the dignitary interests affected and the emergence of distinctive issues of principle, the Court has at times applied the test with bite, holding stigma-implicating classifications unreasonable.[10]

[7] *Obergefell v Hodges*, 576 US __ (2015) (slip op, at 10).

[8] See Frank Michelman, 'Law's Republic' (1988) 97 *Yale L J* 1493, Cass Sunstein, 'Interest Groups in American Public Law' (1985) 39 *Stanford L Rev* 29, Tribe, *American Constitutional Law*, 3rd edn, vol I (New York, Foundation Press, 2000) 1365 (the Court has never accepted that there exists no public interest beyond the summation of competing private interests but has continually pointed to reasons that could justify legislative actions in terms of the public interest) and Dworkin, *Law's Empire* (Cambridge, Harvard University Press, 1986) 345 (a community of principle does not treat legislation simply as a mere matter of compromises). See also, from the takings context, *Kelo v New London*, 545 US 469, 478, 480 (2005), distinguishing between the public purpose requirement and the applicable standard of review ('Nor would the City be allowed to take property under the mere pretext of a public purpose, when its actual purpose was to bestow a private benefit. … The disposition of this case therefore turns on the question whether the City's development plan serves a "public purpose." Without exception, our cases have defined that concept broadly, reflecting our longstanding policy of deference to legislative judgments in this field').

[9] *Cleburne v Cleburne Living Ctr.*, 473 US 432, 439–40 (1985).

[10] See paradigmatically *Plyler v Doe*, 457 US 202, 223 (1982) ('Section 21.031 imposes a lifetime hardship on a discrete class of children not accountable for their disabling status. The stigma of illiteracy will mark them for the rest of their lives. By denying these children a basic education, we deny

Let us move beyond these familiar themes. In *United States v Bajakajian*,[11] involving the forfeiture of currency for failure to report its transportation, the Court developed the doctrinal test governing judicial review of government action under the excessive fines clause of the Eighth Amendment. The Court emphasised that the 'touchstone of the constitutional inquiry under the Excessive Fines Clause is the principle of proportionality'[12] and noted that excessive means 'suppressing the usual, the proper, or a normal measure of proportion'. Yet, the Court accepted that legislative judgment deserves substantial deference, counseling 'against requiring strict proportionality between the amount of a punitive forfeiture and the gravity of a criminal offense', and determined that the applicable standard for judicial review is one of 'gross disproportionality'.[13]

On this line of reasoning, it would be odd to suggest that the Constitution simply requires that the State does not impose grossly disproportionate fines: this is what courts are supposed to examine in the process of judicial review. The applicable doctrinal test reflects a division of labour between courts and legislatures over the specification of the proportionality principle. The requirement of gross disproportionality reflects institutional judgements about the comparative competency of courts and agencies. And as such judgements are often general and overinclusive, there is space for adjustments. In fact, the *Bajakajian* Court applied this test with real bite, holding the forfeiture at issue unconstitutional, after noting that the respondent did not fit into the class of persons for whom the statute was primarily designed.

II. The Dual Character of Constitutional Doctrine

A. The Dual Character

I have presented case law patterns that exemplify the divergence between (judicially under-enforced) constitutional law and judicial doctrine. They are not isolated. In fact, Professor Fallon has expanded upon the insight of under-enforcement and has argued for a fundamental and pervasive distinction between constitutional meaning and the doctrine the Court crafts for the purpose of implementing

them the ability to live within the structure of our civic institutions …') and *United States v Windsor*, 570 US __ (2013) (slip op, at 21) ('The avowed purpose and practical effect of the law here in question are to impose a disadvantage, a separate status, and so a stigma upon all who enter into same-sex marriages made lawful by the unquestioned authority of the States'). On rational basis with bite, see Gerald Gunther, 'The Supreme Court, 1971 Term—Foreword: In Search of Evolving Doctrine on a Changing Court: A Model for a Newer Equal Protection' (1972) 86 *Harv L Rev* 1, 18–19.

[11] 118 S Ct 2028 (1998).

[12] ibid, at 2036.

[13] ibid, at 2037.

the Constitution.[14] For our purposes, it is important to note that constitutional doctrine is the main mechanism enabling the Court to arrange the division of interpretive labour in implementing constitutional norms; not merely in the field of judicial passivity, but throughout the realm of constitutional review. We will examine shortly the operation of this function in areas of heightened judicial scrutiny. But first, let us draw the major theoretical implications from the insight of judicial under-enforcement.

The divergence between (under-enforced) constitutional law and judicial doctrine reflects what we may call the *dual* character of constitutional doctrine. First, doctrine has a substantive function; it provides an interpretation *of the normative content of substantive constitutional law*. Yet, such interpretation sometimes covers only part of applicable law, capturing violations of a certain kind or magnitude. In this sense, constitutional doctrine diverges from exhaustive formulations of applicable constitutional law on the same level of generality. Secondly, it has an institutional function, regulating the applicable scope and intensity of review and thereby organising the judicial interpretive assignment. It specifies *norms of adjudication* governing the role of courts over issues of constitutional specification in the process of resolving disputes. Such institutional norms supply propositions of a higher order. They specify the kinds of substantive constitutional judgements that courts are directed to make themselves and the way they are structured with relevant judgements of the reviewed body, in the process of forming an overall constitutional determination and resolving the dispute at hand.

B. The Justification of Constitutional Doctrine

In crafting constitutional doctrine, the Court employs substantive constitutional interpretation. First, the substantive norms the doctrine specifies have to be tailored to the corresponding area of constitutional law. Secondly, in determining which judgements of the political branches are to be invested with authoritative character over courts, the Court needs some idea about what would count as a good account of the pertinent constitutional requirements.

The second point is crucial for us. It reflects the idea that the institutional scheme shaped by doctrine—the scope and degree of deference, or the rejection thereof etc—is answerable to normative criteria, like the criteria defended in Part Two. The paradigmatic rationale for the doctrine's institutional function is that, overall, compliance with it is expected to make it more likely that the pertinent dispute will be resolved on the basis of an appropriate specification of constitutional law. The point of institutional norms and arguments is to help us better specify and

[14] Fallon, above n 1, at 76 ff. See also Mitchell Berman, 'Constitutional Decision Rules' (2004) 90 *Va L Rev* 1, and Kermit Roosevelt, 'Constitutional Calcification: How the Law Becomes What the Court Does' (2005) 91 *Va L Rev* 1649.

apply constitutional law; not to subvert it! Hence, their paradigmatic justification requires both a more general substantive frame and institutional analysis about the contribution expected from the political branches and the reviewing court in living up to the pertinent ideals and principles.

This has important implications for the responsibility of the Court in crafting and revising doctrine. Rational performance of the task presupposes, even in areas of deference, a general account of at least some of the pertinent substantive principles, including a rudimentary idea of the interplay of considerations of legitimacy and of just content in their specification. Such an account, as we have discussed in chapters nine and ten, should in principle be flexible enough to allow adequate room for meaningful deliberation in public culture and the political process. At the same time, it is continuously subject to specification, refinement, and potential revision in the actual operation of the doctrine, in its confrontation with the contingencies of constitutional practice and in the exercise of discursive reciprocity with political institutions.

Justification, of course, is a normative project. Practised constitutional doctrine, on the other hand, like all practised norms, often fails to meet the applicable justificatory standards. Constitutional doctrine is not always the product of functional design (chapter seven, section III). It is continuously shaped, refined and revised in path-dependent processes, under contingencies of adversarial litigation, interest group conflict and strategic institutional behaviour. Its components are often dressed up in apologetic language or subjected to indiscriminate dismissal. And its institutional or substantive function is often not transparent to practitioners. Even when courts are aware of its deficiencies, their power to revise or discard it is constrained by further norms and, in particular, the rule of precedent. As a result, we need to distinguish (schematically, no doubt) between satisfaction of the paradigmatic justification thesis, mere legitimacy and unacceptability.

Still, constitutional theory has the duty to exercise critique, and to investigate ways for functional reconstruction. In this course, it has to engage in substantive argument and institutional analysis. Otherwise we may not assess, for instance, the highly deferential standard of review in socio-economic matters. Is it based on partial and over-inclusive institutional assumptions (for instance, the idea that failures of the political process are judicially cognizable only in the presence of systemic failures, like those involving suspect groups or classifications)? Does it rest on a simplified understanding of the applicable principles (for instance, the idea that economic regulation is politics as usual)? We will return to this point in discussing the mentality of constitutional jurisprudence towards the end of this book (chapter fourteen, section V).

C. Constitutional Reasoning Beyond Judicial Enforcement

In rejecting uncritical equation of constitutional law with constitutional doctrine, I argued for intelligent deliberation about the appropriate scope of judicial engagement in constitutional implementation. We also need to avoid the antipodal risk of focusing on constitutional doctrine while ignoring the contribution of the political branches to constitutional law. In fact, we need to distance ourselves from a predominant sensibility to the effect that constitutional doctrine is all that matters.

This sensibility has both institutional and conceptual, so to speak, sources. The main determinant is the focus of academic commentary on the judicial process, especially in the light of its reason-giving character. As Lon Fuller has famously claimed, adjudication is, in aspiration, 'a device which gives formal and institutional expression to the influence of reasoned judgment in human affairs'.[15] The political branches, on the other hand—and unless they operate under specific enforcement mandates—normally do not act upon well-articulated constitutional judgements. They make public policy by balancing competing social interests. And their modes of reasoning do not involve precedent-based, common law-like argumentation. As a result, all we have from them are the ways ideas of constitutional justice are specified in the process of shaping public policies. And such specification is subject to wide *variation* (both temporal and subject-dependent, as shifting majorities or different bodies in a federal system make choices of constitutional significance) and to *opacity* with regard to their underlying (sometimes merely projectable) constitutional principles.

This does not mean that the contribution of the political branches is minimal. Constitutional interpretation involves various component judgements, so to speak, that do not have to be presented in doctrinal fashion. Constitutional doctrine, on the conceptual frame defended here, acknowledges the contribution of the political branches in filling that content. At the same time, this frame also explains that the full effect of constitutional law in the United States is often *opaque*. Sometimes, courts provide us with a general description of applicable constitutional law and then proceed with the applicable scope[16] and standard[17] of review. But in many cases, as in economic regulation, they simply start with doctrine. All we have beyond doctrine are some generalisations, a few scattered judicial dicta and the specifications of the political branches as reflected in the content of public policies.

To a large extent, this situation is unavoidable. But this does not diminish the strong reason that the political branches and the citizenry at large have to care and deliberate about all aspects of constitutional law.[18] In fact, the unavailability of judicial safeguard makes conscientious, transparent and accountable performance of the underlying constitutional duty all the more imperative.

[15] Lon Fuller, 'The Forms and Limits of Adjudication' (1978) 92 *Harv L Rev* 353, 366.

[16] *Vieth v Jubelirer*, 541 US 267 (2004).

[17] *Bajakajian*, above n 11.

[18] Paul Brest, 'The Conscientious Legislator's Guide to Constitutional Interpretation' (1975) 27 *Stanford L Rev* 586.

Recognition of the constitutional, though judicially under-enforced, import of the choices by the political branches has judicially cognizable implications as well. They extend to the operation of synergistic schemes of constitutional enforcement (chapter thirteen, section II), to intelligent treatment of constitutional tensions or conflicts (D, below), to statutory interpretation (chapter fourteen, section V(B)), etc. Moreover, the judiciary has reason to address the wider picture in crafting, assessing and revising doctrine, especially doctrine that turns out to perform poorly. In the process of operating doctrinal tests, courts are disbarred from considering whether the dispositions reviewed and upheld under a deferential test would, on independent judgement, be considered unconstitutional. Yet, in assessing the test itself, they are not to ignore poor overall performance. Thus, they need to have an idea about what an appropriate constitutional implementation would look like. Without it, they cannot intelligibly determine which institutional assignment is preferable, and whether the existing one is the preferable one, just legitimate or simply unacceptable.

Beyond such practical concerns, it is of intellectual importance to understand what judges are supposed to be doing in applying settled constitutional doctrine. The justificatory idea is that compliance with doctrine makes it more likely that the overall scheme of public institutions comply with appropriate specifications of constitutional law or, at any rate, that such compliance is required under public reason and political justice. Constitutional doctrine directs judges to *examine* on independent basis whether, say, a legislative provision complies with part of the normative content of constitutional law and *assume* that it complies with the remaining part if it satisfies the applicable standard of review. The judge is supposed to act on such an assumption because, if the doctrine is in fact justified under the paradigmatic thesis, it is more likely that the judgements the legislature relied upon (as to the remaining part) contribute to an appropriate constitutional determination than the ones the judge would have independently constructed; and, at any rate, because, if the doctrine is anyhow legitimate, the judge under public reason has most reason to accept the relevant constitutional judgements of the legislature as applicable (so long as satisfying the standard). This explanation shows why it is misleading to say that the Court is sacrificing part of applicable constitutional law in employing well-functioning deferential doctrine. In this sense, proper understanding of the institutional function of doctrine can liberate us from a vision of the law dominated by failure and by necessary compromise between process and substance. And it invites us, as Larry Sager has long insisted, to attend to the constitutional responsibilities of the overall system of government.

D. The Comprehensive Perspective and Constitutional Tensions

The dual character of doctrine ultimately explains why a comprehensive perspective is necessary in order to understand both the full normative force of the Constitution in the United States and the role of political and judicial institutions in its elaboration and implementation. And this is confirmed even in areas least expected, like domains where constitutional rights stand in mutual tension.

Constitutional tension does not defy under-enforcement analysis. Judicial doctrine does not always dictate unique outcomes in such cases. To the contrary, judicial supervision of the way the political branches moderate constitutional tension will normally single out issues where more or less policy maneuvering is permissible. Within the contours of the permissible, it makes sense to inquire whether the policy choices reflect readings of underlying constitutional commitments and set forth prophylactic schemes to effectuate them. An answer in the affirmative enables us to adopt a comprehensive view of the constitutional landscape and to revisit the very contours of the permissible in an intelligent manner.

For example, the Court has recognised that there is some 'play in the joints' between what the establishment clause of the First Amendment (prohibiting establishment of religion) permits and what the free exercise clause compels. Thus, in *Locke v Davey*, the Court upheld a state scholarship program excluding the pursuit of devotional theology degrees.[19] It reasoned that the state policy not to fund a distinct category of instruction did not require applicants to drop their religious beliefs, but furthered a legitimate 'anti-establishment interest'. The Court noted that the establishment clause of the federal Constitution did not require such exclusion from funding. Yet, it took pains to emphasise that the State interest was inspired by Union-wide anti-establishment concerns, as the use of tax funds to support the ministry was traditionally perceived in most States 'one of the hallmarks of an established religion'. As I see it, the more persuasive rationale for this is that States possess limited power to tailor the outer reach of a core anti-establishment principle to local traditions and bona fide assessments.

At the same time, this State leeway is not supposed to eulogise unprincipled constitutional choices. Rather, the Court frames a scheme of judicial supervision with a view to ensure that political moderation of constitutional tension is principled. For instance, the Court has distinguished *Locke* from cases where provision of a generally available governmental benefit is conditioned upon religious status or identity. Granting that the anti-establishment concerns at *Locke* 'lay at the historic core of the Religion Clauses', it has emphasised that '*Locke* took account of Washington's antiestablishment interest only after determining … that the scholarship program did not "require students to choose between their religious beliefs and receiving a government benefit."' Such a requirement would be so offending against the equal status of religious believers that it would trigger the strictest scrutiny. Accordingly, a mere 'policy preference for skating as far as possible from religious establishment concerns' would not 'qualify as compelling'.[20]

[19] *Locke v Davey*, 540 US 712 (2004).

[20] *Trinity Lutheran Church of Columbia v Comer*, 582 US __ (2017) (slip op, at 13, 14).

Our analysis does not imply that *Locke* was correctly decided. After all, a similar structure can be ascribed to decisions rejecting anti-establishment claims against policies beneficial to religion, on the ground that such policies safeguard free exercise values.[21] The important point is that we may not intelligibly engage in such discussions without adopting a comprehensive conception of the constitutional norms at play and attending to the role of political institutions in joint elaboration and enforcement. And the same may be said with regard to some of the deepest constitutional controversies of the present. A comprehensive view of the First Amendment is a prerequisite for discussing the constitutionality of campaign finance laws. A comprehensive view of equal protection is essential in determining permissible means of racial inclusion in education. And we may not attain such comprehensiveness without attending to the contribution of the political branches of government in the constitutional edifice; to the constitutional significance of their policy choices and to their proper role in the joint process of constitutional construction in the United States.

This same discussion has a noteworthy technical dimension as well. It sheds light on the substantive structure of strict standards of review. The Court did not examine whether the anti-establishment interest in *Locke* was 'compelling'. It rather considered that the constitutional rationale behind State policies had such an integrative character, altering the very nature of the free exercise claims, that strict scrutiny would be inapplicable. We will come back to this issue with regard to affirmative action (section IV(A)). But first, let us examine the institutional grounds for judicial scrutiny.

III. Constitutional Doctrine and Schemes of Scrutiny

A. Independent Modes of Reasoning

The institutional dimension in constitutional reasoning is confirmed also when judicial under-enforcement is rejected. A paradigmatic example is the role the Court has often assumed in identifying and protecting 'certain intimate choices that define personal identity and beliefs',[22] informed by public discourse and emerging national values. As we have seen in *Obergefell*, this approach is deeply contested—as a matter of both substance and institutional role. What the paradigmatic justification thesis may contribute in this debate is that resolution of the institutional issue largely depends on what scheme of assignment is expected

[21] *Walz v Tax Comm'n of City of New York*, 397 US 664, 678 (1970) (upholding property tax exemptions to religious organisations on the ground, among others, that such long established State policies have 'operated affirmatively to help guarantee the free exercise of all forms of religious belief').

[22] *Obergefell v Hodges*, above n 7 (slip op, at 10).

to lead to better constitutional implementation. An affirmative answer may be defended on recognition of comparative advantages of the judicial process (say, judgemental sensitivity) and concern about the political process in the relevant domain; and on a precautionary approach that, given the gravity of moral loss in case such interests are unduly harmed, an additional filter of independent review is expected, on balance, to minimise the stakes of constitutional error.[23] These assessments in turn depend upon a broader substantive frame about what is at stake in the relevant domain.

In some of these cases, as in *Obergefell* itself, quasi-independent constitutional reasoning may suffice for the resolution of the dispute at issue (a paradigmatic issue of principle) and doctrinal intermediation may be unnecessary. But in many other cases, a searching judicial role is framed within complex doctrinal standards for review. In the rest of this section, we will attend to this phenomenon: the employment of judicial doctrine as an operational device for structuring standards for intensive review, often on the explicit basis of institutional considerations about the thematic unreliability of the political process or the importance of the judicial forum.

The obvious example is strict scrutiny. This standard has an evident institutional function, in directing courts to exercise quasi-independent judgement on the substantive issues at stake. It also has a substantive function, in subjecting governmental conduct to a very demanding structure of justification. I will discuss in this section the institutional grounds behind strict scrutiny and in the following section the interplay between the two functions.

B. The Scope of Strict Scrutiny

The Court has expressly linked strict scrutiny in equal protection jurisprudence to institutional suspicion over a narrow category of classificatory judgements of the political branches. It has even classified 'traditional indicia of suspectness' so that strict scrutiny may be warranted whenever 'the class is saddled with such disabilities, or subjected to such a history of purposeful unequal treatment, or relegated to such a position of political powerlessness as to command extraordinary protection from the majoritarian political process'.[24] No doubt, institutional considerations of this sort need further refinement in the light of their over-inclusiveness in capturing the grounds for institutional distrust (in capturing, for instance, critical vulnerability and propensity for subjection to legislative or executive bias).[25]

[23] This line of analysis is an extension of Fallon's precautionary justification for judicial review. See Richard Fallon, 'The Core of an Uneasy Case for Judicial Review' (2008) 121 *Harvard L Rev* 1693, and the text in ch 8, section II(B) for qualifications I would propose.

[24] *Massachusetts Bd. of Retirement v Murgia*, 427 US 307, 313 (1976) (per curiam), citing *San Antonio Indep. Sch. Dist. v Rodriguez*, 411 US 1, 28 (1973).

[25] For an overview of the literature see Marcy Strauss, 'Reevaluating Suspect Classifications' (2011) 35 *Seattle U L Rev* 135.

It is also pretty clear in the case law that they do not exhaust the rationale for judicial attentiveness, nor the full scope of invidious discrimination. Certain classifications are considered by members of the Court as *per se* invidious and other ones not amounting to 'suspectness' trigger a variety of standards for intermediate review. Still, this line of jurisprudence provides a paradigmatic explanation of how institutional distrust underlies a scheme of intensive judicial review, assigning the judicial process a central role in implementing this domain of equal protection.

Strict scrutiny over suspect classifications is also defended on the reason that the pertinent classifications 'are so seldom relevant to the achievement of any legitimate State interest that laws grounded in such considerations are deemed to reflect prejudice and antipathy—a view that those in the burdened class are not as worthy or deserving as others ... [On the other hand,] where individuals in the group affected by a law have distinguishing characteristics relevant to interests the State has the authority to implement, the courts have been very reluctant, as they should be in our federal system and with our respect for the separation of powers, to closely scrutinize legislative choices as to whether, how, and to what extent those interests should be pursued'.[26]

This argument has a prominent substantive interpretation: Certain classifications are considered very likely or unlikely to turn out invidious. No doubt, it is over-inclusive and under-inclusive as well, and remains so, in the light of its context-insensitivity, even as adapted to cover intermediate categories, like gender. 'A sign that says "men only" looks very different on a bathroom door than a courthouse door'.[27] What is of interest though is that this substantive-cum-strategic argument has secondary institutional implications. If cases of a certain sort are very likely to be unconstitutional, then a multi-tier scheme of judicial scrutiny, triggering intensive review over a certain category of substantively suspect classifications, is perhaps superior for equal protection analysis over a unitary standard of review; it may facilitate the judicious use of limited judicial resources and minimise both litigation costs and the likelihood of overall constitutional error.

Finally, there is also a due process argument for judicial scrutiny in cases of this sort. When government decisions 'touch upon an individual's race or ethnic background [the harmed individual] is entitled to a judicial determination that the burden he is asked to bear on that basis is precisely tailored to serve a compelling governmental interest.'[28] This argument presumably lies in the idea that individualised dignitary harms of a certain profundity require access to individualised institutional review and justification by an independent tribunal.

Now, while the relevance of institutional considerations in subjecting certain classifications to strict scrutiny is not in particular doubt in the abstract, determination of the actual scope of strict scrutiny has been a matter of bitter contestation. The paradigmatic example is the choice of the conservative majority of the

[26] *Cleburne v Cleburne Living Ctr.*, 473 US 432, 440–42 (1985).
[27] ibid, at 468–69 (1985) (Marshall, J, concurring in the judgment in part and dissenting in part).
[28] *Regents of the University of California v Bakke*, 438 US 265, 299 (1978) (opinion of Powell, J).

Court to apply strict scrutiny to all racial classifications, irrespective of the race of the benefited group and of the purposes for their employment.

Current jurisprudence goes back to Justice Powell's denial in *Bakke* that the standard of review for racial or ethnic distinctions could vary with the suspect or non-suspect status of the beneficiary group. His premise was largely substantive: distinctions based on one's ancestry are 'odious to a free people whose institutions are founded upon the doctrine of equality';[29] and he expressly held that aiming at racially preferential end-states always constitutes a forbidden state purpose.[30] On this account, subjecting affirmative action to strict scrutiny is based on a judicial interpretation of the underlying equal protection principle.

At the same time, there is also endorsement of institutional reasons to this conclusion. Justice Powell stressed in *Bakke* that it is not the role of an isolated faculty to determine societal discrimination and to formulate remedial policies.[31] Justice O'Connor in *Croson* expressed concern that the Richmond City Council was implicated in racial politics and defended scrutiny of means so 'that there is little or no possibility that the motive for the classification was illegitimate racial prejudice or stereotype'.[32] In *Adarand*,[33] the Court exported this scepticism to Congress. Moreover, all three cases reflected scepticism about the prospects of a highly politicised federal judiciary implementing an opaque standard of review.[34]

Adarand is particularly important, as it is the case that solidified the requirement of strict scrutiny in the field. In *Adarand*, as in *Croson*, the institutional basis was quite prominent. Justice O'Connor did not question the legitimate use of race in governmental decision making, but considered that strict scrutiny is necessary to 'smoke out' illegitimate uses of race. 'Absent searching judicial inquiry into the justification for such race-based measures, there is simply no way of determining what classifications are "benign" or "remedial" and what classifications are in fact motivated by illegitimate notions of racial inferiority or simple racial politics'.[35] Of course, she considered illegitimate uses to be quite pernicious. Still, for her (though not for all members of the majority), the idea was not one of presumptive unconstitutionality; rather it was the institutional concern that 'any retreat from

[29] *Bakke*, ibid, at 290–91 (1978) (opinion of Powell, J).

[30] 'If petitioner's purpose is to assure within its student body some specified percentage of a particular group merely because of its race or ethnic origin, such a preferential purpose must be rejected not as insubstantial but as facially invalid. Preferring members of any one group for no reason other than race or ethnic origin is discrimination for its own sake. This the Constitution forbids.' *Bakke*, ibid. at 307.

[31] *Bakke*, ibid, at 297 and 309 ('Its broad mission is education, not the formulation of any legislative policy or the adjudication of particular claims of illegality … isolated segments of our vast governmental structures are not competent to make those decisions, at least in the absence of legislative mandates and legislatively determined criteria').

[32] *Richmond v J.A. Croson Co.*, 488 US 469, 505 and 493 (1989) (opinion of the Court and opinion of O'Connor, J, respectively).

[33] *Adarand Contractors, Inc. v Pena*, 515 US 200 (1995).

[34] *Bakke*, above n 28, at 290 ('the kind of variable sociological and political analysis necessary to produce such rankings simply does not lie within the judicial competence—even if they otherwise were politically feasible and socially desirable').

[35] *Adarand*, above n 33, at 226 (citing *Croson*).

the most searching judicial scrutiny can only increase the risk of another such error [i.e. failure to detect illegitimate classifications] occurring in the future'.[36]

We will discuss in the next section the difficulties the majority faces in moving from these sensible institutional concerns to the substantive dimension of strict scrutiny. But let us first complete our expository task by considering how the Court grapples with institutional issues in the process of applying strict scrutiny.

C. The Operation of Strict Scrutiny

Considerations of an institutional nature are also relevant in guiding the *operation* of strict scrutiny. The case law on affirmative action in public higher education confirms this point. Recent jurisprudence on this subject starts with *Grutter's* fundamental choice to calibrate strict scrutiny to the peculiarities of the educational setting. Justice O'Connor, writing for the majority, opted for a flexible approach: 'Context matters when reviewing race-based governmental action under the Equal Protection Clause', as 'not every decision influenced by race is equally objectionable'.[37] Evidently, she considered the benefits from calibration to justify uncertainty and litigation costs.

In pursuing a context-sensitive approach, the *Grutter* Court showed some institutional deference to Universities: 'The Law Schools educational judgment that such diversity is essential to its educational mission is one to which we defer. … Our scrutiny of the interest asserted by the Law School is no less strict for taking into account complex educational judgments in an area that lies primarily within the expertise of the university. Our holding today is in keeping with our tradition of giving a degree of deference to a university's academic decisions, within constitutionally prescribed limits'. And the Court gave mixed signals over narrow-tailoring: 'Narrow tailoring does, however, require serious, good faith consideration of workable race-neutral alternatives that will achieve the diversity the university seeks'.[38]

Justice Kennedy had dissented in *Grutter*. His main concern was that an institutional argument from good faith was inadequate to justify such relaxation of strict scrutiny over narrow-tailoring. 'The Court confuses deference to a university's definition of its educational objective with deference to the implementation of this goal.' His institutional concern was linked to a perceptible substantive

[36] ibid, at 236.

[37] *Grutter v Bollinger*, 539 US 306, 327 (2003). Justice Scalia objected that such a context-sensitive approach is 'perversely designed to prolong the controversy and the litigation'. And next to his general preference for rules, Scalia also had a default preference on substance that would support a rule-like standard of review: 'The Constitution proscribes government discrimination on the basis of race, and state-provided education is no exception'. ibid at 348, 349 (Scalia, J, concurring in part and dissenting in part).

[38] ibid, at 328, 339.

differentiation on proper ways to pursue diversity-sensitive educational objectives. 'The concept of critical mass is a delusion used by the Law School to mask its attempt to make race an automatic factor in most instances and to achieve numerical goals indistinguishable from quotas.' For Justice Kennedy, there is a fundamental substantive 'tension between the pursuit of critical mass and the requirement of individual review'. Given this substantive understanding, an institutional assumption of good faith is inadequate to secure constitutional compliance. 'To be constitutional, a university's compelling interest in a diverse student body must be achieved by a system where individual assessment is safeguarded through the entire process'.[39]

After O'Connor's retirement, this sense of dissatisfaction with the *Grutter* standard had to be addressed. The *Fisher I* Court assumed the task of providing a more comprehensive standard. Justice Kennedy, writing for a broad majority, reasoned that a University, taking consideration of the applicant's race in its admissions policies, has the burden to demonstrate with clarity that the interest pursued is unquestionably legitimate and, in fact, compelling, and that the means taken are both necessary and precisely tailored to its service. The Court (or more precisely, pivotal Justice Kennedy) was willing to show some deference to a university's 'educational judgment that [student-body] diversity is essential to its educational mission' provided that 'there is a reasoned, principled explanation for the academic decision', showing, for instance, that the University has not misconceived the nature of the interest pursued by collapsing 'genuine' student body diversity with 'ethnic diversity'.[40]

But what about narrow-tailoring? *Fisher I* warns Universities that on this point they receive 'no deference'. First, 'it remains at all times the University's obligation to demonstrate, and the Judiciary's obligation to determine, that admissions processes ensure that each applicant is evaluated as an individual and not in a way that makes an applicant's race or ethnicity the defining feature of his or her application'. Secondly, 'strict scrutiny imposes on the university the ultimate burden of demonstrating, before turning to racial classifications, that available, workable race-neutral alternatives do not suffice', and requires the reviewing court to 'verify' accordingly.[41] Indeed, this conception of judicial role was one step further in an incremental path toward exacting scrutiny of means;[42] a path presumably

[39] ibid, at 388, 389, 391, 392 (Kennedy, J, dissenting).

[40] *Fisher v University of Texas at Austin*, 570 US __ (2013) (slip op, at 9). Also *Grutter*, ibid, at 328, and *Bakke*, above n 28, at 315 (opinion of Powell, J).

[41] *Fisher*, ibid (slip op, at 11).

[42] *cf Grutter*, above n 37, at 339 ('Narrow tailoring does not require exhaustion of every conceivable race-neutral alternative. Nor does it require a university to choose between maintaining a reputation for excellence or fulfilling a commitment to provide educational opportunities to members of all racial groups ... Narrow tailoring does, however, require serious, good faith consideration of workable race-neutral alternatives that will achieve the diversity the university seeks') and *Bakke*, above n 28, at 318–19 and at fn 53 ('in short, good faith would be presumed ... If an applicant can establish that the institution does not adhere to a policy of individual comparisons, or can show that a systematic

involving, from the substantive standpoint of the prevailing majority of the time, the persistence of grounds for institutional concern, even potential distrust. Universities have experience and expertise over judgements of educational necessity. Yet, they are also subject to more subtle vices, to imperceptible use of means impermissible. Given the tight entanglement of issues of educational policy and principles of fair treatment, judicial attentiveness is crucial—even at the risk of some judicial over-enforcement.

But perceptions change—as do majorities. Thus, the most recent pronouncement on this issue, in the very same case (*Fisher II*), delivered by the same Justice Kennedy for a majority of a different (more liberal) composition, imperceptibly applied the 'reasoned, principled explanation' standard to necessity of means. After 'refut[ing] any criticism that the University did not make good-faith efforts', and reviewing the data collected, the Court determined that 'a reasonable determination was made that the University has not yet attained its goals'; moreover, the University provided a 'reasoned, principled explanation' for its decision to pursue these goals … [articulating why] the use of race-neutral policies and programs had not been successful in providing an educational setting that fosters cross-racial understanding, providing enlightened discussion and learning, or preparing students to function in an increasingly diverse workforce and society'.[43] That majority was apparently more concerned with honouring the competency of educational institutions pursuing educational policy in good faith, and less willing to assume the risks of judicial over-enforcement.

The Court was also satisfied that workable alternative means of furthering the educational benefits of diversity were not available. The standard was framed in *Fisher I* in quite a demanding way; perhaps sidestepping that alternative means have their own repercussions that may only be assessed in overall policy judgements. The point was well understood in *Fisher II*, which accepted policy arguments to the effect that alternative means would have compromised academic excellence or sacrificed other aspects of diversity.[44] And this was made possible by endorsement, on a reasoned explanation standard, of the University's broad conception of the educational goals of diversity.

The conservative minority objected, criticising the Court for its willingness 'to be satisfied by [UT's] profession of its own good faith.'[45] At the same time, this point confirms that standards of reasoned elaboration, while malleable, are flexible enough to satisfy a variety of institutional contingencies, capture those issues of principle calling for judicial attentiveness, and allow space for reasonable policy elaboration.

exclusion of certain groups results, the presumption of legality might be overcome, creating the necessity of proving legitimate educational purpose').

[43] *Fisher v University of Texas at Austin*, 579 US __ (2016) (slip op, at 10, 15, 13).

[44] *Fisher II*, ibid (slip op, at 16–19).

[45] *Fisher II*, ibid (slip op, at 47) (Alito, J, dissenting).

IV. Process and Substance in Strict Scrutiny

We have seen how institutional and substantive argumentation are interrelated in crafting and specifying judicial doctrine. This argumentative entanglement is coupled with the fact that doctrine has both a substantive and an institutional function. This complexity gives rise to important complications. We will single out two difficulties, as they pertain to strict scrutiny.

First, we tend to overlook that institutional argumentation should be tailored to the nature of the substantive determination at issue and that it paradigmatically aims at schemes of review expected to reach appropriate determinations overall. Secondly, we often reason under the false impression that institutional arguments for intensive review operate on the same level with substantive arguments for increased protection. As a result, I fear, much of strict scrutiny analysis misunderstands both the reasons for intensive review and the very relation between intensive review and increased substantive protection, leading to undue overprotection.

A. Service to Substance

We have seen that an argument for judicial scrutiny in equal protection relates to specific grounds for institutional suspicion. A main difficulty here is that institutional distrust cannot justify independent review over all determinants of interpretive judgement. Most importantly, it cannot silence the general duty of the judiciary to engage in earnest dialogue with the political branches over the commitments of the Nation to equal citizenship.

I presented the operation of strict scrutiny in affirmative action in the previous section from the perspective of the majority of the Court and, more precisely, its pivotal justices. In this regard, I treated the substantive principles of the law as exogenous, and examined how the Court has crafted and applied doctrine in pursuing their proper enforcement, while allowing for reasonable policy elaboration. But our thesis about the dual character of constitutional doctrine also provides us with the conceptual tools for critique over the fundamentals of this line of case law; critique extending to the background principle that the educational benefits that flow from a diverse student body constitute practically the only legitimate governmental interest for affirmative action in education. In particular, it invites us to ask whether the Court has paid lip service to the limits of its institutional mandate in shaping the substantive moral principles themselves. And no matter how one settles on these principles, a strong argument may be made that the Court has not made peace with the role of the representative institutions of the American Nation in contributing to a comprehensive vision of equal protection, where proper space for racial integration is duly recognised.

No doubt, various institutional considerations may counsel against the judiciary exercising primary enforcement power over broader integrative visions.

Yet, this does not deprive these visions of potential constitutional import, carried out by the political branches in their constitutional capacities—within judicially supervised limits.

I will not pursue this matter further, as this book does not aim at any specific normative conclusion. But I emphasise that its proper treatment engages the very concerns discussed in chapters nine and ten over the role of public institutions, as agents of free and equal citizens, in responding to reasons that in good faith reach all citizens in such capacity, including their possession of a sense of justice worthy of equal respect. The Court does have a distinctive deliberative role in this process (chapter ten, section I(D)). But in a constitutional democracy, its self-critical role is an element of the very process of public reasoning about constitutional justice; not an external corrective thereto.

Finally, I wish to note that a difficulty of the same nature arises over policy and is particularly troubling in the process of doctrinal implementation. We saw in *Fisher II* how scrutiny for improper means shall allow adequate space for the elaboration of educational policy. We may generalise. Grounds for institutional scepticism do not determine in themselves the degree of overall judicial scrutiny in doctrinal specification.

B. Disservice to Substance

The second complication is equally troubling but harder to apprehend. Let us focus, again, on affirmative action. Under current equal protection jurisprudence, governmental classifications on the basis of race are impermissible unless narrowly tailored to serve a compelling state interest. The majority of the Court has accepted the position that the doctrinal standard of review is the same regardless of the race of the persons harmed or benefited from governmental conduct. We have seen that this doctrinal selection has been defended, at least in part, on institutional scepticism.

Now, the fact that the political process may be prejudiced in employing certain classifications may imply that the judiciary should have a more attentive role in enforcing applicable constitutional principles. We may assume with Justice O'Connor that 'absent searching judicial inquiry into the justification for such race-based measures, we have no way to determine what classifications are "benign" or "remedial" and what classifications are in fact motivated by illegitimate notions of racial inferiority or simple racial politics'.[46] No doubt, such assumptions may be challenged as resting on overbroad institutional analysis, on speculative cross-context generalisations.[47] Still, perhaps, they may justify the position, defended by

[46] *Adarand*, above n 33, at 226 (citing *Croson*).

[47] Roosevelt has relatedly argued that standards of strict scrutiny constitute decision rules adapted to certain institutional and strategic contexts and has warned that failure to appreciate this point leads to constitutional calcification. In this particular example, he has pointed out that the intuitive appeal

Justice Stevens in *Fullilove* and endorsed by the Court in *Adarand*, that the reviewing court must satisfy itself that the reasons for any racial classification 'be clearly identified and unquestionably legitimate'.[48]

Yet, institutional scepticism *does not in itself* imply substantive conclusions, and much less categorical ones like the norm that a suspect classification may be employed only in furtherance of a compelling state interest. That would impermissibly affect the structure of the substantive assessment, over-protecting a legitimate constitutional interest for the mere reason that the political process is not adequately trusted on its proper protection. Similarly, it may not even justify the exacting requirement of necessity stressed in *Fisher I*, demanding that 'no workable race-neutral alternatives would produce the educational benefits of diversity … about as well and at tolerable administrative expense'.

I do not deny that one could argue for linkages between institutional considerations, loosely understood, and substantive conclusions; at a minimum, it is the very history of official discrimination that has tainted the very concept of race, as opposed to various other immutable individual features, with odiousness and with the shadow of social and cultural subjugation. Now, the critical substantive issue is whether this history has transformed that very concept into a purpose-independent, *per se* forbidden policy ground. In this regard, one may have to argue that the history of discrimination has affected applicable social understandings in such a way that it has invested otherwise innocuous (seemingly 'benign') classifications with stigmatising or otherwise status-conferring effects, affecting the structure of substantive assessment; or that, given such history, their employment has the propensity to perpetuate a vicious circle of competing policies of hatred, in pursuit of consequentialist social states on the racial structures they embody;[49] and take captive along this way any bystander with autonomous life-plans. Yet, such linkages have to be defended on their own, and not be inferred from the institutional argument for intensive review. If endorsed, they may provide the substantive backdrop against which institutional considerations may become pertinent in determining the operational intensity of review over, say, the compelling status of the governmental purpose, or the necessity of means.

Of course, Justice Scalia was willing to defend a substantive constitutional judgement along these or similar lines. But this was not the case with Justice Kennedy or Justice O'Connor. Justice O'Connor in *Grutter* expressly noted that 'not every decision influenced by race is equally objectionable'. If so, it is hard to

of their symmetrical application is due to failure to distinguish between them and the underlying constitutional propositions which are subject to the symmetry requirement. Roosevelt, above n 14, at 1702–04.

[48] *Fullilove v Klutznick*, 448 US 448, 533–35 (1980) (Stevens, J, dissenting), *Adarand*, above n 33, at 236.

[49] *cf* Justice O'Connor's concern that racial classifications lead to 'racial hostility' and that the pursuit of racial proportionality assures that 'race will always be relevant in American life'. *Croson*, above n 32, at 493, 495 (plurality opinion).

defend strict scrutiny across-the-board. And this explains Justice Kennedy's point in dissent that the *Grutter* Court 'does not apply strict scrutiny. By trying to say otherwise, it undermines both the test and its own controlling precedents'.[50]

This point is clear to Justice Breyer. Justice Breyer, dissenting in *Parents Involved* (regarding K-12 schools), distinguished affirmative action contexts 'in which race-conscious limits [do not] stigmatize or exclude' nor 'impose burdens unfairly upon members of one race alone' and defended the application there of a standard of review that is less than strict, while providing for careful judicial review of the necessity of race-conscious programs and their tailoring.[51] As he clarified, in such cases the legislature could properly conclude that 'a racial classification sometimes serves a purpose important enough to overcome' countervailing risks. Justice Kennedy has a different view on the stigmatising nature of racial classifications. Yet, his substantive assessment also leads to variations in the standard of review. We saw in some detail the tales of strict scrutiny in *Fisher I and II*. Most importantly, in his concurrence to the judgment of the Court in *Parents Involved*, he emphasised that the pursuit of equal educational opportunity and integration through racially-conscious programmes not involving racial classification of students, is unlikely to demand strict scrutiny.[52] The more genuine way to justify the substantive dimension of strict scrutiny, hence, is by appeal to a correlative substantive understanding of the pertinent constitutional principles.

There is though one further possibility, that is, to employ strict scrutiny as a prophylactic policy purportedly grounded on the idea that rights-overprotection in this area minimises the risk of constitutional error. Let us defer treatment of this option and examine it in the following section V(B).

Closing this section, I note that the foregoing analysis casts doubt more generally on the ability of institutional grounds for intensive review to justify, on their own, the current substantive structure of strict scrutiny in equal protection. We may recall here our earlier argument that uncritical invocation of institutional grounds for non-justiciability or for merely nominal review also has the tendency to silence the applicable substantive principles (chapter eleven, section II(B)). Linking these points together, we may better examine certain substantive infirmities of the currently practised tiers of review: for instance, once we see that there is no natural correlation between institutional grounds for intensive review and the 'degree' of substantive protection, we may appreciate that the structure of the current doctrine is sometimes disturbingly category-dominated and consequentialistic.

[50] *Grutter*, above n 37, at 387 (Kennedy, J, dissenting).

[51] *Parents Involved in Community Schools v Seattle School District No. 1*, 551 US 701, 834–37 (2007) (Breyer, J, dissenting).

[52] *Parents Involved*, ibid at 788–89 (Kennedy, J, concurring), mentioned with approval by the Court in *Texas Dept. of Housing and Community Affairs v Inclusive Communities Project, Inc.*, 576 US __ (2015) (slip op, at 22–23). Relatedly, the more relaxed approach in *Fisher II* was linked to the fact that alternative ways to promote educational benefits of diversity, though racially neutral, were racially conscious, so that further reliance thereupon would not make admissions policy more racially neutral. *Fisher II*, above n 43, at 16–17.

Affirmative action is one side of this coin. The other side is over-emphasis on the suspect nature of the group harmed. Engagement in a futile discussion over, say, the political power or powerlessness of same sex couples and over whether such couples constitute suspect, quasi-suspect or nonsuspect groups, on the assumption that such analysis determines the intensity of the countervailing interest that could justify the classifications imposed against such groups, etc, is deeply alien to what is at stake in an inquiry about the demands of equal protection: not the degree of substantive over-protection that suspect groups deserve or do not deserve (because we are suspicious of the way they are often being treated!), nor the proper balancing of competing category-wide interests. Rather, what was at stake, for instance in the classifications imposed by the Defense of Marriage Act (DOMA) against same sex couples, was the permissibility of a certain classification, its invidious, arbitrary or otherwise undue nature or operation when employed in the exercise of the collective power of free and equal citizens. It is not surprising, in this regard, that the Court's judgment as to DOMA's unconstitutionality bypassed traditional, standard-of-review analysis, and simply held that 'the federal statute is invalid, for no legitimate purpose overcomes the purpose and effect to disparage and to injure those whom the State, by its marriage laws, sought to protect in personhood and dignity'.[53]

V. Constitutional Norms of Prophylactic Nature

A. Institutional Distrust and Constitutional Prophylaxis

We have pointed out that the existence and content of *prophylactic rules* depend upon constructive constitutional interpretation (chapter four, section I(A)). Their purpose is to serve the efficacy of constitutional rules and principles by regulating conduct in ways not required by them. While prophylactic rules are often formulated separately from the primary norm, it is sometimes the case, I want to argue, that judicial doctrine incorporates in a single doctrinal test both the prophylactic rule and the norm served by it.

This is so, I think, when the Court employs presumptions of unconstitutionality to capture conduct that is highly likely to be unconstitutional, as, for instance, in prior restraints to speech.[54] The rationale behind the presumption combines a

[53] *Windsor*, above n 10 (slip op, at 25–26).

[54] See *New York Times Co. v United States*, 403 US 713, 726–27 (1971) (Brennan, J, concurring) ('Our cases, it is true, have indicated that there is a single, extremely narrow class of cases in which the First Amendment's ban on prior judicial restraint may be overridden. …, only governmental allegation and proof that publication must inevitably, directly, and immediately cause the occurrence of an event kindred to imperiling the safety of a transport already at sea can support even the issuance of an interim restraining order.').

substantive judgement with serious distrust in the relevant field towards the non-judicial branches (sometimes even towards the judiciary itself). In such cases, the presumption has a prophylactic function in potentially covering cases that could have satisfied the underlying primary norm.

Actually, considerations of this sort appear, in various more subtle forms, throughout constitutional adjudication.[55] Perhaps the more famous, and infamous, application is strict scrutiny. This is particularly so in fatal variants of the test, resembling presumptions of unconstitutionality. But the point can be generalised whenever the Court is deeply concerned about the institutional trustworthiness of the political branches and, at the same time, appreciates that credible employment of a more balanced standard of review would require expending disproportionate resources and would still run an increased risk of judicial mistake. In selecting the appropriate doctrinal test, the Court is concerned with minimising the overall risk of judicial mistake while channeling most of the remaining risk to the side where potential mistakes are less threatening for the integrity of the political community. The lack of trustworthiness in the performance of public officials and the record of past constitutional violations in the field are important factors to be considered in serving these desiderata.

In this sense, institutional considerations do not (merely) determine the division of interpretive labour between the primary body and the reviewing court; they are factual elements in a complex substantive argument leading to the formation of a substantive norm of prophylactic nature. For this reason, their relevance is dependent upon substantive assessment of what is at stake. Prophylaxis cannot rest on institutional argumentation alone. It needs judgement justifying incurring the risks that overprotection carries to competing legitimate interests and other considerations of constitutional significance.

For instance, in *Employment Div. v Smith*, the Court considered that subjecting generally applicable laws substantially burdening religious freedom to strict scrutiny, as a matter of constitutional right, would be 'a constitutional anomaly'. The majority acknowledged that 'leaving accommodation to the political process will place at a relative disadvantage those religious practices that are not widely engaged in; but that unavoidable consequence of democratic government must be preferred to a system in which each conscience is a law unto itself or in which judges weigh the social importance of all laws against the centrality of all religious beliefs'.[56] Similarly, defence of overprotection shall include reflection about the

[55] Even, for instance, in the field of proscribable speech. See *R.A.V. v City of St. Paul*, 505 US 377, 390 (1992), distinguishing suspect from nonsuspect content discrimination ('to validate such [content] selectivity (where totally proscribable speech is at issue) it may not even be necessary to identify any particular "neutral" basis, so long as the nature of the content discrimination is such that there is no realistic possibility that official suppression of ideas is afoot. (We cannot think of any First Amendment interest that would stand in the way of a State's prohibiting only those obscene motion pictures with blue eyed actresses.)').

[56] 494 US 872, 886 and 890 (1990) (Scalia, J).

fair allocation of the burdens of overprotection, especially if falling unevenly upon certain groups of individuals, and argument about the kind of tailoring respect to the claims of such individuals may demand.

B. On the Prophylactic Function of Strict Scrutiny in Affirmative Action Cases

In this regard, an interesting issue arises over the possibility, denied in principle in the previous section IV(B), to justify judicial scrutiny in affirmative action cases while affirming, again in principle, that racial integration is a legitimate state purpose that could in turn justify limited employment of certain racial classifications.

Indeed, for many citizens, the sensitive and limited employment of classifications on the basis of race does not necessarily disserve the very ideal of equal citizenship given non-ideal social and political conditions. This may be grounded on a proper understanding of the importance of social integration and of the social function of certain institutions, like public universities. And it may provide support in turn to the legitimacy of policies of societal distribution of the burdens necessary in this pursuit, provided that such distribution is equitable and fair, and does not carry with it stigma, victimisation, or a sense of status conferral.

The more natural, and indeed genuine, conclusion from such premises would be a standard of heightened scrutiny aiming to ensure the integrity in the operation of such policies and the fair allocation of their burdens. But what about strict scrutiny à la *Fisher I*? In considering this option, we may entertain the thought that strict scrutiny operates here as a prophylactic rule explained partly by lack of trust in the political and bureaucratic institutions for accommodating the competing concerns,[57] and partly by deep concern over the ability of the judiciary to engage in open-ended balancing.

This option does not suffer from the contradictions we warned against in the previous section. The prophylactic rule would seek defence on ideas that pay due attention to the distinctive force of substance and process. Yet, such justification faces hard, insurmountable I fear, difficulties of content. It would need an assumption that, under a more balanced standard of scrutiny, judicial error in failing to strike down unconstitutional policies would be both more likely to occur and compellingly grave, as compared to error in striking down permissible ones.

This assumption would require a very dim outlook about institutions. Prophylactic overreaching serves a function similar in logic, though reverse in effect, to the political question doctrine. Therefore it is subject to the same critique about abdication of judicial responsibility. And refutation of this critique normally presupposes that the judiciary is incapable of calibrating the standard of review

[57] *cf* Jed Rubenfeld, 'Affirmative Action' (1997) 107 *Yale L J* 427.

in functional manner (as the Court tried to do, for example, in the road from *Fisher I* to *Fisher II*).

More importantly, the justification needed would have to involve a very strange substantive assessment of unilateral gravity of error, given that the pertinent affirmative policies also seek justification in equal protection aspirations. And finally, there is a reminder of institutional integrity. If there is a due process argument to the effect that the profundity of the subject matter requires independent judicial review, this same argument also counsels for specificity in the reasoning leading to the judicial construction of a prophylactic rule.

C. Institutional Distrust and Remedial Prophylaxis

The previous paragraphs discuss prophylactic rules of general applicability that are not conditioned by a litigation-specific violation of another constitutional norm. I now want to suggest the analogy between that category of norms and specific prophylactic norms issued by courts in the form of injunctive relief.

Courts often issue injunctive relief of a restorative or preventative nature. Such relief is prophylactic in the sense that the judicially-issued norms mandate or proscribe conduct that is not in itself mandated or proscribed by the violated norm.[58] Prophylactic norms do not derive from an 'analysis' of the violated norm but reach beyond it. Furthermore, the norms discussed here do not precede the remedial decree. Their validity depends on the authority of the court to issue such relief. However, their justification is to be found in the constitutional or statutory scheme whose principles they are supposed to effectuate.

As a general matter, a remedial measure against a public institution must be related to the nature and scope of the legal wrong. In particular, it must be designed as nearly as practicable to restore the affected parties to the position they would have occupied in the absence of a violation and to reasonably ensure that further violations of the law would not occur.[59] It is beyond the remedial authority of courts to pursue policies that are removed from such remedial objectives.[60] At the same time, there are multiple, alternative structures and techniques that may be employed in pursuing the permissible remedial goal. In the absence of past violation, the defendant would have ample power to specify the appropriate conduct in conformity to the norm. At the other end of the spectrum, when unconstitutional conduct is pervasive or severe, the defendant is deemed untrustworthy with regard to further compliance. In light of the failure of the bureaucratic process, the judiciary assumes the role of a more appropriate forum to make some of these judgements. Accordingly, the court negotiates or unilaterally specifies some of the

[58] The dis-correlation between the invoked right and the remedy was thoroughly discussed by Abram Chayes, The Role of the Judge in Public Law Litigation (1976) 89 *Harvard L Rev* 1281.

[59] *Miliken v Bradley*, 433 US 267 (1977).

[60] *Missuri v Jenkins*, 515 US 70 (1995).

requisite conditions in the form of an injunction. And the degree of judicial intrusiveness varies with the degree of distrust. The worse the past record is or the more the public authority obstructs the remedies already imposed, the more intrusive judicial engagement becomes. In extreme cases, the injunctions needed are structural in the sense that they mandate the restructuring and judicial supervision of an institution associated with repetitive unconstitutional conduct.[61]

There is an obvious institutional implication here. As constitutional law expands to address default, courts have to consider their role in specifying remedial requirements. In this course, past record and institutional distrust affect both prophylactic remedial substance and the degree of judicial engagement in determining it.

There is also another, more subtle institutional dimension. It transpires when the judicial doctrine whose violation triggers the remedial process under-enforces the underlying constitutional principles. In fashioning remedial relief, the court may then take over part of the role the primary decision maker would have in implementing constitutional requirements in the absence of default. In fact, the most prominent example of institutional reform litigation, namely the judicially mandated and supervised desegregation of public schools following *Brown II*, may be understood along these lines.

In the pursuit of school desegregation federal courts faced widespread resistance by state and local authorities and pursued activist remedial policies, scrutinising school facilities, redrawing school districts, grouping noncontiguous school zones, putting local institutions under receivership, even requiring local governments to levy taxes to support judicially mandated programs. The Court justified such intrusive judicial intervention on the ground that institutions operating a discriminatory system are 'charged with the affirmative duty to take whatever steps might be necessary to convert to a unitary system in which racial discrimination would be eliminated root and branch'.[62] And it accepted that policies with segregative effects violate the Constitution 'even though the State has abolished the legal requirement that whites and blacks be educated separately and has established racially neutral policies not animated by a discriminatory purpose'.[63]

But it is unclear what the basis of this duty is. It might seem natural to suggest that such measures were deemed necessary to remedy past de jure or purposeful discrimination; that they were calculated to remove the discriminatory effects of past unconstitutional discriminatory practice and to ensure that such practice would not reoccur. However, this account may not explain why the educational system should become a 'unitary' one with a high degree of integration. The Court

[61] *Morgan v McDonough*, 540 F.2d 527 (1st Cir, 1976) cert. denied 429 US 1042 (1977) (pattern of obstruction justifies imposition of receivership). See generally Owen Fiss, *The Civil Rights Injunction* (1978).

[62] *Green v County School Board of New Kent County*, 391 US 430, 437–38 (1968) (Brennan, J, delivering the opinion of a unanimous Court).

[63] *United States v Fordice* 505 US 717, 731–32 (1992) (White, J).

never conducted any study suggesting that, in the absence of de jure or purposeful discrimination by school authorities, the school system would have been a relatively integrated one. In fact, evidence from the North suggests the salience of other factors like housing allocation, patterns of immigration, etc.[64]

If we are to make sense of this remedial policy, it would be more promising to suggest that there is some further constitutional norm being served here. Justice Powell famously suggested in *Keyes* that equal protection mandates public school authorities to operate integrated school systems and that school authorities have a burden to show compliance with this duty if there is evidence of substantial de facto segregation in their district.[65] Justice Powell did not clearly define what 'integration' signifies, although it is clear from his analysis that the duty to operate integrated school systems does not amount to a duty to retain at every school a racial mixture that would reflect the overall racial mixture in a given geographical area; not even to ensure 'that every school must, in fact, be an integrated unit'. It is rather essential that public policy about both educational substance and structure is reasonably directed at the operation of non-segregated schools. The operational standard shall perhaps relate to making reasonable efforts to create an integrative educational environment, including an environment cultivating the civic virtues of tolerance and reciprocity. The measures needed to fulfil this duty may include a wide variety of facially neutral though racially conscious measures to attract students of minority races and perhaps a limited set of non-neutral ones, especially with a view to minimising segregated conditions.

If one endorses Justice Powell's account of substantive law, there is in principle congruence between the duty to operate integrated schools and the remedial schemes employed in the school desegregation litigation.[66] But *Washington v Davis* has settled that, in the absence of facial discrimination, a finding of purposeful segregation is normally necessary for judicial intervention.[67] How can we accommodate these two propositions in the educational context? One option lies in considerations about institutional structure and judicial under-enforcement.[68]

[64] 'In imposing on metropolitan school districts an affirmative duty … to eliminate segregation in the schools, the Court required these districts to alleviate conditions which in large part did *not* result from historic, state imposed de jure segregation. Rather, the familiar root cause of segregated schools in *all* the biracial metropolitan areas of our country is essentially the same: one of segregated residential and migratory patterns the impact of which on the racial composition of the schools was often perpetuated and rarely ameliorated by action of public school authorities.' *Keyes v School District No.1*, 413 US 189, 222–23 (1973) (Powell, J, concurring in part and dissenting in part).

[65] *Keyes*, ibid, at 225–26. The decision of the Court was based on the idea that judicial intervention is triggered in the presence of intentional segregation, but it emphasised ways in which evidence of purposeful segregation in a substantial portion of a district may ground a district-wide finding of discrimination.

[66] This is not to deny that Justice Powell was also sceptical about remedial overreach, especially on the issue of 'large scale or long distance transportation of students'. ibid, at 238.

[67] *Washington v Davis*, 426 US 229 (1976). See also *Arlington Heights v Metropolitan Housing Corp.*, 429 US 252 (1977) (discriminatory purpose has to be a motivating factor in the decision).

[68] Larry Sager raised my attention to this issue.

The broad constitutional duty to provide integrated educational opportunities is not in principle judicially enforceable. Any decent review of conformity to this duty would require examination of a multiplicity of organisational facts (regarding faculty, administration, facilities, attendance zones etc) that would overburden judicial competence. Considerations of expertise and available resources, as well as fear of systemic judicial overreach indicate more limited doctrinal tests (like de jure segregation and discriminatory intent). The specification of the wider duty shall be left to the political branches. But once violation of the more limited duty is established, we have no more reason to trust the political and bureaucratic process.[69] Violation of the broader constitutional principle may also be presumed. And if default is severe or repeated, courts assume responsibility for the specification and implementation, in remedial form, of both the limited doctrinal duty and, to some extent, the underlying constitutional principle. As the Court emphasised in *Swann* 'remedial judicial authority does not put judges automatically in the shoes of school authorities whose powers are plenary. Judicial authority enters only when local authority defaults'.[70]

My main focus in presenting this argument is explanatory: to explain the normative structure of a line of jurisprudence that shaped post-*Brown* public law litigation. As such, it is also historically situated. It is most illuminating with regard to eras or areas where there is confidence in the aspirational dimension of constitutional law[71] and in the utility of reconstructing complementary institutional processes in furtherance of such pursuit.

VI. Revisiting Substance and Structure

Recognition of the proper relevance of institutional norms structuring the role of the political, bureaucratic and judicial branches in the joint task of constitutional construction does not commit us to any specific constitutional vision. Yet, it exposes us to the force of neglected, though pertinent reasons and the necessity for requisite justification.

[69] When the Court, in its liberal days, felt confident that the wider duty was violated, it was willing to infer purposeful discrimination from substantially disparate impact, inviting Justice Rehnquist to comment that the Court is reducing 'the discriminatory purpose requirement to a discriminatory impact test by another name' (*Columbus Board of Education v Penick*, 443 US 449, 509 (1979)).

[70] *Swann v Charlotte Mecklenburg Board of Education* 402 US 1, 16 (1971) (Burger, CJ).

[71] During the recent conservative control of the Court, the most one could contemplate outside the remedial context would be the recognition of educational integration in K-12 schools as a compelling state interest. 'This Nation has a moral and ethical obligation to fulfill its historic commitment to creating an integrated society that ensures equal opportunity for all of its children. A compelling interest exists in avoiding racial isolation, an interest that a school district, in its discretion and expertise, *may* choose to pursue'. *Parents Involved, above* n 51, at 797 (Kennedy, J, concurring). But while such aspirations are presented in permissive language, a constitutional drive often resonates behind the lines. 'School districts can seek to reach *Brown*'s objective of equal educational opportunity'. ibid, at 788.

The motivating idea behind our inquiry is that appreciation of the distinctive relation between constitutional substance and institutional structure can improve both. We have seen in this chapter how the theory of judicial under-enforcement illuminates that there may be more to constitutional law than limited judicial competence and legitimacy perceives. In fact, judicial cognizance of this fact has important implications for judicially enforced law, as we will see again in the next chapter. Similarly, we have seen how institutional considerations calling for searching review may be confused with overreaching substantive constraints—a finding that urges us to re-examine the substantive parameters of over-protection.

The general principle is that institutional considerations are not supposed to compete with substance, but to serve it. And recognition of their proper space is crucial for avoiding loss in our constitutional visions. At the same time, this elementary principle forces us to be critical over their proper content as well. Reasons for deference or for independent review are not self-justifying, as public institutions do not exercise privileges; they serve public functions, subject to public reason and, at least in the realm of constitutional law, political justice. We have seen that much of the contestation experienced in the field is attributed to conflicting visions of constitutional law and of underlying principles of political justice. We defend this approach and encourage its explicit elaboration, proposing the ideas advanced in Part Two above.

Constitutional construction is a joint, public function entrusted to the institutions of a constitutional democracy; under conditions of reasonable interpretive pluralism, reflecting the self-critical nature of the political community. And the institutional dimension of constitutional doctrine is to be assessed on doctrine's role to structure this functional process; the process of engagement with interpretive pluralism with a view to settlement on appropriate constitutional determinations under public reason and political justice.

13

The Claim to Judicial Supremacy

I. The Judicial Authority over Constitutional Doctrine

A. Judicial Supremacy and Doctrinal Authority

The complex institutional assignment of interpretive labour I discussed in the previous chapter stands in apparent tension with a fundamental claim pronounced repeatedly in American judicial practice: the claim to judicial interpretive authority. The Court has repeatedly used emphatic language regarding its interpretive authority in cases involving attempts by other institutions to question its constitutional holdings. It has added that institutional disagreement with the Court's pronouncements is not a reason to alter its doctrine. And it has even gone further and implied that the very fact of political resistance is an additional reason for the Court to insist on applicable precedent. Indeed, in *Casey*, Justice O'Connor, Justice Kennedy and Justice Souter declared that 'to overrule under fire in the absence of the most compelling reason to reexamine a watershed decision would subvert the Court's legitimacy … It is therefore imperative to adhere to the essence of *Roe's* original decision, and we do so today.'[1]

I will briefly discuss the two most famous cases in the field and argue that, at least upon a fair reading, they are not incompatible with the argument presented in the previous chapter, although their specific institutional conclusions are open to question on the ideas defended in Part Two. I will return to *Casey* in closing.

In *Cooper v Aaron*, signed by each of the nine judges, the Court rejected postponement of judicially decreed remedial plans concerning the desegregation of Little Rock's Central High School. The case was considered of paramount

[1] *Planned Parenthood of Southeastern Pa. v Casey*, 505 US 833, 869 (1992) (joint opinion of O'Connor, Kennedy, and Souter, JJ). It is doubtful whether the appearance of legitimacy in itself is a legitimate concern for the Court. Moreover, on the Court's own terms, if one endorses the claim that 'the Court's role is to discern principles sufficiently absolute to give them roots throughout the community and continuity over significant periods of time' (*Regents of the University of California v Bakke*, 438 US 265, 299 (1978)), authoritative insistence on rules that fail to receive such rooted status implies institutional failure and reinforces public discontent. But see Debora Hellman, 'The Importance of Appearing Principled' (1995) 37 *Tex L Rev* 1107.

significance because the chaos and turmoil that was prevailing was partly induced by the behaviour of Governor Faubus and other state officials in resistance to the plans decreed. The Court pronounced in dicta that under *Marbury* 'the federal judiciary is supreme in the exposition of the law of the Constitution' and that its interpretation of the law is 'the supreme law of the land'[2] that state officers are bound to obey.

This position of the Court was reaffirmed in *City of Boerne v Flores*[3] involving conflict with a federal institution, Congress itself. In 1993 Congress passed the Religious Freedom Restoration Act (RFRA), setting stringent conditions that neutral, generally applicable laws have to satisfy if they burden religious practices substantially. Members of Congress debated issues of constitutional interpretation and concluded that under the Constitution the compelling interest standard is the more appropriate one. Under the federal rule they instituted, federal, state and local government was prohibited from substantially burdening a person's exercise of religion unless it could demonstrate that the burden serves a compelling governmental interest and is the least restrictive means of furthering that interest.

In response, the Supreme Court held the statute unconstitutional as lying beyond the power of Congress to enforce the substantive provisions of the Fourteenth Amendment. The Court reasoned that, pursuant to section 5 of the Fourteenth Amendment, 'Congress has been given the power "to enforce", not the power to determine what constitutes a constitutional violation … When the Court has interpreted the constitution, it has acted within the province of the Judicial Branch, which embraces the duty to say what the law is … When the political branches of Government act against the background of a judicial interpretation of the Constitution already issued, it must be understood that in later cases and controversies the Court will treat its precedents with the respect due them under settled principles, including stare decisis, and contrary expectations must be disappointed'.[4]

The constitutional ideas employed in RFRA diverged fundamentally from the Court's interpretation of the free exercise clause, as settled in *Employment Div. v Smith* (1990). In fact, the rule instituted in RFRA was effectively described in *Smith* as a 'constitutional anomaly' (chapter twelve, section V(A)). However, the Act did not directly affect the judicial enforcement of the free exercise clause. In particular, it did not direct courts to resolve *constitutional* disputes within their jurisdiction on principles that contradict or even differ from judicially crafted doctrine.[5] What was addressed in *Flores* was the power of Congress to enforce

[2] *Cooper v Aaron*, 358 US 1, 18 (1958).

[3] *City of Boerne v Flores*, 521 US 507 (1997).

[4] ibid, at 536.

[5] Like in *Cooper*, the Court might have felt the need to invoke *Marbury* given the political context. Congress had directly attacked a very recent decision of the Supreme Court and had announced that their purpose was to 'restore' Religious Freedom.

certain constitutional provisions by appropriate prophylactic or remedial legislation under section five of the Fourteenth Amendment. When courts are asked to enforce Congressional measures, they are supposed to enforce them as legislative in nature.

Therefore, the issue in *Flores* involved the scope of Congressional legislative authority pursuant to section five (RFRA is still applicable to federal action) and the authority of judicial doctrine in its determination. In resolving this issue, the Court did not repeat the 'law of the land' language, but employed more moderate phraseology including reference to principles of stare decisis. But the underlying idea was the same: Congress has no authority to determine what counts as a constitutional violation; it is judicial doctrine that is controlling over the nature of violations Congress is authorised to prevent or remedy.

I will discuss and criticise the ideas behind the *Flores* conception of Congressional power in the next section II. Here, it is important to deflate its broader implications for judicial supremacy. The Court's determination that Congress may not go beyond the constitutional interpretation specified in judicial doctrine is an interpretation of the constitutional scope of Congressional power. The Court simply held that judicially crafted constitutional doctrine is dispositive on the scope of the Congressional mandate to enforce the Fourteenth Amendment. It does not address the power of the political body exercising general regulatory power (here, the States) to employ a more expansive interpretation of a constitutional right, so long as the right is under-enforced by the judiciary (and, consequently, by Congress as well). The Court simply replicates on section five the institutional division of labour between the primary decision maker and the judicial process and holds judicial doctrine dispositive in both domains. Beyond this, what applies to all political institutions is the general principle that 'when the political branches of Government act against the background of a judicial interpretation of the Constitution already issued, it must be understood that in later cases and controversies the Court will treat its precedents with the respect due them under settled principles'.

This account also helps us make sense of the *Cooper* Court's inflated assertion that the Court's constitutional interpretations constitute the supreme law of the land.[6] Given the chaotic situation in Arkansas at the time, including the promulgation of an amendment to the State constitution holding the *Brown* decisions unconstitutional, as well as the claim before the Court that there has been no judicial resolution over the constitutionality of such State conduct,[7] the Court felt the

[6] See Daniel Farber, 'The Supreme Court and the Rule of Law: *Cooper v. Aaron* Revisited' (1983) *U Ill L Rev* 387 (defending the holding while noting the exaggeration in the formulation).

[7] In the course of the overall litigation (though technically in prior proceedings), State officials had been made additional party defendants and subjected to judicial order enjoining them from interfering with the injunctions decreed. See *Faubus v United States*, 254 F.2d 797 (8th Cir., 1958). The case involved the employment of the Arkansas National Guard to prevent black students from attending the school.

need to 'equate' its constitutional holdings in *Brown* with the law of the land itself. This was perhaps unnecessary since implicated State conduct obstructed, with the purpose of frustrating, the effectuation of the court orders at issue. At any rate, the underlying idea is that the political branches are bound by judicially construed law,[8] like the constitutional rule enunciated in *Brown*; that is to say, in the conceptual framework employed here, they are bound by judicially crafted constitutional doctrine. Beyond that, *Cooper v Aaron* was evidently the paradigmatic case where the potential divergence between doctrine and the full scope of constitutional protection could not be an issue.

Furthermore, the *Cooper* Court evidently thinks that resistance to judicially crafted constitutional doctrine by a political institution does not provide in itself a reason for the Court to reverse its precedent in future cases. In moderate language, Justice Frankfurter clarified in concurrence that 'revision of … errors must be by orderly process of law. The Court may be asked to reconsider its decisions, and this has been done successfully again and again throughout our history'.[9]

Combining these two features, and given the authority of courts over the resolution of specific disputes brought before them, the Court may be understood as 'supreme' in the exposition of constitutional doctrine, at least as regards the application of constitutional law to issues within potential judicial jurisdiction. But it is of critical importance to notice, first, that such doctrine supposedly incorporates in its content the interpretive responsibilities of the political branches, as discussed in chapter twelve, and secondly, that judicial authority so construed, or supremacy if you like, does not cover every constitutional judgement; most importantly, it does not cover constitutional reasoning extending beyond judicial (and, under section 5, Congressional) enforcement.

Let us conclude. The Supreme Court has authority to settle the applicable standard of review and to form constitutional doctrine. Secondly, such doctrine governs both the judicial process (before federal or state courts) and the Congressional enforcement process. Thirdly, constitutional doctrine is authoritative over all public institutions, including the co-equal branches of government. This set of propositions is the most important legacy of the tradition of *Marbury v Madison* and is alive in current judicial practice. And it is fully compatible with the complex institutional division of interpretive labour operationalised by and through constitutional doctrine.

[8] *cf* the moderate way the same point is made in ordinary times: 'It is this Court's responsibility to say what a [federal] statute means, and once the Court has spoken, it is the duty of other courts to respect that understanding of the governing rule of law.' *Rivers v Roadway Express, Inc.*, 511 US 298, 312 (1994), quoted with approval in *James v City of Boise*, 577 US __ (2016) (per curiam) (slip op, at 1–2).

[9] *Cooper*, above n 2, at 23 (Frankfurter, J, concurring).

B. The Scope of Doctrinal Authority as an Institutional Issue

The construal of doctrinal authority advanced here does not settle details over scope and conditions. For instance, it does not settle the potential duty to follow Supreme Court precedent in conduct lying beyond judicial review (ie, a presidential veto invoking constitutional grounds). In areas within the boundaries of judicial enforcement, political bodies have a prudential reason to follow judicial doctrine. The *Cooper* Court holds that they also have a constitutional reason. Yet, the scope of such duty is also subject to interpretive doubt. What can be said for our purposes[10] is that these issues exhibit the reverse form of the one implicated in the process of judicial review: they involve the institutional structure governing the reasoning of the political institutions in exercising primary jurisdiction. Therefore, they are subject to justificatory considerations similar to those discussed in Part Two.

As far as the subject matter is within the scope of potential judicial resolution, there arguably has to be some symmetry in the operation of the pertinent considerations (allowing though for constructive dialogue between the branches). Moreover, attention should be given to the respective constitutional function at issue. A uniform rule may perhaps not be appropriate over the whole spectrum ranging from the coordinate branches of the federal government in their primary constitutional function to lower federal courts bound by the rule of precedent in the exercise of their judicial function.

What about the proper stance of the Court when the political branches deviate from past doctrine? The *Cooper* Court, with the qualifications of Justice Frankfurter mentioned above, held that the refusal of the political branches to follow Supreme Court precedent is treated as not having any normative force over the Court revisiting the issue. And *Flores* added that 'contrary expectations must be disappointed'. The issue naturally falls within the scheme of institutional reasoning discussed in this book and is assessed in light of the pursuit of serving the substantive desiderata of constitutional interpretation. Yet, once we take into account the role of political responsiveness and the importance of encouraging genuine constitutional dialogue in the joint task of implementing the Constitution, the justification of this holding seems, in the categorical form in which it is presented (and without questioning its application in *Cooper* in the least), to be in doubt.

Does this condemn the assertiveness of *Casey*? In a sense, it does. But we do need to keep in mind that constitutional dialogue is promising when it honours the commitments to equal citizenship (chapter ten, section II(B)). That was clearly not the case in *Cooper*. *Casey* is more complex. Still, one may point out, in defence

[10] The literature on the distinction between judicial review and judicial supremacy is vast. See, eg, the review essay of James E Fleming, 'Judicial Review Without Judicial Supremacy: Taking the Constitution Seriously Outside the Courts' (2005) 73 *Fordham L Rev* 1377.

of the plurality, the absence of a clear and sustained majority against *Roe* ('its divisiveness is no less today than in 1973') and, more importantly, the zealotry and intolerance that characterised the public debate on abortion.

II. The Case of Shared Enforcement Power

Our discussion in the previous chapter has been modelled on the assumption that interpretive labour is shared by a political body exercising primary jurisdiction and a reviewing court. In the previous section we added the prior doctrine-setting function of the Supreme Court. In both cases, the stipulation of a political body invested with primary jurisdiction is exogenous to the model. We may now expand our reach and discuss schemes of interpretive assignment including multiple institutions exercising primary jurisdiction or enforcement powers.

An obvious example is the case where primary jurisdiction is exercised by a multiplicity of bodies, acting within their exclusive jurisdiction—say, State legislatures exercising the police powers of the respective State. In such cases, it is important to keep in mind the federal aspects of the pertinent issue. There are subject areas where uniformity of constitutional settlement is critical as the issue involves a moral principle reflecting national commitments. Lack of a uniform solution may generate a further moral harm of unequal standing before federal constitutional law. In cases of this sort, perhaps after adequate time for local experimentation, the appropriate institutional resolution would require the Court, instead of focusing exclusively on the division of labour between the reviewed body and the judiciary, to take account of considerations like national consensus, rate and consistency of change in State policies, etc. The paradigmatic example is the death penalty jurisprudence, where the Court has made uniform determinations on a blending of national valuations and independent judicial judgement.[11] The traditional, bipolar model, on the other hand, may be adequate in issues where appropriate resolution largely depends on the choices local communities have made after due deliberation or in issues where local expertise is of particular relevance. Of course, in such cases, the adoption of a uniform standard of review can accommodate variation in performance and outcome.

Another example of considerable significance relates to the constitutional delegation to Congress of concurrent enforcement powers under the reconstruction amendments. Congress has the constitutional mandate to ensure compliance with and remedy violation of constitutional rights protected by these amendments. To this pursuit, it can regulate areas lying within the regulatory power of States.

[11] *Roper v Simmons*, 543 US 551 (2005) (holding imposition of the death penalty upon juveniles unconstitutional), *Atkins v Virginia*, 536 US 304 (2002) (holding imposition of the death penalty upon the mentally retarded unconstitutional).

The question we face is whether the reviewing court is supposed to defer to Congressional judgement regarding the specification of the constitutional norms served.

A. The *Flores* Declaration of Supremacy

Pursuant to section 2 of the Thirteenth Amendment Congress has authority to enforce section 1 abolishing slavery. The Court has read section 2 expansively to empower Congress to proscribe many forms of private racial discrimination, even though such conduct neither violates the prohibition of slavery nor can be understood as remedial to concrete violations of section 1. In *Jones v Alfred H. Mayer Co.*, it held that Congress has the power 'to pass all laws necessary and proper for abolishing the badges and incidents of slavery in the United States … [and to] determine what are the badges and incidents of slavery'.[12] The Court upheld the provisions under challenge, noting that the determination Congress had made was not an 'irrational' one. And while there is some concern about setting outer limits to Congressional authority, lower courts have generally understood *Jones* to establish a rational determination standard of review.[13]

Now, if Congressional measures pursuant to section 2 are not limited to enforcing, in proscriptive or remedial fashion, what is judicially enforceable under section 1, it is reasonable to assume that Congress has some independent authority to set up and implement a broader account of section 1 (determining and abolishing the badges and incidents of slavery). On this understanding, the *Jones* Court acknowledges Congressional power to rationally specify aspects of the constitutional principle of section 1 (beyond its self-executing core), and to design implementing legislation to serve them.

Things are sharply different with regard to section 5 of the Fourteenth Amendment, empowering Congress to enforce the rights protected by the substantive provisions of that amendment. The Court does accept that Congressional measures may reach conduct that does not in itself violate the Constitution, for the purpose of deterring or remedying violations of the constitutional norms anchored in the Fourteenth Amendment. At the same time, it has always been concerned about the limits of Congressional authority, as section 1 of the

[12] 392 US 409, 440 (1968).

[13] See *United States v Hatch*, 722 F.3d 1193, 1205 (10th Cir., 2013), cert denied, 134 S Ct 1538 (2014) ('Congress met the *Jones* test in rationally determining racially motivated violence to be a badge or incident of slavery that it could prohibit under its Section 2 authority'). The Court of Appeals was sensitive to concerns about Congressional overreach. Still, it emphasised that 'Congress [had] employed a limited approach to badges-and-incidents, applying that concept to: (a) actions that can rationally be considered to resemble an incident of slavery when (b) committed upon a victim who embodies a trait that equates to "race" as that term was understood in the 1860s, and (c) motivated by animus toward persons with that trait.' ibid, at 1206.

Fourteenth Amendment sweeps far broader than the prohibition of slavery. Past rulings of the Court had implied that Congress has limited leeway to proceed on its own specification of the pertinent constitutional norm—even in some reasonable variance from the way the Court would have specified it; or, perhaps, that section 5 invites Congress to enter into constructive dialogue with the Court over the best understanding of the underlying constitutional principles.[14] Nevertheless, the Court made it clear in *Flores* that Congress has no independent interpretive authority and that its role is restricted to deterring and remedying conduct that is violative of judicially crafted constitutional doctrine itself. Furthermore, the *Flores* Court held that courts, in reviewing the way Congress is exercising its power, are supposed to examine whether there is congruence and proportionality between the Congressional measures and the end of State compliance with applicable constitutional rules, as construed by judicial doctrine.

In defence of this position, Justice Kennedy, writing for the majority, claimed that judicial doctrine provides the meaning of the constitutional provisions that Congress is empowered to enforce. The idea is that 'the design of the Amendment and the text of § 5 are inconsistent with the suggestion that Congress has the power to decree the substance of the Fourteenth Amendment's restrictions on the States. Legislation which alters the meaning of the Free Exercise Clause cannot be said to be enforcing the Clause. Congress does not enforce a constitutional right by changing what the right is. It has been given the power "to enforce," not the power to determine what constitutes a constitutional violation'.[15]

This argument is radically incomplete. It collapses two distinct issues, the power to *determine* constitutional meaning and the power to *alter* constitutional meaning. This distinction is relevant in a substantive theory about how to interpret the Constitution. Yet, in itself, it does not settle the separate, institutional issue about who may authoritatively do so. No doubt, we may be reminded that, on the paradigmatic justification thesis, considerations of fidelity and efficacy matter in selecting the appropriate process. In this regard, Justice Kennedy provides a supplementary argument: 'if Congress could define its own powers by altering the Fourteenth Amendment's meaning, no longer would the Constitution be "superior paramount law, unchangeable by ordinary means … Under this approach, it is difficult to conceive of a principle that would limit congressional power. Shifting legislative majorities could change the Constitution and effectively circumvent the difficult and detailed amendment process contained in article V"'.[16]

Technically, these dicta, inspired from *Marbury*, somehow mischaracterise the distinctive and extraordinary role of constitutional amendment in constitutional

[14] See Stephen Carter, 'The *Morgan* Power and the Forced Reconsideration of Constitutional Decisions' (1986) 53 *U Chi L Rev* 819.

[15] *City of Boerne v Flores*, above n 3, at 519.

[16] ibid, at 529.

development. The content of constitutional norms changes over time in various informal ways. And this is to be expected, given the constructive dependence of such content upon interpretive reasoning, involving normative judgements subject to difference of opinion. Constitutional amendments, on the other hand, constitute change in the text of the Constitution, as the quintessential source of constitutional law. Yet, the critical issue is not technical. Justice Kennedy overlooks that the choice is not between Congressional exclusivity and Congressional impotence; rather, it is about the scope of Congress' distinctive interpretive contribution, limited by and monitored through judicial review. Hence, Justice Kennedy's argument is persuasive only upon the assumption that there is no meaningful and judicially manageable distinction between the range of permissible constructions, on the one hand, and circumvention of the amendment process, on the other. And as for the underlying idea that the distinction between informal change and amendment reflects concern for constitutional consistency over time,[17] the argument would necessitate the assumption that courts cannot adequately police the consistency required, or that such monitoring has unacceptable systemic costs.

Justice Kennedy invoked *Marbury v Madison*. But *Marbury* defended the power of courts to exercise constitutional review on the basis of the general judicial power to determine the applicable law in the process of resolving cases and controversies, that is to say, in a process of *enforcing* the Constitution. What is at stake here is the mutual demarcation and adjustment of the interpretive power and authority of two constitutional mechanisms of enforcement. Thus, it is not transparent how *Marbury's* reasoning is applicable when another coordinate branch of the federal government has concurrent enforcement power; especially whenever interpretive divergence in the two enforcement processes does not lead to practical conflict that would necessitate unitary settlement. Hence, even if we take *Marbury* at face value, we need further premises to reach the result adopted in *Flores*. We need further institutional reasoning to conclude that the enforcement power of Congress is limited to the legislative 'enforcement' of judicially crafted constitutional doctrine, shaped in the process of judicial enforcement.

B. The Institutional Landscape of Section 5

Given the fact that the language of section 5 and the arguments discussed above do not settle the issue, we need further analysis. We need to conceive of section 5 as setting up an institutional structure that dovetails with all implicated constitutional principles. Two principles implicated here are the supremacy of federal constitutional law and the appropriate respect for the federal character of the American polity, in which States have broad residuary powers. In their light,

[17] *cf* the emphasis on the settlement function of doctrinal authority attached by Larry Alexander & Frederick Schauer, 'On Extrajudicial Constitutional Interpretation' (1997) 110 *Harvard L Rev* 1359.

an appropriate interpretation of section 5 aims at an institutional structure well suited to reach and implement appropriate constitutional judgements accommodating, in particular, the following three interests: the constitutionally protected interests of the right-holders that Congress aims to protect, the constitutionally protected interests of other persons having claims under the Constitution, and other legitimate interests of free and equal citizens that are represented through States exercising general regulatory power, along with implicated State regulatory policies (what are so inaptly called 'state interests'). Systemic considerations are also important, in particular the coherence and synergy between the Congressional and the judicial enforcement process, and non-instrumental aspects of federalism (like, state autonomy).

This approach to the problem does not necessarily render the solution offered by the *Flores* Court deficient. The defender of *Flores* could claim that considerations of institutional competency and legitimacy are already taken into account at the level of formulating constitutional doctrine. The doctrine assigns a certain interpretive role to the (national or State) political institution exercising primary jurisdiction, while, the argument would go, section 5 does not alter this assignment by giving to Congress any distinctive interpretive authority. One could support this conclusion by invoking the recent tendency of the Court to apply the same standard of review to the conduct of both state and federal government.[18] On this account, and in spite of what we have learnt from the Reconstruction era, perhaps Congress does not possess any *further* institutional competency or legitimacy with regard to the interpretation of constitutional issues vis-à-vis States, or, at any rate, the federal structure of government and related systemic considerations disbar us from making any such assumption. If so, the critical issue is not the interpretive responsibility entrusted to the political branch exercising general regulatory power, which may not vary according to the nature of the enforcement mechanism subjected to. Rather, the critical issue is the enforcement responsibilities. And from that perspective, perhaps Congress does not possess any distinctive hedge over courts regarding determination of the substantive rules to be enforced, or, anyway, such hedge is outmatched by the cacophony introduced by two quasi-independent enforcement processes.

Our task is not to solve the interpretive issue, but to clarify its nature. The critic of *Flores* would argue that section 5 does make a difference. Constitutional doctrine is crafted in the process of judicial review, and is therefore informed by the purposes and limitations of that process, including the limitations in the judicial fact-finding capacity. Perhaps, at that stage, comparative differences between state and national legislatures might not make any significant difference with regard to

[18] That debate was conducted two terms before *Flores* in the equally highly contested case of *Adarand Constructors, Inc. v Pena* 518 US 200, 212–31 (1995) (holding that equal protection analysis in the Fifth Amendment area is the same as that under the Fourteenth Amendment).

the appropriate standard of review connecting the reviewing court and the body exercising primary jurisdiction. However, such considerations may make a difference once we move into a triangular model. Perhaps the very rationale behind section 5 was based on the premise that Congress, instituted as an independent guardian of certain constitutional requirements of nation-wide significance, and given historical experience, can better be entrusted with resolving some of the constitutional issues that, in the process of judicial review, are ordinarily reserved within the competence of the primary decision maker. In fact, this has been implied in past dicta explaining judicial deference over state classifications in the field of social and economic regulation on the idea that judicial standards serve a subsidiary function.[19]

Of course, even under this alternative approach, there is need for judicially guarded limitations upon Congressional interpretive authority. For instance, Congressional constructions may be held to lie outside the range of permissibility if they *conflict* with judicial doctrine, or *frustrate* its purposes, especially when doctrine exhausts constitutional meaning and no under-enforcement is present. Perhaps *harmony* with doctrinal principles (and their underlying substantive ideas) may also be required, to control for Congressional overreach. And considerations of this sort are particularly relevant when Congressional policies in furtherance of a constitutional pursuit burden judicially enforced rights of others.

The governing idea aims to accommodate the distinctive and complementary contribution of each co-equal branch of the federal government in giving effect to constitutional guarantees. In this regard, following Eisgruber and Sager, I note that the *outcome* in *Flores* is compatible with an alternative institutional account that is more sensitive to the institutional role of Congress.[20] The Court could have held the federal law at issue unconstitutional as disharmonious with or even frustrating to the underlying doctrinal principles.[21] And it could have insisted that Congressional distinctive contribution is faithful to the constitutional scheme when Congress acts as a partner with the judiciary in a community of principle.

[19] *Cleburne v Cleburne Living Ctr.*, 473 US 432, 439–440 (1985) ('Section 5 of the Amendment empowers Congress to enforce this mandate, but absent controlling congressional direction, the courts have themselves devised standards for determining the validity of state legislation or other official action that is challenged as denying equal protection. The general rule is that legislation is presumed to be valid').

[20] Christopher Eisgruber & Lawrence Sager, 'Congressional Power and Religious Liberty after *City of Boerne v. Flores*' (1997) *Supreme Ct Rev* 79.

[21] In passing RFRA, Congress attempted to effectively overrule *Smith*. And while *Smith* expressly held that nondiscriminatory exemption laws are not in principle unconstitutional (*Employment Div. v Smith*, 494 US 872, 890 (1991)), there is in the background clear understanding that *Smith* does not merely set a minimal floor of protection against other legitimate interests, but also reflects considerations about the appropriate balance that any reasonable federal constitutional rule shall strike between the establishment and the free exercise of religion clauses, an understanding that RFRA's sweeping scope unsettles. See in this regard the text above ch 12 n 56. Finally, one should also keep in mind the institutional friction that was involved in *Flores*. Congress was attempting a front attack against a recent decision of the Court in order to 'restore' religious freedom.

Similarly, if both States and the federal government are under some strict, judicially enforced constitutional duty, it would defy reason to assert that the federal government has the power, in enforcing some other constitutional right, to direct or authorise States to violate the said duty.[22] Such federal policy would in principle both violate the substantive right burdened and overstep section 5. Yet, if the Court is willing to perceive, in dialogue with the political branches of the federal government, that the very structuring of competing constitutional rights is at issue, Congressional engagement under section 5 could make some (judicially supervised) difference; for instance, it could facilitate judicial acceptance that a constitutional interest specified by Congress is compelling, or that the measures mandated in its pursuit are necessary.[23]

This last point sheds light on the opportunities and limits of a partnership conception of constitutional implementation. Yet, it is important to take cognizance of a third conceivable institutional theory. An institutional scheme of checks and balances is based on the understanding that public decision-making processes are prone to error. This applies to the judiciary as well. Section 5, on this account, does not merely contemplate Congressional involvement in the space left open by judicial under-enforcement. It also responds to the likelihood of erratic judicial under-enforcement, by institutionalising a plural scheme of constitutional implementation. Courts would still have to watch for Congressional overreach, and ensure coherence and synergy of enforcement. Yet, given the structure of US-style judicial review and the supremacy the Court claims over judicial doctrine, this alternative scheme may well improve the overall flexibility of the structures entrusted with implementing the Constitution; by facilitating free-flow of ideas and mutual learning among institutions, and by improving long-term correctability and adaptability of the overall system. Admittedly, the current state of the case law is far removed from this vision. Yet, the ideas behind this alternative conception raise concerns that current orthodoxy needs to grapple with.

[22] As the Court unanimously held the day it decided *Brown*, 'in view of our decision that the Constitution prohibits the states from maintaining racially segregated public schools, it would be unthinkable that the same Constitution would impose a lesser duty on the Federal Government'. *Bolling v Sharpe*, 347 US 497, 500 (1954).

[23] *Adarand*, above n 18, at 253 (Stevens, J, dissenting) ('But it is one thing to say (as no one seems to dispute) that the Fifth Amendment encompasses a general guarantee of equal protection as broad as that contained within the Fourteenth Amendment. It is another thing entirely to say that Congress' institutional competence and constitutional authority entitles it to no greater deference when it enacts a program designed to foster equality than the deference due a state legislature'). The issue is also of particular relevance with regard to the friction between disparate impact liability and equal protection claims of others. See the famous concurrence of Justice Scalia in *Ricci v DeStefano*, 557 US 557, 594–96 (2009) (Scalia, J, concurring) ('Disparate impact provisions place a racial thumb on the scales, often requiring employers to evaluate the racial outcomes of their policies, and to make decisions based on (because of) those racial outcomes. … The war between disparate impact and equal protection will be waged sooner or later, and it behooves us to begin thinking about how—and on what terms—to make peace between them').

C. *Flores* and Argumentative Transparency

Be that as it may, it should be stressed that the institutional rigidity of *Flores* affects the transparency of substantive constitutional debate. The problem, of course, is not recent and is linked to the conservatism that traditionally characterises the scope of the Court's equal protection jurisprudence. Thus, title II of the Civil Rights Act of 1964 (prohibiting racial and religious discrimination in places of public accommodation), a quintessential equal protection statute, was defended and upheld under the Commerce clause.[24] Yet, the institutional monism of *Flores* (along with recent state immunity jurisprudence) has exacerbated it to the effect of jeopardising judicial candour itself.

For instance, the liberal wing of the Court is often pressed to pigeonhole disparate impact liability imposed by federal anti-discrimination laws into disparate treatment pursuits. Sometimes language is cryptic: 'When Congress seeks to remedy or prevent unconstitutional discrimination, § 5 authorizes it to enact prophylactic legislation proscribing practices that are discriminatory in effect, if not in intent, to carry out the basic objectives of the Equal Protection Clause'.[25] But what are these 'objectives', given the narrow scope of intent-focused judicial doctrine? I discussed a similar difficulty with liberal approaches to judicial remedies in the previous chapter (section V(C)). At the background of that line of jurisprudence rests a broader constitutional drive for equal opportunity and social inclusion, at least in the sense of combating policies that perpetuate exclusion or pertinent inequalities. And I suggested that judicial engagement in pursuit of the broader principle has been implicated once government if found to default under much narrower doctrine. That same constitutional drive operates behind Congressional anti-discrimination plans pursuant to section 5, and should be acknowledged and defended as such.

It is no wonder, in this regard, that the majority opinion in *Inclusive Communities Project*, authored by Justice Kennedy himself, expressly blended narrow prophylactic with broader aspirational purposes in projecting disparate impact liability upon the Fair Housing Act (FHA). The opinion emphasised that the statutory purpose relates to the 'removal of artificial, arbitrary, and unnecessary barriers' to housing. While it linked disparate impact liability to the eradication of discriminatory practices, it concluded that 'the FHA must play an important part in avoiding the … grim prophecy that "[o]ur Nation is moving toward two societies, one black, one white—separate and unequal." … The Court acknowledges the Fair Housing Act's continuing role in moving the Nation toward a more integrated society.'[26] And although the case was decided on statutory interpretation grounds,

[24] *Heart of Atlanta Motel, Inc. v United States*, 379 US 241 (1964).

[25] *Tennessee v Lane* 541 US 509, 519–20 (2004).

[26] *Texas Dept. of Housing and Community Affairs v Inclusive Communities Project, Inc.*, 576 US __ (2015) (slip op, at 18 and 24).

the decision was coupled with various constitutional caveats to secure that impact liability and consequent remedial measures do not violate equal protection claims of others (do not require defendants to consider race in a pervasive manner in order to justify their policies, etc). In effect, Justice Kennedy, leading here a liberal Court, perceives a legitimate federal commitment to secure against arbitrary, artificial and unnecessary barriers to basic opportunities in pursuit of integrative aspirations. But if the Court 'acknowledges' this important federal role, while supervising its outer substantive reach, there is an issue with *Flores*.

D. Congress as an Instrumentality of the Court?

Even under the limited understanding of Congressional role adopted in *Flores*, there could be space for Congress to provide its own *specification* of the abstract interpretation the Court adopts. That was indeed implied in preexisting law. In *Katzenbach v Morgan*, the Court held that Congress had permissibly banned literacy requirements barring Puerto Ricans from voting. The Court accepted that the Congressional measures were appropriately enforcing the equal protection clause. It noted that Congress might have questioned whether the voting qualifications aimed at providing an incentive for immigrants to learn English and assuring the intelligent exercise of the franchise, and might well have concluded that they constituted invidious discrimination. The Court went even further and stressed that since Congress acted 'in the context of a general appraisal of literacy requirements for voting ... to which it brought a specially informed legislative competence, it was Congress' prerogative to weigh these competing considerations. Here again, it is enough that we perceive a basis upon which Congress might predicate a judgment ... [of] invidious discrimination in violation of the Equal Protection Clause'.[27]

After *Morgan*, the Court has consistently been narrowing Congressional latitude. For example, in *Oregon v Mitchell* three members of the Court reasoned that *Morgan* 'does not hold that Congress has power to determine what are and what are not compelling state interests'. Yet, they acknowledged that Congress may override state laws that are instruments of invidious discrimination 'even though a court in an individual lawsuit might not have reached that factual conclusion'.[28]

[27] 384 US 641, 655–56 (1966). *Morgan* has been understood more broadly to cover the very scope of constitutional principles. See *Adarand*, above n 18, at 255 fn 11 (Stevens, J, dissenting) ('We have read § 5 as a positive grant of authority to Congress, not just to punish violations, but also to define and expand the scope of the Equal Protection Clause. *Katzenbach* v. *Morgan* ...'). In a strikingly opposing direction, the *Flores* Court accommodated *Morgan* noting that the 'Court perceived a factual basis on which Congress could have concluded that New York's literacy requirement "constituted invidious discrimination" in violation of the Equal Protection Clause'. 521 US at 528.

[28] 400 US 112, 295, 296 (1970) (Stewart, J, joined by Burger, CJ and Blackmun, J, concurring in part).

It is arguably not difficult to draw a coherent picture accommodating both *Morgan* and *Mitchell.* Congress has some latitude in specifying judicially crafted constitutional doctrine in light of the social problem at issue and its factual pattern. The scope of the latitude cannot be determined in advance in easily drawn categories. Rather, one has to ask whether it would be more appropriate for a judgement lying beyond ordinary judicial competence to be made by the national legislature.

Now, one can read *Flores* in a way that accommodates that frame of analysis, subject of course to compliance with the 'congruence and proportionality' requirement. However, subsequent case law has almost eradicated Congressional latitude in specifying judicial doctrine and has narrowed even further Congress' power to reach beyond doctrine for remedial or preventative purposes. The two issues, though conceptually distinct, are linked together as proportionality presupposes an adequate pattern or risk of constitutional violations and as such adequacy aims to ensure, under *Flores*, that legislation does not alter the substance of the law in operation and effect.

For instance, in *College Savings Bank* the Court held invalid the Congressional abrogation of state immunity in patent infringements.[29] A 5–4 majority concluded that the statutory scheme of a uniform remedy for patent infringement against States and private parties was not proportionate to the goal of deterring or remedying unconstitutional conduct by States. The majority defined such conduct with specificity. It determined that the Fourteenth Amendment is violated only by unremedied State patent infringements and refused to give Congress any benefit of doubt in challenging the constitutional adequacy of State remedies. It then required that Congress should have provided findings of fact establishing a widespread pattern of deprivations ('no evidence that unremedied patent infringement by States had become a problem of national import'). And it even questioned the reach of remedial power, at least in the absence of such a widespread pattern, beyond 'arguable constitutional violations'.[30] The decision is unfortunate in downplaying even the institutional advantages that Congress has over issues of strategy! It is unclear whether the majority conceded any advantage to Congress other than the absence of the 'case or controversy' limitation.

Indeed, even if we put the issue of constitutional specification aside, the Court seems to sidestep the fact that the proportionality of preventative or remedial measures largely depends upon issues of social fact and policy. No doubt, the pertinent judgements also involve assessments of value, for instance, about the gravity of the wrongs to be deterred by sweeping legislation and about the optimal

[29] *Florida Prepaid Postsecondary Ed. Expense Bd. v College Savings Bank*, 527 US 627 (1999). See also *Board of Trustees of Univ. of Alabama v Garrett*, 531 US 356, 376 (2001) (Breyer, J, dissenting) ('Reviewing the congressional record as if it were an administrative agency record, the Court holds the statutory provision before us … unconstitutional').

[30] *Florida Prepaid*, ibid, at 645–46, 646.

balance between deterrence and costs of over-inclusion. Still, assuming no conflict of fundamental rights is implicated, this Congressional assessment is reviewable within a frame of analysis different from fundamental rights review. What is at stake is not whether a fundamental liberty interest may be sacrificed to further a compelling public interest, but whether the burdens imposed upon affected interests and state policies are justified given the national interest that Congress may legitimately decide, as a matter of constitutional policy, to pursue. And in inquiries of this sort, it is highly questionable whether heightened judicial review is justified. It is in fact quite doubtful whether it provides any distinctive hedge to better assessments, or whether the error of under-enforcing 'State interests' is so grave to warrant prophylactic frames of review.

Be that as it may, the sharp division within the Court, replicated in subsequent cases,[31] shows that the debate over the exact interpretive assignment of States, Congress and the Supreme Court is as lively as ever. And as happens to be the case with contested issues of institutional allocation, substantive assessments about the sensitivities and priorities of different institutions lurk in the background.[32]

E. The Standard of Judicial Review and the Congressional Process

A noteworthy feature in recent case law is the tendency of the Court to link the evidentiary burden Congress faces to the standard of judicial review governing the discriminatory patterns at issue. This provides us with an appropriate perspective for a more comprehensive discussion of the relevance of standards of judicial review for section 5 analysis.

As Chief Justice Rehnquist explained in *Hibbs*, 'under our equal protection case law, [age- or disability-based] discrimination … is not judged under a heightened review standard, and passes muster if there is "a rational basis for doing so at a class based level, even if it 'is probably not true' that those reasons are valid in the majority of cases." *Kimel* … Thus, in order to impugn the constitutionality of state discrimination against the disabled or the elderly, Congress must identify, not just the existence of age or disability-based state decisions, but a "widespread pattern"

[31] See the narrow majority in *Nev. Dep't of Human Res. v Hibbs*, upholding the Congressional measure in review as it was 'narrowly targeted at the fault line' and involved conduct subjected to heightened judicial scrutiny (538 US 721, 738 (2003)), and the casuistry dominating the equally contested case of *Coleman v Court of Appeals of Maryland*, 566 US __ (2012).

[32] See *Shelby County v Holder*, 570 US __ (2013) striking down section 4(b) of the Voting Rights Act of 1965 for not speaking to 'current conditions'. While the rationale sounds quasi-procedural, pointing out that the provision is not supported by an updated record, the majority is heavily influenced by an implicit substantive assessment of the magnitude and intensity of the constitutional evil Congress purportedly combats: 'In 1965, the States could be divided into two groups: those with a recent history of voting tests and low voter registration and turnout, and those without those characteristics. Congress based its coverage formula on that distinction. Today the Nation is no longer divided along those lines, yet the Voting Rights Act continues to treat it as if it were' (slip op, at 18).

of irrational reliance on such criteria. … Here, however … because the standard for demonstrating the constitutionality of a gender-based classification is more difficult to meet than our rational-basis test … it was easier for Congress to show a pattern of state constitutional violations. Congress was similarly successful in *South Carolina v. Katzenbach* …: Because racial classifications are presumptively invalid, most of the States' acts of race discrimination violated the Fourteenth Amendment.'[33]

This explanation provoked the reply by Justice Breyer, on behalf of the four liberal justices, that the rational basis standard is partly explicable on institutional considerations not applicable to Congress. 'The problem with the Court's approach is that neither the "burden of proof" that favors States nor any other rule of restraint applicable to judges applies to Congress when it exercises its § 5 power. Limitations stemming from the nature of the judicial process … have no application to Congress.'[34]

Careful attention to the matter shows that both lines of argument are rather incomplete. The main deficiency is that the majority fails to recognise that standards of review should not be equated with constitutional substance. They have an institutional dimension. Without attending to the institutional function, any congruence and proportionality analysis is heavily distorted. At the same time, the minority, while pointing out to institutional aspects, does not examine their implications for the Congressional process. Here is why:

'Age classifications, unlike governmental conduct based on race or gender, cannot be characterized as so seldom relevant to the achievement of any legitimate state interest that laws grounded in such considerations are deemed to reflect prejudice and antipathy.'[35] On this line of jurisprudence, an age classification is presumptively rational. Now, this argument has both a substantive and an institutional dimension. On the substantive dimension, such classifications are perhaps thought not to carry with them inherent, status-conferring properties of the sort encountered, say, in racial discrimination. No doubt, sometimes they are in fact arbitrary and unreasonable. Still, institutional review has an inherent propensity to err and we need to care about how to minimise error. Judicial review provides an institutional layer on top of the process governing the formation of judgement by the State body exercising primary jurisdiction. Thus, considerations of expected gravity and likelihood of error may perhaps provide the extra argumentative resources to uphold a presumption of constitutionality.

Now, it is pretty obvious that the mechanics of this assessment invite attention to the institutional process at issue. For instance, the relative degree of over-enforcement and under-enforcement is related to the ability of the judiciary to

[33] *Hibbs*, above n 31, at 735–36 (while technically part of the majority opinion, this dictum reflects the views of the Chief Justice and Justice O'Connor).

[34] *Garrett*, above n 29, at 383 (Breyer J, dissenting).

[35] *Kimel v Florida Bd. of Regents*, 528 US 62, 83 (2000).

exercise discriminate judgement under a more flexible standard. A heavy presumption of constitutionality would normally imply a bleak view of such an alternative. At any rate, Justice Breyer is certainly correct in claiming that the minimal standard of review was initially designed against the backdrop of the judicial process. Yet, if a kind of classification is normally taken not to be arbitrary and unreasonable, perhaps the calculus would turn out similarly with regard to the Congressional enforcement process as well. On this assumption, Congressional enforcement should perhaps also be a species of under-enforcement, like the judicial one.

In fact, if the judicial standard is optimal in minimising enforcement error, one would need further argumentation to support aggressive Congressional enforcement. To this conclusion, it is not enough to point out that the process for designing the applicable standard is different (Supreme Court v Congress). In contrast to *Morgan*, in the line of cases discussed here, what is at stake is not a specific Congressional determination specifying the substantive import of equal protection to a set of facts, but a generic legislative standard that competes with judicial doctrine on the same level of generality: a legislative rule subjecting general conduct to heightened scrutiny, whereas constitutional doctrine subjects it to a deferential standard. If so, we also need to inquire on the process charged with implementing the Congressional standard. If the legislative standard will be implemented by the very same processes operating constitutional review, that is by the federal courts (or by processes of equivalent competency), we need further reason to explain why the calculus would be different. And this burden is quite onerous if the Congressional standard is fundamentally different from the judicial one (as in *Kimel*). Furthermore, we need to discount the fact that the process enforcing the legislative standard is a third institutional layer, on top of the operation of minimal judicial review. For reasons of this sort, it may turn out that broad Congressional alterations to the generic standard of judicial review cause substantially more error overall. And, finally, they may unsettle the substantive constitutional settlement that the judicial standard may have formed or create cacophony in the operation of the processes of review.

Having made these qualifications, I suppose that in many cases the calculus in the two enforcement processes would be different. There are two fundamental reasons to that. First, our discussion so far has focused on how to capture violations of equal protection in an optimal manner. But Congress has authority to reach conduct that is not violative of equal protection—for preventative or remedial purposes. Thus, we need to be able to re-assess the calculus by adding the prophylactic and remedial benefits. Congruence and proportionality analysis applies to the overall scheme. Of course, proper analysis presupposes some rational basis in apprehending the mischief of constitutional violations Congress aims to remedy. Yet, proportionality review shall accommodate the fact that Congress, in determining proper reach, employs complex assessments of social fact and constitutional policy, which are not applicable to the judicial process operating within the context of resolving specific disputes.

There is also a second ground for valuing an expansive legislative enforcement process. On the very criteria discussed above, it may well turn out that, under a focused test, the Congressional process captures—say, at acceptable cost—a significant sub-set of unconstitutional conduct that the judicial process may not capture under the minimal rationality test. It is entirely plausible to argue that Congress has a unique deliberative responsibility in advancing national commitments to equal citizenship and in highlighting criteria of reasonableness, especially in territory the judicial process may often lack confidence, resources or judicially manageable standards to enter. In those areas, both the lessons of history and the value of a national dialogue for equal citizenship may well support the bounded authority of Congress, pursuant to section 5, to determine that certain classifications in well-defined contexts stand in need of special justification. And finally, on a more radical conception, this may be permissible even if the Court is confident of its own substantive approach. Confidence should be accompanied with cognizance of one's own fallibility and of the fact that plural schemes of constitutional implementation may well improve long term correctability and systemic adaptability. Either way, I would suggest that we need to question as quite dogmatic the obsessive insistence that the end state of Congressional preventative or remedial legislation shall always be conduct violative of judicial doctrine itself.[36]

III. Institutional Reciprocity and the Joint Project of Constitutional Construction

The preceding discussion brings to the surface the tension between absolutist claims to judicial supremacy and a main normative argument advanced in Part Two of this book: the value of institutional reciprocity over the joint task of constitutional construction. To the broader aspects of this issue, we may now turn.

A. From Civic to Institutional Reciprocity

A driving idea of this book is the commitment that, in a political democracy, public power is power held and exercised in trust. Public officials are supposed to exercise public power in their capacity as the collective arms of the free and equal members of the political community. Constitutional implementation is such a public task, entrusted to a scheme of public institutions. Given the constructive nature of constitutional interpretation and the fact of reasonable interpretive pluralism, there is

[36] *Kimel*, ibid, at 86 ('The Act, through its broad restriction on the use of age as a discriminating factor, prohibits substantially more state employment decisions and practices than would likely be held unconstitutional under the applicable equal protection, rational basis standard').

a genuine normative issue about the proper assignment of the interpretive labour to judicial and non-judicial institutions.

I have discussed this normative issue, with particular focus on the standard of judicial review. The main normative argument, defended in Part Two, is that the institutional norms governing the intensity of judicial review are paradigmatically to be assessed in the light of the functional synergy that they may create with a view to expounding and implementing the Constitution in appropriate manners under the pursuit of public reason and political justice. In chapters nine and ten I added that the commitment to political democracy urges us, in this normative inquiry, to appeal to reasons that reflect the bonds of reciprocity among co-equal and free members of a political community with diverging views about political justice. Accordingly, the process of authoritative constitutional exposition should, among other desiderata, exhibit fair democratic responsiveness and be well suited, in this regard, to engage in a dialogue with the citizenry, a dialogue that is open and conducted on reasons that in good faith reach all citizens as free and equal.

This implies in turn an inter-branch counterpart: a call for reciprocity between the judicial and the political branches, the latter being treated, in principle, as quintessential areas of public engagement. Of course, institutional reciprocity is neither absolute, nor substance-blind. It is to be understood as an element of an overall institutional frame, also including considerations of comparative institutional analysis, occasional institutional distrust, and management of risks of error. Moreover, the qualification about the nature of the civic dialogue contemplated (open and conducted on reasons that in good faith reach all citizens as free and equal) further colours the institutional frame in substance-sensitive desiderata: it reminds us that the bonds of civic reciprocity among free and equal citizens are honourable so long as the outcomes reached do uphold the substantive preconditions of such reciprocity and lie within a range of sufficient justice.

So, evidently, institutional reciprocity would not require the kind of servile projection of public purpose that sometimes we encounter in minimal rationality review. But, at the very least, it would imply a good faith engagement of the judiciary with the legislative plan at issue for the purpose of unearthing underlying judgements of principle; and a duty to substantiate why, if so, such judgements turn out to be unsustainable in a community of free and equal citizens with diverging views about political justice. It would also entail an earnest commitment to correctability, including sensitivity to the responses the judiciary gets from the political branches and the citizenry at large. Laurence Tribe has powerfully claimed, in defence of judicial review, that the 'unending constitutional discourse, and the role it plays in subjecting governmental practices to continuing critique' gives the institution of judicial review legitimacy.[37] Institutionalisation of critique can sustain this function so long as it is based on argumentative interaction and mutual correctability.

[37] L Tribe, *American Constitutional Law*, 3rd edn, vol I (New York, Foundation Press, 2000) 311.

If these considerations are relevant in assessing the appropriate standard of judicial review, they also have a distinctive bearing with regard to the proper scope of Congressional power in enforcing the Reconstruction amendments. Civil Rights Acts constitute rare instances where Congress has articulated constitutional vision. More importantly, these Acts have marked modern American history in promotion of national values of equal citizenship. In this process Congress has often built upon judicial milestones, but has sometimes circumnavigated around rearguard judicial doctrine. In the latter category of cases, progress was not obtained by doctrinal supremacy; but by mutual learning, and by the force of national culture, enabling all three federal branches of government to leave traumatic mistakes behind.

Indeed, ever since 1883, when the Supreme Court invalidated the public accommodation provisions of the Civil Rights Act of 1875,[38] the Court has been sceptical on the reach of national legislation prohibiting discrimination in the private sector. In 1906, it held that only conduct reducing individuals to a condition of slavery can be subjected to punishment under legislation enacted to enforce the Thirteenth Amendment.[39] The latter decision was overruled by *Jones* in the heyday of the Warren Court. And it took 20 more years for the conservative side, then and now in the majority, to acknowledge the relevance, for the reach of civil rights legislation to private conduct, of 'our society's deep commitment to the eradication of discrimination based on a person's race or the color of his or her skin'.[40]

In discussing judicial reasoning about constitutional justice in chapter ten, we recalled Alexander Bickel's admonition that the Court lead public opinion without imposing its own. Given the historical record, it does not make much sense to deny Congress a distinguished role in national dialogue about constitutional values. The pursuit of constitutional justice is arguably better served through a smoother process, where Congress would have a fair opportunity to participate, as an esteemed partner, in the formation of national values of equal citizenship; and where a plural, while coherent, scheme of constitutional implementation would keep the dialogue open, and serve the virtues of long term correctability and systemic adaptability.

We may of course be reminded of the distinctive sensibilities of the judiciary and of the risks of error in matters of moral gravity. But when constitutional anomalies are not at issue, judicial scrutiny of potential Congressional overreach here cannot easily be justified by ordinary institutional considerations that are dispositive in mainstream cases of strict or heightened scrutiny. Whenever the government regulates speech on the basis of viewpoint, or classifies citizens on the

[38] *The Civil Rights Cases*, 109 US 3 (1883), reaffirmed in *United States v Morrison* 529 US 598, 621–24 (2000).

[39] *Hodges v United States*, 203 US 1, 17–19 (1906), overruled in *Jones*, *above* n 12, at 441 n 78.

[40] *Patterson v McLean Credit Union*, 491 US 164, 174 (1989).

basis of their colour, it makes sense to appeal to distinctive judicial sensibilities and to institutional detachment. Of course, Congressional constitutional policy that crates havoc in the structure of competing constitutional claims is an anomaly. But when we assess structural arguments about concurrent authority we need some sense of balance. 'There is no constitutional right, for example, to discriminate in the selection of who may attend a private school or join a labor union.'[41] At any rate, assuming that Congressional legislation in expansion of equal protection rights does not give rise to serious concerns of constitutional conflict, it is highly questionable whether the judiciary possesses distinctive sensibilities in policing vague federalism boundaries against expansive constitutional vision. And ending up with somehow loose outer boundaries does not normally implicate error of utmost moral gravity.

In any case, the Constitution does contemplate synergy between the judicial and the Congressional process in enforcing the respective principles of constitutional justice. To a large extent, the imperatives of *Brown* were not actualised before Congress—with a time lag of a decade—enacted broad remedial policies.[42] But synergy requires reciprocity. As Justice Jackson has famously noted, 'the actual art of governing under our Constitution does not and cannot conform to judicial definitions of the power of any of its branches based on isolated clauses or even single Articles torn from context. While the Constitution diffuses power the better to secure liberty, it also contemplates that practice will integrate the dispersed powers into a workable government. It enjoins upon its branches separateness but interdependence, autonomy but reciprocity'.[43]

The exact institutional division of interpretive labour in judicial review is a rather dynamic issue. It is shaped by the continuous interactions between the political branches and the judiciary and by the doctrinal, path-dependent quasi-equilibria sustained by the role of the Supreme Court in American constitutional practice. Accordingly, upholding the bonds of reciprocity requires continuous effort by all branches; yet, given the privileged position of the Supreme Court in unilaterally setting the judicially enforceable terms of reciprocity, it implies a heavy justificatory burden to the Court itself.

In carrying out this burden, the Court is invited, in all respect, to pay due attention to the fact that public institutions are to be understood as the collective arms of free and equal citizens, joint tenants in sovereignty. In elaborating the terms of reciprocity among the federal branches of government in particular, especially with regard to constitutional principles reflecting national value commitments, the Court is asked to uphold the importance of genuine and constructive dialogue between the judiciary and the political branches of the federal

[41] *Hishon v King & Spalding*, 467 US 69, 77 (1984).

[42] Mark Tushnet, *Taking the Constitution Away from the Courts* (Princeton, Princeton University Press, 1999) 145.

[43] *Youngstown Sheet & Tube Co. v Sawyer*, 343 US 579, 635 (1952) (Jackson, J, concurring).

government, provided that such dialogue is conducted on reasons that in good faith reach all citizens as free and equal; and to give effect, within the contours of such dialogue, to Congressional distinctive contributions in safeguarding the principles and realising the ideals of equal citizenship.

B. A Joint Project of Plural Construction

The account of constitutional interpretation employed throughout this book builds upon a fundamental feature of pluralistic institutional life: its reflective and argumentative character. The constructive nature of constitutional interpretation is an offspring of this social fact. And the same applies to reasonable interpretive pluralism. At the same time, I have warned against interpretive relativism, invoking an implicit commitment to standards of interpretive failure and success. And, in Part Two, I defended a normative commitment to the joint nature of constitutional construction, operated by the scheme of public institutions as agents of a political community of free and equal citizens.

This conception of constitutional interpretation invites two fundamental questions. What makes it possible to understand constitutional law as something more than a temporary overlap of interpretive idiolects? How is it possible to conceive of an institutional scheme of joint constitutional construction in a world of independent minds?

I approached the first question in chapter four, section IV, explaining how the constructive dependence of constitutional law upon practical deliberation is not incompatible with the sense of stability and minimal convergence that enables us to treat constitutional practice as an institutional normative practice. I indicated various mutually reinforcing factors to this conclusion (web of interpretive loci treated as settled in the practice, judicial culture, considerations of constitutional legitimacy, and the substantive value of discursive reciprocity). And I claimed that the operation of these factors explains how both convergence and discursive argument in the face of divergence reflect a joint commitment of participants to treat constitutional practice as a shared normative practice. At the same time, I emphasised the limitations of such factors. The commitment to correctability operates within substantive ideas we have about the applicable standards of reasonableness. And even discussants of good faith exhibit sensitivity towards a certain range of acceptable arguments. Thus, interpretive disagreement is unavoidable—often of irreconcilable nature.

The question we now face is how interpretive pluralism is compatible with the normative idea that institutional actors are invited to see themselves as engaged in a joint project of constitutional construction. The basic idea would be that democratic constitutional construction implies a strong substantive commitment to discursive reciprocity and a corresponding commitment to institutional reciprocity. Political justice and political democracy require a certain normative attitude. First, an acknowledgment of institutional fallibility and an understanding that civic engagement over fundamental commitments of constitutional justice is not reduced to any single-branch process of decision making. And secondly, the appreciation that, in determining the kind of synergy and reciprocity apposite, institutional actors are supposed to appeal to institutional reasons that are reasonably available for broader endorsement in a community of free and equal citizens. In the face of reasonable disagreement, such reasons would normally ground *nuanced standards of judicial review* and qualify *absolute claims to interpretive supremacy*. If relied upon, these reasons would reflect a commitment of institutional participants to the joint nature of constitutional construction—including a joint commitment to doctrinal tests that are more inclusive in content, and to the operation of complementary schemes of constitutional implementation.

There are obviously limitations upon this function. The import of institutional norms, including institutional reciprocity, is subject to practical deliberation itself and, hence, to difference of judgement. More importantly, any sensible account of institutional reciprocity, within the context of meaningful judicial review, would include substantive standards of reasonableness. Yet, different minds would often differ on what reasonableness permits. What appears to a committed legislative majority as a balanced corrective policy to remove racial stigma might appear to an equally committed judicial majority to be an unreasonable policy of racial balancing. Thus, we have to accept irreconcilable institutional interpretations as a possibility inherent in the operations of free democracies with US-style judicial review.

In cases of this sort, interim resolution is provided by mechanisms of institutional settlement, like judicial decisions equipped with the force of res judicata. The operation of such processes of settlement may signal that the political community is failing to realise the joint potential of the constitutional project. But our overall assessment cannot be agnostic as to the substance of the matter. The implementation of *Brown* was conflictual. And this was so because of unreasonable resistance. What we can say from a detached perspective is that, as a general matter, reasonable procedures for reversibility should be available. In the US case, beyond interim closure, the political branches can engage in various strategies to promote their constitutional visions, ranging from judicial selection to endeavours for non-conventional constitutional transformation. And as constitutional stability is ultimately a self-enforcing quality of the overall scheme of law-applying institutions, it is reasonable to expect, one way or another, long term alignment over fundamentals.

Now, whereas constitutional theory has by and large been preoccupied with Promethean inter-branch conflicts, we also need to be sensitive to predicaments of a different nature: the kind of entrenched and perpetuating polarisation that has inflicted current constitutional practice throughout the nation. Indeed, we cannot make sense of much of recent constitutional controversy without noticing a cross-cutting cleavage between sharply contrasting and quite comprehensive visions of equal protection and federalism. What is more, what for some appear to be large scale remedial measures to ensure equal protection, for others they stand in inherent, sharp tension, or even direct conflict, with this very principle—out of irreconcilable conceptions thereof. For some, equality grounds the policy, if not the duty, to protect against State practices that reinforce social patterns of racial exclusion. For others, it commands strict governmental neutrality. And similar clashes of principle resurface on a consistent pattern throughout constitutional law: what for some are well-balanced measures 'to *facilitate* First Amendment values by preserving some breathing room around the electoral "marketplace" of ideas'[44] and to safeguard the integrity of elected institutions are, for others, policies whose 'purpose and effect are to silence entities whose voices the Government deems to be suspect'.[45]

This cross-cutting cleavage has acquired a cultural dimension, bundling a wide-variety of constitutional issues together and creating large normative distance between the poles. It is entrenched both within the judiciary and the political branches, while no side has managed to gain wide and transformative social support. And it is accompanied by deep mutual distrust with profound implications for the reach of argument. Even temperate justices have sometimes repudiated the burdens of civility in judicial exchange.[46]

This environment explains hesitancy to acknowledge constitutional space beyond judicial enforcement and reluctance to engage in formative dialogue about the proper contours of such enforcement; more generally, it challenges both the actual scope and utility of discursive reciprocity and the very inclusiveness of the constitutional project. Still, it does not discredit the importance of institutionalising discursive rationality and reciprocity—to the extent that can reasonably be accomplished. Without them, constitutional settlements are precarious; and democratic institutions cannot flourish.

[44] *Citizens United v Federal Election Comm'n*, 558 US 310, 473 (2010) (Stevens, J, dissenting in part and concurring in part).

[45] *Citizens United*, ibid, at 339 (Kennedy, J, delivering the opinion of the Court).

[46] See *Kimel*, above n 35, at 79–80 (O'Connor, J, delivering the opinion of the Court) ('Indeed, the present dissenters' refusal to accept the validity and natural import of decisions like *Hans*, … makes it difficult to engage in additional meaningful debate on the place of state sovereign immunity in the Constitution') and at 98–99 (Stevens, J, dissenting in part and concurring in part) ('the decision of five Justices in *Seminole Tribe* to overrule that case was profoundly misguided. … I am unwilling to accept *Seminole Tribe* as controlling precedent …. The kind of judicial activism manifested in cases like *Seminole Tribe* … represents such a radical departure from the proper role of this Court that it should be opposed whenever the opportunity arises').

14

Constitutional Sensibilities

Our analysis so far has focused on explaining the institutional function of constitutional doctrine. In this process, we have encountered the occasional conflict of substantive visions, the local interplay between institutional confidence and mistrust, and a high degree of judicial commitment spiced up with a flavour of institutional complacency, especially as reflected in claims to judicial supremacy. Yet, we have not attempted to single out any underlying leitmotiv that would bring together these features.

As is often the case, progress requires epistemic distance. The institutional division of interpretive labour is not an exclusive privilegium of constitutional litigation. We will briefly step out the rugged constitutional landscape and take note of the adjacent field of administrative law. An emerging contrast with that field will enable us to unearth dominant sensibilities underlying the multi-faceted constitutional domain and pave the way for informed doctrinal assessment and reconstruction.

I. Deference to the Administration over the Interpretation of Statutory Law

A. The *Chevron* Rule

In *Chevron v Natural Resources Defense Council*, the Supreme Court frankly acknowledged that in resolving cases within its jurisdiction it is not always supposed to proceed on the basis of an independent judgement about the interpretation of applicable statutory law. As framed, it is hard to imagine any clearer divergence from *Marbury's* perceived rationale that judges are supposed to resolve cases on the basis of independent interpretations of applicable law. Here is what the Court said:

> When a court reviews an agency's construction of the statute which it administers, it is confronted with two questions. First, always, is the question whether Congress has directly spoken to the precise question at issue … If, however, the court determines Congress has not directly addressed the precise question at issue, the court does not simply impose its own construction on the statute as would be necessary in the absence

> of an administrative interpretation. Rather, if the statute is silent or ambiguous with respect to the specific issue, the question for the court is whether the agency's answer is based on a permissible construction of the statute.[1]

The *Chevron* doctrine is firmly established as providing applicable rules of decision, although there is debate over its grounds, with one strand of jurisprudence treating it as judicial common law and another as based on implicit Congressional delegation of interpretive authority to agencies.[2] In fact, although I think that the latter view, if defended on an across-the-board basis, does not fit institutional reality,[3] it is reasonable to presume that the rule combines elements of both features. Like *Marbury*, it is a judicially crafted jurisdictional norm, aiming to best effectuate the policies and principles of applicable statutory schemes in a way consistent with the corresponding Congressional assignment of policy-making powers.

Yet, the important point is that *Chevron* is institutional law; it does not govern the substantive content of applicable statutory law; rather, it assigns to the administration the conditionally authoritative task of interpreting ambiguous statutory law[4] and accordingly orders courts to under-enforce it. As Justice Scalia had emphasised, within the scope of judgement assigned to it, 'it is up to the agency to specify the *correct* meaning'.[5] And such meaning is taken as binding, the Court tells us in a frank acknowledgment of reasonable interpretive pluralism, 'even if the agency's reading differs from what the court believes is the best statutory interpretation'.[6]

In defending this rule of judicial under-enforcement, the *Chevron* Court did in fact engage in institutional analysis and determined that *Chevron* step two (resolving statutory ambiguity) involves contested issues of policy that lie within the expertise and political legitimacy of agencies. It explicitly acknowledged that 'judges are not experts in the field and are not part of either political branch of government. Courts must, in some cases, reconcile competing interests, but not on the judges' personal policy preferences. In contrast an agency to which Congress has delegated policy-making responsibilities may, within the limits of that delegation, properly rely upon the incumbent administration's views of wide policy to inform its judgment. While agencies are not directly accountable to the people, the Chief Executive is, and it is entirely appropriate for this political branch of the Government to make such policy choices'.[7]

[1] *Chevron v Natural Resources Defense Council*, 467 US 837, 842 (1984).

[2] *Smiley v Citibank (South Dakota), N.A.*, 517 US 735, 740–41 (1996).

[3] See David Barron & Elena Kagan, '*Chevron's* Nondelegation Doctrine' (2001) *Supreme Ct Rev* 201, 212–25.

[4] See *National Cable & Telecommunications Assn. v Brand X Internet Services*, 545 US 967, 983 (2005) ('the agency remains the authoritative interpreter (within the limits of reason) of such statutes').

[5] Antonin Scalia, 'Judicial Deference to Administrative Interpretations of the Law' (1989) *Duke L J* 511, 518 (the emphasis is mine).

[6] *Brand X*, above n 4, at 980.

[7] 467 US at 865.

B. Specification of *Chevron's* Scope

The institutional analysis that the *Chevron* Court performed is of course not over. The Court has subsequently grappled with clarifying the scope of application of *Chevron* and specifying its import, by revisiting and supplementing the pertinent institutional reasoning. The emphasis has been to single out those processes that are likely to contribute to reasoned statutory elaboration[8] within statutory policy mandate.[9]

Under *Mead* (2001), the Court understands *Chevron* as an application of a more general institutional principle to the effect that 'the fair measure of deference to an agency administering its own statute has been understood to vary with circumstances, and courts have looked to the degree of the agency's care, its consistency, formality, and relative expertness, and to the persuasiveness of the agency's position'. *Chevron* is held applicable whenever the agency is authorised 'to speak with the force of law when it addresses ambiguity in the statute or fills a space in the enacted law [it administers]',[10] whether in rulemaking or adjudicatory capacity. In all other circumstances, courts would have to inquire whether the agency's interpretation deserves some kind of deference under *Skidmore's* more generic, though amorphous test.[11]

The *Mead* Court understands the distinction in terms of implicit Congressional delegation. On this rationale, presumed Congressional purpose has to be grounded on presumed institutional reasoning. But presumed choices and reasons are always subject to interpretive refinement. And such refinement is subject to the dilemma over the appropriate balance between institutional rigidity and flexibility (chapter seven).

Indeed, as Justice Souter, writing for an 8–1 majority, famously remarked in *Mead* itself, 'JUSTICE SCALIA's first priority over the years has been to limit and simplify. The Court's choice has been to tailor deference to variety'.[12] Yet, sometimes uniformity of treatment prevails. In *City of Arlington*,[13] *Chevron* deference was held to cover agency constructions of statutory ambiguities that concern the very scope of the agency's statutory authority, so long as the agency has general authority to administer the statute. The majority under Justice Scalia reasoned against any sensible distinction between jurisdictional and nonjurisdictional

[8] See *Smiley*, above n 2, at 741 (distinguishing between agency litigating positions of suspect deliberateness and 'full dress' regulations, issued 'pursuant to the notice and comment procedures of the Administrative Procedure Act designed to assure due deliberation').

[9] See *Metropolitan Stevedore Co. v Rambo*, 521 US 121, 138 (1997) ('The APA is not a statute that the Director is charged with administering').

[10] *United States v Mead Corp.*, 533 US 218, 228 and 229 (2001).

[11] ibid, at 234–38. See *Skidmore v Swift & Co.*, 323 US 134, 140 (1944) ('The weight [accorded to an administrative] judgment in a particular case will depend upon the thoroughness evident in its consideration, the validity of its reasoning, its consistency with earlier and later pronouncements, and all those factors which give it power to persuade, if lacking power to control.').

[12] 533 US at 236. For criticism see Cass Sunstein, '*Chevron* Step Zero' (2006) 92 *Virginia L Rev* 187.

[13] *City of Arlington, Texas v FCC*, 569 US __ (2013), 133 S. Ct. 1863 (2013).

agency interpretations; the former as well as the latter involve 'archetypal *Chevron* questions, about how best to construe an ambiguous term in light of competing policy interests'.[14]

Still, there is always a line of jurisprudence, sometimes majoritarian, willing to revisit and refine the general scheme in the light of structural concerns about the division of policy making responsibilities in the regulatory state. This is nicely exhibited in *King v Burwell* (2015), where the majority boldly announced that 'in extraordinary cases, however, there may be reason to hesitate before concluding that Congress has intended such an implicit delegation … This is one of those cases. … [addressing] a question of deep "economic and political significance" that is central to this statutory scheme; had Congress wished to assign that question to an agency, it surely would have done so expressly. … It is especially unlikely that Congress would have delegated this decision to the IRS, which has no expertise in crafting health insurance policy of this sort. … This is not a case for the IRS'.[15]

The language provides a fascinating interchange of both rationales behind *Chevron*. But whether the intent is ultimately attributed to Congressional intent or to the exercise of judicial reason, the conclusion is the same: This is not a case for the IRS. The IRS has no expertise in crafting policy of this sort[16] and, at any rate, the interpretive issue in question is not one of ordinary policy specification, but one of deep significance, involving the very integrity of the underlying Congressional plan: 'But in every case we must respect the role of the Legislature, and take care not to undo what it has done. A fair reading of legislation demands a fair understanding of the legislative plan. Congress passed the Affordable Care Act to improve health insurance markets, not to destroy them. If at all possible, we must interpret the Act in a way that is consistent with the former, and avoids the latter.'[17]

Most recently, the Court applied the *Mead* rationale to hold that procedural defects, including the failure by the agency to articulate its reasoning path

[14] ibid, at 1873.

[15] 576 US __ (2015) (slip op, at 8).

[16] Similarly, in *Gonzales v Oregon*, 546 U.S. 243 (2006), the Court denied *Chevron* deference to the Attorney General's interpretive determination that 'controlled substances' could not medically be used for the purpose of physician-assisted suicide even when the latter is permitted by state law. The Court in particular reasoned that Congress could not have intended to give the Attorney General interpretive authority to determine whether doctor assisted suicide is a 'legitimate medical purpose': 'Because historical familiarity and policymaking expertise account in the first instance for the presumption that Congress delegates interpretive lawmaking power to the agency rather than to the reviewing court, we presume here that Congress intended to invest interpretive power in the administrative actor in the best position to develop these attributes. … The authority claimed by the Attorney General is both beyond his expertise *and* incongruous with the statutory purposes and design. … [W]e are confident that Congress could not have intended to delegate a decision of such economic and political significance to an agency in so cryptic a fashion. … The issue of physician-assisted suicide … has been the subject of an earnest and profound debate across the country'. ibid, at 266–67.

[17] *King*, above n 15 (slip op, at 21). See also Abbe Gluck, 'Imperfect Statutes, Imperfect Courts: Understanding Congress's Plan in the Era of Unorthodox Lawmaking' (2015) 129 *Harv L Rev* 62, 96 ('perhaps *Chevron* lives on, but only for mundane or confined questions that do not implicate the functionality of the overall statutory structure').

(in notice and comment rulemaking), preclude *Chevron* deference.[18] The underlying idea is a legal process conception fitting *Chevron* deference to a functional division of policy-making responsibilities in the regulatory state. The process of agency-rulemaking is tied to the pursuit of reasoned decision making. Thus, if fulfilment of institutional expectations by the agency is structurally questionable, deference may frustrate *Chevron's* rationale.

C. Specification of *Chevron* Steps

Chevron step one is supposed to curve out an important category of judgements where independent judicial determination is warranted. We may roughly accept that, under *Chevron*, judgements about 'whether Congress has spoken to the precise question at issue' include judgements about the statutory text and about clear legislative purpose. The conventional approach has it that the judiciary 'employing traditional tools of statutory construction' is the final authority over the determination of possibly 'clear legislative intent'.[19] Yet, there is considerable disagreement in the practice over the scope of permissible tools (the text v purpose debate being the most prominent example) and prevailing views about the substantive aims of statutory interpretation affect the way the judiciary specifies step one.

Similarly, the plasticity of the 'reasonableness' standard in step two invites supplementary institutional argumentation, contextualising and updating the institutional variables. In this course, it may even matter, though in silence, whether the agency is perceived as a trustworthy partner in a collaborative project or an expert body that nevertheless has been consistently cool to some of the statutory values.[20] And there is no doubt that such judgements are ultimately influenced by the regulatory vision one adopts,[21] often located in historical patterns of contested policy success or failure.[22]

[18] *Encino Motorcars, LLC v Navarro*, 579 US __ (2016). The opinion offers a dithyrambic account of the process model of reasoned elaboration (slip op, at 9–10).

[19] *Chevron*, above n 1, at 843 fn 9.

[20] See W Eskridge & L Baer, 'The Continuum of Deference: Supreme Court Treatment of Agency Statutory Interpretations from *Chevron* to *Hamdan*' (2008) 96 *Geo L J* 1083 and Robert Glicksman & Richard Levy, 'Agency-Specific Precedents' (2011) 89 *Tex L Rev* 499 for an analysis of agency-specific deference patterns. See also Richard Pildes, 'Institutional Formalism and Realism in Constitutional and Public Law' (2013) *Supreme Ct Rev* 1, 21–30, for the relevance of institutional realism in assessing deference regimes.

[21] For instance, concern about the agency's credibility in reasoned analysis, combined with substantive concern about regulatory overreach, explains cases like *Michigan v Environmental Protection Agency*, 576 US __ (2015) (EPA acted unreasonably in not considering cost—including cost of compliance—before deciding whether regulation of emissions of hazardous air pollutants from power plants is 'appropriate and necessary').

[22] See the account of 'systematically disfavored agencies' in the history of progressive and libertarian administrative law patterns, as reflected in the case law of the DC Circuit. Cass Sunstein and Adrian Vermeule, 'Libertarian Administrative Law' (2015) 82 *U Chi L Rev* 393.

II. The Discontinuity Thesis

A. *Marbury* and *Chevron*

Marbury and *Chevron*, the most famous cases in their respective fields, appear to support two disharmonious propositions: that judicial review of the political branches is supposed to rest upon independent constructions of the Constitution and deferential accounts of ambiguous agency-administered statutory law. Technically, both doctrines have built-in interfaces enabling surface compatibility: first, *Chevron* is supposedly based on implicit or presumed Congressional delegation and therefore purportedly has the force of Congressional law, to be interpreted authoritatively by the judiciary. And members of the Court have emphasised that in specifying the scope of *Chevron* deference, the judiciary is exercising *independent* interpretive judgement.[23] Even on the account that *Chevron* constitutes judicially crafted common administrative law, it is crafted and interpreted on the basis of independent judicial judgement. Secondly, Congress is not considered entrusted with 'administering' the federal Constitution (with some noteworthy and embarrassing exceptions, see chapter thirteen, section II) and thus, no corresponding, constitutional delegatory intent could be presumed.

Beyond such formal compatibility, our analysis so far shows that the apparent disharmony shall be reduced to its actual scope. In both fields the Court claims authority over the determination of the applicable standard of review. In constitutional law, such determination is norm-specific and the applicable standard of deference is built into the doctrinal explication of the law, whereas in administrative law the *Chevron* rule applies across the board and has an explicitly institutional nature. In constitutional law, doctrine often reflects and requires a high level of judicial scrutiny over issues of principle, whereas under *Chevron* agencies are entrusted with conditionally authoritative responsibility over applicable issues of policy. Judicial bite in administrative law is normally experienced either on generic process-based grounds or whenever there are strong textual or purpose-based grounds against agency constructions.

[23] *City of Arlington*, above n 13 (Breyer, J, concurring, 'The question whether Congress has delegated to an agency the authority to provide an interpretation that carries the force of law is for the judge to answer independently.') (slip op, at 4) and (Roberts, CJ dissenting, 'a court should not defer to an agency on whether Congress has granted the agency interpretive authority over the statutory ambiguity at issue.') (slip op, at 5). The majority does not dispute this fact, but understands the scope of the presumption on a categorical basis ('*Chevron* is rooted in a background presumption of congressional intent: namely, that Congress, when it left ambiguity in a statute administered by an agency, understood that the ambiguity would be resolved, first and foremost, by the agency'. 'Congress has unambiguously vested the FCC with general authority to administer the Communications Act … and the agency interpretation at issue was promulgated in the exercise of that authority.') (slip op, at 5, 16).

B. And their Flip Sides

At the same time, there exist pockets of constitutional jurisprudence characterised by extreme judicial passivity, like rationality review of economic regulation. When the Court says, first, that 'social and economic legislation ... must be upheld against equal protection attack when the legislative means are rationally related to a legitimate governmental purpose' and, secondly, that such legislation 'carries with it a presumption of rationality that can only be overcome by a clear showing of arbitrariness and irrationality',[24] it defers to Congress over the specification of rationality requirements. Commentators have compared the deferential standard of review employed in economic due process cases to deferential judicial review over agency interpretations of their organic statutes.[25] In fact, the Court is more deferential under its economic due process jurisprudence than under *Chevron* step two.

Moreover, the submissive language of *Chevron* does not always reflect the actual degree of deference the Court shows in statutory interpretation. *Chevron* has not been applied in one uniform way and differentiations in deference do not follow a uniform principle.[26] Whereas the Supreme Court usually invokes the deferential standard, in a few cases it has ignored *Chevron* and in other cases it applies it in a way that is not faithful to its original rationale. In some cases, courts are so deferential that they in fact abdicate even their *Chevron* step one function.

Two more mainstream doctrinal linkages are particularly relevant here. First, we have already noted the trend of the Court to qualify the scope of *Chevron* deference on generic process-based or theme-oriented grounds (section I(B), above). As Thomas Merrill has suggested, *Chevron* is largely explicable under a process model of reasoned elaboration subject to judicial accountability.[27] The *Mead* line of jurisprudence links the intensity of judicial policing to the formality of agency process and other insignia of reasoned decision making. But the pursuit of 'process review' in the post-war period and its discontents are implicated in constitutional law as well. In areas or eras of value consensus and institutional trust, such an account may support a partnership conception of judicial review in both constitutional and administrative law. As we already seen, the idea of reasoned elaboration can penetrate tiers-of-review constitutional analysis, smoothen even strict scrutiny, or single out issues of principle in rational basis review.[28]

[24] *Hodel v Indiana*, 452 US 314, 331–32 (1981).

[25] Henry Monaghan, '*Marbury* and the Administrative State', (1983) 83 *Colum L Rev* 1, 34 concluding that, in the end, 'there is far less discontinuity' (at 33).

[26] See Thomas Merrill, 'Judicial Deference to Agency Precedent' (1992) 101 *Yale L J* 969, 980, and Eskridge & Baer, above n 20, at 1130–36.

[27] Thomas Merrill, 'Presidential Administration and the Traditions of Administrative Law' (2015) 115 *Colum L Rev* 1153, 1164–66.

[28] See *Fisher v University of Texas at Austin*, 579 US __ (2016), and the line of cases cited in ch 10 n 7 above, respectively.

Secondly, intensity of review is tied to the confidence the judiciary has in carrying out itself its preferred interpretive modes. In the *Chevron* context, both conservative and liberal members of the Court have notoriously attempted to strengthen the determinacy of step one, where the judicial role reigns supreme, on their respectively preferred methodologies. For instance, in *INS v Cardoza-Fonseca* the majority flirted with a restricting interpretation of *Chevron* to the effect that a term is considered ambiguous and subject to deference only if the court determines by the use of traditional tools of statutory construction that Congress does not actually have an intent on the issue under review,[29] provoking Justice Scalia to reply that such an implication 'would make deference a doctrine of desperation, authorizing courts to defer only if they would otherwise be unable to construe the enactment at issue'.[30] In the 1990s, and under the influence of Scalia himself, the conservative wing of the Court pursued a dramatic change in the prevailing methods of interpretation, to the same effect: easy invocation of closure under step one, now under a strong version of 'textualism', based on dictionary definitions, treatises, judicial opinions and terms' legal usage. As a result, in a number of cases, the Supreme Court rejected the agency's interpretation as contrary to the plain meaning of the statute.[31] Even today, both 'hypertextualism' and 'intentionalism', as they develop in various refined forms, often make it difficult to rationalise the actual scope of agency interpretive authority.

C. A Discontinuity in Sensibility

The emerging picture is one of complexity as competing claims of judicial independence and deference entangle with competing methodological and substantive visions and find their way in both areas of law. Yet, the features discussed above (under A) can fairly be characterised as exhibiting a partial discontinuity of treatment that in turn reflects a perceptible difference in sensibility. A discontinuity reaching its peak when juxtaposing *City of Boerne*, involving express delegation of enforcement powers to Congress (chapter thirteen), with *Chevron* and *City of Arlington*, and confirmed in the fact that constitutional interpretive innovation is mainly effected by the federal judiciary operating in a common law fashion,[32]

[29] 480 US 421, 445–6 (1987).

[30] 480 US 421, 454 (1987) (Scalia, J, concurring).

[31] *MCI Telecommunications Corp. v AT&T*, 114 S Ct 2223 (1994), *NLRB v Health Care & Retirement Corp.*, 114 S Ct 1778 (1994), *Central Bank of Denver v First Interstate Bank*, 114 S Ct 1439 (1994). See Thomas Merrill, 'Textualism and the Future of the *Chevron* Doctrine' (1994) 72 *Wash U L Q* 351, 362 and Richard Pierce, 'The Supreme Court's New Hypertextualism: an Invitation to Cacophony and Incoherence in the Administrative State' (1995) 95 *Colum L Rev* 749, 754–55 and 763.

[32] A similar point has been made by Strauss, arguing though that 'the common law elements are provided mostly by administrative agencies'. David Strauss, 'Foreword: Does the Constitution Mean What it Says?' (2015) 129 *Harv L R* 1, 27.

whereas interpretive innovation in regulatory law is mainly performed by agencies in policy oriented exercises.

Indeed, in contrast to the countermajoritarian rhetoric of constitutional law and the idea that constitutional norms structure the realm of permissible reasons of public policy, the Court has recognised agency interpretive authority even over ambiguous statutory provisions of a restrictive purpose, including those of jurisdictional nature. As the *City of Arlington* Court reminded us, 'our cases hold that *Chevron* applies equally to statutes designed to *curtail* the scope of agency discretion'.[33] On this reasoning, jurisdictional limitations make no difference since 'the question a court faces when confronted with an agency's interpretation of a statute it administers is always, simply, whether the agency has stayed within the bounds of its statutory authority'.[34] And in contrast to *Obergefell's* emphasis on independent judicial judgement over 'constitutional provisions that set forth broad principles rather than specific requirements',[35] the majority of the day found the insignia of delegatory intent in statutory ambiguity: 'Congress knows to speak in plain terms when it wishes to circumscribe, and in capacious terms when it wishes to enlarge, agency discretion',[36] with Justice Breyer counter-arguing in eclectic fashion that statutory ambiguity is 'not always a conclusive sign' and that a variety of other considerations may turn out to be relevant, like the 'subject matter of the relevant provision—for instance, its distance from the agency's ordinary statutory duties or its falling within the scope of another agency's authority'.[37] Far removed from the constitutional realm, these debates may well be understood as quarrels over the scope of the most 'archetypal *Chevron* questions', involving agency 'interpretive decisions about how best to construe an ambiguous term in light of competing policy interests.'[38]

If a broad-brush contrast is permissible, there is a perceptible underlying sensibility conceiving much of constitutional law as a domain particularly fit for judicial interpretive guardianship, while relegating agency-administered statutory law to the realms of policy compromises and instrumental rationality. Circuit Courts find it natural to pronounce, despite exaggeration, that '[i]f the issue falls outside the area generally entrusted to the agency, and is one in which the courts have a special competence, i.e., the common law or the constitutional law, there is little reason for the judiciary to defer to an administrative interpretation.'[39] And the High Court has no difficulty to distinguish, in various contexts, between 'the most prototypical exercise of judicial power: the entry of a final, binding

[33] *City of Arlington v FCC*, above n 13 (slip op, at 12).
[34] ibid, at 5.
[35] *Obergefell v Hodges*, 576 US __ (2015) (slip op, at 10).
[36] *City of Arlington*, above n 13 (slip op, at 5).
[37] *City of Arlington*, ibid (Breyer, J, concurring) (slip op, at 2,3).
[38] *City of Arlington*, ibid (slip op, at 13).
[39] *Maloley v R.J. O'Brien & Assoc., Inc.*, 819 F.2d 1435, 1441 (8th Cir, 1987), quoting *Hi-Craft Clothing Co. v NLRB*, 660 F.2d 910, 915 (3d Cir, 1981).

judgment *by a court* with broad substantive jurisdiction, on a common law cause of action, when the action neither derives from nor depends upon any agency regulatory regime'[40] and the most 'archetypal *Chevron* questions' involving agency '*interpretive decisions* about how best to *construe* an ambiguous term in light of competing *policy interests*.'[41]

We need to unearth the intellectual ideas behind these sensibilities. We will restrict ourselves to the constitutional landscape, putting this revealing digression to an end. But in this pursuit, we will direct our attention to the considerations that the *Chevron* Court did invoke: political legitimacy and expertise;[42] and we will attempt to explain how prevalent constitutional sensibilities don't fit well with *Chevron's* stated rationale: 'Judges are not experts in the field and are not part of either political branch of the Government'.[43]

III. Institutional Competency and Moral Conflict

A. The Political Process and the Common Law Model

Institutional competency has been an issue of heated controversy in the history of American constitutional law and, in particular, in the history of economic due process. In the early twentieth century courts and legislatures were competing in claiming superior institutional competency over the constitutional legitimacy of regulatory policies and the rationality of legislative means. In *Lochner v New York* (1905), for example, the Court claimed authority to give concrete form to the notion of police powers on traditional common law understandings. Police powers 'relate to the safety, health, morals and general welfare of the public', the Court declared,[44] and any economic regulation that promotes other ends is constitutionally suspect.

The Court's theoretical outlook internalised the ideology of the common law. Since judges were supposed to be experts in common law reasoning, the story went on, they also had expertise over the constitutional legitimacy and rationality of economic regulation. Accordingly, they crafted and employed various

[40] *Stern v Marshall*, 564 US 462, 494–95 (2011) (discussing the constitutional limitations in vesting legislative courts with jurisdiction over 'private' as opposed to so-called 'public' rights, in light of the status of article III judiciary as 'the guardian of individual liberty and separation of powers').

[41] *City of Arlington, above* n 13 (slip op, at 13).

[42] The relative importance of the two rationales is both time-contingent and contested. *cf* Peter Strauss, 'From Expertise to Politics: The Transformation of American Rulemaking' (1996) 31 *Wake Forest L R* 745 with Jody Freeman & Adrian Vermeule, '*Massachusetts v EPA*: From Politics to Expertise' (2007) *Supreme Ct Rev* 51.

[43] 104 S Ct 2778, 2793 (1984).

[44] 198 US 45, 53 (1905).

highly intrusive standards of review ranging from permissible public purposes, as in *Lochner*, to the reasonableness of regulatory rates.[45] On the latter, the Court extended its imperial claims over the administrative process, employing the doctrine of constitutional fact to justify 'hard look' review over administrative rate-making. The Court explicitly declared that, pursuant to the due process clause, 'the State must provide a fair opportunity for submitting that issue to a judicial tribunal for determination upon its own independent judgment as to both law and facts'.[46] Even in *Crowell v Benson*, a 1932 case that marks judicial acquiescence with extensive agency fact-finding, the Court reasoned that substituting for constitutional courts an administrative agency as to the 'final determination of the existence of the facts upon which the enforcement of the constitutional rights of the citizen depend, … would be to sap the judicial power as it exists under the federal Constitution, and to establish a government of a bureaucratic character alien to our system'. The Court flatly concluded that '[i]n cases brought to enforce constitutional rights, the judicial power of the United States necessarily extends to the independent determination of all questions, both of fact and law, necessary to the performance of that supreme function. The case of confiscation is illustrative, the ultimate conclusion almost invariably depending upon the decisions of questions of fact. This court has held the owner to be entitled to a fair opportunity for submitting that issue to a judicial tribunal for determination upon its own independent judgment as to both law and facts.'[47]

Defenders of the legislative process responded invoking a competing conception of constitutional reasoning with different institutional implications. Dean Pound from Harvard wrote a seminal article about the limitations of common law reasoning and the institutional advantages of legislation. What matters is empirical verification, not armchair judicial speculation. 'There is coming to be a science of legislation [based on] long and patient study by experts, careful considerations by conferences or congresses or associations'.[48] As this new outlook was gaining support, 'a shift in the understanding of the locus of science in government [occurred and] … the Court [was seen to have] less of a claim to science and rationality than legislatures and administrative agencies did'.[49] Arguments of expertise were associated with other process-based ideas. Although Congressional members are not 'experts' in economic organisation, they have their own bureaucracies. Oversight Committees, for example, receive a steady flow of information from agencies and independent expert communities. In *Nebbia v New York* (1934), the Court finally recognised the institutional capacity of the legislature in conducting hearings, listening to hundreds of witnesses, examining expert reports, etc.

[45] *Smyth v Ames*, 171 US 361 (1898).

[46] *Ohio Valley Water Co. v Ben Avon*, 253 US 287, 289 (1920).

[47] 285 US 22, 56–57 and 60 (1932).

[48] Roscoe Pound, 'Common Law and Legislation' (1908) 21 *Harv L Rev* 383, 384.

[49] Paul Kahn, *Legitimacy and History: Self-Government in American Constitutional Theory* (New Haven, Yale University Press, 1992) 126.

As the regulatory state was to prevail, this new outlook extended to agency expertise, forcing courts to loosen the intensity of judicial review over agency rate-making. Thus, in *St. Joseph Stock Yards Co. v United States*, which was an intermediate step before the demise of the constitutional fact doctrine in the area of economic regulation, the Court noted that 'in a question of rate-making there is a strong presumption in favor of the conclusions reached by an experienced administrative body after a full hearing.'[50]

Yet, Congressional understanding of the likely consequences of regulatory proposals does not imply commitment to pursue constitutionally legitimate policies. Moreover, there is no such thing as Congressional expertise on moral judgement; or anyone's expertise for that matter. Moral reasoning is a critical activity open to all citizens, perceived as free and equal partners of a democratic polity.[51] The pertinent concept here would be *trust* in a collective endeavour, which normally presupposes some convergence on the criteria of justification.

Accordingly, endorsement of Congressional competency to settle the constitutional legitimacy of socioeconomic policy largely presupposed some wider endorsement of the ideas behind the regulatory state. It was ultimately the actual predominance of New Deal policies and the subsequent value consensus of the 1940s and 1950s that secured judicial deference to Congressional determinations about the rationality and legitimacy of economic legislation. Thus, if we are to understand judicial passivity in economic due process, we need to take into account a combination of factors, including scepticism about the ability of courts to comprehend complex regulatory schemes and acquiescence, if not comfort, with the regulatory state. The ensuing condemnation of the *Lochner* Court had cultural repercussions within legal academia and public culture, and a lasting, devastating effect in judicial practice to these days; disabling any meaningful judicial review of ordinary economic legislation in the absence of systemic failures in the political process (as in areas involving suspect groups or classifications). No doubt, the value consensus of the 1940s and 1950s no longer exists and the partisan and conflictual nature of Congressional choices is in the last few decades all too transparent. Thus, as we will see in the next section, judicial passivity in the field cannot be explained without appeal to democratic legitimacy in the light of policy conflict. Yet, the historical demise of any special claim that judicial reasoning could sustain in assessing the constitutional legitimacy of economic legislation is an indispensable element of any genealogical explanation of the doctrinal state of affairs in the field.

[50] 298 US 38, 53 (1936). By 1940 the Court had accepted that a Commission's judgement on allowable oil production is conclusive 'even in the face of convincing proof that a different result would have been better'. *Railroad Comm'n of Texas v Rowan & Nichols Oil Co.*, 310 US 573, 584 (1940).

[51] Christopher Hookway, 'Fallibilism and objectivity: science and ethics', in JEJ Altham & Ross Harrison (eds), *World, Mind and Ethics: Essays on the Ethical Philosophy of Bernard Williams* 46, 63 (Cambridge, Cambridge University Press, 1995) ('it would be a confession of moral failing were I to act on others' judgments of justice while unable to form such judgments for myself').

B. An Evolving Sensibility of Moral Significance

This institutional and intellectual background could not, and did not justify bracketing constitutional contestation altogether. The more American society left behind the solidity of prevailing sociopolitical conventions, or at least the appearance thereof, the more one would recognise the relevance of value judgements in the resolution of various constitutional disputes and consider doubts about the *trustworthiness* of political and bureaucratic institutions to translate institutional competency into public-spirited output. The pivotal event was *Brown v Board of Education of Topeka* (1954), signifying a fundamental change in the attitude and role of the federal judiciary.

In the course of holding that segregation in public education on the sole basis of race violates equal protection, the *Brown* Court emphasised the retarding effect of segregation upon the mental and educational development of children of a minority class and cited relevant literature in psychology and education. The Court concluded that 'this finding is amply supported by modern authority. Any language in *Plessy* v. *Ferguson* contrary to this finding is rejected. We conclude that in the field of public education the doctrine of "separate but equal" has no place'.[52] The Court related the holding to the state of scientific knowledge and did not comment on the morality of segregation per se and, technically speaking, did not overrule *Plessy v Ferguson*.[53]

In this sense, it has been argued that 'the *Brown* decision symbolized the confrontation between mythology and empiricism … [and] confirmed [that] … constitutional law [should be] propounded in the light of reliable extralegal data rather than of arbitrary judicial biases … The Court used modern social science to overturn the *Plessy* decision and its pseudoscientific factual assumptions … What Warren unequivocally challenged and rejected was Justice Brown's finding of fact'.[54] Let us accept that the Court's conclusions of fact were correct and that the state of educational theory in the 1950s had discredited the 'scientific' basis of *Plessy*.[55] Is the adoption of the 'new' findings of science the best way to understand the importance of *Brown* in American constitutional law?

Examining *Brown* in retrospect, one has to acknowledge that its outcome was a quintessential exercise in what Ronald Dworkin has called the moral reading of the Constitution, based upon recognition that judicial review involves the protection of fundamental commitments of political justice. General clauses like the equal protection clause 'refer to abstract moral principles and incorporate these

[52] 347 US 483, 494–95 (1954).

[53] 163 US 537 (1896).

[54] Paul Rosen, *The Supreme Court and Social Science* (Urbana, University of Illinois Press, 1972) 156–57, 163–64.

[55] The issue was contested in the academic literature of the time, and the Court has been criticised for its use of scientific literature. See Edmond Cahn, 'Jurisprudence' (1955) 30 *NYU L Rev* 150.

by reference'.[56] In fact, a literal reading of *Brown's* stated reasoning would lead to counterintuitive results; it would allow, for example, district courts to accept local scientific research showing that in a particular setting segregation is not detrimental to the mental and educational development of black children.[57] It would conflict with various Supreme Court decisions that have held segregation in a wide variety of public services (from beaches to restaurants) per se unconstitutional.[58] And it would diminish its role as a turning point in American constitutional jurisprudence, as confirmed by the subsequent revolution in fundamental rights review under the Warren Court.

Post-*Brown* constitutional jurisprudence of course does not ignore the relevance of social facts in constitutional specification.[59] Yet, it has cultivated a by now prevailing sensibility to the effect that much of constitutional disagreement is not explicable in terms of disagreement over the implicated issues of fact and over effective policies to deal with them. Rational discussants do not give up their diverging positions even after they agree on the underlying assumptions about relevant social facts. Contestation is about the substantive requirements of political justice and, sometimes, about their institutional implications. And this feature is quite fundamental in constitutional practice; whether praised or deplored; whether genuinely channeled through convergence-seeking and stability enhancing doctrine, or dressed up in doctrinal facade.

Even in areas where constitutional doctrine is fact-dependent, for instance over the health implications of abortion regulation, the very reason for taking a closer look upon contested issues of fact relates to the importance of the moral issue at stake.[60] And differences of opinion over issues of moral value affect both the assessment of the implicated issues of fact, and, more importantly, the reasonableness of the policy treatment once the factual record—its uncertainties included—becomes transparent.[61]

[56] Ronald Dworkin, *Freedom's Law: The Moral Reading of the American Constitution* (Cambridge, Harvard University Press, 1996) 7–8. In Dworkin's more specific opinion, the pertinent clauses 'commit the United States to the following political and legal ideals: government must treat all those subject to its dominion as having equal moral and political status; it must attempt in good faith, to treat them all with equal concern'. ibid.

[57] See, nevertheless, *Stell v Savannah-Chatham County Board of Education*, 220 FSupp. 667 (SD Ga, 1963), for such a preposterous holding.

[58] For instance, segregation in a restaurant in a public airport was held unconstitutional under *Brown* in *Turner v City of Memphis*: '[O]ur decisions have foreclosed any possible contention that such a statute or regulation may stand consistently with the Fourteenth Amendment'. 369 US 350, 353 (1962).

[59] See Richard Fallon, *Implementing the Constitution* (Cambridge, Harvard University Press, 2000) ch 2.

[60] See *Gonzales v Carhart*, 550 US 124, 165 (2007) (the 'Court retains an independent constitutional duty to review factual findings where constitutional rights are at stake').

[61] Compare *Gonzales v Carhart*, 550 US 124 (2007) (sustaining a statute proscribing partial birth abortion without a health exception against facial attack) with *Stenberg v Carhart*, 530 US 914 (2000) (striking down a statute criminalising partial birth abortion for lacking a health exception). See also the text above ch 8 nn 26–27.

C. An Evolving Awareness of Moral Contestation and Institutional Distrust

A sensibility of moral significance is the first step towards awareness of institutional scepticism and potential distrust. That was clear in the trajectory from *Brown* to *Cooper* (chapter thirteen, section I), which epitomised the failure of the legal process school's thin institutional theory to appreciate the incentive structure of political institutions and to accommodate a more turbulent linkage between competency and public spirited output (chapter eight, section V). And it was reinforced by the sensitivity, already exhibited in famous footnote four of *Carolene Products* (1938), that the New Deal era presumption of constitutionality may not be apposite with regard to statutes 'directed at particular religious ... or national ... or racial minorities ... [and that] prejudice against discrete and insular minorities may be a special condition, which tends seriously to curtail the operation of those political processes ordinarily to be relied upon to protect minorities, and which may call for a correspondingly more searching judicial inquiry'.[62]

The institutional underpinnings of subsequent Supreme Court jurisprudence are well noted to need special reference.[63] We point out here that awareness of moral contestation and institutional scepticism and distrust are all too apparent in prophylactic reasoning throughout constitutional law. We have already touched upon strict scrutiny in equal protection cases (chapter twelve, section III). Another prominent example is First Amendment jurisprudence. The Court applies intensive judicial review over both issues of law and fact. For instance, the Court does not defer to a governmental determination that an expression of a provocative idea will incite a riot, but carefully examines the actual circumstances surrounding such expression;[64] it examines whether the exercise of First Amendment rights constitutes a danger to the President: 'the expertise of those entrusted with the protection of the President does not qualify them to resolve First Amendment issues, the traditional province of the judiciary';[65] and it often crafts constitutional doctrine from what Professor Blasi has famously called the 'pathological perspective'.[66] The idea is not merely that the subject matter is important or that value judgements

[62] *United States v Carolene Products Company*, 304 US 144, 152 fn 4 (1938).

[63] The locus classicus of course is John Hart Ely, *Democracy and Distrust: A Theory of Judicial Review* (Cambridge, Harvard University Press, 1980).

[64] *Texas v Johnson*, 491 US 397, 409 (1989). See also *Landmark Communications v Virginia*, 435 US 829, 843 (1978) ('Deference to a legislative finding cannot limit judicial inquiry when First Amendment rights are at stake').

[65] *Quaker Action Group v Hickel*, 421 F.2d 1111, 1118 (DC Cir, 1969).

[66] Vincent Blasi, 'The Pathological Perspective and the First Amendment' (1985) 85 *Colum L Rev* 449–514. See also *Citizens United v Federal Election Comm'n*, 558 US 310, 340 (2010) ('Premised on mistrust of governmental power, the First Amendment stands against attempts to disfavor certain subjects or viewpoints').

of importance are implicated. This may not in itself justify intensive review. It also needs an element of value conflict and an element of institutional distrust, or the potentiality thereof;[67] and normally a variety of further considerations (including institutional expectations, the fact of judicial independence, the culture of the office, the deliberative setting of judicial review, etc) grounding some reasoned expectation that judges would be sensitive in a distinctive way to the underlying moral principles.[68]

D. Complex Sensitivities to Constitutional Facts and Values

I have offered the outline of a genealogical argument regarding the diminished importance of institutional competency in the prevailing constitutional sensibility. But it is not my intention to present the sketched sensibility as a balanced one. In fact, both fact and value-sensitivity are often under-emphasised and remain in the backdrop behind unarticulated institutional assumptions and inadequately explained doctrines.

First, moral dependence is more ubiquitous than the case law recognises. Pertinent value judgements often affect how we treat disputed issues of fact. And they guide us in both approaching and dealing with uncertainty about them. Let us consider, for example, the doctor-assisted suicide cases. An important concern raised involved the risk that the legalisation of doctor-assisted suicide would facilitate performance of euthanasia to patients without an informed and voluntary will to die. As Justice Souter emphasised, the Court was faced with uncertainty over the ability of States to provide adequate regulation with teeth. Justice Souter concluded that the degree of uncertainty is such that 'the legislative institutional competence [is] the better one to deal with that claim at this time'.[69] Yet, once a legislature has made a reasonable finding of fact, we need difficult evaluative judgements in order to assess it and draw a normative conclusion. Suppose that a legislature reasonably claims that any feasible regulatory scheme would not secure a low rate of impermissible assistance to death. How are we to assess this finding? We have to make, among others, the following *moral* judgements: is there morally significant distance between the end of preventing assistance to impermissible suicide and the prophylactic means of prohibiting assistance in the exercise of an otherwise valid moral right of terminally ill patients to hasten their death? Does prevention of the former justify prohibition of the latter kind of assistance? If so,

[67] Fred Schauer, *Free Speech: A Philosophical Inquiry* (Cambridge, Cambridge University Press, 1982) 80–86.

[68] There is also a more mundane, systemic reason in delimiting areas for heightened judicial scrutiny: the efficient management of limited judicial resources. In the end of the day, the Court has to settle over the areas where employment of the judiciary's resources is reasonably effective. In this course, path dependence and happenstance often make a difference.

[69] *Washington v Glucksberg*, 521 US 702, 789 (1997) (Souter, J, concurring).

are rates substitutable? Does it justify complete prohibition?[70] Thus, confidence in the institutional capacity to understand the implicated risks does not necessarily justify confidence in handling them in accordance with fundamental constitutional commitments to political justice.

Nonetheless, this very point was well-understood by all sides in the abortion setting, as the case law on regulations lacking a health exception testifies. In *Stenberg v Carhart*, for instance, the majority expressly claimed that '[medical] uncertainty means a significant likelihood that those who believe that D&X is a safer abortion method in certain circumstances may turn out to be right. If so, then the absence of a health exception will place women at an unnecessary risk of tragic health consequences',[71] and Justice Kennedy replied that 'the most to be said for the D&X is it may present an unquantified lower risk of complication for a particular patient but that other proven safe procedures remain available even for this patient … Where the difference in physical safety is, at best, marginal, the State may take into account the grave moral issues presented by a new abortion method'.[72]

What then distinguishes the assisted suicide from the abortion setting and explains universal deference in the former versus the ordinary confrontation over both standard of review and substance in the latter? Perhaps there is some difference in the degree of uncertainty over the underlying facts and fair concern about the irreversibility of judicial error. But we may reasonably suppose that there is also a difference in the public nature of the debate: in the abortion field there is actual moral contestation, overconfidence by both sides, and institutional distrust.

At the same time, this last comment invites us to concede that the role of judgements about social fact is also under-emphasised. The prevailing sensibility in areas of conflicting certitudes often underestimates the pertinence of *consequentialist* considerations. Even under a deontological conception of fundamental rights, we may not determine the requisite protection without examining whether the questioned element is conducive to the free, informed and full exercise of our fundamental interests. Similarly, in specifying the place of a right in a coherent scheme of equal liberty, we have to examine collateral consequences that affect the exercise of other rights. Most importantly, we need to consider the implications for the wider scheme of effective freedom available to citizens. This scheme is not limited to the negative rights of individuals. It also includes their educational and

[70] The same week, the same Court that ruled against the right to doctor-assisted suicide had no trouble putting, in a First Amendment case, a heavy burden upon government to show why a less restrictive provision would not be as effective as the one adopted. See *Reno v American Civil Liberties Union*, 117 S Ct 2329 (1997).

[71] 530 US 914, 937 (2000).

[72] 530 US 914, 967 (2000) (Kennedy, J, dissenting).

social opportunities and other public goods. Performance of inquiries of such sort is fundamentally incomplete without proper understanding of consequences—including uncertainties.

But it remains the case that the institutional relevance of considerations of this kind is more easily appreciated when courts are not moved by perceptions of institutional distrust. This was illustrated in *Fisher II's* turn to standards of reasoned decision making (chapter twelve, section III(C)): even within the formal frame of strict scrutiny the majority of the Court was attentive to the competency of the reviewed body and careful not to frustrate the latter's judgements of necessity in good-faith pursuit of legitimate policies.

Let us conclude. I have argued that moral contestation and institutional distrust have made the moral dimension of constitutional reasoning more visible and have qualified the relevance constitutional practice attaches to institutional competency—sometimes to the effect of under-estimating the role of the factual dimension of constitutional reasoning itself. I have also suggested that a balanced institutional approach needs to appreciate how the factual and the moral dimension are entangled. But we cannot make progress here without attending further to those constitutional disputes, taken to be paradigmatic of the field, that are not particularly fact-dependent.

Most of us are prepared to affirm the outcome of *Brown* in various possible social environments. That is not so, on the other hand, with the specific injunctions implementing *Brown* or with ordinary educational legislation. How are we to understand this differentiation? One conjecture is that the fundamental constitutional choices do not address the full content of the reasons guiding public policy or their optimal interrelation. They rather aim to secure that the reasons employed are permissible in a political community of free and equal citizens and they indicate certain major implications that follow from the commitment to equal liberty. Within this frame, public officials reason about just and effective public policy in light of competing social claims and pursuits, contingent social facts and other strategic and prophylactic considerations. No doubt, principle and policy are entangled throughout that process. But we cannot understand the constitutional domain, without comprehending the salience of principle: crystallised in the high choices, though pervading the whole realm.

IV. The Domain of Principle

Much of constitutional law jurisprudence exhibits an awareness of moral contestation and institutional scepticism. But why is institutional scepticism applicable here in the first place? The *Chevron* Court expressly invoked *political accountability* to disclaim judicial guardianship over policy choices. Why is this line of reasoning unpersuasive in much of constitutional jurisprudence?

A. The Deontic Structure of Constitutional Rights

The more plausible reason I may propose is the more obvious one: much of constitutional law is seen as instituting fundamental principles of *political justice*. One may be hesitant in endorsing this argument since, first, the differentiation between issues of policy and issues of principle is schematic and largely dependent upon substantive conceptions of public reason and, secondly, there is wild disagreement in judicial practice and academic commentary over both issues of substance and issues of methodology. But neither of these factors contradicts this account.

In fact, I think a fair argument may be made that fundamental rights jurisprudence, which is taken as paradigmatic in the exposition of constitutional law, exhibits distinctive structural features of a deontic nature, in line with the account proposed here. This is quite apparent with regard to the often dominant position that the substantive provisions of constitutional law establish a basic scheme of equal liberty, or equal dignity, if you like.[73] But appreciation of a distinctive deontic nature is compatible with a variety of positions about how comprehensive one takes the scope of fundamental rights to be as a matter of positive constitutional law, of what rights one takes to be fundamental, or of whether one is originalist or not in determining the range of issues of principle falling under constitutional coverage. And although the conception one endorses about privileged interpretive materials (original meaning, tradition, doctrinal reasoning, moral dialogue, etc) affects the way judicial engagement operates, it does appear that this distinctive feature can accommodate to quite an extent such variation (for instance, by justifying non-deference over original meaning as regards commitments of principle of the founding generation).

I have warned against the idea that constitutional doctrine is a functional construct of rational design (chapter seven, section III); its content is subject to competing claims and interests, to criticism and apology, to path dependence, adaptation and strategy. Moreover, its function is not always transparent to the practitioners, who may have an amorphous or unarticulated idea thereof. Yet, it would be fair to say that much of the fundamental rights jurisprudence can best be rationalised as premised on the supposition that the Constitution protects a set of fundamental rights crucial for the authenticity, autonomy and equal status of persons, whose operation limits the pursuit of legitimate state policies. And concern for equal status evidently drives equal protection.

This is evident in *Obergefell*. It drives both the majority and the conservative minority in *Fisher II*. The underlying substantive matter in all such cases relates to the special nature of the *wrong* inflicted in the violation of the respective

[73] Laurence Tribe, 'Equal Dignity: Speaking its Name' (2015) *Harvard L Rev Forum* 129, 16–32 (*Obergefell's* chief jurisprudential achievement is to have tightly wound the double helix of Due Process and Equal Protection into a doctrine of equal dignity).

fundamental right, which is dramatically different from the *loss* incurred in unwise or unbalanced combinations of ultimately substitutable components of public policy. And the connection between the liberal and the democratic dimension of this idea rests on the further supposition that the protection of such fundamental rights reflects the elementary relation between free and equal citizens as joint tenants in sovereignty. It is respect for this commitment that, in one prominent version of this sensibility, *structures* the very idea of the common good.[74]

On this account, the specification of fundamental rights often involves explanations about the respect political institutions are required to show to highly unpopular individual exercises of fundamental human interests. In determining the protective scope of freedom of speech against content-based policies, for instance, we are paradigmatically disbarred from balancing all sorts of conflicting utilities; rather, we are supposed to give effect to the equality and authenticity of our personhood and to the commitment that public power is normatively understood as the collective power of free and equal citizens with a fundamental interest in developing and responsibly carrying out their life-projects, and in exercising their sense of justice. In this process, the protection we recognise to certain forms of social conduct, say speech expressing dissent from deep-seated social customs and political traditions, is not supposed to be 'proportionate' to either the utility gained by those who are likely to exercise them, or their contribution to collective goods.[75]

It is this feature that explains, for instance, how cases so extreme in public perception, like the flag burning cases, can be seen to be quite straightforward in principle and doctrine, inviting Justice Kennedy to note that 'so great is our commitment to the process that, except in the rare case, we do not pause to express distaste for the result, perhaps for fear of undermining a valued principle that dictates the decision … The case here today forces recognition of the costs to which those beliefs commit us'.[76] And it clarifies why we feel uneasiness when we look back to the kind of arguments the minority of the time invoked, in stubborn resistance to the formation of modern First Amendment jurisprudence: 'But as the statute's dampening effect on associational rights is to be weighed against the asserted and

[74] The philosophical locus classicus of this idea is Immanuel Kant, *Kritik der praktischen Vernunft* (1788) (KpV § 5:64). Of course, appreciation of the main insight does not require any tendentious philosophical commitment. On the special character of the deontic nature of moral principles see, among others, Frances Kamm, *Intricate Ethics* (Oxford, Oxford University Press, 2006) 227 ff., and R Jay Wallace, 'The Deontic Structure of Morality' in David Bakhurst, Margaret Olivia Little & Brad Hooker (eds), *Thinking about Reasons: Themes from the Philosophy of Jonathan Dancy* 137 (Oxford, Oxford University Press, 2013).

[75] *West Virginia State Bd. of Educ. v Barnette*, 319 US 624, 634 (1943) ('validity of the asserted power to force an American citizen publicly to profess any statement of belief, or to engage in any ceremony of assent to one, presents questions of power that must be considered independently of any idea we may have as to the utility of the ceremony in question.').

[76] *Texas v Johnson*, 491 US 397, 421 (1989) (Kennedy, J, concurring).

obvious government interest in keeping members of Communist-action groups from defense facilities, it would seem important to identify what interest Robel has in joining and remaining a member of a group whose primary goals he may not share. … The Court is left with a vague and formless concept of associational rights'.[77] It is precisely the abstract concept of equal liberty that explains why, as a matter of principle, it would be impermissible, for the purposes of that case, to consider what interest Robel had in joining that party.

Of course, the deontic nature of fundamental rights does not imply constitutional maximalism across-the-board, nor extremism. Much depends on subject matter. And its effect is, anyway, tempered by the operation of multiple competing visions of legitimacy, also emphasising democratic responsiveness, doctrinal stability and constitutional efficacy. But we would fail miserably in understanding fundamental rights jurisprudence if we were to let such forces silence this driving motif.

B. The Fora of Principle

This sensibility is coupled with a corresponding institutional scheme perceived well-suited to specify the pertinent principles. It is a scheme of primary jurisdiction exercised by the political branches and subjected to intensive judicial review, though not on a uniform basis. How are we to think of the linkage between this sensibility and such an institutional scheme?

Once again, the more plausible rationale is the more obvious one, inviting us to return to the opening case of this book, *Obergefell*. In the aspirational words of Justice Kennedy, 'the identification and protection of fundamental rights is an enduring part of the judicial duty to interpret the Constitution. That responsibility, however, "has not been reduced to any formula." … Rather, it requires courts to exercise reasoned judgment in identifying interests of the person so fundamental that the State must accord them its respect.'[78]

But immediately after presenting *Obergefell*, we also warned against looking at constitutional adjudication through Manichean lenses. And we cited the more formulaic approach of *Fisher* and the conflicts over the proper degree of deference. The question naturally arises whether this outlook of 'reasoned judgment' conflicts with the multi-faceted doctrinal terrain we surveyed in chapter twelve. And whether this in turn discredits the relevance of the sensibilities we quest after.

Justice Kennedy's judicial approach is certainly self-confident and aspirational, recalcitrant to doctrinal pigeon-holes. Yet, we need to understand his claim in conjunction with well-established perceptions of judicial authority over judicial

[77] *United States v Robel*, 389 US 258, 287–88 (1967) (White. J, dissenting).
[78] *Obergefell v Hodges*, 576 US __ (2015) (slip op, at 10).

doctrine (chapter thirteen, section I). In this light, the core message of this statement is that it is an essential element of the judicial duty to single out fundamental issues of principle and to craft standards of judicial scrutiny well-suited to capture pertinent constitutional wrongs. It is the province of the judicial department to single out, for instance, the prima facie impermissibility of governmental purposes suppressing the free expression of ideas and to devise a set of standards facilitating judicial implementation, in the light of the likelihood that such purposes are implicated, the ease of judicial discernment, the reciprocal risks of error, etc. In this sense, judicial independence in pursuit of constitutional principle can accommodate the complex scheme of judicial doctrine, and the tailoring of the standard of review to theme-specific substantive considerations and institutional assumptions, including, ideally, the virtues and vulnerabilities of the political, the bureaucratic and the judicial process.

Once we employ such a more nuanced approach to the judicial role, we may better grasp how a deontic outlook about constitutional substance may be seen to justify an institutional scheme of judicial authority over issues of principle associated with corresponding, though subtle and theme-specific standards of judicial scrutiny. First, there is a negative argument. The requirement of political responsiveness to the political judgements of the citizenry is less demanding here (chapter nine, section II) and, anyway, may be taken care of through political primary jurisdiction and the calibration of applicable standards of review. Secondly, on the prevailing mentality, the Supreme Court is perceived, out of organisational culture, institutional expectations, process of operation (with emphasis on focused deliberation and provision of reasoned answers to individual claims, etc.[79]) and in comparison with the political process, more likely to exercise certain virtues and sensibilities critical in this pursuit and to 'reflect the sober second thought of the community',[80] so as ultimately to act as a forum of political principle—or at least as a 'distinctively valuable hedge against errors of [rights] underenforcement'.[81] And thirdly, an argument regarding fair allocation of risks of error can be made in defence of standards of strict and heightened scrutiny: given the grave injustice incurred in violating a commitment of constitutional principle, the risk of judicial over-enforcement (implying risk of under-enforcement of implicated legitimate policy interests pursued by the government) may be considered less troublesome than the risk of rights under-enforcement.[82]

Perhaps neither of these considerations justifies rigid or overbroad schemes of constitutional prophylaxis. As *Fisher II* illustrates (chapter twelve, section III),

[79] See Jonathan Siegel, 'The Institutional Case for Judicial Review' (2012) 97 *Iowa L Rev* 1147.

[80] Albert M Sacks, 'The Supreme Court, 1953 Term- Foreword' (1954) 68 *Harvard L Rev* 96, 96. In fact, as Justice Kennedy noted in the flag-burning case, there are issues where 'we cannot … ask another Branch to share responsibility'. *Texas* v *Johnson*, above n 76, at 421.

[81] Richard Fallon, 'The Core of an Uneasy Case for Judicial Review' (2008) 121 *Harvard L Rev* 1693, 1709.

[82] Fallon, ibid, at 1704–15.

issues of principle are often entangled with issues of policy and the deontic structure of constitutional reasoning has to accommodate this feature. Accordingly, standards of scrutiny can serve their functions provided they are narrowly tailored themselves to capture concerns of principle and to minimise risks of judicial overreach.

Most importantly, the institutional outlook associated with the deontic nature does not justify judicial complacency and half-hearted attention to public deliberation and to the reflected judgements of the political process. I have argued that the institutional synergy between the political and the judicial process shall acknowledge each citizen as having the capacity for a sense of justice that is worthy of equal respect, and a fundamental interest to affect, through the exercise of deliberative responsibility, the formation and specification of public commitments of political justice (chapter ten). And on this ground I have criticised attitudes of judicial supremacy (chapter thirteen, section III). Yet, the nature of what is at stake in issues of constitutional principle sometimes explains the assertive predisposition of the judiciary in its dialogue with the political process. For instance, the moral gravity of the subject matter and the irreversible and focused nature of the wrong disabled the *Obergefell* majority from postponing independent review and letting the political process reform policy 'one step at a time', as is the case in much of social and economic regulation.[83]

These two points help us come to terms with the uneasiness many of us feel with the distinction between issues of policy and issues of principle. Bernard Williams, for instance, has noted 'the intense moralism of much American political and indeed legal theory, which is predictably matched by the concentration of American political science on the coordination of private or group interests: a division of labour which is replicated institutionally, between the "politics" of Congress and the principled arguments of the Supreme Court … They represent a Manichaean dualism of soul and body, high-mindedness and the pork barrel, and the existence of each helps to explain how anyone could have accepted the other'.[84] The best reply to this kind of criticism is not to deny the distinction, but to emphasise that issues of policy and issues of principle are often tightly entangled and that, at any rate, decision-making bodies are to be treated as trustees; they act in the name of a political community of free and equal citizens, ideally on reasons that reach all citizens as free and equal, and against the backdrop of reasonable, and sometimes unreasonable, pluralism about political justice. These normative considerations, in turn, matter as to the proper institutional space and the proper doctrinal rule for judicial enforcement.

With these qualifications, we may feel safe in our conviction about the relevance and critical force of principle. Constitutional justice operates in the context of policy contest and policy formation, as the political process gives content to the

[83] *Williamson v Lee Optical of Okla., Inc.*, 348 US 483, 489 (1955).

[84] Bernard Williams, *In the Beginning Was the Deed: Realism and Moralism in Political Argument* (Princeton, Princeton University Press, 2007) 12.

joint pursuit of fair and functional policies. What constitutional norms require in this process is adherence to certain principles. As a result, the interplay of principle and policy operates throughout the various deliberative stages implicated in giving content to the constitutional mandates. We saw in *Fisher II* the tension between scrutinising policy implementation to ensure that unconstitutional purpose is not at play, and allowing the flexible synthesis of plural educational goals. Similarly, without background conceptions of moral principle, we are at complete loss to distinguish, along with Justice Kennedy, or refuse to distinguish between the malign Denver constitutional amendment prohibiting special protection against discrimination on the basis of sexual orientation[85] and the 'policy determination' of the Michigan Voters 'that programs designed to increase diversity—consistent with the Constitution—are [not] a necessary part of progress to transcend the stigma of past racism'.[86] And we need principle to single out for separate constitutional treatment, or refuse to do so,[87] policies Congress deems compelling to further constitutional commitments.

Most importantly, we need to be aware that failure of principle is a distinctive failure of public policy, challenging the very commitment to equal citizenship. Williams presents a competing conception of the political where the non-moralistic 'political decision—the conclusion of a political deliberation which brings all sorts of considerations, considerations of principle along with others, to one focus of decision— … does not in itself announce that the other party was morally wrong or, indeed, wrong at all. What it immediately announces is that *they have lost*'.[88] No doubt, the value of institutional settlement makes it inevitable that, at the end of the day, rights claimants are told whether they have won or lost. But, does it make sense to tell the claimants in *Obergefell*, or in *Brown*, that all they deserve are decision-making processes which, after political argument is heard but without examining specifically whether claimants are being *wronged*, declare to them that they have simply *lost*?

C. Contested Principle

The deontic account discussed here does not imply value neutrality. On the contrary, dominant perceptions about constitutional principle are contingent upon contemporaneous judicial culture and upon underlying substantive visions of political justice.

85 *Romer v Evans*, 517 US 620, 631–33 (1996).

86 *Schuette v Coalition to Defend Affirmative Action*, 572 US __ (2014) (slip op, at 18).

87 'States can, and do, stand apart from the citizenry. States act as neutral entities. … The failure of a State to revise policies now seen as incorrect under a new understanding of proper policy does not always constitute the purposeful and intentional action required to make out a violation of the Equal Protection Clause'. *Board of Trustees of Univ. of Alabama v Garrett*, 531 US 356, 375 (2001) (Kennedy, J, concurring).

88 Williams, above n 84, at 13.

The *Lochner* Court, let us remember, thought that it was faced with an unjust and arbitrary interference with individual freedom favouring an organised interest group 'equal in intelligence and capacity to men in other trades'.[89] It was the same Court that invoked, in (concededly a rare) defence of *intellectual* freedom and against the objections of Justice Holmes, the more general principle that constitutional liberty 'without doubt, … denotes … the right of the individual … generally to enjoy those privileges long recognized at common law as essential to the orderly pursuit of happiness by free men' and demands that any legislative interference thereupon is 'subject to supervision by the courts'.[90] And it was the same Court that held in 1910 that 'in interpreting the Eighth Amendment, it will be regarded as a precept of justice that punishment for crime should be graduated and proportioned to the offense';[91] against the dissent of Justices White and Holmes, claiming that 'the word "cruel," as used in the Amendment, forbids only … inhuman methods for causing bodily torture, like or which are of the nature of the cruel methods of bodily torture which had been made use of prior to the Bill of Rights of 1689, and against the recurrence of which the word "cruel" was used in that instrument'.[92]

The situation today over liberty of contract is reversed partly because of radically different conceptions of principle in the field of economic regulation; not out of a radically different sense of the structural force of liberty in public reason. The design and specification of statutory schemes regulating the production of milk or subsidising railway transportation is no longer thought to raise fundamental issues of political principle. Rather, the pluralist model underlying the legislative process and 'notice and comment' agency rulemaking are thought better suited to handle legal problems that ask for functional compromises and for social input about how the people themselves rank various social goods.

At any rate, we shall not forget what we noted in discussing the political question doctrine, and, in particular, the jurisprudence on political gerrymandering: what, for a majority of the day, is politics as usual, may, for a stubborn minority, hide instances of grave injustice.[93] This very point, confirming the self-critical and contestable nature of constitutional practice, coupled with the expectation of every minority one day to become majority, explain why the deontic account presented here, while inspired by the paradigmatic core of constitutional rights jurisprudence, may be taken to capture, at least in part, the sensibility of the field.

It is perhaps easy to miss this point while locked within our engaged perspectives. But constitutionalism has a long history stretching far beyond current

[89] 198 US 45, 57 (1905).

[90] *Meyer v Nebraska*, 262 US 390, 399 and 400 (1923) (A state law forbidding the teaching in any private, denominational, parochial or public school, of any modern language, other than English, to any child who has not attained and successfully passed the eighth grade is unconstitutional).

[91] *Weems v United States*, 217 US 349, 373 (1910).

[92] ibid, at 409 (White, J, dissenting).

[93] See the exchange between the plurality and Justice Stevens in *Vieth v Jubelirer*, 541 US 267 (2004). Ch 11 n 31 ('excessive injection' of politics) and n 40 ('extreme abuses').

perceptions and arrangements. It took roots in the English soil before the Civil War, reflected in section 39 of the Magna Carta, as re-interpreted by Chief Justice Coke, and in the forceful, though perhaps misty, distinction between *iurisdictio* and *gubernaculum*: the realm of justice guaranteed to all freemen and delivered by the royal courts of justice under the supervision of the High Court of Parliament, and the realm of public utility pursued by Council.[94] Neither realm was beyond the power of the Sovereign. In fact, the political theology of the early days of this process stressed that the King was supposed at the same time to be 'debitor iustitae' (debtor of justice) and 'auctor iuris' (author of the law), acting through institutional processes reflecting the idea that his power is the power to give and make law, not commit iniuriae.[95] But, in contradistinction to imperial Roman law, and to the duty of judges to refer back to the Emperor in case of interpretive doubt, in these processes, royal courts of justice claimed all too often the 'liberty and authority that Judges have over laws, especially over statute laws, according to reason and best convenience, to mould them to the truest and best use'.[96] In this sense, and despite flagrant shortcomings and contradictions, anglo-american constitutional tradition at its best combined certain fundamental rights against the government with processes for their protection unimaginable at the time in the rest of the world.

This constitutional tradition, or at any rate its reconstructed reminiscence, in a polity where sovereignty has purportedly 'devolved on the people' as free and 'equal tenants' therein, finds its present reflection in the sensibilities we here strive to unearth; and in the current forms that neverending conflicts over constitutional legitimacy and institutional structure take—conflicts like those that captured our attention in the opening pages of this book, in Supreme exchanges of ideas; in the debates over the locus of constitutional principles that have not received explicit textual endorsement, in the common law, in the history and traditions of the nation, or in the learning of present generations; and in the parallel debates about the respective role of the political and the judicial process in expounding such learning amidst disagreement—reasonable and unreasonable.

D. The Perception of Coherence and Determinacy

The moral gravity of the subject matter, coupled with associated institutional perceptions, is perhaps not adequate in itself to explain the prevailing sensibility.

[94] Charles McIlwain, *Constitutionalism: Ancient and Modern*, 2nd edn (Ithaca, Cornell University Press, 1947) 67 ff. While meticulous scholars have debated McIlwain's more specific attribution of this distinction to late medieval scholars, they have not challenged the core idea. See Brian Tierney, 'Bracton on Government' (1963) 38 *Speculum* 295, 306–10.

[95] See Ernst Kantorowicz, *The King's Two Bodies: A Study in Medieval Political Theology* (Princeton, Princeton University Press, 1957) 143–64.

[96] *Lord Sheffield v Ratcliffe* (1615) Hob 334, 346 (Chief Justice Hobart).

There is a second reinforcing element. We can get a grasp of it once we ponder on the tendency of the judiciary to be less reserved whenever it thinks that a principled and well-articulated normative scheme underlies a legal field and provides determinacy within it. The intellectual process of elaborating such a scheme is traditionally deemed to fit the institutional role of the judiciary.[97] And this is particularly so once that scheme has managed to receive recognition in the case law.

Much of the critique advanced by realist and, more recently, critical legal thinkers aimed to debunk the perceptions of neutrality behind schemes of legal coherence, and to reveal their ideological nature. This critique has discredited the perception of interpretive determinacy in policy-laden fields of law.[98] Yet, in constitutional justice, there persists, indeed flourishes, confidence over access to appropriate and well-articulated normative schemes that supposedly underlie the pertinent principles; and such schemes have in fact received recognition in the case law—at least as forming the basis for legitimate, though deeply contestable interpretive arguments.

On this perception, many constitutional norms are understood as establishing a principled scheme of requirements of political justice. Much of the case law is inspired by relatively coherent, though contested accounts of political justice or, at least, by perceptions of such coherence.[99] And one of the most celebrated accounts of constitutional philosophy in our times, Dworkin's law as integrity, precisely attempts to interpret constitutional law as committed to a principled set of abstract principles of political morality that offers an appealing and coherent justification of constitutional practice.[100]

[97] Variants of this model have been employed to distinguish judicial from political reasoning. For example, the legal process school specified the function of the court in interpreting a statute on the model of 'reasoned elaboration' of the underlying principles and policies. See Henry Hart & Albert Sacks, *The Legal Process: Basic Problems in the Making and Application of Law* (ed William Eskridge & Philip Frickey, Westbury NY, The Foundation Press, 1994) 1374–80. Ronald Dworkin has advanced a conception of adjudication based on the model of 'coherent and principled extension' of such principles and policies. See Dworkin, *Law's Empire* (Cambridge, Harvard University Press, 1986) 134–35.

[98] Duncan Kennedy, 'The Disenchantment of Logically Formal Legal Rationality or Max Weber's Sociology in the Genealogy of the Contemporary Mode of Western Legal Thought' (2004) 55 *Hastings L J* 1031, 1076 ('policy is always a potential Trojan horse for ideology, just because of the patently weak rationality of choosing policies by universalizability').

[99] It is an open question whether similar considerations apply to structural constitutional provisions. Structural issues need institutional settlement and stability, as frequent controversy leads to social distrust and political turmoil. John Rawls, *Political Liberalism* (New York, Columbia University Press, 1993, 1996) 228. But a further issue arises over the proper forum to provide settlement. Moreover, the substantive debate over formalist versus functionalist approaches to structural issues affects the degree of judicial enforcement in the sense that functionalist approaches, say to the non-delegation doctrine, invite judicial deference. But once again, considerations of constitutional efficacy often move the Court to settle on independent grounds even issues of constitutional policy. See *Zivotofsky v Kerry*, 576 US __ (2015) ch 4 n 7, above.

[100] Dworkin, above n 56, at 7–8.

No doubt, controversy exists over both method and specification, over doctrinal tools, assessments of social and economic fact, and strategic considerations. Yet, even with regard to issues of focused contest, many of us think that some (though not the same for each of us) principled vision of constitutional theory explains much of the constitutional text and judicial doctrine by way of justification. In this regard, the role of moderate justices cannot be downplayed. They often provide us with doctrinal common ground, as in *Fisher I*, enabling visionaries of contested principle to project upon the web of precedent what they perceive to be its more appealing justification, as in *Fisher II*.

V. The Domain of Competing Policy Interests

A. Sensibilities of Deference and Despair

The sensibility that prevails in policy discourses over the reasonableness and legitimacy of economic legislation is largely different. On the one hand, the demise of the *Lochner* Court jurisprudence has left courts bereft of any coherent normative structure that they could reasonably impose upon the political process. On the other, the main policy contests over the regulatory state (when they do not implicate suspect classifications) are well internalised in the political process. As a result, there is a strong sense, first, that considerations of democratic legitimacy are particularly pertinent in the field, disallowing judicial substitution of policy judgement in the absence of a very strong case of constitutional unreasonableness and, secondly, that such a case is almost impossible to make. As a result, the *Chevron* assumption on the importance of political accountability amidst policy conflict is perceived particularly applicable here.

There are strong philosophical arguments that may be summoned to rationalise this outlook. First, major issues of regulatory policy are sensitive to public judgement in a fundamental manner; their appropriate resolution largely depends upon responsiveness to the political judgements prevailing in public political discourse under conditions of equal political liberty. And such responsiveness is promoted through processes of political representation and accountability. Secondly, constitutionally legitimate reasons normally allow for ample space for reasonable disagreement over such policy. Thus, major competing conceptions of rational economic legislation are largely thought to be, at least in principle, defensible on the basis of such reasons. Finally, if restraints of principle appear to be illusory and policy effectiveness to be of primary importance, particular emphasis is attached to virtues like policy coherence and adaptability, as well as to systemic considerations disfavouring judicial engagement. Hence, under the prevailing sensibility, the desiderata thought pertinent in evaluating the constitutional reasonableness of policy schemes are both quite permissive and considered better served by ordinary politics and better specified by a reasoned administrative process.

B. Injections of Principle in the Domain of Policy

One may wonder whether the picture I have presented, in its procrustean form, is a virtue or a predicament. Public policy needs both rationalisation and sensitivity to justice. And there are claims to this effect from both the right[101] and the left,[102] demanding rationality and fairness. Such issues may not be resolved by a blanket reference to political responsiveness and by deferential doctrines of despair.

Yet, we are quite far from incorporating these concerns in judicially manageable standards for review that would not raise suspicion of partisanship. Indeed, in contradistinction to the New Deal era, it is policy conflict and its internalisation in polarised political process that reinforces mutual suspicion against any judicial attempt on the constitutional level to rationalise the regulatory leviathan or to instill a commitment to fairness in socioeconomic regulation.

For instance, the Court has recently attempted to supervise regulatory overreach as to the flow of commercial ideas and information, on free speech grounds. 'Unlike content based discrimination, discrimination based on viewpoint, including a regulation that targets speech for its offensiveness, remains of serious concern in the commercial context. … To the extent trademarks qualify as commercial speech, they are an example of why that term or category does not serve as a blanket exemption from the First Amendment's requirement of viewpoint neutrality. … To permit viewpoint discrimination in this context is to permit Government censorship'.[103] Governmental censorship in the economy is constitutionally troubling. Nonetheless, the transplantation of a doctrinal frame designed for the marketplace of ideas into the marketplace of commercial information is a notoriously precarious exercise and has given rise to concern and sharp criticism for hidden policy agendas.[104]

As this book draws to its end, having expended much of the author's imagination and challenged the reader's patience, it would be unwise to venture upon substantive constitutional reconstruction. But we may not let the argument rest without indicating, in conjectural and closing tone, challenges and options we face.

[101] See *Michigan v Environmental Protection Agency*, 576 US __ (2015), where the Court held consideration of cost to be a necessary element of 'rational' decision making ('One would not say that it is even rational, never mind "appropriate," to impose billions of dollars in economic costs in return for a few dollars in health or environmental benefits') (slip op, at 7).

[102] See *Goldberg v Kelly*, 397 US 254 (1970) and Frank Michelman, 'On Protecting the Poor through the Fourteenth Amendment' (1969) 83 *Harv L Rev* 7.

[103] *Matal v Tam*, 582 US ___ (2017) (slip op, at 5–6) (Kennedy, J, concurring).

[104] See the sharp exchange of views in *Sorrell v IMS Health*, 564 US 552 (2011), subjecting to heightened scrutiny content- and speaker-based restrictions upon the sale and use of commercial information.

The pervasiveness of the regulatory state has largely reshaken fundamental convictions about the role of government in respecting and protecting liberty. Regulatory schemes not only regulate our social and economic interaction, but provide the relevant institutional domains making the very exercise of human choice meaningful. On this ground, a powerful argument may be made that, in principle, governmental interference with our effective freedom requires *rational* regulatory schemes and *legitimate* classificatory distinctions. This of course does not justify judicial substitution of judgement over what policy mixture the political branches have most reason to pursue in the public interest. Yet, it could justify, on the long tradition of 'reasoned process', more focused and nuanced inquiries into whether, for instance, a class of persons is uniquely harmed on arbitrary grounds, suffering a constitutionally cognizable wrong.

We have seen that the Court has engaged in such inquiries in extreme cases involving conferral of separate status and stigma. Such cases are arguably safely placed within the ambit of judicial cognizance. Still, they are dramatically underinclusive of the category of cases where a court of law would be adequately suited to adjudicate, under a presumption of constitutionality, a claim that an individual or a designated class of persons has been unduly singled out to carry an undue burden or suffer undue harm by the impersonal forces governing the regulatory leviathan.

Justices Brennan and Marshall attempted, but failed to sensitise the Court on this issue a generation ago. Part of the reason for their failure was their underlying ideological backdrop and its institutional repercussions. Justice Marshall, the author of *Hodel v Indiana*, involving coal mining operations, was honest enough to tie judicial attentiveness to a distinction between business interests and vulnerable individuals: 'The extremes to which the Court has gone in dreaming up rational bases for state regulation in [business regulation] may, in many instances, be ascribed to a healthy revulsion from the Court's earlier excesses in using the Constitution to protect interests that have more than enough power to protect themselves in the legislative halls. This case, involving the literally vital interests of a powerless minority—poor families without breadwinners—is far removed from the area of business regulation.'[105] The majority of the *Burger* Court was not persuaded, disclaiming any institutional mandate to substitute for the political process along such lines and to upset social welfare policies, in the absence of a narrow class of status-conferring classifications.

But it is frustrating to concede that judicial culture may not make, at least in principle, a distinction between respecting the plenary powers of legislatures to make compromises and settle upon policy mixtures, and employing a focused arbitrariness standard of review to reach cases where a narrow class of persons is specified for suffering a unique harm or burden. And it is disturbing to accept, as the majority effectively did, without at least a sense of discontent, that the judicial

[105] *Dandridge v Williams*, 397 US 471, 520 (1970) (Marshall, J, dissenting).

process is silent over an equal protection claim advocating that 'the fortuity of one day of employment in a particular year should not govern entitlement to benefits earned over a lifetime'. That was the case in *Fritz* concerning retirement benefits.[106] Justice Stevens appreciated the difficulty and remarked: 'JUSTICE BRENNAN is also correct in reminding us that, even though the statute is an example of "social and economic legislation," the challenge here is mounted by individuals whose legitimate expectations of receiving a fixed retirement income are being frustrated by, in effect, a breach of a solemn commitment by their Government. When Congress deprives a small class of persons of vested rights that are protected … for others who are in a similar though not identical position, I believe the Constitution requires something more than merely a "conceivable" or a "plausible" explanation for the unequal treatment'. He went on to argue that 'Congress had a duty—and surely it had the right to decide—to eliminate no more vested benefits than necessary to achieve its fiscal purpose. Having made that decision, any distinction it chose within the class of vested beneficiaries would involve a difference of degree, rather than a difference in entitlement'. On the merits, he confirmed, against Justice Brennan, that 'a distinction based upon currency of railroad employment represents an impartial method of identifying that sort of difference'.[107]

Even assuming that there are strong institutional arguments for letting the legislative process supreme in handling claims of policy fairness, courts may still employ constitutional considerations in interpreting the scope of agency policy discretion and reviewing its exercise. In fact this option is latent, though not acknowledged, in much of rationality review; in cases holding, for instance, that an agency interpretation needs to be 'cognizant that longstanding policies may have engendered serious reliance interests that must be taken into account'.[108]

A less latent, but more troubling mechanism is provided by the avoidance-of-constitutional-questions canon of statutory construction. The canon is often employed to allow extension of constitutional values beyond their doctrinal scope. For example, in *Kent v Dulles*,[109] the Court interpreted the law governing the issuing of passports so as to make it compatible with the constitutionally protected right to travel. The Court then quashed an administrative rule prohibiting issuance of passports to members or supporters of the Communist party. Yet, there are significant difficulties of both candour and legitimacy with that canon, illustrating

[106] *United States R. Retirement Bd. v Fritz*, 449 US 166, 197 (1980) (Brennan J, dissenting).

[107] *Fritz*, ibid, at 190, 192 (Stevens, J, concurring in the judgment).

[108] *Encino Motorcars*, n 18 above. The Court considered that 'the retail automobile and truck dealership industry had relied since 1978 on the Department's position … Dealerships and service advisors negotiated and structured their compensation plans against this background understanding. Requiring dealerships to adapt to the Department's new position could necessitate systemic, significant changes to the dealerships' compensation arrangements', and concluded that 'in light of this background, the Department needed a more reasoned explanation for its decision to depart from its existing enforcement policy'. ibid, at 10–11.

[109] 357 US 116 (1958).

the broader difficulties our endeavour faces. In *Rust v Sullivan*,[110] the Court upheld a regulation requiring family planning clinics that receive grants to refuse giving advice on abortion. It appealed to *Chevron* and noted that the statute, as interpreted by the agency, did not raise 'grave doubts' of constitutionality,[111] sharply distinguishing between applicable constitutional law and some vague constitutional penumbra. Indeed, it is unclear why the judiciary may constitutionally restrict the Executive branch in the exercise of its constitutional functions, by tinkering around with constitutional doubt, while refusing to remove it.

For reasons of this kind, any legitimate injection of constitutional principle in the domains of policy has to be transparent and justified accordingly. In this regard, the institutional dimension of constitutional reasoning discussed in this book provides an appropriate conceptual toolkit. Judicial reasoning may take note of the discrepancy between constitutional law and constitutional doctrine. It may well be that Congressional deliberation could have settled a judicially underenforced issue of constitutional significance. Yet, if Congress has avoided addressing the issue in drafting statutory text, the court may be justified to engage, as a junior partner, in the constitutional deliberation needed for the purpose of construing the text.[112]

No doubt, in eras of sharp partisan conflict and divided bench, proposals of this kind invite the risk of the judiciary running afoul of its institutional role; and bootlegging policy visions into the law. From our perspective, next to transparency, we need to invoke another fundamental virtue we have already touched upon: reciprocity with the political branches. Courts are well-advised to approach the task of constitutional elaboration in socio-economic regulation in a dialogic, argumentative manner: by encouraging further reflection, under appropriate process or at a more appropriate forum. An illuminating example of this technique is given in the case of *Hampton v Mow Sun Wong* (1976) where the Court held unconstitutional a Civil Service Commission rule banning the employment of noncitizens in competitive civil service. The Court, taking into account the impact of the rule on the millions of lawfully admitted resident aliens, and while 'assuming without deciding that the national interests identified by the petitioners would adequately support an explicit determination by Congress or the President to exclude all noncitizens from the federal service', concluded 'that those interests cannot provide an acceptable rationalization for such a determination by the Civil Service Commission'.[113]

Is this a feasible endeavour? We need to concede that doubt is justified. The rise and fall of the legal process school testifies that successful performance of this

110 111 S Ct 1759 (1991).

111 ibid, at 1771 (1991).

112 See also Gillian E Metzger, 'Ordinary Administrative Law as Constitutional Common Law' (2010) 110 *Colum L Rev* 479 and Ernest A Young, 'Constitutional Avoidance, Resistance Norms, and the Preservation of Judicial Review' (2000) 78 *Tex L Rev* 1549, 1585.

113 426 US 88, 116 (1976).

endeavour entails a degree of genuine reciprocity by all implicated actors and joint concern over the implicated issues of principle. And both conditions are not easy to fulfil in current, highly polarised, institutional landscape.

C. On Means and Ends

Even if the broader constitutional debate the previous paragraphs envisage can be transparent and conducted on terms of genuine reciprocity, is it not likely to lead to inadvertent policy substitution or to increase institutional cacophony? The short answer is in the affirmative. In particular, it is likely to affect the effectiveness of the policy mixture the political process would most favour. In assessing this risk, we need to return to the argument about the risks of mistake associated with alternative institutional schemes. At the core of fundamental rights jurisprudence lies the idea that, given the grave harm from constitutional injustice, the risk of judicial overreach (implying risk of under-enforcement of legitimate policy interests pursued by the government) is normally considered less troublesome than the risk of rights under-enforcement. Can we extend this argument here?

Policy effectiveness is an important desideratum. We often have reason to prefer interpretations of the law that would otherwise fall short of the ideal in order to secure policy effectiveness. When fundamental issues of political justice are at stake, the permissible distance from an ideal interpretation is much narrower. This shows what is ultimately so special about constitutional law. The effective implementation of *some* constitutional order cannot justify distancing ourselves from the fundamental commitment to political justice.

The range of the reasonably just in areas dominated by issues of policy is wider. However, it is fallacious to think that in those areas issues of constitutional principle do not arise. First, there is always the question of appropriate means. Means that are effective vis-à-vis a set of operational goals may be unjust, or may exhibit a mixture of virtues contradicting the sense of integrity for a political community of free and equal citizens. The means a political community deems appropriate often symbolise its very character,[114] as a community grounded in the principles of liberty and equal citizenship. And fractures in this character may obtain even if they do not implicate personal freedom, privacy, expression, or suspect classifications. Secondly, both the stipulation of operational goals and the design of means to these goals partake in a continuous process of specifying the ends themselves. Our thought is partly directed at what qualifies as an adequate and practically realisable specification of just ends given the situation we face.[115] In this endless process, we aspire to determine and make real the deepest commitments to political justice.

[114] See Robert Nozick, *The Nature of Rationality* (Princeton, Princeton University Press, 1993) 135.
[115] See David Wiggins, *Needs, Values, Truth*, 3rd edn (Oxford, Oxford University Press, 1998) 225.

And some of our noted failings in this regard manifest themselves in unconstitutional conditions, undue classifications or regulatory entrapments.

Policy effectiveness is a virtue so long as it is effectiveness for a right reason. As our operating goal gets distanced from that end, our action lacks in value. And once we miss the right end completely, the very idea that we have an instrumental reason to pursue our operating ends becomes incoherent.[116]

[116] Wiggins, ibid, at 385.

INDEX